# Educative Assessment

# GRANT WIGGINS

# Educative Assessment

## Designing Assessments to Inform and Improve Student Performance

JOSSEY-BASS PUBLISHERS ▪ San Francisco

Chapter Three excerpt from "True or False: Testing by Computers Is Educational Progress," *The New York Times*, June 15, 1997, Business section, p. 10, is reprinted with permission.

Chapter Three excerpt from J. Peterman catalog is reprinted with permission.

Figure 3.2 is one of four different rubrics used for reading assessment in Harrison School District Two, Colorado Springs, Colorado, and is used by permission.

Figure 3.3 is reproduced from *Primary Purposes: Assessing*, with permission of Fairfax County Public Schools, Fairfax County, Virginia.

Figure 7.3 is used by permission of School Qualifications and Curriculum Authority, Newcombe House, London.

Figure 9.1 is used by permission of Daniel Beaupré, a teacher in the DaVinci program at the Gailer School, Middlebury, Vermont.

Figures 10.4 and 10.14 are reprinted by permission of Patrick Griffin, Patricia G. Smith, and Lois E. Burrill: *The American Literary Profile Scales: A Framework for Authentic Assessment* (Heinemann, a division of Greenwood Publishing Group, Portsmouth, NH, 1995).

Figures 10.11 and 10.12 are from Chapter 11, by Grant Wiggins from *Communicating Student Learning*, 1996 Yearbook, Alexandria, VA: Association for Supervision and Curriculum Development. Copyright 1996 by ASCD. Used with permission. All rights reserved.

For sales outside the United States, please contact your local Simon & Schuster International Office.

Jossey-Bass Web address: http://www.josseybass.com

Manufactured in the United States of America.

**Library of Congress Cataloging-in-Publication Data**

Wiggins, Grant P.
    Educative assessment : designing assessments to inform and improve
student performance / Grant Wiggins.—1st ed.
        p.    cm.—(Jossey-Bass education series)
    Includes bibliographical references and index.
    ISBN 0-7879-0848-7
    1. Educational tests and measurements.  2. Examinations—Design
and construction.  I. Title.  II. Series.
LB3051.W495   1998
371.26—dc21                                                        97-49935

FIRST EDITION
PB Printing        10 9 8 7 6 5 4 3 2 1

The Jossey-Bass Education Series

# CONTENTS

# LIST OF FIGURES

# PREFACE

This book presents a rationale for learning-centered assessment in our schools and an overview of the tools, techniques, and issues that educators should consider as they design and use assessments focused on learner needs. It argues that we need a different kind of student assessment than the one most schools now use. It explains what this new system looks like and how it satisfies learner needs rather than sacrificing them to demands for efficiency and expediency. And it presents standards and criteria we can use to judge the value and effectiveness of this or any other assessment system.

The proposals presented in this book are all based on a simple principle: assessment should be deliberately designed to improve and educate student performance, not merely to audit it as most school tests currently do. Regardless of their technical soundness, audit tests (typically indirect multiple-choice or short-answer tests, be they national or teacher-designed) cannot serve the chief "clients" of assessment, the students, because these tests are inherently incapable of giving students the access to models and the feedback that are central to all real learning. Nor can these typical tests help teachers to improve their own performance. Because each major test is a one-shot effort, and because much secrecy surrounds these questions and test scoring, conventional approaches to testing cannot provide what we most need in our schools: a way to help students systematically to *self-correct* their performance.

To achieve increasingly better and ultimately excellent performance, students need *educative assessment*. Such assessment always has at least two essential qualities: it is anchored in *authentic* tasks—namely, tasks that teach students how adults are actually challenged in the field—and it provides students and teachers with feedback and opportunities they can readily use to revise their performance on these or similar tasks.

There is nothing radical or even new here, really. In one sense this book merely reminds us of what Benjamin Bloom and his colleagues said years ago about the genuine "application" of knowledge and about synthesis; namely, that application requires novel problems, and synthesis requires contextualized performance and unique products.[1] What is noteworthy is that we are no closer to honoring the lessons of Bloom's Taxonomy of Educational Objectives than we were forty years ago. *Educative Assessment* might therefore be said to be an update of Bloom's analysis (with corrections and changed emphasis where needed, especially in the failure to distinguish between academic exercises and the most sophisticated and performance-based forms of understanding). The book describes what it would mean for assessment design, instruction, curriculum, teacher accountability, and grading and reporting if educative assessment were made central to student and teacher work.

I attempt in this book to meet two criteria that are in perpetual tension: to be both provocative and helpful. Some readers will no doubt desire step-by-step assessment design guidelines. Readers who want concrete tutorials, worksheets, and design exercises are referred to our organization—the Center on Learning, Assessment, and School Structure (CLASS)—which offers print, video, and software materials as well as training workshops in assessment design. The aim of this book is to provide readers with the standards for design that underlie any such training. In the long run, these standards are more important than training by itself because the standards prevent the work from ending in rigid orthodoxies or thoughtless design. Design is also a self-correcting standards-based activity, just as performance is for students.

## Audience

*Educative Assessment* is addressed to educators at all levels: classroom teachers; superintendents, principals, and other administrators; curriculum and assessment specialists; professors and students of educational assessment and reform; and teachers of educators. Anyone directly involved with students in a school or college and anyone teaching or studying in a graduate program in education has to assess and report results, and thus can profit from the ideas and practices discussed here. Anyone who has responsibility for professional or technical assessment or measurement can benefit from this book. Those who think that current testing often sacrifices performance improvement and the needs of the student as client for the sake of technical precision and adult concerns will find much here that they can use to make changes in how they assess.

## Overview of the Contents_____

In Chapter One I lay out a vision: What does educative assessment look like? What happens when students are assessed with authentic tasks, given useful feedback, and expected to use it? In the three chapters comprising Part One, we look at the elements of educative assessment.

In Chapter Two, I define and explore the first of two essential qualities, or principles, of educative assessment: authentic tasks. Authentic tasks simulate adult tasks; they give students worthy work and they produce useful feedback so that students can progressively improve their understanding and performance, that is, their application of subject-matter content.

In Chapter Three, I consider part two of educative assessment—feedback—and why it must be built into the assessment process rather than just being made richer and more user-friendly when the assessment is over. How does useful feedback differ from blaming and praising? How and why is feedback in relation to a known goal an essential part of fair assessment and eventual excellence? These questions focus the chapter. Assessment and feedback used to be thought of as something that came *after* teaching. Ongoing assessment for understanding with authentic tasks and useful feedback that help students to self-assess and self-adjust will radically change our view of what teaching itself involves. We need a theory of instruction that recognizes the importance in learning and assessment of having the student react to results—to carry out purposeful trial, error, and adjustment, as it were.

Chapter Four explores the question of why understanding is the achievement that conventional testing cannot adequately test and so does not improve. What *is* understanding? Why after all our teaching do so many students lack understanding or misunderstand? Why is conventional assessment not well suited to test for it? This chapter suggests a provocative new theory of understanding, whereby understanding is seen as composed of five distinct but interdependent facets: sophisticated accounts, contextual application, perspective, empathy, and self-knowledge.[2] Although a variety of implications for assessment follow from this proposed theory of understanding, many of them derive from the ideas in the preceding chapters, namely, that understanding is revealed through authentic work and feedback response, through the student's ability to justify answers, self-assess, and authentically use knowledge in diverse contexts.

In Part Two, I move on to a consideration of design in assessment. Central to Part Two is an explanation of a logical order for considering assessment design elements, a set of design constraints that serve as criteria for judging any assessment design. It does not tell you specifically how to design a particular assessment task but rather how to know whether and when your tasks are sound. To make assessment valid, designers need to ask a series of questions prior to teaching that can be summed up as follows: What evidence do we need to determine whether learning was successful? and What kinds of work requirements will yield that evidence?

Chapter Five discusses the design of authentic assessment using the elements discussed in Chapters Two through Four (authentic tasks, feedback, and understanding). Local educators must learn to think more like assessors—a dramatic shift—and to ask, What is evidence of learning and how will I teach toward it? instead of implicitly asking, as we now do, What will I cover and have students do? This chapter and the two that follow lay out the design standards that underlie an educative assessment system, and it clarifies the difference between content standards, performance standards, and assessment standards—all of which are central to improved schools.

Chapter Six focuses on performance tasks and the issue of authenticity. Questions central to the discussion are, What is an authentic task? Why isn't it synonymous with performance assessment? and What is the relationship between authenticity and validity?

Chapter Seven explores scoring rubrics and criteria. It addresses many questions that are often asked about rubric design and use. Both good and bad rubrics are illustrated. Here as in earlier chapters the focus is on fully informing the student about the desired impact of performance—Was the writing engaging? the proof persuasive? the solution effective? and so on—instead of merely focusing the student on the accuracy of the content and the organization and mechanics of a work, as we now too often do. A purposeful view of performance means that students must learn to bring tasks to completion and meet criteria—not to be confused with pleasing the teacher or merely obeying recipes or procedural instructions.

Part Three looks at the implications of the design work.

Chapter Eight suggests a powerful new use of portfolios—the course of study can be reconceived as leading toward a valid and revealing portfolio of work—and considers the "macro" problems of assessment through this lens. How might we design student portfolios to ensure sound assessment? What kinds of portfolios are there? And how do different purposes shape design? The problem of ownership is central to the discussion: Whose portfolio is it? ours or the student's? and How do the answers affect our work?

Chapter Nine considers curriculum: What are the curriculum implications of performance-based educative assessment? How must courses and programs be designed to produce ongoing student progress toward and achievement of high standards? The questions suggest the answer: curriculum is not separate from assessment, and it cannot precede it. I propose a way of thinking "backward" about curriculum: designating what we want the student to understand and the assessment tasks that will improve that understanding, and *only then* deciding how best to develop lessons and instruction leading to mastery. Such a performance-based view of curriculum also makes it possible for students (and teachers) to prioritize content and time use, and to see the larger purposes for lessons and activities. In other words, an assessment-driven curriculum system makes learning more purposeful and self-evident for the learner. This curriculum has coherence; it has direction; and key concepts, theories, challenges, and genres of performance recur, so students develop an in-depth understanding and mastery of core knowledge. Sample templates for curriculum design and peer curriculum review conclude the chapter.

Chapter Ten examines a practical consequence of new forms of assessment and curriculum, one much on people's minds: new forms of grading and reporting. The current typical report card and grading system is incapable of telling us what honesty and fairness demand we should know about inherently complex performance: how the student is doing against standards and relative to reasonable expectations. New report cards are examined and new approaches to grading are described and justified, showing where we might more helpfully and validly distinguish progress, achievement, and intellectual attitudes.

In Chapter Eleven, I argue that teachers should embrace accountability rather than resist or tolerate it. If feedback is central to all learning, then it must also be central to teaching; accountability systems should be built on feedback and on the requirement that teachers more aggressively solicit it and respond to it (whether from clients or from assessment results). We will have real, not simply political, accountability when we are required to seek and use feedback as part of our daily practice. Teachers as well as students must come to recognize that seeking and receiving feedback on their performance is in their interest, and different from their previous experience with so-called supervision and evaluation, which has too commonly been counterproductive or useless. The chapter concludes by describing a rewarding and professional structure at the heart of such accountability: the process of peer review, whereby draft assessment designs are refined, debugged, and improved. We must practice what we preach. We routinely demand that students work in teams and learn to help each other meet standards. The same approach should be taken to adult design work. Indeed, honoring the logic of design discussed in earlier chapters is almost impossible without a disinterested review of our design work by others. Such review is truly professional and it is extraordinarily rewarding when we engage in it openly, honestly, and responsibly.

The final two chapters deal with feasibility and next steps. Where does an individual teacher or an entire school system begin? What might get in the way and which of the anticipated impediments are real or illusory? What kinds of ideas or models exist for making the changes in schedules and policies that are needed to honor the vision laid out in the previous chapters? What are the most likely strategies for success and what common mistakes ought to be avoided? These are some of the questions addressed.

I am a realist, not a romantic. Nothing recommended or discussed in this book will come easy. My recommendations may well seem impossible within your current circumstances. My challenge here is to provide you with direction and guiding principles for overcoming obstacles rather than capitulating to them. All of the ideas in this book are taken from experiences at real schools, many of which lacked the time, the money, or the talent that skeptics "know" are central to success.

The view that underlies all these chapters is that all students, but *especially* the least and most able, are capable of far better performance than they now accomplish—not because students and teachers are flawed or lazy and irrespective of the other societal and school problems that interfere with our doing our jobs, but because our schools are mostly ineffective performance systems.

This book's novel claim is that most of the students in our schools are underachievers because the schools' implied theory of performance is false, namely, that teaching and hard work cause mastery. Teaching and hard work are necessary but not sufficient, because mastery never results from pieces of discrete teaching and learning piling up in a logical sequence. Rather, mastery requires iterative and purposeful performance by students who are given clear and worthy performance targets, good feedback, coaching, and many opportunities to make incremental and sometimes idiosyncratic progress toward excellence. Obviously not all students can meet what we call the *highest* standards (a contradiction in terms), but we still fail to see how ineffectual (because input-driven) are our approaches to teaching and testing. For as long as assessment is viewed as what we do "after" teaching and learning are over, we will fail to greatly improve student performance, regardless of how well or how poorly students are currently taught or motivated. (This book says more about the opportunities needed for excellence than about incentives for students. Readers who wish to know more about incentives and about how students can acquire better intrinsic and extrinsic motives for learning through better assessment may want to read my 1993 book, *Assessing Student Performance*.)

My thinking on assessment is always evolving, subject to feedback from readers, clients, and the visible effects of my ideas. Most of the material here should be thought of as new even though half of the chapters have their roots in earlier articles (and may seem to have a different slant than the original pieces, for those readers who are familiar with them). The material in Chapter Ten, for example, has been rewritten three times in five years. The book's usefulness stems less from any final truth it might contain than from the questions, discussions, and investigations it should spark.

The book is therefore somewhere betwixt theory and practice. It is theoretical in its discussion of principles of design, standards of assessment, and the intellectual justification for a different approach to assessing students. (Readers familiar with *Assessing Student Performance* may usefully think of this book as Part Two.) It is practical in that it presents design templates, strategies of design and of troubleshooting, and numerous examples of assessment tasks and scoring rubrics. My colleagues and I have developed and repeatedly refined these materials in response to constant feedback from clients and from their use in the consulting we do to schools, districts, and state departments of education. Readers can use these design standards and templates as they draft or revise work in progress. However, this book is not a workbook or tutorial.

"What can I do Monday?" is the cry understandably uttered by teachers and heard across the land. But the cry for immediate relevance has a dark side, even if it must eventually be honored. Teachers are often too eager to plug in a tool instead of working to grasp the strategies, logic, and principles that underlie reform. I know from a decade of work that powerful and self-corrective assessment of student and school performance cannot occur without a clear conception of the principles of good assessment. Assessment design, like assessment itself, is mastered only by providing ourselves with feedback that is based on a clear conception of *ideal* assessment, that is, on a standard or vision. There are no windup techniques, no foolproof recipes. We do not improve much when we lean on mere habits and hunches. Our designs and our efficacy improve when we judge our work against standards and feedback. This is the most useful point I can make to the reader.

Finally, additional concrete design tools, full sets of worksheets, training materials, samplers of tasks and rubrics, videos, and software for self-directed assessment design are available from CLASS. For further information on CLASS materials, training, and programs, contact us in the following ways:

*By mail:* CLASS, 56 South Main Street, Pennington, NJ, 08534

*By telephone:* (609) 730–1199

*By e-mail:* info@classnj.org

*On the World Wide Web:* www.classnj.org

## Acknowledgments

This book could not have been written without the wonderful thinking and colleagueship of Everett Kline, my senior associate at CLASS. So many of the ideas in the book grew from our conversations, from our self-assessment of work in progress, from his designs and their use with our clients, and from our feedback to each other. Everett practices what this book preaches: he thrives on receiving good feedback, is clear about standards and works hard to meet them, and gives excellent feedback. His assistance and friendship are treasured. So is his humor and constant good cheer.

Though distance now makes our colleagueship less face-to-face, Deborah White has also been a vital contributor to these ideas. Her keen eye and ear for what is most useful and intelligible to clients, her exuberance for the work, and her increasing expertise as a task and rubric designer and critic have helped make my ideas clearer, better developed, and more useful.

Other consultant-colleagues who have contributed to the ideas in these pages include David Grant, Pat Jacoby, Michael Katims, and Bill and Anne O'Rourke. Their feedback, ideas for material, and support of our work at CLASS have given me a clear sense that we are a community of associates working together, even if distance typically separates us.

Thanks, too, are due to my staff at CLASS. Through thick and thin, former and current staff members have tirelessly and cheerfully helped us to produce and refine all our materials and programs. Carol Wander is second to none. Her good cheer and assistance helped make possible the assembly of this book into a whole.

Jay McTighe is a wise and trusted friend and coconspirator. We have had memorable lengthy conversations, with synapses firing; his feedback and sharing of work in progress for the Maryland Assessment Consortium greatly clarified my thinking about many design matters and greatly improved the user-friendliness of CLASS products. Thanks, too, to Heidi Hayes Jacobs for her insights and guidance, especially on the subject of design. Our joint workshops and conferences provided invaluable opportunities for sustained and insightful dialogue. Her passion for the work is an inspiration. Rich Strong and Fred Newmann also have been wonderful, critical friends and conversants along the way.

Far too many practitioners to mention are responsible for the best ideas in this book—namely, the specific tasks, rubrics, and portfolios. Many teachers and administrators in the New Jersey Consortium on Assessment helped refine the templates, as did educators from North Carolina in our work during the past three years for the Standards and Accountability Commission.

A special thanks to Sam Houston, the head of that commission. He had the crazy idea to hire CLASS to help build a state-of-the-art learning-focused assessment system for North Carolina. His unwavering enthusiasm, support of our work, political smarts, and feedback were chief reasons why many of the ideas contained herein progressed from design to practice. Necessity was the mother of invention: in such a high-profile and complex venture, we needed to have good stuff, and we had to self-assess and self-adjust early and often. I am grateful to Sam and the members of the commission for their unwavering belief in our work, even as critics and naysayers were suggesting that our ideas would never work.

Thanks, too, to the good folks at the Association for Supervision and Curriculum Development, especially Sally Chapman, Mikki Terry, and Ron Brandt. Sally in particular has been a tireless and enthusiastic supporter of my work while also being a constant no-holds-barred, critical friend, always challenging me to make things more user-friendly when the ideas threaten to get too highfalutin.

In terms of support, the Geraldine R. Dodge Foundation has been without peer. The good folks at Dodge—Scott McVay, Robert Perry, and Alexandra Christie in particular—have been there when we have needed them, have enthusiastically supported and promoted our work, and have provided us with many opportunities for doing the sustained research and development (especially through funding of the New Jersey Consortium on Assessment) that led to the ideas presented in this book.

Supporters in another sense, Ron Thorpe and Rick Love have been stalwarts. Each has been consistently enthusiastic about what we do and each has worked hard to ensure that more people become aware of CLASS and its projects. Marue Walizer and Rick Cowan of the CLASS board have given loyal and generous support and wise counsel. And thanks to Lesley Iura at Jossey-Bass for having the patience to see the book through to fruition, and to Christie Hakim for helping me negotiate the horrors of responding to the editor's queries and the technical publication requirements.

Finally, there would be no book worth the mention without the unwavering love and wisdom of my wife and business partner, Holly Houston. I shudder to think about what kind of incomplete and slapdash stuff the reader might have found here without her feedback, high standards, praise, and ability to keep our wonderfully rich and crazy lives on a steady keel when I become the neurotic and cranky writer. I dedicate the book to her and to my intellectual hero, Jerome Bruner.

*December 1997*                                                      Grant Wiggins
*Pennington, New Jersey*

# AUTHOR

Grant Wiggins is the president and director of programs for the Center on Learning, Assessment, and School Structure (CLASS), a not-for-profit educational organization in Pennington, New Jersey. CLASS consults with schools, districts, and state education departments on a variety of reform matters; organizes national conferences and workshops; and develops video, software, and print materials on assessment and curricular change. Wiggins and his CLASS colleagues have consulted to some of the most influential assessment-reform initiatives in the country (including Kentucky's performance-based system and Vermont's portfolio system). They have established two statewide consortia devoted to assessment reform, and have recently designed a performance-based and teacher-run portfolio assessment system plan for the North Carolina Commission on Standards and Accountability.

Wiggins earned his B.A. degree from St. John's College in Annapolis in 1972 and his Ed.D. degree from Harvard University in 1987. He is the author of *Assessing Student Performance: Exploring the Purpose and Limits of Testing* (1993), also published by Jossey-Bass. His many articles on curriculum and assessment reform have appeared in such journals as *Educational Leadership* and *Phi Delta Kappan.* His work is grounded in fourteen years of secondary school teaching and coaching. He is married to Holly Houston; they have three children: Justin, Ian, and Priscilla.

## CHAPTER 1

# Educative Assessment
## A Vision

The only way we can properly judge where we are is relative to where we want to be. But beyond some general principles, we do not really know what assessment reform would look like if it were successful. We need a vision, in short, of exemplary assessment in action—in the same way that students need models, not just a set of criteria, in order to understand concretely the performance for which they are aiming. Just what is our goal in reform? What would assessment sound and look like if reform were successful? When we get beyond arguments for and against large-scale testing, what do we imagine any comprehensive and effective assessment system should and could be like? Let us imagine an educative assessment system that is designed to improve, not just audit, student performance.

## Classroom Sounds

Where assessment is educative, we hear classroom and hallway conversations that are different than those heard in schools that use traditional assessment methods. Students are no longer asking teachers, "Is this what you want?" or "Is this going to be on the test?" Instead, learning goals and standards are so clearly spelled out that students understand what they are expected to learn. Moreover, these goals and standards are spelled out in terms of performance so that students know how they are expected to demonstrate their learning. All students are aware of their current personal levels of performance, and their talk reflects it: "I need to complete two more tasks at Score 4 if I'm going to make it to the intermediate level in history," says Moira. "I'm missing only two pieces of problem-solving work from my math portfolio," says Josef.

All students can *accurately* self-assess their work, irrespective of their performance ability, and they unendingly self-assess their work on specific tasks: "My essay is strong on voice but weak on organization," Dara says a bit dejectedly. "I think our theory about the identity of these mystery chemicals is good, but we need to check our portfolios to see if those earlier labs on density support our claims," says Bobby to his lab partners. Even small children can be heard talking about their stories in this analytic way: "Remember what we said: good stories paint pictures in your head. Ours doesn't do it," says Jayna to our work group, "so we can't circle the smiley face yet." Students can be heard routinely seeking and taking feedback provided by adults or peers and then revising their work, explaining which feedback they did and did not take and why. The importance of expecting and receiving feedback and using it is so well established that all teachers build formative assessment and revision days into each unit plan. Major performance tests are always in a multipart form to ensure that there is time and opportunity for revision and improvement based on feedback and self-assessment.

We hear teachers' conversations change, too, when assessment is educative. They talk more about students' levels of expertise, as illustrated by shared language in staff rooms and corridors about performance levels and tasks, than about students' scores on traditional tests and grade point averages. "Too many of our seventh graders are still performing at the novice level on these research and presentation tasks," says Manny to his colleagues in a team meeting. "What can we do about the trend?" responds Dorothy, the team leader. "Well, do we know it to be a downward trend?" asks Cilla. "Let's look at the data from the last few cohorts." They find that the trend for their students over the three-year period in fact shows a slippage, using the district novice-expert rubrics in science for grades 7 to 12. Teachers then make changes according to this feedback before it is too late—that is, before students reach exit-level exams. The team ultimately decides to devote a week to a complex science-and-presentation task on pollution with seventh and eighth graders, downloading the task and rubrics they had in mind from the district database.

Outside of school, what we *don't* hear is significant: policymakers no longer judge and discuss programs, schools, districts, or states on the basis of a single, simplistic test score. They now seem to understand that no single generic test can adequately measure the learning that has taken place in a particular school, nor can it establish the most basic aspect of accountability: the *value added* by schools. National and state comparisons continue, but talk in policy circles centers on whether schools are making *appropriate* gains over time when the current performance of students at a school is compared to their past performance and to other cohorts' past performance at the same school and at similar schools. Local transcripts have become more reliable and credible as faculties within regions have established common grading standards, further decreasing the importance of and need for a single test score.

The most noticeable difference in all that we hear is that assessment is no longer discussed as a test that is done once, *after* teaching and learning are over. Instead, discussions among students, teachers, and policymakers center continually on the full range of assessment modes employed, and on whether the blend of local and state results is the most valid and credible mix. They talk about how and why current results occur and about how they can be improved. Revision of work, once a choice offered to students by only a few teachers of writing, is now required of all students and built into many exams: quality work is not an option. The system, the curriculum, and the school support teachers as they focus class time on cycles of performance, feedback, and revision, and as they evaluate not only levels of performance but also how well students self-assess and self-correct their work against high standards.

## Classroom Sights

Although we *see* nothing out of the ordinary, assessment is taking place. This is not just the familiar sight of students busy at work in their rooms or in the library, alone as well as in small groups. The assessment process is often so unobtrusive to students and teachers, so seamless with teaching and learning, that it is visually indistinguishable from what takes place during good instruction. Gone for the most part are silent examinees sitting in rows, answering uniform questions with orthodox answers in blue books or on answer sheets with number 2 pencils. Gone are arbitrary calendars that dictate that all students must be examined simultaneously, regardless of readiness. Instead, students are being given the kind of challenges, diversity, and flexibility that make assessment far more realistic and educative—and professional. They are working together and critiquing one another's writing, bringing science experiments to fruition, finishing art exhibits, honing debate points, and even making presentations to panels of outside judges. These authentic tasks—challenges that more closely resemble the ways students will be expected to use their knowledge and skills in the real world—are built on careful protocols and elaborated scoring systems, but they appear to the novice observer to be enjoyable and challenging activities.

As a teacher and a small group of students hold a lively debate, an administrator functions as assessor, using a faculty-designed scoring system to make a formal and rigorous assessment. The assessor scores the students' responses to the teacher's scripted and impromptu questions that carefully probe the progress the students have made in understanding the solar system, in building a three-dimensional model to scale, and in simple computer animation. The teachers want to know not only what assumptions the students started with and what decisions they have made but also why the students thought these assumptions were valid and how they justify their decisions. Teachers record a discussion like this and have it transcribed so they can analyze it in more detail later, to better gain insight into the most common student misconceptions. At times, two distant classrooms hold such discussions over the Internet, with additional participants acting as judges.

We also see some students working on portfolios that bring together the elements required by each student's learning plan. Purposeful control over work is stressed: first the students, then their teachers, select materials for their portfolios that demonstrate what they are learning and the district benchmarks they have met. These materials include papers, test results, and video or audio recordings of selected performances. As they work on their portfolios, these students also complete a self-assessment process that reveals how well they understand the benchmarks and standards they are to meet and that prompts them to think about what they are learning, to recognize quality work, and to plan how they can perform better in the future.

Other students are building balsa wood bridges, staging plays, and mounting museum exhibits, using computer simulations as well as physical materials, and demonstrating their understanding of subject areas, skills, and ideas by using them in particular contexts. As the students work, teachers are gauging each student's ability to self-adjust in response to the typical problems of each context (what happens for example, when the simulation buffets the balsa bridge with eighty-mile-per-hour winds). Students get immediate feedback, just as they would on the job or the playing field, and they are also assessed on the degree to which they solicit, ponder, and effectively use this feedback.

Available to teachers over the World Wide Web are hundreds of standardized test questions, prompts, performance tasks, scoring rubrics (guidelines), and exemplary work samples from local, regional, and national sources. Standardized national tests are now almost completely customized and adaptive to student responses. These tests form a piece of the student portfolio: student work on local assignments, districtwide performance tasks, and state and national tests is collected; the data is *triangulated*, (in other words, results are compared and anomalies are investigated); no single score is taken as gospel, whereas state assessment used to demand this. Teachers make a summary judgment about the student's performance level. Use of these tests also helps teachers to keep their grading standards consistent with other teachers' standards. Teachers are trained in the standards and sophisticated criteria to use in judging student performance (a scoring system used for decades for Advanced Placement examinations) so that judgments are fair and students' performances can be effectively compared.

Using portfolio requirements and on-demand performance tasks designed for repeated use over time, teachers build a profile of individual and cohort achievement that they use to chart student progress over the years and to predict patterns of performance based on multiyear trends, just as other results-oriented professions do. Instead of seeing cumulative student work represented by only a summative grade or score given in isolation by individual teachers, we see scores that correspond to rubrics in use statewide. (Indeed, the rubrics and "anchoring work samples" [student samples that typify each level of performance] are available to any person with access to the state department of education's Web site.) Teachers, students, and parents review students' work samples and compare them with other samples that represent the complete range of possible quality.

We see teachers personalizing assessments and using a student's previous achievements as a benchmark for assessing new gains and for providing apt challenges over the years as the student moves along a continuum from novice to expert—much as students track their own scores on computer games and their performance in athletics. Both teachers and parents have access to long-term achievement profiles of each student. When these profiles are kept electronically, they provide detailed data and documentation at the click of a mouse.

Most of all, what we both hear and see are students and teachers deeply engaged in work that relates to real-world activities and results, confident that they know what various levels of achievement should look like and that school accountability is finally centered on performances that matter to them and to others around them.

## Administrative and Policy Implications_____

As educative assessment motivates students to improve performance in accordance with worthy and public standards and criteria, it becomes easier to hold schools and districts accountable for the results of assessment, which are now more credible to everyone. Consequently, states no longer give tests as a rule. They evaluate local tests for their value as assessment tools. Random state audits monitor local assessment processes and tasks to make sure they meet established criteria for good assessment. Sets of student papers are also audited to make sure that performance standards are high and that there is consistent scoring within each subject area. Based on these audits, state personnel make recommendations and provide assistance in improving local assessment systems, because everyone now sees that, as in politics, all school reform is local.

At the local level, teams of teachers routinely collaborate on assessments to ensure consensus and consistency in the scoring of work. (Most state guidelines now require such collaboration and inter-rater reliability.) Teachers visit one another's schools periodically to judge performance and help conduct audits to ensure validity and reliability. Administrators now have a primary responsibility to ensure that the quality of local assessment is high.

In evaluating student work and setting standards for performance and assessment, school educators and administrators are aided by others. College professors help develop and administer assessments that ensure students are prepared for college work, and businesspeople help set specific performance standards and tasks related to business and professional needs. They are also often recruited to participate on the teams of judges used in major assessments of student portfolios and performance. In fact, educative assessment is a community-wide affair, so teachers do not hesitate to ask for help from anyone whose expertise might be valuable during a particular task. These guests in the classroom (either in person or over the Internet) do not simply impart their wisdom and leave; they stick around to help evaluate what was learned by students, teachers, and even themselves.

Employers and college admissions officers have devised various ways of interpreting candidates' portfolios of student work. In place of limited and one-size-fits-all transcript information, they can review applicants' academic profiles, which are grounded in the novice-expert continua for all core subjects that schools' clients have helped validate to ensure the quality and usefulness of the schools' data. Some employers and admissions officers combine quantifiable results into a single score; others take the time to look more deeply at specific qualities needed for success. Either way, few pine for the days when all the information they had about a candidate's education was a grade point average that was not linked to a known or shared standard.

In short, when our schools practice educative assessment, our children and our teachers come to see assessment as central to learning, as linked to real-world demands (and hence to incentives), and as worthy of attention. Thus, rather than seeming to be a fearful and onerous set of hoops to jump through, assessment now seems more like the other performances that educate and motivate while testing: the game, the recital, and the play. It becomes anchored in challenges worth mastering; it becomes enjoyable; and it becomes more able to accommodate an appropriate diversity of talents, aspirations, and interests while supporting high standards.

## The Core Premise: The Purpose of Assessment

The vision just presented illustrates the core premise of this book: the aim of assessment is primarily to *educate and improve* student performance, not merely to *audit* it. I use the terms *auditing* and *audit test* to describe checking up on activities after they are over, as accountants audit a business's books to check that all the financial records match over a fiscal year. People do not run their businesses only to satisfy an auditor's requirement for records that appear accurate. But schools too often worry about the equivalent: we focus on teaching students to pass simplistic, often multiple-choice tests composed of "items" that neither assess what we value nor provide useful feedback about how to teach and how to learn.

We sacrifice our aims and our children's intellectual needs when we test what is easy to test rather than the complex and rich tasks that we value in our classrooms and that are at the heart of our curriculum. That is, we sacrifice information about what we truly want to assess and settle for score accuracy and efficiency. That sacrifice is possible only when all of us misunderstand the role assessment plays in learning. In other words, the greatest impediment to achieving the vision described is not standardized testing. Rather, the problem is the reverse: we use the tests we do because we persist in thinking of assessment as not germane to learning, and therefore best done expediently.

Assessment reform is thus neither as easy nor as simple as throwing out conventional tests. Before we can change our system into one that serves all our needs, we require something more educative and exemplary to which to aspire—something vivid and provocative that makes us see the deficiencies in our time-honored practices, something designed to promote excellence, not just to measure efficiently.

The vision serves as a standard against which we can measure and adjust change; its seeming impossibility is not a defect but a spur to more focused work, as with all standards.

The vision is not fanciful or idle, in other words. The images that began this chapter are essential to more effective self-adjustment on our part. And almost every one of the scenes described can be witnessed somewhere in the world right now. Many districts are using longitudinal rubrics both to assess students and to report progress to parents. The Province of Quebec already builds the getting and using of feedback into its writing exam.[1] The New Standards developed by Marc Tucker and Lauren Resnick at the National Center on Education and the Economy and the University of Pittsburgh lay out a comprehensive system for achieving high-level performance against credible standards.[2] The assessment system recently built in prototype form for the state of North Carolina by the Center on Learning, Assessment, and School Structure, described in further detail in Chapters Two and Eight, is built on a state portfolio of work and a nonsecure, statewide database of performance tasks and rubrics that provides one source of performance evidence relative to state standards. Longitudinal rubrics on a novice-mastery continuum exist in all subjects in Great Britain.[3] Such continua in literacy can be found in dozens of school districts, and in *The American Literacy Profiles,* based on a decade of research in Australia.[4] Many folks are finally coming to understand that assessment *is of no value* unless it is educative—that is, instructive to students, teachers, and school clients and overseers. They see that, despite the significant energies required to change how, what, when, and by whom we assess, it is worth the effort.

And once assessment is designed to be educative, it is no longer separate from instruction; it is a major, essential, and integrated part of teaching and learning. Once we see how achievement of excellence depends not only on the quality of the tasks that students undertake but also on the quality of the feedback they get, we will better marshal the energy and resources needed to honor this vision.

In part, this book is devoted to showing you how we have wrongly construed assessment as a problem of tinkering with testing techniques, and how school and assessment reform depends on our grasping the moral and intellectual imperatives embedded in a new vision of the *purposes* of teaching, of the ways students acquire understanding, and of the corresponding methods and goals of assessment. From such an educational vision all technical, technological, and restructuring solutions will follow.

The remainder of this chapter looks at some current realities of testing and assessment, and at the primary characteristics of an educative, or learning-centered, assessment system. It also introduces the key ideas on which assessment reform must center.

## Seeing Current Testing Differently

Sometimes we need a negative vision. Sometimes we need to cast current practice in a different light—to make the familiar strange—to enable us to see that practice and the need to change it more clearly. As part of thinking about why, how, with what, and by whom students are typically assessed today, and about why changes of a wholesale kind are required, imagine the following scenes:

1. Imagine that a person in your state can get a driver's license merely by doing well on the paper-and-pencil part of the test. Then imagine further that your state department of motor vehicles (DMV) does not administer a road test for new drivers because it thinks the test would not be worth the time, money, and hassle and that the DMV officers administering the test would be likely to make "subjective" (and thus controversial) judgments. Instead, drivers' education involves extensive book work, paper-and-pencil tests of driving strategy, and lots of practice on different forms of written tests. (Is this a state you would feel safe driving in?)

2. Imagine that high school bands have no rehearsals or recitals. Instead they have lots of book learning, with paper-and-pencil tests on the strategies of playing, the history of music, and the rules of composition. Then imagine that the final exam consists of a one-shot performance, a single-event, external test at semester's end, in which bands in competition with each other play not whole pieces of music but only tightly structured drills and exercises designed to test bits of discrete teaching. The exam is "secure"—that is, the band members do not know what musical segments they have to play until they see them on the test. And the players cannot hear themselves play (the instruments are digital and the sound is turned off). The musicians have to wait a week or more to find out how they did on this test; they get back a personal, norm-referenced score. (Will this system produce high-quality musicianship or passion to play?)

3. Imagine a performance appraisal system for teachers that at the end of each year tests them only in writing on a variety of teaching skills and knowledge about instruction, curriculum, and assessment. The test varies from year to year and is secure, so only the supervisor knows the small sample of questions to be asked and how the results will be scored. (Will this system improve teacher performance?)

These scenes seem absurd, yet they reflect students' and teachers' current plight in the classroom, even in good schools, where students are given one-shot secure tests that audit a sample of the content they are expected to have learned during a year, and that give them a numeric score telling them where they stand compared to other students taking the same test, and not much else. If the function of assessment is to improve student (and teacher) performance, then testing of the kind described in these three scenes is dysfunctional, no matter what area of endeavor we are testing and no matter how technically sound the scores. It is ineffective because even if such instruments are technically sound, they can never adequately inform or direct the energies of students and teachers to improve their work.

Worse, because of its political authority, traditional large-scale testing causes teachers to mimic locally the *format* of test items, even though such mimicry turns validity on its head and lowers intellectual standards over time. A steady dose of simplistic tests in school then unwittingly teaches the student an incorrect view of intellectual performance in the adult world while also undercutting the student's need for and right to user-friendly feedback from ongoing assessment on clear and worthy achievement targets. The vision presented earlier is built on the principle that we need to safeguard the learner's needs, even when meeting other needs in the educational system seems more pressing or cost-effective. But as long as assessment is conceived of as what we do *after* teaching and learning are over, and as long as it yields a hard-to-fathom score too late to be useful, assessment will never serve its primary client, the student, or its primary purpose, improvement leading to excellence. Cost-effectiveness will win out as the key criterion.

Our excessive reliance on short-answer or multiple-choice testing has landed us in a world I describe as "teach, test, and hope for the best." Teachers typically cover a great deal of material, test once, and move on. But it should not be our job to *hope* that by teaching a bunch of stuff some of it will stick. Our job ought to be seen (by everyone) as maximizing learning on worthy tasks that require enduring knowledge and skill. That requires us to anchor instruction in authentic work, to use feedback loops and better coaching, not more content coverage based on higher content standards.

The vision and the crazy vignettes suggest a vital overlooked consequence of traditional assessment habits. Most teachers feel a mixture of unrelenting faith in kids and depressing fatalism about their own and other teachers' inability to get most students to meet high academic standards. The fatalism is "justified" by the results teachers see on most tests, be they local or national. Dramatic gains of whole cohorts are rare (often by design in the large-scale test). In fact, today the socioeconomic status of a student's parents is the best predictor of that student's performance (according to data on Scholastic Achievement Tests provided by the Educational Testing

Service[5]). Given this information, why should we not believe that our net effect as teachers is more dependent on students' native talent and opportunity than on anything else?

By contrast, if our assessment system were actually *working* to teach students, what would we see? We would see strong performance gains over time for *all* students. We would see the feedback loop working so well that what was once considered outstanding performance, reached by only a few people twenty years ago, would now be commonplace (as is the case today in the arts and athletics).

This is not far-fetched. Look at the sheer bulk of audit tests we use. Then consider that U.S. schools spend well over $100 million on commercial standardized testing per year.[6] Then ask, What evidence is there that this massive amount of traditional testing is helping us to improve student performance on worthy, challenging tasks? Practically none, if we are to believe the test data from the National Assessment of Educational Progress (NAEP) for the past twenty years. They show flat and shockingly poor performance on demanding tasks, even by students with high scores in relation to other students. For example, despite student gains in basic science knowledge over the past decades, "their ability to apply scientific knowledge, design an experiment themselves or clearly explain their reasoning is 'disappointing,'" as found in the most recent NAEP results.[7] In fact, teaching to simplistic tests makes dramatic gains unlikely.

When we fail to find evidence that massive amounts of conventional testing improve student performance, we can better understand why schools do not improve much. Learning to master something requires constant receipt and use of feedback. Giving a single-unit or year-end test on the heels of content coverage has as little likelihood of causing significant performance gains over time as one-recital secure-test semesters of playing in a school band have of yielding many future musicians. We must come to see the irony that few now see: teaching (and testing once) does not cause learning. Learning from assessment and standards—that is, "teaching as coaching"—is what ultimately causes the performer to meet a standard.

Moreover, what conventional teaching and testing hide is the enormous misunderstanding that many students have about things the generic standardized tests say they "know." As we shall see in Chapter Four, it is not contradictory to say that students possess a good deal of knowledge that hides a great deal of misunderstanding. The gap between our teaching intent and our teaching effect is profound—more wide and deep than many educators imagine. We can close it only by learning to think as assessors of our own and students' skills and understanding, and by becoming better researchers into our own practice.

## Educative Assessment Defined_____

In this book I argue that assessment should be educative in two basic senses. First, assessment should be deliberately designed to teach (not just measure) by revealing to students what worthy adult work looks like (offering them authentic tasks). Second, assessment should provide rich and useful feedback to all students and to their teachers, and it should indeed be designed to assess the use of feedback by both students and teachers. Other requirements surround these two central characteristics. The following outline offers an overview of these additional elements of a learning-centered assessment system:

1. An educative assessment system is designed to teach—to improve performance (of student and teacher) and evoke exemplary pedagogy. It is built on a bedrock of meaningful performance tasks that are credible and realistic (authentic), hence engaging to students. This system must also
    a. Be open—that is, based on tasks, criteria, and standards known to students and their teachers. Educative assessment is hence far less reliant on audit testing methods, which require that test questions be kept secret.
    b. Model exemplary instruction, encouraging rather than undercutting desirable teaching practice, showing all teachers how the most rich and vital educational goals and pedagogies can be properly assessed.
    c. Use grades that stand for something clear, stable, and valid. These grades must also be linked directly to credible and important state or national standards for assessing performance on authentic tasks.
    d. Measurably improve student performance over time so that standards once thought very high and reachable by only a few become reasonable expectations for many students. Assessment systems should themselves be assessed against this standard.
2. An educative assessment system must provide useful feedback to students, teachers, administrators, and policymakers. A useful feedback system must
    a. Provide data and commentary that are rich, clear, and direct enough to enable students and teachers to self-assess accurately and self-correct their own performances increasingly over time. It must not center on praise and blame.

b.  Provide ample opportunities to get and use timely and ongoing feedback. This implies a longitudinal or iterative system of assessment in which tasks, criteria, and standards recur over the years, frequently alerting students and teachers to how the students' current performance compares to exit-level standards, thereby permitting intervention and adjustment before it is too late.

This view of educative assessment has many implications, some of which strike at time-honored habits, practices, and policies. Some of the most important ones—the impact on curriculum design, accountability, performance appraisal, grading and reporting, and scheduling—are considered in the chapters that make up the latter half of the book. But we can note a key policy implication now: school performance, like student performance, must highlight the value added by schooling, using measures credible to the performers and teacher-coaches. To ensure improvement and not just table thumping, comparisons of students and schools to one another should involve meaningful accounts of progress (gains over time against standards) in terms of credible performance tasks and criteria (just as we now do in college athletics by putting schools in separate divisions based on school size).

## Teaching as Coaching: Feedback and Guidance

Educative assessment implies that teaching sets possibilities in motion; the quality of the assessment (the challenge set, the feedback obtained, and the adjustments made) and of the coaching determine how far students will take those possibilities. Achievement depends on the learner attempting, through successive approximations (based on many performance-feedback-guidance cycles), to match or even exceed model performance. Think of being coached in chess or basketball, or recall efforts at losing weight: the "teaching" is meaningless unless we learn to internalize methods, insights, and standards through the feedback from the results of our attempted performances and through the coach's targeted guidance. Unless we attend carefully to the effects of our attempts at performance, no genuine achievement is likely to occur except by luck or native talent (hence, once again the fatalism of so many educators about raising standards).

If the goal of an assessment system is to educate, to improve performance on difficult tasks, then getting students to self-assess and self-adjust their performance effectively is key. No task is mastered the first time out; no one has twenty-four-hour access to coaches or teachers. And no task is mastered without lots of trials and errors. But the errors are instructive only if we learn to understand them as errors: long before we master a task we must learn whether we are on the road to mastering it. Long before I consistently hit the tennis ball properly, for example, I need to know (and feel) the difference between hitting it properly and improperly. I must (slowly) learn to coordinate where the ball went with what my body was doing (or not doing) just before the ball was hit. Students must be taught the standards, criteria, and key tasks; they must be given practice in judging performance the way the adult judges do it; and they must then be assessed in part on whether they have learned to assess their work reliably and make adjustments to it.

This sounds obvious enough, but consider the implications. What do students need to know in order to self-assess and self-adjust? What kinds of information and opportunities are required to build an effective self-correcting performance system based on a significant self-assessment component? At the very least, students need four things that challenge conventional assessment at its roots: (1) they need a complete demystification of the standards and performance test tasks against which they will be evaluated (as already occurs when people work at a job, play music, or participate in sports); (2) they need multiple opportunities with accompanying feedback to learn to master complex tasks; (3) they need progress reports in which current performance is judged against exemplary adult performance; and (4) most of all, they need to know how they are doing as they do it.

These needs run headlong into hundreds of years of testing habits. To honor those needs, we must undo test security as we know it and we must stop using one-shot tests that provide no ongoing feedback and opportunity to improve performance. I have previously argued in more detail how test security is an ugly holdover from the premodern era of schooling, a time when educators unthinkingly and with impunity treated students as objects.[8] Extensive secrecy or mystery runs counter to the core premise mentioned earlier—that assessment's primary purpose is student improvement, not auditing for adults. Who could improve their performance under such a system?

## Authentic Performance Tasks

Another implication of an assessment system that is designed to teach is that educators should never rely primarily or exclusively on test items that are proxies for genuine and worthy performance challenges, that try to measure performance indirectly by sampling content knowledge. Instead, we should routinely assess students' ability to perform on complex tasks at the heart of each subject, scaffolding the task as needed when we are dealing with novices—in the same way that T-ball scaffolds the complex game of baseball for six-year-olds. To use a different analogy: instruction and assessment must be designed to function more like using training wheels than like riding a tricycle for years. The aim is to get the student to understand and attempt to master the whole performances that give purpose and direction to isolated skill and knowledge work. Further, the curriculum should be designed primarily to lead to mastery of key performance tasks; curriculum design and assessment design should be merged (a view outlined in Chapter Six). We would expect the student to learn what the athlete and musician learn at a very young age—namely, the kind of problem-based work that "big people" do when they are challenged in their fields. Regardless of the psychometric value of indirect test items, their overuse undermines a good education because it hides from students a key purpose of an education—namely, excellence at worthy tasks.

This sounds reasonable and not very controversial. It should. The vision is not utopian but a return to common sense and core purposes. Of course we learn to do something complex only through good guidance and through receiving and using good feedback. Of course nothing worth understanding is mastered the first time, the first year, or the first course of study. Of course we need powerful and worthy purposes to become competent and stay motivated. Only when we fully grasp the correctness of the vision will we endure the hard work of school reform to honor that vision.

Yet one apparent obstacle needs rethinking. A reason that educators sometimes think they cannot move beyond the short-answer expedient test is revealed when you hear people talk wistfully about the need for more time and when you hear that they fear the potential loss of "coverage." But the argument that there is no time for the kinds of intensive, judgment-based assessment described here gets the matter completely backward. We might as well say we have no time for soccer teams to travel to other schools to play games given the pressing need to cover all the soccer curriculum. We might as well say we have no time for the difficult and time-intensive business of preparing and presenting music recitals featuring just a few pieces of music given the amount of music available to study and learn. Because assessment must anchor teaching and because it enables learning if done well, we must make time for it if we are ever to meet our goals. Instead of saying, "But we don't have enough time!" we must ask, "How are we going to redeploy the limited time we have so that we can make our work truly effective?"

## Incentives to Learn, Incentives to Change Teaching_____

Part of the case for more direct and realistic assessment of performance is that students get greater incentives to perform, hence to improve and achieve. The assessment I envision implies, in other words, that the student question "What can I do with this?" is not an anti-intellectual question (when asked in the right tone of voice). On the contrary, this question alerts us to the fact that coverage-focused work and testing based on a sample of items out of context can have no self-evident meaning to the student. By contrast, all adult work is purposeful (not the same as relevant) in the sense that small jobs clearly support larger projects and overarching job responsibilities. Assessment is properly authentic when it places a particular test in a larger context and provides a rationale for mastering it: I need to know that this exercise or drill helps me do something of importance. Many assignments fail this standard in our world of sampled short-answer testing.

Here is a simple example of the idea that testing, even large-scale testing at the state level, can be more performance based. In the first year of New York State's hands-on fourth grade science test, the director of science for the state heard from numerous teachers that students actually pleaded for more such work in the future. Can most teachers and test directors claim that students feel similarly about the assessments they proffer? (And the New York test was a modest one, nowhere near as fascinating as the better local performance tests in science now in use.) What, then, are we losing in the way of interest and passion—and the better performance that would result—because of our typically dull and superficial test questions? When we set higher standards by making mastery the goal and when we build into the assessment system greater opportunities for students and teachers to meet those standards and to see them as worthy, we create a system that is not only technically defensible but also inspiring.

Thus we should ask of any school, district, or state assessment, Does it adequately motivate students to meet high standards? Does it give students the incentives provided by worthy work and real-world requirements? Simplistic, one-shot, secure, "Gotcha!" tests may get students' attention but they do not get their respect nor inspire their passion and persistence.

Teachers, too, must have greater incentives, particularly as results become more public and high-stake, if the vision is to happen. Teachers, too, need models, design standards, and multiple opportunities to get feedback about their performance against state standards so they can practice what they preach here. They also need incentives and opportunities to improve their performance as assessors, something prevented by a constant reliance on external secure testing systems. Teachers not only need to have access to high-quality assignments, tests, and performance standards for use in local instruction and assessment, but they also need the opportunities and incentives to make greater use of such high-quality tasks and demanding standards in their own assessments.

Any assessment system that would improve itself must therefore make all teachers co-owners and co-operators of high-stake testing. At present they are more often out-of-the-loop victims of it. There must be a more explicit linkage between state and district performance and mastery standards, and local testing and grading of student work. The quality of grading from school to school and from teacher to teacher varies far too much, and too few teacher tests reliably measure the performance described here. Historically, it was in part inconsistencies in teacher grading and the poor quality of local assessment that gave rise to the prominence of standardized testing and the mistrust of local reports. Now we must reverse that situation. We need an assessment system that over time is self-correcting and deliberately engineered, based on design and use standards, to improve the quality of local standards and measures. We need a system that makes it as much in the classroom teacher's interest to use state standards in local grading as it is in the interest of the track and field coach to remind students that winning times and distances in dual track meets may not yield excellent results in state meets.

## Conclusion

This chapter has introduced five key ideas about assessment and assessment reform:

1. *Assessment reform must center on the purpose, not merely on the techniques or tools, of assessment.* That purpose is to help the student to learn better and the teacher to instruct better. All other needs, such as accountability and program evaluation, come second and must not be allowed to override the first need, as so often happens now. Thus, merely shifting assessment tools from multiple-choice questions to performance tasks changes nothing if we still rely on the rituals of year-end one-shot secure testing.

2. *Assessment reform is essentially a moral matter.* Students are entitled to a more educative and user-friendly assessment system. By extension, teachers are entitled to an assessment system that facilitates better teaching.

3.  *Assessment is central, not peripheral, to instruction.* Indeed, learning depends on the goals provided by assessment and on the adjustment based on its results. We learn through receiving and using feedback.

4.  *Assessment anchors teaching, and authentic tasks anchor assessment.* Students in the classroom are thus enabled to see what adults really are called on to do with their knowledge, and to learn what the student athlete or musician already knows—that genuine performance is more than drill work that develops discrete knowledge and skill.

5.  *All performance improvement is local* (to paraphrase former Speaker of the House Thomas P. O'Neill on politics). Of course we will continue to have state and national comparisons and state standards that guide local standards, but it is the daily local cycle of performance and feedback that produces most of students' learning and most improvement of schools.

Our current methods of testing and grading are, I believe, deep-seated but unthinking habits. All too often we give contrived tests, hand back scores that have little meaning to students, and move on to the next lessons, irrespective of the assessment results. Assessment can be much more than this. It can inspire and focus work to yield the kinds of student improvement we are always hoping for but rarely see.

As described in the preface, the chapters that follow explain how the vision presented in this chapter can become reality. Chapters Two and Three define authentic tasks and useful feedback, the two essential elements in educative assessment. Chapter Four looks at what we need to assess, with special focus on understanding, which is the quality we all prize but do not currently assess for properly. Chapter Five discusses the logic by which we can weave assessing for understanding, authentic tasks, feedback, and other assessment elements into sound assessment design. The rubrics we will need to score our assessments are described in Chapter Six, and the way curricula must change to reflect the use of ongoing assessment and performance improvements tasks is addressed in Chapter Seven. Portfolios are discussed in Chapter Eight; the new report cards demanded by assessment reform are outlined in Chapter Nine. Chapter Ten then talks straightforwardly about teacher accountability and peer review, made more necessary but also more practical and predictable by assessment reform. Finally, Chapters Eleven and Twelve discuss the development of strategy for honoring the vision.

# PART ONE

# Essential Elements of Assessment

## CHAPTER 2

# Ensuring Authentic Performance

Testing that is deliberately designed to teach and improve, not just measure, is the essence of educative assessment. But what does this mean in practice? As mentioned in the preface, two elements are fundamental: *authentic tasks* and built-in *performer-friendly feedback*. Assessment must be anchored in and focused on authentic tasks because they supply valid direction, intellectual coherence, and motivation for the day-in and day-out work of knowledge and skill development. Such tasks are never mastered the first time out. Eventual excellence at all complex tasks depends on how well we adjust to meeting high standards, that is, how well we learn to use feedback and guidance as we confront such tasks repeatedly. Thus we ultimately develop excellence and autonomy by getting progressively better at self-assessment and self-adjustment. Assessment must make authentic work and use of feedback more central to the learning process—whether we are talking about the learning of students, teachers, or administrators. In other words, student self-adjustment must become central to teaching, learning, and testing.

Assessment is authentic when we anchor testing in the kind of work real people do, rather than merely eliciting easy-to-score responses to simple questions. Authentic assessment is true assessment of *performance* because we thereby learn whether students can intelligently use what they have learned in situations that increasingly approximate adult situations, and whether they can innovate in new situations. This chapter introduces the first element of educative assessment: authenticity; the following chapter then looks at how feedback and its use become central to the assessment, rather than merely taking place afterward.

## Authentic Tasks

Though some folks I have spoken with over the years regret or resent the use of the word *authentic* in describing assessment, it remains an apt adjective. Conventional test questions, be they from national tests or the teacher down the hall, do not replicate the kinds of challenges that adults face in the workplace, in civic affairs, or in their personal lives. This is not to condemn such questions but to identify them as a certain type: in the language of psychometrics (the science of intellectual measurement), typical questions are *indirect* ways of testing performance *directly*—that is, in context. Whether because of cost, time, feasibility, or purpose, test "items" serve as proxies for or preludes to real performance. While test items have a use in assessment, in the same way that drills have a place in coaching, the sum of the items is not performance, whether we are considering intellectual or athletic mastery. Assessment ought to be educative in the basic sense that students are entitled to direct testing that educates them about the purpose of schooling and the nature of adult work. Authentic tasks thus supply greater incentives for students to persist with day-in and day-out learning and insight into the reasons for specific lessons. The chart in Figure 2.1 summarizes some of the key differences between authentic tasks and typical tests.

I propose the following standards for authentic assessment.[1] An assessment task, problem, or project is authentic if it

1. *Is realistic.* The task or tasks replicate the ways in which a person's knowledge and abilities are "tested" in real-world situations.

2. *Requires judgment and innovation.* The student has to use knowledge and skills wisely and effectively to solve unstructured problems, such as when a plan must be designed, and the solution involves more than following a set routine or procedure or plugging in knowledge.

3. *Asks the student to "do" the subject.* Instead of reciting, restating, or replicating through demonstration what he or she was taught or what is already known, the student has to carry out exploration and work within the discipline of science, history, or any other subject.

## Figure 2.1 Key Differences Between Typical Tests and Authentic Tasks

| *Typical Tests* | *Authentic Tasks* | *Indicators of Authenticity* |
| --- | --- | --- |
| Require correct responses only | Require quality product and/or performance, and *justification*. | We assess whether the student can explain, apply, self-adjust, or justify answers, not just the correctness of answers using facts and algorithms. |
| Must be unknown in advance to ensure validity | Are known as much as possible in advance; involve excelling at predictable demanding and core tasks; are not "gotcha!" experiences. | The tasks, criteria, and standards by which work will be judged are predictable or known—like the recital piece, the play, engine to be fixed, proposal to a client, etc. |
| Are disconnected from a realistic context and realistic constraints | Require real-world use of knowledge: the student must "do" history, science, etc. in realistic simulations or actual use. | The task is a challenge and a set of constraints that are authentic— likely to be encountered by the professional, citizen or consumer. (Know-how, not plugging in, is required.) |
| Contain isolated items requiring use or recognition of known answers or skills | Are integrated challenges in which knowledge and judgment must be innovatively used to fashion a quality product or performance. | The task is multifaceted and non-routine, even if there is a "right" answer. It thus requires problem clarification, trial and error, adjustments, adapting to the case or facts at hand, etc. |
| Are simplified so as to be easy to score reliably | Involve complex and non-arbitrary tasks, criteria, and standards. | The task involves the important aspects of performance and/or core challenges of the field of study, not the easily scored; does not sacrifice validity for reliability. |
| Are one shot | Are iterative: contain recurring essential tasks, genres, and standards. | The work is designed to reveal whether the student has achieved real versus pseudo mastery, or understanding versus mere familiarity, over time. |
| Depend on highly technical correlations | Provide direct evidence, involving tasks that have been validated against core adult roles and discipline-based challenges. | The task is valid and fair on its face. It thus evokes student interest and persistence, and seems apt and challenging to students and teachers. |
| Provide a score | Provide usable, diagnostic (sometimes concurrent) feedback: the student is able to confirm results and self-adjust as needed. | The assessment is designed not merely to audit performance but to improve future performance. The student is seen as the primary "customer" of information. |

4.   *Replicates or simulates the* contexts *in which adults are "tested" in the workplace, in civic life, and in personal life.* Contexts involve specific situations that have particular constraints, purposes, and audiences. Typical school tests are context-less. Students need to experience what it is like to do tasks in workplace and other real-life contexts, which tend to be messy and murky. In other words, genuine tasks require good judgment. Authentic tasks undo the ultimately harmful secrecy, silence, and absence of resources and feedback that mark excessive school testing.

5.   *Assesses the student's ability to efficiently and effectively use a repertoire of knowledge and skill to negotiate a complex task.* Most conventional test items are isolated elements of performance—similar to sideline drills in athletics rather than to the integrated use of skills that a game requires. Good judgment is required here, too. Although there is, of course, a place for drill tests, performance is always more than the sum of the drills.

6.   *Allows appropriate opportunities to rehearse, practice, consult resources, and get feedback on and refine performances and products.* Although there is a role for the conventional "secure" test that keeps questions secret and keeps resource materials from students until during the test, that testing must coexist with educative assessment if students are to improve performance; if we are to focus their learning, through cycles of *performance-feedback-revision-performance,* on the production of *known* high-quality products and standards; and if we are to help them learn to use information, resources, and notes to effectively perform in context.

A call for greater authenticity in tests is not really new. Benjamin Bloom and his colleagues were onto the importance of such work forty years ago, as evidenced in their description of *application* ("situations new to the student or situations containing new elements as compared to the situation in which the abstraction was learned. . . . Ideally we are seeking a problem which will test the extent to which an individual has learned to apply the abstraction in a practical way")[2] and of tests to assess *synthesis* ("a type of divergent thinking [in which] it is unlikely that the right solution to a problem can be set in advance").[3]

In later materials, Bloom and his colleagues characterized synthesis tasks in language that makes clear the need for authentic assessment as I have defined it:

1. The problem, task, or situation involving synthesis should be new or in some way different from those used in instruction. The students . . . may have considerable freedom in redefining it.
2. The student may attack the problem with a variety of references or other available materials as they are needed. Thus synthesis problems may be open-book examinations, in which the student may use notes, the library, and other resources as appropriate. Ideally, synthesis problems should be as close as possible to the situation in which a scholar (or artist, engineer, and so forth) attacks a problem in which he or she is interested. The time allowed, the conditions of work, and other stipulations should be as far from the typical, controlled examination situation as possible.[4]

Educational researcher Fred Newmann and his colleagues at the University of Wisconsin have developed a similar set of standards for judging the authenticity of tasks in assessments and instructional work, and they have used those standards to study instructional and assessment practices around the country.[5] In their view, authentic tasks require

**Construction of Knowledge**

1.    Student organization of information (higher order skills)

2.    Student consideration of alternatives

**Disciplined Inquiry**

3.    Core disciplinary content knowledge

4.    Core disciplinary processes

5.    Written communications to elaborate understanding

**Value Beyond School**

6.    Connecting problems to the world beyond the classroom

7.    Involving an audience beyond the school

To understand the implications of these standards, the limits of current testing (in which assessment overemphasizes scripted behavior separated from natural context), and the performance that authentic assessment tasks require, compare Figures 2.2 and 2.3. Figure 2.2 shows four items on a recent state test in eighth grade mathematics.[6] These items are all of the questions used to assess the students' knowledge of volume. Figure 2.3 shows a performance-based challenge that implicitly requires the same *knowledge* as the conventional test, but also requires students to use their *understanding* of volume effectively. The authentic task thus does not replace the first test; it supplements it.[7]

## Figure 2.2 State Test of Knowledge of Volume

34. What is the surface area of the cylinder shown below?

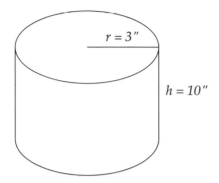

    A       13 π square inches

    B       18 π square inches

    C       60 π square inches

    D       78 π square inches

35. A can of Goofy Grape Soda has a diameter of 5 cm and a height of 10 cm. What is the volume of the can of soda?

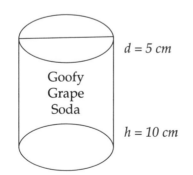

    A       78.50 cm³

    B       157.00 cm³

    C       196.25 cm³

    D       392.50 cm³

36. What is the volume of the cone?

    A       4710 cu ft

    B       1570 cu ft

    C       942 cu ft

    D       300 cu ft

37. The area of the base of a triangular pyramid was doubled. How does the new volume compare with the old volume?

    A       one-forth

    B       one-half

    C       two times

    D       four times

## Figure 2.3  Authentic Task for Assessing Understanding of Volume

*That's a Wrap.*

You are in charge of the gift-wrapping of purchases in a large department store. On average, 24,000 customers make clothing purchases in your store each year. About 15 percent of the customers want their purchases gift-wrapped. In a month, the store typically sells 165 jackets, 750 shirts, 480 pairs of pants, and 160 hats. The price of all boxes is the same, and wrapping paper costs 26 cents per yard. Each roll of gift-wrap is one yard wide and one hundred yards long.

As the manager of gift-wrapping, you naturally want to plan for the year's gift-wrapping costs *and* you want to save money where possible. What box shape for pants, shirts, jackets, and hats would require the *least amount* of wrapping paper?

*Your task*:

Recommend to the purchasing agent in a written report:

- The size of boxes that should be ordered for pants, shirts, jackets, and hats when ordered separately

- The number of rolls of wrapping paper needed

- The approximate cost of wrapping paper for a year's worth of sales of pants, shirts, jackets, and hats

*Questions to consider*:

1. When the clothes are folded, how big does the box need to be? Of course, the way you fold makes a difference in the shape of the box you could use without messing up the clothes.

2. Experiment with measuring, folding, and boxing clothes in the typical light-cardboard boxes that clothes come in (or make boxes out of large pieces of paper with which to experiment).

3. Consider whether some package shapes are easier to wrap than others, with minimal waste. Yet maybe those easy-to-wrap shapes require more paper—even though less is wasted. Are there any rules or generalizations you can come up with about the amount of paper a box shape ideally requires versus the waste that might be eliminated if a larger box were used? Or are the savings in using the easier-to-wrap box offset by the increased costs in wrapping the new shape?

4. No one can wrap a package without wasting some paper. Figure in the cost of the extra paper and the unused or wasted paper on the roll required, given the needs of real-world wrappers.

*Your work will be judged against the following criteria*:

- Mathematical sophistication
- Mathematical methods and reasoning
- Effectiveness of work
- Quality of reports
- Accuracy of work

Figure 2.4 charts examples of tasks on a continuum from inauthentic to authentic, suggesting that authenticity is a matter of degree. There is a place in assessment for tests such as those exemplified in the first column, but they are properly either subordinate or supplementary to the tasks presented in the third column.

Figure 2.4 Degrees of Authenticity

| Inauthentic | Somewhat Realistic | Authentic |
|---|---|---|
| Explain a data set. | Design a house using specific mathematical formulas and shapes. | Design and build a model house that meets standards and client demands. |
| Write a paper on laws. | Write a persuasive essay on why a law should be changed. | Write a proposal to present to appropriate legislators to change a current law. |
| Read a teacher-chosen text segment. | Read to class a self-selected text. | Make an audiotape of a story for use in library. |

## Impact and Context: Beyond Mere Good-Faith Effort

As the examples suggest, and as the standards for authenticity make explicit, authenticity is not merely synonymous with hands-on work. The work must replicate how people actually confront problems and performance challenges in the field. A performance task will be authentic only to the extent that the contexts of performance—the goals, roles, situations, ambiguities, and constraints facing performers—are realistic. The aim in assessment design should be to honor the results-focused, often messy, audience-influenced ways in which typical adult performance invariably occurs.

It is thus vital to score such tasks using criteria that are central to real performance and its purposes. Situational performance is always about a desirable impact. Did the performer accomplish the appropriate results? What good is writing—even well-organized and mechanically sound writing—if it has nothing to say? If it is boring? If it is ineffectual? If it does not reach the intended audience with the desired impact? So authenticity is not just about finding application tasks. Thoughtfully constructed tasks grounded in real purposes teach students that their efforts and attitudes are appreciated, but ultimately performance is about results. (The typology developed by me and my colleagues at the Center on Learning, Assessment, and School Structure, or CLASS, to underscore the importance of this idea by highlighting impact criteria in scoring performance is discussed in the next two chapters.)

It is only through a results-focused attitude, in fact, that the importance of the second key element in educative assessment, feedback, becomes clear. It is only by attending to context and feedback while planning and performing that excellence is achieved. Such an approach stands in sharp contrast to the demands of testing in which the student plugs in answers, receives no feedback en route, and learns to hope passively for the best. The end result is a student who thinks that performance means just a good-faith effort to do what one has been taught. Set aside for a minute the current hoopla over national content and performance standards, then. What so upsets noneducators about current schooling is far more mundane, I believe: the perception that students, even good ones, seem unwilling and unable to meet demands for quality in the adult workplace, and are therefore willing to hand in subpar work.

These points are reminders that a test can be performance based but inauthentic. The student may be performing (that is, providing a constructed response) when writing an essay in a sixty-minute statewide writing test, but such a test clearly falls on the inauthentic side of the continuum and criteria. (As we shall see later, however, an inauthentic test can nonetheless be a valid test.)

As noted earlier, context matters in assessment and instruction, and not merely for reasons of engagement or aesthetic design. Unless we are faithful to the demands of context, students will come away from school believing that giving back merely what was taught is a sufficient indicator of mastery and understanding, or that performance is merely ritualized response to an academic prompt. This is why Norman Frederiksen, senior researcher at the Educational Testing Service, once declared that the "real" bias of the Scholastic Achievement Test and similar tests is related not to content but to format: the neat and clean character of test items does not reflect the messy and uncertain character of the challenges put before us in life.[8]

To appreciate the significance of context in assessment design, consider this complaint made in a federal report criticizing the testing program of a national organization: "These programs are lacking in 'real world' scenarios and result in non-thinking performance, where the ability of the student to demonstrate a mastery of complex problems, good judgment, situational awareness, . . . and leadership skills have all been removed."[9] The sobering fact is that this quote is from a Federal Aviation Administration (FAA) report on deficiencies in the annual pilot testing and rectification program for a major U.S. airline. It is even more sobering to realize that the FAA is criticizing the airline for its use of an airplane simulator in annual recertification testing—a challenge more authentic than almost all school testing.

To make the production of excellence more likely on tasks that are realistic, the following questions should be asked during the design of performance tests:

- Is there an obvious-to-the-student and constantly present and overriding purpose to guide performance and adjustment?

- Is there a distinct audience for the work that will determine the shape and focus of the work and adjustments en route?

- Are the options and constraints in the task realistic?

- Are appropriate resources available? Does the task require an efficient as well as effective use of notes, materials, and repertoire?

- Is secrecy of desirable performance strategy, criteria, and standards minimized?

- Is the setting realistically noisy and messy?

- Are there clear and obvious standards for self-assessment?

- Are there opportunities for feedback and self-adjustment en route?

An unending diet of academic tests that are removed from such contextual considerations leaves the student with a merely academic education, in the pejorative sense of that phrase. When school testing denies students such conditions and remains content with testing through decontextualized items, we end up testing something other than performance, and we end up miseducating students about genuine work and its challenges. What we are really testing when we ask students to sit in silence, without their resources, not knowing the test questions (the answers to which are known and unproblematic) until test day, and without any concurrent feedback is the power of their memory and the habituation of discrete skills. These may well be necessary elements of performance, but they are not sufficient (and may not even have priority) to determine intellectual success in life (as theories of multiple or multidimensional intelligence such as those promoted by Howard Gardner and Robert Sternberg[10] make clear).

## Assessment Tasks: Not Instructional Activities

Authenticity is essential, but authenticity alone is insufficient to create an effective assessment task. The design of assessment tasks will depend on a host of related decisions (discussed in Chapter Four) and, most important, the tasks must tell us how students are doing in relation to specific achievement targets. Thus, *assessment tasks are not instructional activities*.

We all know that well-defined instructional activities are central to learning, because a good activity brings an idea to life; it causes the student to find meaning in an abstraction. To put the wolf from *Little Red Riding Hood* or the Socrates of Plato's *Apology* on trial, for example, is both engaging and illuminating. Done well, such a trial makes clear, much more than a teacher's explanation ever can, the nuances and multiple layers of meaning derivable from the text. Conversely, students who read the text in a superficial way can easily conclude that in narratives or philosophy there are obvious "good guys" and "bad guys."

A mock trial works for instruction but will not easily work as sound assessment by itself, for a variety of reasons. The following general questions that assessors must ask of all would-be assessment tasks suggest why:

- What desired understandings and competencies should occur as the result of students' reading?
- What evidence do we need to infer whether each student now has those understandings and skills, and to an acceptable standard?
- What kinds of performance are best suited for collecting that evidence?
- What diversity and redundancy of evidence are needed to ensure validity and reliability of results?

Novice teacher-assessors almost universally want to jump from a content standard (in the latter case, for example, to "understand Socrates, Athens, and Plato's *Apology*") to a performance task built on a favored or attractive activity—in this case, a simulated trial of Socrates. But the assessor questions tell us why this may be a mistake. Consider the following implications of the questions in relation to the instructional activity of putting Socrates on trial:

- Although the desired achievement involves the text and its implications, the activity can be done engagingly and effectively by each student with only limited insight into the entire text and its context. If a student merely has to play an aggrieved aristocrat or playwright, he or she can study for that role with only a limited grasp of the text. Also, the student's trial performance need not have much to do with Greek life and philosophy. The question of assessment validity (Does it measure what we want it to measure?) works differently, requiring us to consider whether success or failure at the proposed task depends on the targeted knowledge (as opposed to fortunate personal talents): the performance of the student playing, say, one of the lawyers may be better or worse relative to his or her debating and lawyering skills rather than relative to his or her knowledge of the text.
- It is highly unlikely that we will derive apt and sufficient evidence of understanding of the text from each individual student through this activity, even if we can hear an understanding of the text in some comments by some students. In fact, in the heat of a

debate or mock trial, students might forget or not be able to use what they understand about the text, depriving themselves and us of needed assessment evidence. This is a crucial problem, common to many proposed assessment tasks: when we employ a particular performance genre, such as a trial, essay, or report, as a means to some other assessment end, we may fail to consider that the performance genre itself is a variable in the task and will affect the results.

- Although the trial may provide some evidence, it is far more likely that in this case a thorough and thoughtful piece of writing, combined with an extensive Socratic seminar on the text, would tell us more of what we need to know about students' knowledge and understanding. Such writing and discussion can certainly supplement the trial, but in considering such an idea we should be alert to the fact that no single complex performance task is sufficient for sound assessment.

This example suggests a simple two-question technique for ongoing analysis of any possible assessment task, especially one derived from an activity. These queries should always be made of every task as it is being designed, to check for its potential validity and reliability:

1.  Could the student do well at the task for reasons that have little to do with the desired understanding or skill being assessed?

2.  Could the student do poorly at the task for reasons that have little to do with the desired understanding or skill?

If the answer to either question is yes, the task is either an invalid measure or the evidence it will produce will be insufficient or misleading.

Here are three similar examples of how easy it is to jump to activity ideas before thinking through what evidence is required to assess understanding:

1. A fifth grade teacher proposes to assess students' understanding of the Civil War by having each student build a diorama of one of its key battles. All the teacher needs to ask to see the problem is the assessor's pair of questions about linking the task to the desired outcome. Could a student build an adequate diorama but still not understand the Civil War in its entirety? Or could a student build an inadequate diorama but still have a complex understanding of the war? Yes and yes—which shows that the task as it stands is invalid. At worst, what the teacher might really be assessing with this task is students' small motor skills and the habits of mind called patience and perseverance.

2. A second grade teacher proposes, for a major marking-period test of students' emerging literacy, to ask them each to pick a book for oral reading, read it out loud, and say why they like the book. First, by allowing each student to choose any book, the teacher loses all assessment validity because each student will presumably choose a book that she or he likes and can read reasonably well. Unless the teacher limits the choices to grade-level texts or other books of the teacher's choosing, the result may well be a skewed sample. The situation is akin to asking each competitor in the high jump to choose the height he will attempt, with the intention of treating all who clear their chosen heights as having demonstrated the identical high-jumping ability. Second, reading is composed of many skills, and merely reading out loud is both a limited test and potentially misleading. What about the student who might read well but is shy, stutters, or is not a native English speaker?

3. A tenth grade history teacher wants to assess his Russian history unit through a debate. A key objective of the unit is to have students know and explain the rise and fall of the Russian Communist empire, so the debate is to center on the question *Who blew it?* and the students, in teams of four, are to simulate Yeltsin, Gorbachev, Khrushchev, Stalin, Lenin, Trotsky, Catherine the Great, and Tolstoy. Great activity! But it will not work as the only assessment task for the same reasons mentioned in the previous examples. The teacher is not assured of getting evidence from each student, and the students' performance as debaters may or may not signal an understanding of the subject and of the debate question.

In this case, I worked on the problem with the teacher. What kind of evidence do we need from each student? I asked. My feedback and his thinking out loud led him to determine that he needed the following written materials from each student (some before and some after the debate): student-produced sections of a "debate briefing book"; an editorial for a hypothetical newspaper arguing who had won and who had lost the debate and why; a news article on what was said and by whom; and later letters to the editor disagreeing with the editorial.

Then the teacher looked sheepish, grinned, and said, "You're going to be mad at me."

"Why?" I asked.

"Because I think we should have a quiz on the century in Russia," he said.

"I'm not going to flunk you," I said, laughing, "because now you're thinking like an assessor instead of like a teacher trying to be politically correct about authentic assessment." Given the initial question, Who blew it? the answer to which would require a breadth of knowledge, giving a quiz was wise—particularly in light of the teacher's choice of a debate as an activity, which might focus on only a few questions and a few answers.

Could all these activities be designed to be assessment tasks and to assess some related targets? Well, of course. But in practice that is not how it works, because teachers typically do not sufficiently clarify for themselves what specific understandings and skills they are after and what kinds of specific evidence their goal requires. We educators typically state what we want to teach or what we wish students to encounter, then we assume that we can derive evidence of learning from the way students perform whatever activity seems appropriate. That is very different from stating precisely what new skills the student should be able to perform as a result of the encounter, and what the needed evidence is and where we must look for it. This is the gist of the assessor's point of view when designing not simply learning activities but assessment tasks.

## Performance as Intelligent Trial and Error

Worthy, engaging, and realistic tasks are key to a better system, but they are ultimately not the most important ingredients of educative assessment. More important is learning how to make our system of teaching, learning, and assessing self-corrective instead of a linear march through content coverage or scripted behavior, in which we end up hoping that the result is excellence. Yes, we need more rigorous content and performance standards; yes, more authentic tasks will help make assessment more focused and instructive. But student (and teacher) performance will improve only when we make adjustments-based-on-results more central to what is taught, learned, and tested. Authentic work involves achieving high-quality results, and such success depends on multiple opportunities to perform. Adjustments to assessment are based on comparing the gap between actual work and standards through feedback. Let us consider how to deliberately build such self-adjustment opportunities and requirements into the assessments we design.

Even when we call on internalized knowledge and skill, in the real world we must innovate when we perform. No real task or context is like the one before; no real problem is ever unambiguous, and hence solvable by the mere use of scholastic lessons. That is why Bloom and his colleagues who developed the Taxonomy of Educational Objectives described *synthesis* as creative and *applications* as requiring novel situations or problems.[11] Any genuine intellectual challenge requires the intelligent testing of our ideas and skills in an idiosyncratic context. Success is determined not merely by what habits of discrete knowledge and skill we bring, but also by our ability to seek, obtain, and employ feedback intelligently, using those habits as a repertoire from which to draw aptly. We constantly feel our way, based on a clear sense of the goal and on where we stand at any moment, as revealed through feedback.

In the world of professional work and civic or social life, self-assessment and self-adjustment are vital skills based on sizing up unfolding situations and bringing work to successful fruition by comparing where we are to where we need to be. An educative assessment system would therefore deliberately build in and make central challenges that require the student to attend to feedback and make adjustments accordingly in authentically complex situations.

Consider the following situations as simple examples of the constant need to make intelligent adjustments based on feedback when faced with real challenges:

- *All design work and new product development.* Through constant trial and error and the use of client feedback, a new camera or piece of software is conceived, refined, and developed.

- *Legislation and public policy.* Problems and needs are identified, and competing interests and proposed solutions are considered. No simple road map exists, and ideas must be constantly floated so that the constituencies affected can respond and play a role in shaping the law.

- *A business or personal financial plan.* By definition, such plans are predictions of the unpredictable—attempts to develop detailed and multiple "What if. . . ?" scenarios based on data, projections, protection against worst-case scenarios, and feedback from other experts, analysts, and market research.

- *Raising children.* Little need be said about the difficulty of this challenge, which is far removed from plugging in truisms or the "facts" of developmental psychology. Attending carefully to feedback from what does and does not work in childrearing is central to success. It is also key to respectful relationships with children.

- *Winning games (as a player or a coach).* Game strategy is a complex mix of judgment and expertise, in which attention to ongoing performance is vital to success, irrespective of one's prior game plans. As Marv Levy, coach of the Buffalo Bills, once said impatiently in a post-game interview when he was asked to explain the Bills' surprising comeback in a playoff game: "Don't you guys get it? Coaching is about adjustment!"[12]

Rather than seeing a performance as involving merely the testing of our ability to call up from memory and employ fixed routines (as in plugging in knowledge and skill in narrow academic prompts), we must come to see all performance as basically adaptive (innovative, efficient, and effective) use of knowledge in differing and new contexts.

These points may suggest that I am arguing in favor of the elimination of traditional tests. No, educative assessment is not either/or. Just as the student must learn to play from a repertoire, so too must teachers; they must know when to test and when not to test, based on purpose and other context factors; and they must know which kind of test—quiz, prompt, task, constructed response/selection, and so on—to use in which kind of situation. The aim of educative assessment is not to eliminate test items but to make them properly subordinate to complex performance demands, in the same way that coaches do simple sideline drills in preparation for games, as noted earlier. The analogy is apt: no player or coach would forget that drills are not the game, and the sum of the drills rarely adds up to effective performance. Yet drills (problems taken out of context, like test items) are helpful in working on and testing specific knowledge and skill. As Newmann and his colleagues have noted, "Even if authenticity were accepted as a key indicator of intellectual quality, one would not expect all instruction and assessment activities to meet all three standards all the time. For example, repetitive practice, retrieving straightforward information, and memory drills may be necessary to build knowledge and skills as foundations for authentic performance. . . . The point is not to abandon all forms of inauthentic work in school, but to keep authentic achievement clearly in view as the valued end."[13]

Newmann might also have said "as the *visible* end," because the student, unlike the athlete or musician, rarely sees the purpose to all those drill-like test questions. In our use of both direct and indirect test questions or tasks, we typically get the balance wrong, with negative consequences for learning. The upshot is that we need design standards in assessment (proposed in greater detail in Chapter Five) to guard against long-standing bad habits. We need to establish better safeguards against students leaving school without knowledge or control of the most important kinds of authentic performance tasks, be they subject-matter specific or related to general performance genres that cut across subjects.

The design challenge is thus best understood as equivalent to the design of a new world of performance demands—new complex academic "games" that justify and make meaning of the discrete drills found in typical tests. So, although it may be vital in the early stages of learning to confront simple tests, the aim in assessment design is to ensure that students (and teachers) always know the difference between preparatory quizzes and genuine tests of purposeful and adaptive performance, and that they are taught and assessed in such a way as to make them able performers in the latter context.

Again, the issue is not just one of closed versus open-ended tasks, or paper and pencil versus hands-on work, as many think. The challenge is to design tasks that require thoughtful responsiveness, not just plugged-in knowledge and skill. To see the difference, consider the pairs of performance challenges presented in Figure 2.5. The first column is composed of tasks that either follow directly from drill work or are learned and perfected as straightforward routines or habits. The tasks in the second column can be done well only by responding efficiently, effectively, and creatively to the emerging results, which obviously builds on the skills and knowledge listed in the first column. The second set of tasks, unlike the first set, can be carried out only by innovative and intelligent trial and error, using one's drilled knowledge and skill as a kind of database. Put differently, the first set of tasks can be mastered through traditional practice and study techniques; the second set can be mastered only through judgment and adjustment.

Schools should ensure that students have mastered the art of task analysis and intelligent adjustment that is at the heart of the second column. Performance knowledge and practice cannot be unendingly postponed in the name of simple discrete knowledge and skill development; at a certain point the low-level work is without direction or meaning, and more powerful mastery is short-circuited. In other words, the work of the first column does not lead inexorably to the expertise of the second column, nor must exhaustive low-level drill on all performance elements precede all purposeful performance. Indeed, both views have mistakenly informed teaching and testing in the forty years since the creation of Bloom's taxonomy: what was originally a way of characterizing the degree of cognitive difficulty of exam questions became mistakenly viewed as a prescription for the chronology of teaching. By contrast, if you want to produce performers, you had better start having them perform as soon as possible, as is done in all youth arts, athletics, and clubs. Yes, students need the basics; but they do not know why or what the basics enable them to do unless they practice the performances those basics enable.

## Dealing with the Consequences: Reality Therapy Through Assessment

The aim of teaching is effective and efficient learning. Excellence depends on confronting students not merely with high standards and exhortations but with the effects of their work, and with the requirement to improve on an undesired or undesirable effect. A

Figure 2.5  Skill Execution Versus Intelligent Adjustment

| *Straightforward Execution of Skill* | *Intelligent Adjustment Essential* |
| --- | --- |
| Follow the recipe. | Prepare a meal using available ingredients, while addressing specific varied likes and dislikes. |
| | Fix an overcooked dish. |
| Assemble a model from parts. | Create a sculpture using a given piece of wood or marble. |
| Speak in public. | Speak to raise funds and get elected. |
| Do the science lab as mapped out. | Design and debug an experiment. |
| Take a history test. | Conduct an oral history, write up findings, and respond to criticism. |
| Take a test on polynomials and graphing. | Examine AIDS data and calculate the trend for fatalities, finding the "best fit" curve. |
| Take a vocabulary test in French. | Take an immersion challenge to communicate successfully in a target language with speakers who speak no English. |
| Write an essay. | Get an op-ed piece published. |
| Take a written test on auto mechanics. | Enter the annual national competition on student teams repairing cars with unknown defects. |
| Do a graphics assignment. | Satisfy a design client. |
| Build a product. | Build and finance an affordable and desirable product based on a business plan and market research. |
| Take a test on percents and compounded interest. | Choose the most effective investment plan from three presented options. |
| Know the facts of history. | Research a controversial historical account to determine the facts. |
| | Build a successful museum exhibit. |

grade is not an effect; it only stands for one. The challenge is to engineer schooling so that students have far more direct and powerful experiences of the actual effects—on themselves, people, and situations—of their work. An authentic education is one with consequences—an intellectual Outward Bound.[14]

Performance is ultimately about results. It is cause for delight that process now gets a better hearing in education, but the frequent failure to link process to results causes many students to believe that making lots of effort and following procedures are sufficient. "I worked on it for eight hours, and I did everything you said!" ("So give me an A" is the message.) This repeated comment by students to teachers is not seen, ironically, for what it is: the direct feedback of an assessment system that overrewards effort and unmoors consequences from actions. All real performance is ultimately about impact, intended or otherwise.

Students will work to improve performance only when they are motivated by a real hoped-for (or feared) result, using real standards and criteria as references for feedback, and using empirical observation (what happened) as the primary source of feedback. This is why athletes, actors, and musicians can improve so much: they get direct feedback from their own actions (regardless of whether a coach yells out during the unfolding action), and they want to learn from that feedback so they can experience the happy feelings and consequences of genuine public competence (and avoid the painful feelings and shame of public incompetence). These motives—wanting to appear competent and to make an impact—are vital to learning. Assessment must build on these motives, and it must do more to avoid the unreal and intimidating realm of grades and scores divorced from legitimate consequences and results.

Failure to assess using real-world consequences (rather than teacher or test grades) explains a ubiquitous phenomenon that angers the general public greatly: students' failure to take an adequate interest in work quality and results. Here are three examples of the problem:

1.    A graphics design teacher at a vocational high school brought in a real potential client for design jobs and had the students bid on the work. They listened to the client explain his product needs, they went to work (without asking questions), and they worked very hard, much harder than usual, to produce what they thought he wanted. The client came back the next week, inspected the work, and politely turned down all the efforts. The students' reaction? Anger. "We worked so hard. . . ." Yes, but did they ever check with the client about whether they were on the right track? Did they put a variety of design styles before the client to tease out his tastes, as all good designers do? No. The teacher had taught these students technical skills but not how to accomplish results in the marketplace.

2.    The second example comes from work I and two others did with high school students in a performance-based laboratory summer school to try out numerous ideas for authentic curricula and assessment. One of the student tasks was organized around the question, How does a bill become law? We asked each student to begin by taking on the persona of a candidate for Congress. Students had to choose a district, research it, develop a platform and campaign likely to succeed in such a district, and develop campaign literature and a "winning" television commercial. Then, as new members of Congress, they took stands on various issues to get a

voting record, and they requested committee assignments. Each committee was charged with bringing a bill out of committee to the entire Congress.

Here was the catch: the Congress was composed of not only students' peers on other committees but also the eighty adults who visited the CLASS summer institutes. The adults took on roles representing both geographical and ideological interests. The students then discovered how the making of legislation really works as they met with the adults twice over lunch to discuss the emerging legislation and to horse trade. (The students found this a horrifying but illuminating process, a far cry from the balderdash in their civics lessons about how bills become law.) The student committees then had two days to decide how to retain their ideas (and principles) as they made their bills as palatable as possible for undecided members.

One group failed miserably. Though composed of bright, conventionally well-educated students, this committee brought before the Congress a bill that did not consider the feedback the students had received from the role-playing adults. The bill was defeated by a five-to-one margin. The students were crushed—and for all the wrong reasons. They honestly believed that their good-faith research, writing, and presentation effort was sufficient for success in the task. Instead they discovered that there are consequences of failure to consider audience, context, and purpose. It took them weeks to come to understand (ruefully) that the experience was educative.

3.   The final example involves an experience I had while working for a year in a small school district with a group of six teachers representing the district's language arts–English faculty. Our goal was to develop some common prompts and scoring rubrics that the district could use to get a better handle on student progress and achievement. When we reviewed the existing prompts and student papers and then sought to generate some possible criteria for scoring, the teachers initially proposed only such formal writing dimensions as organization, support, and the like. It took three meetings of two hours each before they all admitted out loud what they felt: that what they most hated about students' work was that it was boring. "But of course we could never assess them for that," said one of the teachers while all the others nodded.

"Why can't you assess the work for its engagement?" I asked.

"Because that's so subjective!" they said. Ironically, they were arguing against impact criteria as they cited papers that they all agreed had the specific impact of being boring. This is how teachers often respond to proposals to assess memorable or psychologically astute storytelling. But is it really always difficult to agree on what is memorable or psychologically astute? As lists of best-selling books and movies indicate, a story that has an impact on audiences is easy to identify (irrespective of whether it is "great art"). Finding out if a piece of writing moves its readers or provokes their thinking is not an esoteric challenge: ask the readers. (Am I saying that the reader is always right? No. I am saying only what is obvious: if you are boring your reader and you do not wish to, you need to know. How to better understand and engineer genuine feedback is the subject of the next chapter.) Once impact criteria lose their mystery for teachers and students, they can be used to give formerly vague assignments specificity.

I find that an assessment of "boring" is actually less subjective than an assessment of "coherent"; it is formal traits that are more abstract and prone to cause disagreement among evaluators. Hidden and deep ideological disagreements about form as well as content always come out in training sessions on group scoring for writing assessments. I recall one woman assertively announcing, to the surprise of her colleagues, when the issue of format was raised that she flunks any paper by any of her students in which block paragraphing is used instead of indenting.

In short, students do not seem sufficiently bothered by sloppy, ineffective, or incomplete work in school, and that bad habit may well continue on into the home and the workplace. My claim here is that students' feelings about their work often result from an alienated scoring and grading system that separates student work from its natural workplace or home consequences. Students are rarely confronted by the effects of their sloppiness or incompletely thought-through work in the way that an adult might have a direct encounter with an angry client or be held responsible for a bridge that falls down. (Not so surprisingly, by contrast, the same students will often work like dogs, including on weekends, to make sure that a play is performed well in public.) That is why I propose here that such intellectual Outward Bound consequences should be built into our schools' assessment systems, so that consequences can almost always be felt—in the same way they are felt on the playing field or in the auditorium.

Consider the following basic impact questions that might be asked about a project, performance, or product, whether a simulation or a real experience, and that ought to be at the heart of any authentic and valid assessment:

- Was the client satisfied?
- Was the audience moved, enlightened, or otherwise engaged?
- Was the proposal accepted?
- Was the campaign successful?

All of these achievement-related questions teach students that effort, content, and process are necessary but not sufficient. That is why we must build an assessment system that asks these questions.

Authentic assessment is simply a fancy way of describing what performers in the world beyond school face each day: they are tested on their ability to do a known job well and in a variety of circumstances in which the performer has a right to receive or seek utter clarity about purposes, audience, standards, and criteria; they are also quizzed or challenged to cope with isolated facts, decisions, or needs; but there is invariably nothing unknown about the purpose of the challenges they face, about how to prepare for them, and about how to link them to larger objectives. They get better at their jobs because they know what is expected of them, and they can check their understanding and skill as they go, adjusting on the basis of feedback from bosses or clients that can be sought at any time. Why should school testing be any different?

## CHAPTER 3

# Providing Ongoing Feedback

If assessment is to improve performance, not just audit it, the techniques of measurement must be accompanied by quality feedback provided to learners. The feedback needs to be of two kinds: in addition to better feedback *after* the performance, feedback must also be provided during (concurrent with) the assessment activities, as discussed in the previous chapter. While we know that helpful feedback enables a performer to revise performance to meet high (yet clear and stable) standards, the novelty proposed in this chapter is that we should stop construing feedback and its use as what occurs *between* assessments and start construing it as at the core of what we need to assess. In other words, we must come to see deliberate and effective self-adjustment as a vital educational outcome, hence more central to how and what we test.

Feedback is not merely useful, in other words. It is an essential part of any *completed* learning. As William James described it one hundred years ago, we "receive sensible news of our behavior and its results. We hear the words we have spoken, feel our own blow as we give it, or read in the bystander's eyes the success or failure of our conduct. Now this return wave . . . pertains to the completeness of the whole experience."[1] This emphasis on the "whole experience" is significant because so much of the student's intellectual experience is, unfortunately, fragmentary. Essentially, constant isolated drill work and testing without concurrent feedback means that answers are isolated from actual effects, causes, and purposes in the student's school experience. That is why the "reality therapy" of authentically contextualized assessment is no luxury. One cannot improve or learn to improve unless one knows how one is doing in performance.

This may seem commonsensical but in traditional school testing it is a radical idea to give the student self-evident feedback while she or he is still being tested or as one stage in a multipart assessment that requires the student to use feedback. Indeed, in many instances it would be considered cheating or perversion of the validity of the results (just as it is also considered radical to give students before-hand knowledge of the tasks and criteria by which their work will be judged). But safeguarding the core premise that assessment should improve performance, not just audit it, requires that assessment embody and demand self-adjustment based on good feedback. To state it more pointedly, we cannot know if students are competent unless and until we see them respond to effects and results.

In Chapter One I asked you to imagine what getting a driver's license, playing in a band competition, and being evaluated as a teacher would be like if these tests were designed to be like most school tests. Here is a similar analogy that suggests just how dys-functional the present system of testing divorced from feedback is for student learning and improvement: Imagine that the school bas-ketball season consisted of one game, played on the last day of the year, and that the players do not know which of the hundreds of plays they have learned will be tested. Imagine further that this one game is not basketball as the adults play it, not basketball as profes-sional coaches and players see it, but consists instead of a series of drills (a different selection of isolated moves and plays each year) devised by measurement experts and valid to them. Imagine a scor-ing system therefore fully understandable only by the assessors, not by the student players and the coaches. Finally, imagine further that students do not know until weeks later which plays, which have been taken out of game context and isolated from the shooting and making of baskets, have been judged successful. *Who would improve at the game under these conditions? Who would understand the game and his role—the purposes at work—in such an assessment?* Yet this is what typical testing does. The so-called feedback it provides cannot be easily deciphered or used by players and coaches to carry out real performance or real improvement.

To grasp from the learner's point of view how debilitating such a system can be, consider the remarks of recent test takers who expe-rienced the latest innovation in large-scale testing: so-called adap-tive computer testing. It would seem that a test that adapts its questions to your responses in order to better ascertain the level of difficulty and complexity you can reliably achieve would be wel-come. Not so, as far as the test-taker is concerned, especially due to the complete absence of user-directed feedback in such testing:

Only one question appears on screen at a time, and test-takers must answer it before moving on. This means you can't skip around or go back to change an answer. . . .

It is a system that cannot help but fluster test-takers. It is almost impossible to tell how well you are doing, and unpleasant surprises can occur. Edie Sagenkahn, a 30-year-old nurse at Johns Hopkins University Hospital in Baltimore, recalled her panic at being cut off less than a third of the way through 265 questions on a licensing exam last year.

"I was just cruising along, and then the computer just shut off after I had answered the 75th one," she said. "I didn't know if I had passed or failed. I just sat there saying, 'Oh, God, what does this mean?'" Later she found out a friend had plowed through 210 questions, and she felt even worse. Two weeks later she learned that she had passed; the computer shuts off early if the test-taker is performing very well.[2]

This example is just an extreme case of a universal problem. Access to and quality of feedback is often the last thing on the test designers' minds (be they in a testing company or in a classroom). They are looking merely to obtain credible results in an efficient way. Regardless of the purpose (such as licensure, college admissions, accountability, or summative assessment of achievement), almost all tests work the same way: the student must address random questions without knowing how they are doing or without being able to clarify the question and its purpose. What, then, is the unwitting lesson of school testing? Answer, hope, and move on—a view antithetical to quality work. How can the student learn to get better and want to get better if testing does not allow it? Never mind the further absurdity of much test feedback coming after the coursework and school year are over! When all formal assessment is viewed as what one does *after* teaching and learning are over—no matter how performance-based the task—the battle for excellence is lost.

Another reason the computer testing story matters is that most teachers have come to design their tests in accordance with large-scale test formats, which are never designed with anything more than superficial auditing in mind. When students' learning is simply audited, they cannot and do not improve much over time. This is also true, ironically, of the standardized tests being held over teachers' heads. As I shall argue in the next-to-last chapter, educators often misunderstand the feedback from indirect testing; local teaching and testing should not imitate the structure of large-scale testing if the goal is better scores. "Teaching to the test" can lead to worse, not better, student performance on standardized tests—in much the same way that student musicians would worsen over time if all they were taught to worry about were isolated fingering exercises and paper-and-pencil questions about their instruments and music.

## What Is Feedback?

We do not get very far in assessment reform without realizing that many educators act as though they do not understand what feedback is. If I had to summarize what I have seen over the past decade in all kinds of schools (public and private; elementary, secondary, and collegiate; with and without state testing programs), I would have to report that many educators seem to believe that feedback means giving lots of approval, and some disapproval and advice. In classrooms, the most common piece of so-called feedback I hear is "Good job!" or an equivalent phrase. It is of course important to praise students because it often satisfies and encourages them, but it cannot help them to improve their performance. Praise keeps you in the game; real feedback helps you get better. Feedback tells you what you did or did not do and enables you to self-adjust. Indeed, the more self-evident the feedback, the more autonomy the performer develops, and vice versa.[3]

Feedback is information about how a person did in light of what he or she attempted—intent versus effect, actual versus ideal performance. In the more formal language of systems theory, feedback is evidence that confirms or disconfirms the correctness of actions. *Facts* about a performer's performance are fed back to him or her, without the addition (or worse, the substitution) of an adult's view of the *value* of the performance. The audience fidgeted when I spoke; that was not my goal. I sought to keep them on the edge of their seats, and saw that my effect did not match my intent. The pasta meal was too salty (which I did not intend) but was cooked al dente (which I did intend). My clients' body language while I presented my proposal told me it was time for some humor, vivid stories, or helpful examples; I adjusted my approach on the basis of that feedback and they became more engaged.

*The best feedback is highly specific, directly revealing or highly descriptive of what actually resulted, clear to the performer, and available or offered in terms of specific targets and standards.* Put this way, the challenge is not merely one of having more adults at the ready with fancy verbal or written feedback—a solution that we cannot really afford and would not want to encourage. In light of the previous chapter's discussion of reality therapy in testing, the challenge instead is to ensure that performance tasks place students in the position of having to confront the effects of their actions directly, as suggested by the William James comment quoted earlier in this chapter. In fact, a system of learning and testing that requires a constant reliance on adult interpretation of all student work (instead of making the results and their meaning as self-evident as possible) ensures that learning will be slow and unpredictable.

We thus misunderstand the nature and role of feedback in learning if we think of it as primarily adult commentary. The student needs to see that adult commentary is grounded in what works. In order to see this, the student must gain experience from tasks that permit many "loops" that reveal how his or her adjustments do or do not make a difference in terms of a desired effect. Feedback in healthy systems is thus always timely, continual, and user friendly. Among the most obvious examples of situations in which we seek and use system feedback loops effectively are playing computer games, adjusting the shower water temperature, tasting a meal as we cook, and seeking comments from peer reviewers as we write or perform. Or recall how often a music or athletic coach gave you a steady flow of feedback to tell you how your actions caused this or that result, or did something as simple but helpful as pointing out to you something you did ("There! That time you kept your knee over the ball, and your shot on goal stayed low"). The best feedback is purely *descriptive*, in other words. By contrast, most school test feedback is like the children's game of "hot and cold," where the adult's grades and comments amount to saying "You're getting warmer." Students know that they are close to or far from the goal, but they do not know what or where the goal is; what's worse, they never have sufficient opportunities to play the game long enough and fast enough to ensure success on every major test.

We all need such goal-based perceptions and description of our work, even when the final results are obvious. As the description of what we did is fed back to us (or to a coach who translates it), we come to understand better what we did and did not do, and what we need to do more and less of to cause the desired result next time. We can use that information to close the gap between our intent and the effect we produced.

Consider this feedback from a pitching coach to a major league baseball pitcher who recently began to perform poorly: "Of the 28 pitches he threw," said Red Sox pitching coach Joe Kerrigan, "Heathcliff hit his location only eight times. When I see 8–28, there must be something in his delivery that is keeping him from getting the ball where he wants it. On the videotape, it shows he is opening up his stride by about 4–6 inches. His body direction is actually geared to go into the left-handed batter's box. That's actually taking him away from the plate."[4] No praise, no blame, no vague interpretations—just feedback. Heathcliff Slocumb knew that his effect did not match his intent. Merely knowing that he was not throwing strikes and getting batters out was of limited use as feedback, however. He needed to understand why he was getting that result, just as a student whose writing is vague or whose arguments are fallacious needs to understand exactly what needs to be fixed and how to fix it.

Effective feedback can come from many sources. But as the Kerrigan quote reminds us, even when complex performance is at stake, feedback can come from a camera and replayable tape if we know what we are looking for. (Indeed, we might say that one long-term goal of teaching is for teachers to make themselves obsolete as the only feedback givers.) A videotape cannot only tell a pitcher that he failed to stride and release the ball properly; it can also reveal to students that their speech was mumbled and their words were unfocused, or it can reveal to teachers that far fewer of their students were engaged in discussion than it seemed at the time or that Vance's understanding of the quadratic formula was more solid than it seemed in class. Even in the absence of video, performance will improve if we become more habituated to asking When did it work? Why? When did it not work? Why not? The point in this chapter is that assessment must demand that we ask and answer such questions if performance mastery is our goal.

Our goal in assessment reform is thus not merely to design more engaging and authentic tasks but to build in the kind of frequent feedback and opportunities to use that feedback that are found in all effective performance systems. Road signs do this for drivers. Otherwise we would have to stop and ask for directions or check our maps each time we came to an unfamiliar intersection.[5] Software manufacturers do this for computer users (and minimize costly and time-consuming user telephone calls for assistance) by selling self-correcting systems with on-line tutorials and help files. Assessment should be designed to provide such information to students and teachers. When tasks are designed to maximize the availability of direct evidence and to require self-adjustment, we also come to see that using adult assessors at every step is not necessary (a realization that is an important part of feasibility, as discussed further in the last chapter of the book).

Yet even with better designs, teachers often argue that there is no time to do the kind of assessment proposed here. I fear that these teachers have lost sight of their purposes. The goal is not to teach and hope that it works out; it is to optimize results, just as any coach would. Repeated attempts to teach with good models as concrete examples of goals, with descriptive feedback, and with targeted guidance are what cause excellence. It stands to reason that an unending dose of scattered content, no matter how rigorous, will not by itself produce the educational results demanded. How, then, can there be no time for the giving and using of feedback? We might as well say that there is no time for giving feedback to the trumpet player because there is so much to teach about music and trumpets.

Figure 3.1 sums up what feedback is and what it is not.[6]

### Figure 3.1  What Feedback Is and Is Not

| *Effective Feedback* | *Ineffective Feedback* |
| --- | --- |
| Provides confirming (or disconfirming) useful evidence of effect relative to intent, for example, a map and road signs; compares work to anchor papers and rubrics. | Provides nonspecific advice, praise/blame, or exhortations, for example, "Try harder," "Your writing is awful," or "Good job!"; a mere score on the paper. |
| Compares current performance and trend to successful result (standard), for example, the taste and appearance of the food, not the recipe, guarantee the meal will come out as described; student work is compared against exemplars and criteria. | Naively assumes that *process* (instructions, hard work, and advice) is sufficient to reach goal, for example, planting seeds and diligently watering according to package directions does not ensure a successful garden; students given only directions on how to complete assignment, not guidance on specific standards of final products. |
| Timely: immediate or performer-friendly in its immediacy, such as feedback from audience and conductor during a recital. | Not timely: too long a delay in usability, or too late to use; feedback on a standardized test provided weeks later, in the summer. |
| Frequent and ongoing. | Infrequent, given once. |
| Descriptive language predominates in assessing aspects of performance, for example, you made a left turn onto Main St. instead of a right turn; rubrics describe qualities of performance using concrete indicators and traits unique to each level. | Evaluative or comparative language predominates in assessing performance, for example, you made many correct turns and one incorrect turn, or your navigating is greatly improved and better than that of most of your peers; rubrics basically amount to "excellent," "good," "fair," and "poor," with no insight into the characteristics that lead to such value judgments. |
| Performer perceives a specific, tangible effect, later symbolized by a score that the performer sees is an apt reflection of the effect, such as the score given by a band judge in competition, based on specific criteria; the grade or score confirms what was apparent to the performer about the quality of the performance after it happened. | No tangible effect or useful result is visible to the performer other than a score, such as a grade at the top of a paper handed back; the evaluation process remains mysterious or arbitrary to the performer, no matter how valid and reliable the test and score are to the expert. |
| The result sought is derived from true models (exemplars), for example, a first grade evaluation of reading is linked to the capacities of a successful adult reader: the reading rubric is longitudinal and anchored by expert reading behaviors; feedback is given in terms of the goal, such as the specific accomplishments of those who effectively read to learn. | The result sought is derived from a simplistic goal statement, for example, the feedback to first grade readers relates only to checklists: the reading rubric is limited to age-grade skills; there is too much feedback in terms of learning to read, not enough in terms of reading to learn. |
| Enables performers to improve through self-assessment and self-adjustment. | Keeps the performers constantly dependent on the judge to know how they did. |

## Assessment as Software

Instead of thinking of assessment as a test (and the student as the test subject), we would be better off thinking of it as activity having the goal of getting students to use our designs to produce high-quality work. Thus we might think of assessment as software that enables students to master complex performance "programs." This view blurs the boundaries between instruction and assessment in a useful way, because it helps us to see that taking stock of progress against standards and using that knowledge to improve performance is both what we want to teach and what we want to assess.

Consider the following example of a system that encourages and assesses student self-correction.[7] In Ralph's welding course he works with thirty students at once and uses a system of effective feedback that requires no adult intervention. The first task is straightforward. Each student must produce a ninety–degree corner weld to industry specifications. The standards for this weld are written out on paper, but the feedback system involves something more. Ralph tells the students that when they believe their weld is up to standard, they should bring it over to a table, pick up a magic marker, and write their name on the weld. By so doing they signify, first, that they understand the standards, and second, that they believe their work is up to standard. There is a catch, however. On the table are welds from previous years, ranging from the excellent to the awful. Students routinely come up to the table thinking they have finished the task and then think twice after inspecting other welds. I watched one boy look around furtively to see if Ralph was watching before he snuck back to his station. This is a feedback system that works, based as all good feedback systems are on activating each person's ability to self-assess and self-adjust when he or she gets clear feedback and sees clear standards.

What a student thinks is a fine weld, essay, or musical performance may be shown to be inadequate once the student views the work through the eye or ear of a judge and in reference to comprehensible standards and criteria. And as long as such feedback is timely, it is welcomed rather than feared because it tells students soon enough (before it is too late to change their work) and unambiguously that their intent is unlikely to be realized unless they make a change.

## Feedback Is Not Guidance

If a common misunderstanding about feedback is that it is synonymous with praise or blame, an even more common misunderstanding is the view that feedback is the same as guidance. Feedback and guidance are quite different; they represent complementary parts of a self-correction system. Feedback tells you what resulted from your action; guidance tells you how to improve the situation.[8] When we teach and comment on performance, we tend to give too much guidance and not enough feedback. In fact, we sometimes jump over feedback and go directly to giving advice—guidance that often does not make much sense unless it is seen as a logical response to feedback.

Here is an illustration of feedback—how it differs from encouragement or criticism, how it is not guidance, and why both feedback and guidance are essential to eventual mastery and autonomy. My son Justin was four years and seven months old when he first wrote his name without prompting, like this:

He had just a few weeks earlier discovered his control over a pencil and the differences between the letters that he could produce by writing, so like many kids he practiced writing his own name. We happened to be sitting at the table and he was doing work while I was doing work. He finished and looked at me. Fortunately I had seen what he was up to out of the corner of my eye and had time to consider my response.

"That's really interesting, Justin." (I said this with enthusiasm, but he was puzzled by the word interesting.) "What does it say?"

"It's my name!" he said, somewhat surprised by my reaction.

"Hmmm, show me," I said.

He read off each letter: "J, U, S, T, I, N, spells Justin!"

On another piece of paper I wrote N and H as big block letters and then placed them below where he had written his name. "What's this letter?" I asked, pointing to my N.

"N," he said.

"What's this?" I asked, pointing to the H.

"H," he said, getting a little impatient.

"Hmmm. Well, then," I asked, pointing to his letter N, "What letter is this?"

Long pause. Furrowed brow. "But it is not what I wanted!" he exclaimed, looking at his N.

*That's* feedback: no praise, no blame; just evidence that asks the learner to consider his intent versus his (unwitting) effect, evidence that talks about what the *product* does or does not do. The feedback is a visible fact, not a judgment. Justin could see for himself, once he was shown a standard, that his N was less well-defined than he had intended. Note also that it is *his* intent we are talking about, not mine. No adult was laying an agenda on him. Feedback causes learners to attempt to improve because it derives from and then addresses their intent to accomplish some specific thing. Justin intended to form a well-written N. What he wrote looked more like an H. He was shown timely feedback that allowed him to compare a well-written H and N and helped him to discover that he had not achieved his intent. Without this feedback, it might have been much longer before he had seen the need to be more careful in his writing. No overt guidance was provided here, and certainly no disapproval in my words or tone: I did not tell Justin what to do about the feedback, and I made no explicit value judgment. I only provided the feedback, that is, I caused him to attend to the gap between his intent and the actual effect of his efforts.[9]

Moreover, when feedback is specific and relates to a learner's intent, the learner does not feel anger, fear, or loss of self-esteem. Learners of all ages crave such feedback because they are put in a position to recognize what they have done and they are empowered to decide what they want to do about it in light of their own objectives. Students can accept even the most sobering and difficult feedback if it is stripped of all subjective and blaming value judgment and cast in terms of their aim. Why? Because the teacher is taking the time to understand and make careful observations about their work and their intent, perhaps even more than *they* did! (At a recent conference on higher education, a professor remarked to me that her athlete students sought and accepted feedback far better than her nonathlete students, even though the feedback to the athletes often indicated more significant problems of performance. This is presumably due to the athletes' happy experience with direct feedback.)

Most students never get this kind of vital feedback. We too quickly tell them that an answer is correct or incorrect. Or we jump to giving advice. Or we spot a mistake, apply a label to it in the margin, and move on. (I have often told the story of Mike, a student who waited until the end of the year to ask his teacher the meaning of the word she kept writing on his papers—"vagoo" was how he pronounced it.[10]) All these strategies overlook the vital moment of genuine learning when the learner sees his or her work through the assessor's eyes and understands a mistake as a mistake, of a particular kind and cause. The moment when the student understands why some part of his or her work is a mistake is entirely different from the moment when the student perceives that the teacher *does not like* that part of the work. In the second case the teacher understands the mistake but the student does not. If students are to see mistakes as mistakes, we must confront them with clear feedback and constantly ask them to self-assess, like the students in the welding example.

At the elementary level the technique of *miscue analysis* in reading assessment assumes the power and importance of feedback loops. In miscue analysis we make readers' strategies and renderings explicit, helping them to see where they succeeded and where they did not and why, to see where a misreading is plausible and sensible and where not, so that both learner and teacher come to understand reading performance better. But we rarely do such miscue analysis at higher grades in any subject, despite its power for the learner, as shown in the following description of how some mathematics students were taught to self-assess their work through an error analysis after a test: "After we graded their tests, students were asked to evaluate their own performance. . . . Each student was required to submit a written assessment of test performance that contained corrections of all errors and an analysis of test performance. . . . We directed our students to pay particular attention to the *types* of errors they made. . . . They were to attempt to distinguish between conceptual errors and procedural errors."[11]

The teachers found this process extremely useful: "Student self-assessment and the resulting student-teacher dialogue were invaluable in drawing a clear picture of what students were thinking when errors were made."[12] But they also reported that students found the task demanding. In particular, students "had difficulty weighing the seriousness of an error" and seemed "to have difficulty assigning grades to their work. . . . Many had a tendency to weigh effort heavily regardless of the quality of the product."[13]

Many educators who are still unfamiliar with teaching students techniques of self-assessment imagine that this kind of work requires age and intellectual maturity. Not so. Figures 3.2 and 3.3 present scoring rubrics for teacher assessment and student self-assessment that are used in two different elementary schools. Figure 3.2 contains a chart from which the teacher reads descriptions of student performance out loud, after which students place cardboard smiley faces in the appropriate column.[14] (In a videotape on assessment reform, a little girl who was asked why she judged herself to be only "proficient" and not "advanced" in "Response to Literature through Conversations/Conferencing" said matter of factly that "there are some things there that I don't do yet. I *try*, though."[15]) In Fairfax County, Virginia, teachers and supervisors have developed a comprehensive handbook for assessing literacy development. In addition to a narrative section on assessment policies and practices, the handbook contains numerous tools and strategies for assessing student performance, including student self-assessment forms such as the one contained in Figure 3.3.[16] And Figure 3.4 contains an

## Figure 3.2  Scoring Rubric for Reading Conduct and Attitudes

*Standards: The Levels at Which Students Perform the Task.*

|  | *In Progress* | *Basic* | *Proficient* | *Advanced* |
|---|---|---|---|---|
| Self-Selection of Books | Reading is painful. Reading takes too much time. Doesn't like to choose books. Would rather do other things. Chooses only picture books. | Likes or needs help to choose a book. Chooses picture books or "easy" familiar books. | Initiates own selection of books. Chooses books that are "just right." Chooses books of different lengths. Chooses books by different authors. Chooses different types of books. | Initiates own selection of books. Chooses some "challenging" books. Reads widely. Knows many authors of different types of books. |
| Sustained Reading Engagement | Easily distracted during reading time. Requires monitoring to ensure on-task. Flips through pages. Quits or gives up when text is encountered. | Complies with reading when assigned or requested. Concentrates on reading for brief periods of time. | Concentrates on reading for periods of time. Chooses to read as one option. | Concentrates on reading for lengthy periods of time. Chooses to read when has free choice. |
| Response to Literature Through Conversations/ Conferencing | Answers questions with a few details. Retelling of content is not correct or complete. Often does not understand main idea, even if only represented in pictures. | Needs teacher prompt clues to talk about book. Volunteers some additional details when answering questions. Retells details with near accuracy—but may include details that are not important. Seldom offers own opinions or feelings. Sticks to telling facts. | Shares information and feelings about books in response to discussion. Retells details with accuracy. Is aware of humor. States opinions in response to questions. | Shares information and feelings about books freely. Retells details accurately. Enjoys and appreciates humor. Raises questions and opinions. Uses language expressions from book. |

## Figure 3.3 Fairfax County Self-Assessment Instrument

*Student Self-Assessment in Reading*

This is how I think about my reading.

Name: _____Date: _____

Circle the face that best describes your thinking about each statement. Circle the smile if you *really agree* with the statement, a straight face if you think it's *sometimes true*, and a frown if you *disagree*.

- I like to read.

- I can tell you about what I have read.

- I know that stories have a beginning, middle, and end.

- Sometimes I know how to fix it when I make a mistake.

- I like to guess about what may happen in the story.

- I look at the pictures for clues to the story.

- I read books about a topic I like even if the books are hard.

*Student Self-Assessment in Writing*

This is how I think about my writing.

Name: _____Date: _____

Circle the face that best describes your thinking about each statement. Circle the smile if you *really agree* with the statement, a straight face if you think it's *sometimes true*, and a frown if you *disagree*.

- I like to write.

- I like to pick my own topics.

- I go back to a story to add to it or to change it.

- I go back to a story to change words to improve it.

- My writing makes sense to others.

- My punctuation is correct.

- I check my spelling.

### Figure 3.4 Student Book Tapes

After a semester of reading, a unit on plays focusing on characters' actions and moods, and a study of the use of exclamation points and question marks, the students in my class were asked to produce a book tape that would become a part of our class's book tape collection.

Each student was asked to

1. Select a book appropriate to his or her independent reading level.

2. Take part in an interview led by myself and a parent in which the child stated the reasons he or she could use expression in the reading of the selected text, for example, changes in character's mood, changes in the size of letters used, types of punctuation.

3. Write the changes in tone (defined by feeling word) the child would go through as he or she read the book.

4. Record the book tape, check for errors by listening to it a second time, and retape if necessary.

*Assessment:*     Assessment will be based on the appropriateness of the book selection given the student's reading level, the interview, and the book tape. A three-point scale is given within each category. I assess the first and second categories. The children, the parents, and I assess the third together.

- Was the book appropriate to the child's reading level?

  3 = on target                                    1 = inappropriate

- Response to interviews: one point for each reason mentioned.

- The book tape is scored as follows:

| | |
|---|---|
| 3 | The child read with appropriate expression, substantiated by the changes the child described he or she would use. The child read fluently so as not to confuse the flow of the story. The child paid attention to punctuation. The child made the book fun and interesting to listen to. |
| 2 | The child read with some expression, substantiated by the changes the child described he would use. The child read fairly fluently. The child paid attention to some of the punctuation. The book was fun to listen to once. |
| 1 | The child used little expression. The reading was choppy. The child paid little attention to the punctuation. The child did not make the book tape interesting to listen to. |
| 0 | The child did none of the above. |

assessment activity of one elementary teacher in a New York school district who develops her assessments to involve not only an authentic task (such as making an audiotape of a book reading) but also a requirement that students listen to the tape and self-assess and self-adjust their reading as needed.[17]

As learners, all of us have to be taught to check our work objectively and to experience the benefits of doing so. But assessments must reinforce the lesson. They must be designed to require learners to self-assess and self-adjust.

## Making Assessment Honor Excellence: Writing as Revision

What does assessment look like when getting and using feedback is built into it? Assessment of writing offers one of the best examples because effective writing is an achievement target in many school subjects. "Writing as revision" has become something of a mantra in our schools, and the same writing genres recur in student assignments over the years of schooling.

Yet according to the last twenty years of National Assessment of Educational Progress (NAEP) results, student writing across the country is not very powerful or polished. Despite gains in basic skill at the lowest levels, scores have been flat and disappointingly low for years at the higher levels. One horrifying statistic arising from an NAEP portfolio project was that only 1 percent of student papers collected from classrooms contained "major" revisions after the first draft.[18]

After twenty years of emphasis on the idea of writing as revision, why are we seeing little evidence that students have learned how to revise in order to produce a better piece of writing? Because large-scale school district and state tests are not routinely structured to honor the truth that writing is revision. Our tests do not practice what we preach; they seem, in fact, to undercut it. Formal writing tests that ask students to turn out a completed product in a single sitting only reinforce our schools' unwitting message that writing is jotting. When student writing performance is formally judged on single-sitting timed pieces written in response to prompts, no feedback is permitted or even possible, of course.

Before going further, we need to say exactly what "writing is revision" means. As any writer who revises can report, ideas never quite end up on paper with the lucidity they seem to have in one's head. Every writer, from novice to expert, is guilty of projection, of imagining that what she or he was thinking came out clearly and coherently on paper. It is rarely so. There is almost always a gap between our intent and our effect, between our ideas and our execution. This is not merely a "communication" problem, of course, a mere searching for the right words. The importance of writing as a cognitive act is that we learn that our thoughts are in fact less clear than they seem. Put more positively, we think ideas through by writing. No writer has more than a germ of an idea when she or he first puts pen to paper.

That is why we come to need a reader's perspective. Even after we have clarified our ideas or developed what now strikes us as a good story line, we have to get feedback to find out if our ideas have been grasped as we intended. We must think through our ideas, but then think like a reader—or find good readers willing to look at our draft. We need to try out our ideas routinely on others and of course on ourselves (using the mental trick of getting distance by letting some time pass before we reread what we have written).

Writing is revision because excellence emerges only through many cycles of writing and reading, performance and feedback. But few students are taught to perform both acts. It is unlikely that a writer is seeking to bore readers, that an essayist is pleased if no one is persuaded, that a writer wants a reader to say, "I can't figure out what you're up to." But even the best writers get such responses. And getting beyond the ego most of us invest in our writing is profoundly difficult. We are perpetually self-deceived into believing that what we meant was what we said. It takes feedback, some temporal distance from our aims, and opportunities to revise our work before we can find out how rarely this is so. The phrase "writing is revision" should remind us that writing is reflection, not musing; writing requires empathy with the reader, not just egocentric thought.

If we were to honor this understanding of writing as revision in our assessment, we would require student writers to self-assess and self-adjust their writing in light of both self-imposed and sought-out feedback. Without such educative assessment their writing will never become excellent. Requiring students to write one-shot efforts in timed silence teaches them that they do not need an editor—not even themselves. Grading them on the basis of rubrics that score only for obedience to rules of syntax and logic teaches them that writing must be clear and organized. It fails to teach them that writing also needs to be engaging and insightful.

It need not be this way. Consider an example from the Province of Quebec, alluded to in Chapter One. The provincial writing assessment occurs in grades 6 and 10 and takes one week. It is designed to provide students with opportunities to draft, rethink, seek feedback on, and rewrite their work. Students have multiple tasks, some focused on writing, others on editing. In addition to writing to a standardized prompt, with opportunities to revise over three days, students are required to bring pieces of prior writing, already completed and graded, for possible revision. Finally, they are asked to self-assess all their written work for the week, to comment on their revisions, the degree to which they improved their work, and how they improved it.

Building the getting and using of feedback into testing in this way admittedly raises havoc with conventional security and ease of testing. As long as we think in conventional terms, the specter of cheating and unauthorized coaching raises its ugly head. At the very least it becomes harder for outsiders to discern whether or not a student can write when the student is allowed to get and give feedback and revise. But thinking in these terms gives people excuses for not building feedback into assessment. In Quebec they simply ask teachers to certify in writing that administrative conditions were followed and that the final work is that of the student. Why are we so untrusting of such methods in our country?

If we really want powerful models of writing to be our standard, the only way for students to meet that standard is through feedback and self-adjustment. Currently we far too often sacrifice effectiveness for efficiency in testing, and exchange ongoing learning and understanding for extremely precise measurement of certain kinds of knowledge. We then lower our standards because we are unwilling to change assessment structures in ways that would lead students to do better work. However, as the example from Quebec and other examples suggest, the problems of fairness and of getting results that allow us to make inferences about student learning and arrive at meaningful and accurate scores can be adequately addressed if we stick to our principles, and if we are willing to endure some hassles.[19]

The virtues are undeniable and outweigh the difficulties if excellence is our aim. Consider this finding from Harvard University's Assessment Seminar, an ongoing multiyear study of undergraduate education. When asked to report on the most *effective* courses at Harvard,

> Students and alumni overwhelmingly report that the single most important ingredient for making a course effective is getting rapid response on assignments and tests.
>
> Secondly . . . an overwhelming majority are convinced that their best learning takes place when they have a chance to submit an early version of their work, get detailed feedback and criticism, and hand in a final revised version. . . . Many students report that their most memorable experiences have come from courses where such a policy is routine.[20]

## Assessing and Teaching Self-Assessment and Self-Adjustment

What the Harvard research and Quebec assessments suggest is that the receipt and use of feedback must be an ongoing, routine part of assessment. The reason for making feedback concurrent with performing is that this is the only way students can learn to self-assess continually and then self-adjust their intellectual performance, just as musicians, artists, athletes, and other performers continually self-assess and self-adjust.

Providing feedback in the middle of an assessment is sometimes the only way to find out how much a student knows. Yet as William James pointed out, we treat the student who tells us, " 'I know the answer, but I can't say what it is' . . . as practically identical with him who knows absolutely nothing about the answer." This is a mistake because "the vaguer memory of a subject . . . and of where we may go again to recover it . . . constitutes in most men and women the chief fruit of their education."[21] Because memory and mastery often depend on situational cues that enable us to locate what we "know" but have "forgotten," we know things conditionally rather than unconditionally. It is in given situations that we reconfirm and verify to others and to ourselves what we know or do not know. Put in terms of the discussion of feedback, competent performers recover quickly from memory lapses or mistakes when they are made aware of them. But if testing permits no feedback, how will we know all of what the student can do?

This is true not only in writing. The British Assessment of Performance Unit (APU) in mathematics deliberately made oral interviews central to assessment to get at understanding more effectively.[22] In many cases, for example, a student seemed at first not to know the formulas for area and perimeter, but feedback provided merely by reframing the question often enabled these students to "remember" what they had "forgotten." Such feedback enables the performer as well as the assessor to distinguish between what has and has not been accomplished. This performer recognition is an essential element of an assessment process that is not only valid but trustworthy—a distinction perpetually blurred by conventional testing.

Consider also this example from an APU science assessment in which ten-year-olds were asked to conduct simple experiments using windup toys that included designing ways of measuring the relation between number of winder turns and linear distance traveled. As students did their research, assessors noted the following performance qualities on detailed checklists:

- Makes good use of available space.
- Turns winder the exact number of complete turns, holding wheels.
- Allows no unwinding before run begins.
- Uses tape measure accurately (nearest half cm).
- Makes reasonable prediction of distance with extra turns.
- Uses quantitative pattern in evidence to predict.
- Reports results consistent with evidence.[23]

Then the students are asked a "debugging" question that checks their ability to self-assess and self-adjust: "If you could do this experiment again, using the same things that you have here, would you do it in the same way or change some things that you did, to make the experiment better?"

Student responses to these questions were scored as follows:

3 Shows awareness of variables which were not controlled, procedures which turned out to be ineffective, the need to repeat measurement, or criticizes factors which are central, not peripheral to the investigation

2 Shows awareness of alternative procedures but is unaware of particular deficiencies of those used (does not have very good reasons for suggesting changes)

1 Uncritical of procedures used, can suggest neither deficiencies nor alternative procedures[24]

We should want to know not merely whether students grasp some important ideas and skills and can try them out but also whether they can adjust their own performances in a timely and effective manner in response to puzzles, failures, audience reaction, and client demands. Self-adjustment is not something we can leave to chance between tests if our aim is to determine whether students are effective in the use of knowledge and skill.

Back to writing: consider as an exemplary case the questions related to self-adjustment and effectiveness used in the Arts Propel work in Pittsburgh (undertaken by the Project Zero team led by Howard Gardner and Dennie Palmer Wolf from the Harvard Graduate School of Education) a few years ago. These questions were used by teachers to assess student portfolios, and given to students as an aid to self-assessment:

- Range of work: What does the student understand about "tuning" writing to fit different circumstances and audiences? Can the student see the difference between different genres—how you write up labs vs. stories?
- Development of work: Is this a student who can revise, not just recopy? Is this a student who can make good use of criticism? Is this a student who can pursue and persist with a complex project?
- Style: Can a student write something which is more than an amalgam or imitation of the writings of others? In particular, what evidence is there of questioning, imagining, or playing with ideas?
- Reflection: Is this a student who can think about writing in a way that is likely to inform learning? Does the student recognize his/her own strengths and weaknesses? Does the student know effective strategies?

- Craft: Does the student have enough control of the forms of written English to make his/her ideas understood?
- Audience: Does the student show sensitivity to or awareness of the needs of the reader or listener? Are key details, transitions missing?[25]

The student variant of these questions asked them to identify the most satisfying and dissatisfying pieces in their portfolios, to explain their choice, and to self-assess their work. Often the reasons for their choices and their analyses were more revealing of students' insights about writing or its absence than were the work samples themselves.

It is important here to distinguish between different kinds of student self-reflection, because this can help us see how to move students from self-assessment to self-adjustment. In writing, for example, reflection is too often viewed as passive metacognition (that is, students are asked to reflect on what writing is and about their own preexisting interests and styles) when it would be more helpful to their development for them to reflect on ways to make clearer what they are trying to say. If writing is revision, then we should be assessing self-adjustment more often, not merely self-assessment. It is not enough to ask, Do the students engage in self-reflection about their writing (or any other subject)? Instead, as suggested by the Arts Propel questions about development of work listed earlier, we must ask, Are students profiting from self-assessment and the feedback of others? Are they using the feedback effectively to improve their performance? Are they developing a better grasp of what does and does not work? Are they getting better at judging the value of the feedback they receive?

One English teacher I know has most of this down to a science. He teaches his students two cardinal rules of peer review, and part of their grade reflects how well they follow the guidelines when reviewing each other's writing. The first rule is that they must judge the writing's effect, given the statement of purpose (or intent) the author has attached to the draft, and comment to the author on the extent to which he or she has accomplished that purpose. The statement of purpose describes the particular audience the author was aiming to reach and the reactions sought from those readers. The second rule (the one that causes my workshop audiences to gasp a bit) is that peer reviewers must mark the paper at the point where they lost interest, and they must explain why. In the final draft to be turned in to the teacher the writer must attach a self-assessment and an explanation of which feedback was used and why and which was not used and why. Here, I believe, is a teacher who knows how to cause excellence in writing. And this formative assessment process, accompanied by a high standard, is the key.

Such a system is not restricted to small classes and school systems. In the Toronto Benchmarks program, students are videotaped as they deliver editorials (similar to television news commentaries) on an ecological theme derived from a previous science unit. After their first attempt, they self-assess and get feedback from an adult. Their subsequent revision of the talk culminates in a second delivery and a final self-assessment. The following rubric for scoring describes the range of performance:

| | |
|---|---|
| **Level Five** | The student is aware of the importance of both content and delivery in giving a talk. The content is powerfully focused and informative. . . . The talk is delivered in a style that interests and persuades the audience. Questions, eye contact, facial expressions and gesture engage the audience. . . . Causes and effects are elaborated. The second version of the talk reveals significant changes based on revision after viewing. . . . |
| **Level Four** | The student is aware of the importance of both content and delivery in giving a talk. . . . The student's talk is well shaped and supported with pertinent information. . . . Delivery is improved after viewing the first draft of the talk. . . . |
| **Level Three** | . . . The talk displays a noticeable order and some organization primarily through lists. The student includes some specific information, some of which supports or focuses on the topic. . . . There is evidence of revision as a result of viewing the first version of the talk. . . . |
| **Level Two** | The student's talk contains some specific information with some attempt at organization. The main idea is unclear. Some paraphrasing of text is evident. The student uses no persuasive devices. . . . Little improvement is shown in the talk after watching the first version. . . . |
| **Level One** | The student chooses one or two details to talk about but the talk lacks coherence. The talk is confused and illogical. There may be no response.[26] |

Like all good rubrics (as discussed in Chapter Seven), this one contains statements that describe the performance traits at each level; the statements go beyond the typical "excellent," "good," "fair," and "poor" scores to define what good and poor and so on actually look like. This rubric assumes that assessment and self-adjustment are central to performance improvement. Note that the students given the higher scores saw a need to self-adjust their talk after viewing the first version, and they did so; students whose performances were ranked lowest either saw no need to improve their performance or chose not to. In the work my colleagues and I do at the Center on Learning, Assessment, and School Structure, we see that for students who do not self-adjust, more often the problem is oversight or ignorance rather than lack of will: students are not adequately trained to understand and analyze their own performance against standards, and they are not given built-in opportunities and incentives to self-adjust. They typically do not grasp what is wrong with their work, and thus disregard the guidance that might improve their performance.

## Using Models with Feedback

As all the examples cited in this chapter reveal, effective feedback exists only relative to standards, thus to models or model specifications. Whether we are helping young children learn their letters, older students learn to weld, or any students learn to do math, science, or social studies, all effective feedback systems depend on standards and models that exemplify them. With no well-formed N's and H's next to his own letter N, Justin would not have known that his N did not come up to standard, and instead of saying "It is not what I wanted," he would have said something like "Why isn't this what you wanted?" If we do not have models, we cannot get or give feedback. Without models, we are just guessing, mucking around and hoping for the best. Models tell students what to do. When we hear students asking, "Is this what you want? Is that what we're supposed to do?" it typically means there is no systemic feedback system at work.

Models set the standards that we want students to achieve. They anchor feedback. In the best systems of learning and performance, students attempt a performance in light of a known standard or specification. As part of ongoing assessment, they then compare their work against the standard. In more formal assessments, other judges also compare the work against the same standard. Those comparisons are the basis for feedback, and that is how people improve—by comparing their work to model performance. Students must have routine access to the criteria and standards for the tasks they need to master; they must have feedback in their attempts to master those tasks; and they must have opportunities to use the feedback to revise work and resubmit it for evaluation against the standard. Excellence is attained by such cycles of model-practice-perform-feedback-perform.

Many teachers balk at this idea. But I defy anyone to show me an expert airline pilot, corporate lawyer, internist, basketball player, or bassoon player who learned his or her craft merely by "brains," by mucking around on his or her own, or by acing a single simplistic secure test of performance.

Perhaps a simple example of the power of good models will help remind us of their value. The J. Peterman clothing catalogue had been coming to our house for a few years before I began to read it with any care. One day, as I was leafing through it upon its arrival, I was struck by a particularly wonderful write-up on a fairly ordinary product:

### Listening to Big Yellow

Hobsbawn (not his real name) no longer plunges into deep depression when he flips on the Weather Channel. Betty, once incapacitated by feelings of vulnerability, now seeks out the most challenging muck.

Harry, once angry and irritable, feared he'd "go berserk" at work some April morning. Now he has a smile for everyone.

What does it mean when vulcanized rubber can alter what we think of as personality? Should we question our concept of the self?

Big Yellow. Galoshes with the fortitude of a Caterpillar tractor and the cheerfulness of a school bus. Just-below-the-knee length. Slip them on over shoes or boots (there's lots of room to tuck in your pants), then cinch tight. Cotton jersey lining. Heavy-duty tread. Totally and absolutely waterproof. Wearing them through rain, snow, slush, mud, mire, and muck is like eating a bowl of McCann's oatmeal topped with butter churned from your own cow's milk.[27]

This is wonderful writing: vivid, rich, and as seemingly persuasive as advertising copy can be.

Two arguments typically are made against the use of models in anchoring assessment and instruction. The first is that if we use as exemplars not just better-than-average student work but excellent adult work, students will become depressed or debilitated if they still have a way to go in achieving those standards. According to this argument, no one should ever excel. We should become depressed when seeing or hearing expert performers or knowing the best possible scores on computer games. But instructors and coaches in all public programs know the value of routinely holding out model performance for emulation and analysis. Even students with talent in a particular area need to discover how much more others have done and why study of the great is desirable. Faculties should always calibrate local standards to excellent exemplars. This is the only way for both teachers and students to have valid, inspirational, and stable targets.

The second argument is that anchoring instruction and assessment with models can only inhibit students' genuine creative talent. This argument is perhaps plausible if we think of supplying only one model for students to emulate. However, this is not what educative assessment entails. The easiest way to teach students effectively without inhibiting their creativity is to purvey multiple, diverse models of excellence. Let students read Jane Austen and James Joyce as well as Peterman's catalogue to master description; let them hear the speeches of Desmond Tutu, Ronald Reagan, Jesse Jackson, and Barbara Jordan; let them learn from Stephen Jay Gould, John McPhee, Lewis Thomas, and Oliver Sacks how to describe phenomena and make findings interesting to the reader. The superficial or stylistic differences will in fact force students to dig deeper, to ask, What do these works have in common despite their differences? What in your work shares these traits? This question is at the heart of using assessment as good instruction.

Indeed, teachers have routinely told me that minor adjustments in their lessons to focus on analysis of models (including poor models) and derivation of criteria and indicators from samples have led to dramatic improvement in performance from all manner of students. As one fourth grade teacher put it, "I am no longer resigned to getting the good, bad, and the ugly. Students have revealingly said to me, 'Oh! So that is what you want!'" So often what we are after is unclear to students; the purveying of models ends the mystery or confusion.

Beyond building in consequences and requiring students to face them in assessment, to ensure that they understand the standards and feedback based on those consequences, we must train students to assess work. To understand the desired impact and the success or failure at meeting it, students need to be given the training that the performance judges receive. The school district of Carleton, Ontario, outside Ottawa, provides such training, and has done so for many years in many subject areas.[28] Carleton teachers train their students the way we train advanced placement or statewide writing teacher-judges. They give students (and parents) a big book called the "Exemplar Booklet," filled with many samples of scored work (from the sublime to the ridiculous) and written commentaries explaining the scores given. They then supply a dozen more papers with grades and commentary removed that students can use to learn to score work reliably against the provincial standards. Regular sessions of scoring and self-assessment against these standards are part of the syllabus. Similar work is currently occurring in many elementary schools, such as those in South Brunswick, New Jersey, where students receive detailed rubrics for writing and commenting on sample papers.[29]

If our goal is the kind of understanding that can be achieved only through feedback, self-assessment, and self-adjustment, there is only one way to reach it. We must supply and teach from a full range of possible performances, along a scoring scale of significant range, with rubrics that vividly summarize the differences. This approach directs us to the need for fine discrimination and iteration in an assessment system for excellence.

## Educative Rubrics and Criteria: Aiming at Impact

If we are to obtain effective performance, then our scoring rubrics and criteria have to do a far better job than they do now. Effective feedback and student self-adjustment depend on the aptness of the scoring criteria and the scoring rubrics built on the models. And as noted in the previous chapter, real performance and all enterprising behavior is about causing a desired impact. Much current school performance testing, however, uses criteria that merely address the correctness of content, formats, or procedures. Students learn from this testing only that they need to write up labs a certain way, that they need to use a five-step proof in geometry, or that they need to write essays to specified lengths. These tests teach students that formalism and effort matter more than results. They teach students not to solicit or use feedback.

To improve students' understanding and performance, it is vital that we help them learn to assess their work regularly against the question at the heart of performance: Did the performance work? Were the purposes achieved, regardless of the manner, whether orthodox or unorthodox? The point of student performance is never merely to emulate the surface or mechanical traits of exemplary performances and performers but to achieve their effect, their ability to persuade an audience, satisfy a client request, or solve a problem. When we fail to teach this, we stifle creativity by overemphasizing arbitrary methods and procedures. Many state writing assessments run the risk of undercutting good writing by scoring only for focus, organization, style, and mechanics without once asking judges to consider whether the writing is powerful, memorable, provocative, or moving (all impact-related criteria, and all at the heart of why people read what others write).

In performance testing, efficiency issues can easily drive out pedagogical concerns, and thus everywhere we look today we see safe rubrics that focus on the superficial traits of student products. We need only look at the NAEP pilot writing portfolio assessment project mentioned earlier to see the problem.[30] We look in vain for language in safe rubrics that seeks evidence of the student's narrative powers. Such rubrics do not encourage or evoke an engaging or psychologically astute story; in fact, they penalize anyone who deviates from a crude chronological storytelling format. (Modern fiction would never get a good score.) All the qualities thus scored are formal traits (so called because they relate to the form of the writing, not to its impact, process, or content). The repeated use of such rubrics will inevitably cause students and teachers alike to aim for the formulaic.

When impact criteria are highlighted in assessment, and form and process criteria are appropriately downplayed (not ignored), we overcome one great fear mentioned earlier: the loss of students' creativity. In assessing impact we open the door to greater creativity, not less. The performer asked to make an impact is free—challenged, in fact—to find a new way to achieve that impact. Unless we highlight impact criteria, in other words, the student really has no authentic performance goal other than to please the teacher, obey formulas, or mimic orthodox approaches. Too few students understand writing or any other intellectual performance because they are so rarely instructed in performance purposes. Instead they are taught a grab bag of out-of-context techniques and processes.

## Iterative Tasks and Longitudinal Assessment

As we have said, educative assessment requires not only true models and standards but also multiple opportunities to meet them, opportunities resulting from feedback and guidance after the initial teaching and performing. The best assessment is iterative; it functions longitudinally, that is, over time. In a healthy system of feedback loops in which assessment is iterative, results always improve over time. This is true whether we are talking about people or pigeons, writing or Wiffle ball. The corollary is that test scores that remain pretty much unchanged over time signify a dysfunctional or absent feedback system, not incompetent students and teachers.

Not only does performance improvement occur in an effective feedback system, variability in performance also decreases over time. That is the message of all modern work in quality control and increased production in modern organizations, after all, and performance improvement through feedback in relation to specific standards is being obtained in the military and at McDonald's—which are effectively training our supposedly immature students in both cases.

Earlier in this chapter I presented rubrics that function as novice-to-expert continua for skills (see Figures 3.2 and 3.3). What we presently lack are similar scales for students' mastery of ideas. For example, how might we describe novice-to-expert levels of an understanding of the Declaration of Independence? Or the causes of the Civil War? Presumably the ongoing work at the national level on standards in each subject will provide us with the grist if not the actual descriptors for such rubrics, and recommended benchmarks are already emerging in science and social studies.[31] (This point is pursued in the next chapter, on assessing for understanding.)

Accustomed to our traditional tests for breadth of subject-matter knowledge, and often tending to feel, fatalistically, that large-scale performance gains are not possible, we have lacked reasons and motives for developing continuous-progress and standard-referenced assessment systems. I have argued here that there are critical reasons and impressive motives to change our ways. It is possible for most students, both more and less naturally talented, to improve and to achieve eventual excellence. But they will not do so in a norm-referenced one-shot testing system, in which we anchor our assessment in the current norms of achievement. This is a strategy that must always fail, for both the individual and the system. Our goal needs to be to build a system not out of what is normal but out of what ought to be the norm. A goal based on the best models and lots of feedback initiates a rising tide that lifts all boats.

Real educational progress is possible only through an assessment system that makes feedback and opportunities to use it central to design. Excellence is always achieved by self-adjustment in reference to known standards. The fatalism so often heard in schools about what students cannot do may be justified on the basis of conventional testing schemes, but in a healthy assessment system all students can and will overcome their current best performance, can and will progressively approach and even surpass the expectations we set for them. That individual and aggregate student test scores do not change much over time should be seen for the feedback it is: an indictment of our current approach to assessment.

# CHAPTER 4

# Promoting Student Understanding

Authentic tasks and better feedback will improve learning only if we assess all that we value instead of what is merely easy to test, and certainly a central goal in teaching is to cause genuine understanding rather than to require mere rote behavior or superficial familiarity. We also know that assessment for understanding is inseparable from performance assessment, as Benjamin Bloom and his colleagues argued years ago in describing *application:* "Teachers frequently say: 'If a student really comprehends something, he can apply it.'... Application is different in two ways from knowledge and simple comprehension: the student is not prompted to give specific knowledge, nor is the problem old-hat."[1] Thus, to grasp the real value and challenge of authentic assessment we must consider more carefully what we mean by "assessing for understanding."

However, I offer a cautionary note at the outset to forestall misunderstanding. Understanding is only one aim, and not necessarily the most important, at every turn of schooling. I am thus not suggesting here that all teaching be geared at all times toward deep and sophisticated understanding of everything. There are clearly phases when and topics for which this is neither feasible nor desirable, sometimes on developmental grounds, other times due to the nature of the work (such as when we target the internalization of technical skills in beginning language or computer classes) or simply due to emphasis and priorities. Conversely, without a constant focus on understanding, much of what we learn will never become a fluent and powerful repertoire. Worse, we may find that we have misunderstood things we thought we really knew.

To make this point clearer, the full domain of intellectual achievement targets, or educational goals, can be conveniently divided into five types: subject-matter knowledge, technical subject-matter skill, performance competency, mature habits of mind and conduct, and understanding make up the intellectual goals of schooling. Subject-matter knowledge involves the "content," the declarative and propositional "stuff" that is taught, learned, and, eventually, used authentically. Technical skills are subject-matter-specific abilities, such as writing sonnets, solving simultaneous equations in algebra, translating German text, or critiquing a historical research paper. Performance competencies are cross-disciplinary and focus on generic abilities relevant to complex research and communication of ideas, such as agenda setting, teamwork, problem posing, skill in finding information, public speaking, exhibit building, use of audiovisuals, and so on. Mature habits of mind include perseverance, tolerance of ambiguity, and respect for craftsmanship—in other words, the "discipline" underlying competent and autonomous performance in all the academic disciplines. Due to the assessment reform movement and a more thorough consideration of content and performance standards, discussion in recent years has focused on improving integration of performance competency, technical skill, and subject-matter knowledge. (With respect to habits of mind, many of the best performance tasks do not so much directly measure for habits of mind as indirectly require them for complex task success.)

This chapter focuses on assessment of *understanding*, because understanding is arguably the intellectual achievement we are poorest at improving—and not coincidentally, the achievement we have the most difficulty assessing. Understanding is in fact central to *all* the other achievements: unless we eventually understand the deeper meanings and import of what we know and the skills we develop, we cannot make the most effective and wise uses possible of our knowledge. Without understanding, our thinking is constrained, habit bound, and borrowed; genuine innovations, better solutions, or thoughtful critiques will not likely come to us once we are removed from the highly focused prompts of teacher questions.

There is also irony here: one reason we assess understanding so poorly, I think, is that we do not have a clearly thought-out understanding of understanding, even though we use the word constantly, and we particularly do not realize that understanding and knowledge are not synonyms. That may explain, in part, why our assessment systems are so often ineffective. Our tests of "knowledge" may be hiding from us students' deeper understandings—and misunderstandings—which lurk behind pat answers. Indeed, we have perhaps gotten the whole matter backward in testing: any hope of having an educative assessment system may well depend on our ability to better ferret out, discover, and target the *misunderstandings* that lurk behind many, if not most, of students' correct answers.

Describing understanding, its various facets, and the ways we can better assess it is the aim of this chapter, which begins with an examination of the difference between understanding and knowledge, and of the current state of our students' understanding.

## Knowledge Versus Understanding

The problems that many educators encounter when trying to develop intellectually rigorous tasks suggest that subject-matter knowledge and subject-matter understanding are often confused. Tests of knowledge are simple and straightforward, after all. Whether they are composed of selected or constructed-response questions, they ask the student to recall and use what was encountered, and to distinguish between correct and incorrect propositions or techniques. But does such recall and use signify understanding? Teachers are often surprised to discover that perfectly able and seemingly competent students have an apparently shaky or poor understanding of what they know when the questions become more like "probes" than tests, when more authentic application is required.

Consider the method of probing called Prediction-Observation-Explanation (POE) in science assessment. Richard White and Richard Gunstone provide an elegant account of the difference between this method and traditional test questions about the same phenomena. They note that in a typical test question on gravitational force, "students merely have to explain a completely described phenomenon. Often this will involve a rather unthinking reproduction of textbook knowledge. On the other hand, a prediction is more likely to require genuine application." The explanations are often inadequate—from students who get traditional test questions correct: "A key characteristic of POE is that the student must decide what reasoning to apply. We have found [that] students frequently support predictions . . . by knowledge which is at odds with physics such as 'gravity pulls equally hard on all objects.' This illustrates the greater power of the POE task than more usual approaches to probe the nature of the beliefs which students use to interpret real events."[2] The phenomenon of student misunderstanding obscured by typical testing will turn out to be of fundamental importance in educative assessment.

At the very least we are alerted by the discrepancy in answers to an important fact of teaching: important ideas and their meaning are not self-evident. For example, it is a commonplace in mathematics that students have great difficulty multiplying and dividing fractions, even after lots of practice in problem solving and with knowledge of algorithms. However, when one appreciates the truly counterintuitive nature of both actions—multiplying two things makes them smaller and dividing them makes them bigger—the surprise begins to turn into wonder: Why don't we teachers see how a good deal of what we teach is so easily misunderstood?

It is not surprising that we are unclear about what distinguishes understanding from knowledge and skill. For one thing, understanding clearly depends on both of these achievements. In fact, Ray Nickerson concluded in a fine paper a few years back that understanding was roughly *synonymous* with expert knowledge.[3] That is, if students know key facts and theories and use them accurately in response to challenging questions and problems, should we not conclude that they understand them? Well, perhaps not. A person may *know* the First Amendment and the Supreme Court cases relating to it; and he or she may *know* Darwin's theory of evolution, which purports to explain species' development through adaptation, in contrast to Biblical creationism. But it does not automatically follow that the person *understands* these ideas, that is, that he or she could describe how they work or what makes them valuable or what insights they represent over competing ideas. For example, Thomas Kuhn, the philosopher of science who coined the idea of *paradigm shifts* to explain the revolutionary nature of scientific development, argued that Darwin's truly radical idea was not that of species evolution (which had already been in the air for many years in biology and botany) but the abolition of *teleology*, the notion that all life (and hence the evolution of life) has a purpose: "The *Origin of Species* recognized no goal set either by God or [by] nature. . . . The belief that natural selection, resulting from mere competition between organisms, could have produced man . . . was the most difficult and disturbing aspect of Darwin's theory. What could 'evolution,' 'development' and 'progress' mean in the absence of a specified goal? To many people, such terms suddenly seemed self-contradictory."[4] In fact, Frank Sulloway, Darwin's biographer and author of the recent best-selling book *Born to Rebel: Birth Order, Family Dynamics, and Creative Lives*, puzzled for years over Darwin's achievement: "Darwin knew far less about the various species he collected on the Beagle voyage than did the experts back in England who later classified these organisms for him. Yet expert after expert missed the revolutionary significance of what Darwin had collected. Darwin, who knew less, somehow understood more."[5]

To ask, Do you understand what you know? is thus not redundant. If we understand an idea, we grasp its significance, its implicit connections with other important ideas—its meaning, as the Darwin account shows. Darwin's achievement also involved being able to explain his radical ideas clearly and support them with apt evidence and argument (that is, his account of vestigal organs and traits). Indeed, to Aristotle, understanding rather than know-how was indicated by the ability to simplify and teach a complex idea, and to know causes: knowledgeable "men of experience know the fact but not the *why* of it."[6] When we understand, we are able to adapt knowledge to novel situations because we grasp causal relations, and we can connect seemingly disparate elements of knowledge into a coherent account.

Assessment of understanding must therefore involve more than response to the cue of a specific test item grounded in an unproblematic question. We must be able to do more than just repeat phrases of official explanation; we must be able to do such things as justify the ideas involved, use those ideas effectively, and explain their value. It is not enough to know that gravitational force is related to distance in terms of an inverse square relationship. If a student can reveal a grasp of the proof, explain the principle's applicability, and consider its importance (for example, by explaining how Kepler's and Newton's formulation differed from their predecessors' and did a better job of prediction), that would presumably demonstrate some of what we mean when we say we want students to understand these principles.

But we need not resort to such esoteric examples to see that knowledge does not automatically yield meaning. Listen to any first grader read a storybook out loud. He can all too easily know what each word says without grasping the meaning of the sentence, or he can know all the facts without grasping the moral of the story. Consider a simple sentence that twice misled my son: *The dog flew down the street.* In his first reading, he misread it as "fled" down the street—a sophisticated miscue but a mistake nonetheless. On being prodded to look at it again, he got the word correct but then asked how a dog could possibly fly. Reading is in fact the constant testing of theories as to what the text might mean, and there is often, alas, no unambiguous answer but rather multiple possibly valid interpretations. This has significant implications for assessment of understanding: the student must confront ambiguous or problematic material or experiences.

## How Well Have Schools Been Teaching Understanding?

If understanding were simply a body of knowledge, we would have a real puzzle on our hands because many successful students do not seem to understand (or even to recall accurately after a while) what they ought to understand given what they know (as judged by test results) based on probing and tasks involving application. However, any teacher who has seen what Harvard educational researcher David Perkins so aptly characterizes as "fragile" (forgotten, inert, naive, and ritual) knowledge sufficiently grasps that there must be a difference between correct answers on a test of knowledge and evidence of understanding.[7]

In fact, misunderstanding about what is known is surprisingly common. As Howard Gardner, Perkins's colleague and distinguished psychologist at Harvard, showed in *The Unschooled Mind*, recent educational research reveals that many seemingly competent graduates of courses, programs, and institutions leave without having had their knowledge truly tested, and thus their lack of understanding has not been rooted out or altered by years of formal schooling and probing—even at the level of advanced studies in college: "[What] an extensive research literature now documents is that an ordinary degree of understanding is routinely missing in many, perhaps most students. It is reasonable to expect a college student to be able to apply in new context a law of physics, or a proof in geometry, or the concept in history of which she has just demonstrated acceptable mastery in her class. If, when the circumstances of testing are slightly altered, the sought-after competence can no longer be documented, then understanding—in any reasonable sense of the term—has simply not been achieved."[8]

Later testing of even a conventional kind can reveal earlier failures to understand. Consider this result in mathematics: almost all U.S. teenagers study Algebra I, and most get passing grades. Yet National Assessment of Educational Progress (NAEP) results show that only 5 percent of U.S. adolescents perform well at tasks requiring higher-order use of Algebra I knowledge.[9] The recent Third International Math and Science Assessment reached a similar conclusion about adolescents' understanding of science knowledge in one of the most exhaustive studies to date.[10] So did NAEP's most recent test—a mixture of multiple-choice, constructed response, and performance task questions—which showed "a stark gap between the ability of students in general to learn basic principles, and their ability to apply knowledge or explain what they learned."[11] The message is clear: we are getting what we ask for, namely, relatively unthinking responses to low-level questions.

What makes matters more complicated than just overuse of simple test questions is that misunderstanding often appears more as student thoughtlessness than as lack of wisdom. Another widely discussed result from the NAEP is that one-third of U.S. eighth grade students taking the NAEP math test a few years back answered the question, "How many buses does the army need to transport 1,128 soldiers if each bus holds 36 soldiers?" with the written-out answer, "31 remainder 12."[12] The math was accurate, but the answer was wrong; the students had not grasped the meaning of the question nor apparently understood how to use mathematics in context to reach an answer of thirty-two buses.

The problem of failing to contextualize work to accomplish the best result despite having the requisite mathematical knowledge is not restricted to novices struggling to learn arithmetic. Think of most people's experience with calculus. Many advanced mathematics students become technically skilled at computing derivatives and integrals but seem totally unclear about what it all means or why their actions are warranted. I remember once having to set aside my plans to discuss *King Lear* with seniors in an English class in order to deal with the anger of eight students who had just come from calculus class. They were utterly frustrated due to lack of understanding of their work, and like most math students in this country they were being asked to work without any historical or scientific context, or larger intellectual aim. Most did not even know the straightforward astronomy and physics problems of graphing and calculating velocity, time, and distance that gave rise to the science of calculus.

Consider a somewhat different example from an elementary science classroom to see how conventional assessment may hide student misunderstanding and how, therefore, teachers who rely on typical test questions may misunderstand what students really understand. After a thorough lesson on energy, the sun, radiation, and heat, followed by a quiz, a third grade boy who had done quite well on the quiz piped up: "Yeah, but heat is caused by blankets!" This is, of course, a plausible theory, which the teacher had the good sense, despite her shock, to turn into a "teachable moment" by asking students to do a little experiment designed to clarify that the blanket on one's body only *appears* to cause heat to come into being. The point is that what should concern us is that the boy had compartmentalized his real views and gotten a high score on the teacher-designed test on the causes of heat! This story epitomizes the difficulty inherent in all intellectual inquiry, whether that of novice or veteran scientists. We bring both understandings and misunderstandings to our work; as it turns out, our plausible but wrong ideas are surprisingly resistant to modification through instruction and are somewhat hidden by conventional teaching and testing cycles (never mind being abetted by the common student inclination to "give them what they want").[13]

Thus what appears to be thoughtlessness on the part of students may be something more deep, more complex: that is, student failure to understand may be due to the failure of teaching and testing to tap the understandings that students bring to the classroom and hold on to underneath the lessons they learn superficially. Consider understanding of basic astronomy. To see how naive theory can be longer-lived than extensive knowledge learned in school, simply ask college and high school students, "Why is it colder in winter and warmer in summer?" Every student in the United States has been taught that the earth travels around the sun, that the orbit is elliptical, and that the earth tilts about twenty degrees off its north-south axis. But even when graduating Harvard seniors are asked this question (as occurs in a provocative science education video on the phenomenon of failing to understand), we discover that few explain correctly.[14] They either have no adequate explanation for what they claim to know or they hold the erroneous view that the temperature changes are due to their part of the earth being farther away from the sun in winter than in summer. Similar findings occur when people are asked to explain the phases of the moon.

Or consider the concept of error in science. A very bright and able student once argued with me that error in science was a function only of sloppiness or crude instruments. When the "big boys and girls" did science, using better equipment than this student had access to, their work was without error, he claimed. He was not confused or equivocating on the word *error*, please understand; rather, he honestly and earnestly believed that the concept of "margin of error" referred to a problem of quality control in technology. (This boy had taken Advanced Placement chemistry and physics and received the highest score of 5 on each exam.)

There is now a twenty-year-old literature on such so-called science misconceptions. But as Gardner points out, there are equivalent findings in mathematics in regard to rigidly applied algorithms (as in the NAEP bus example), and in the social sciences and English (if we translate "misunderstanding" into "stereotypes" and "caricatures").[15] Nor are straightforward athletic challenges exempt from ongoing failure to understand or from incorrect understanding, and thus from disappointing performance. I think here of my experience with soccer both as a parent and as a former varsity coach. My young son is led through countless drills without once being taught about the purposes of the drill or the underlying strategies of the game. I then watch children congregate around the ball, drawn like little buzzing bees to honey, without being helped to understand from the outset that working in small teams to create passing opportunities is key to success. (The incessant exhortation "Don't bunch!" from sideline coaches at all levels reveals the problem nicely, I think. No one seems to see that such a command offers no clear direction to students who lack a sense of purpose.) As a varsity coach, I saw the same phenomenon, and puzzled over its persistence. Few players on any team seem to have a clear plan in mind when they are on offense.

This is apparent in both their behavior and their later answers to questions about their actions.

Too few performers, be they soccer players or science students, seem to understand their purposes deeply as they perform. Rather, they obey directions, muddle about, and hope it all works out. Is it any wonder, then, that they can be shown to have fragile, patchwork knowledge? In soccer, for example, being purposeful means knowing what you are trying to accomplish, especially when you do not have the ball (which is almost all the time). The aim is to create open space or numerical advantage to advance the ball. Coaches often seem oblivious to developing such game understanding—an ability that is universally valued and (misleadingly) called *anticipation*—among players. But coaches ought not to be surprised, then, when performance in a game rarely seems deliberate or effective. If we are waiting around for intuition and anticipation instead of developing it, performance will amount to hoping that good luck will occur and that insights will reveal themselves like Alice's cakes that say "Eat me!" And if this is true in the game of soccer, what does it mean for academics—particularly when the performances at the heart of the subject are so often never directly experienced by the student in assessment and assignments? The answer is clear: few students will have a clear understanding of what they know and of how to use it, given the grab bag of isolated skills and facts they possess—a phenomenon we see in every school at every level, including college and graduate school.

Misunderstanding and thoughtlessness are thus related. Both thrive when students do not have to explain and justify what they know and do (that is, what makes what they know and do true or apt). In other words, as suggested in the previous chapters, the absence of purposeful (that is, authentic) challenges abets the mindlessness we see when our students are supposed to have acquired learning: when testing is routinely composed of dozens of items that permit no more than a few minutes' thought or do not force thoughtful connection with other knowledge, why think deeply or carefully? These are just a few of the reasons that suggest the need to rethink what we mean by understanding and how to—and how not to—assess for it.

How wide is the gap between teaching and learning? How can people with a great deal of knowledge not understand what it means? Clearly these are complex questions with no easy answers. But surely we are on solid ground when we say that a significant factor must be the predominance of purposeless drill or play in sports or of multiple-choice and short-answer questions in school testing—that the most ubiquitous tests are designed to bypass explanation, justification, and true judgment-based application.

## The Inevitability of Failing to Understand and of Misunderstanding

Whatever understanding is and however we come by it, it is not an all or nothing affair. Understanding is not a sudden "Aha!" whereby we go from ignorance to deep understanding. Even if there are moments of insight, we typically come slowly and sometimes unsteadily, or two steps forward and one back, to a deeper, more sophisticated understanding. Understanding is a matter of degree, a matter of more or less sophistication, rigor, insight, and tact. Indeed, there has always been irony attached to the course of understanding: those who understand often state how little they understand the more they understand (with Socrates as the spiritual father of the idea). To not understand, to know why, and to be able to explain it clearly has always been the mark of a highly educated person.

Preliminary implications for assessment are clear: no system of testing for only "right" answers will adequately tap into what is understood and not understood by the student. Students who have deep understandings can answer simple multiple-choice questions incorrectly, and students with simplistic knowledge can answer such questions correctly—a phenomenon as old as Plato, who described it so powerfully in his parable of the cave.[16] The now-enlightened philosopher, returning from the light to the darkness, cannot see at all as he takes his old seat in the cave. He looks more foolish than his comrades, who with eyes and intellect adapted to the dimly lit cave are expert at what passes for knowledge, namely, the identification of the shadows cast on the wall. Thus it can happen that a student who makes a mistake on a test later provides a good explanation for the mistake, a self-correction, and a more sophisticated framing of things than a student who has merely learned the right answer and gotten the item correct. This phenomenon alone should make us leery of overreliance on test formats that permit no explanation of the answers by the student.

But then the challenges of teaching, learning, and assessing must go deeper still. Misunderstanding cannot perhaps ever be avoided. As Friedrich Schleiermacher said when arguing in favor of hermeneutics as the "the art of avoiding misunderstandings" in textual interpretation, "misunderstandings follow *automatically* and understanding must be desired and sought out at every point."[17] The sophisticated reader or scientist is no different from my son: our "sensible" interpretations and analyses always depend on incomplete information, the simplified lessons and theories we first encountered as novices, and the self-projected ideas that we put into the text or experience.

Coming to an understanding will thus invariably require a careful rethinking and revising of what we thought we knew in light of further evidence, analysis, and reflection. As we shall see in later chapters, this insight has profound instructional and curricular implications, not just assessment ones: a linear scope and sequence, predicated on a view that treats learning as additive and nonproblematic—as though we could inoculate students against misunderstanding—will likely fail to develop student insight and mastery. We may end up teaching more, but causing far less understanding than is possible. (This, too, has implications for the common fear that one loses precious time by engaging in more complex performance-based work than can be afforded in this test-driven world. As I argue in Chapter Twelve, some of this fear is based on a false view of our current effectiveness—the poor yield of coverage-dominated teaching in test results—and a misunderstanding of how validity in testing works.)

One of the more thought-provoking exercises used in workshops lead by the staff of the Center on Learning, Assessment, and School Structure builds on this inevitability, as well as on the idea that understanding is a matter of degree. We ask teachers to target an important idea or text in their teaching and to begin by considering two questions: What are the predictable misunderstandings students have about this idea and bring to their studies? and What might a "sophistication rubric" for this idea look like, whereby we describe the words and actions indicative of a naive, average, and sophisticated understanding of the same idea? Teachers are highly engaged by the questions but disturbed by the results. Though they can provide lots of examples of predictable misunderstandings when prompted, they see that they rarely gear their teaching and testing to anticipate, ferret out, and actively work to overcome these misconceptions. Similarly, although teachers can build draft rubrics in the exercise, they realize that they have rarely assessed for the degree of student insight or power in addition to correctness and skill. Many participants actually seem stunned by the realization that the misunderstandings are predictable and the understandings are typically diverse, but both facts are ignored in their usual instructional and assessment designs.

Some implications for assessment become clearer from such experience. The need is not merely for performance tests but for a different assessment philosophy. We need to probe more than quiz, to ask for students' resulting theories and criticisms more than for correct answers if we want to reveal understanding or its absence. Students must be confronted with challenges that make them face such questions as, What does this answer mean? What does the question assume? Why does this phenomenon occur or not occur? What does this knowledge enable me to do or not do? What is the power and the limit of this way of thinking? How else might this idea be grasped? What feedback do I need to find out if I am on the right track? Might this approach work in one setting but not another? and (as one teacher put it to me years ago) Do I know what to do when I do not know what to do?

Thus it is not the technique of short-answer testing that is the problem. It is our thoughtless overuse of the technique. Our problems in assessment stem from an ironic lack of clarity about purpose on our part as assessors: Why do we and why should we assess? If we were clearer that our aim is to produce people who can use knowledge effectively and wisely, we would more often deliberately design probes and tasks based on ferreting out mere recall from thoughtful use, and we would be happy to take the time needed to do it well. We would design rubrics that sharpen the discrimination between those who understand and those who seem to but do not. Short-answer testing, when well-designed, can actually help us do this, in fact. This is what has happened in physics, which has the longest and richest history of inquiry into student misunderstandings. Multiple-choice tests exist, for example, to help teachers assess for the degrees of understanding of the concept of force. In the Force Concept Inventory, a widely used test designed by three educators, students are asked thirty questions deliberately posed to reveal whether they have overcome the most common misconceptions.[18]

Another look at the problem of reading assessment reveals the challenge of assessing for understanding regardless of the testing method used. Either a multiple-choice or simple constructed-response test on a reading passage can determine whether a student knows the "correct" response to a relatively straightforward question on a matter of valid interpretation. If analytic comprehension is what we want to measure, then the cloze method (whereby words or phrases are deleted from passages and the student must propose an apt phrase or choose from alternatives) is adequate to the task. It is quite another purpose and method to see whether students can interpret and evaluate texts when we ask them first to read a text, then to read excerpts from criticism in which other readers or even experts disagree on what the story meant, and then to join the conversation. (That is why, in part, evaluation is the highest level of Bloom's Taxonomy—not because it is the most important but because it is the most cognitively difficult, because it assumes understanding of multiple points of view and of criticism in reference to standards.)

Similarly, well-meaning reformers can unwittingly sidestep the assessment of students' understanding even as they call for new methods. Consider, for example, reader-response approaches in modern language arts instruction. Getting a thoughtful response from a reader is vital for helping him or her to develop meaningful connections with a text, and for giving teachers an insight into the student's ability to find value in a text. But merely seeking a thoughtful reaction from a reader is not the same as assessing that reader's understanding of the text. Students are too often encouraged to be reactive at the expense of understanding what provoked their response. Literature then becomes only a test of self-projective ability, moving much too quickly away from understanding the text and too quickly toward an egocentric—though interesting and heartfelt—response. Leaving aside the literary criticism wars about the possibility of "true" or valid interpretations, the fact remains that students can have an interesting response to a text without really understanding it (that is, they may be unable to defend their view using evidence from the text). This fact takes on added significance when faculties blur the difference between engaged and skilled readers in their reporting systems to parents. In many current report cards, one sees the category "reader response" used as though it covered reader understanding.

These initial images, puzzling phenomena, questions, and analyses suggest that we need to practice better what we preach. We should carefully rethink what we are after when we say we want students to understand. Understanding is neither the inevitable residue nor perhaps even the goal of a traditional education (as judged by our common testing practices). But insofar as all teachers want to make it possible for students to develop sophisticated insights, meanings, and uses, we will need to understand better what counts as evidence of understanding (the assessment challenge) and how to cause self-understanding through inherently educative work that is designed to cause and elicit such understanding (the instructional and curricular design challenge).

## Understanding Understanding: Five Facets

As Gardner ironically notes, "Understanding is itself a complex process that is not well understood."[19] He offers us, however, a clear and pithy definition. He defines understanding as "a sufficient grasp of concepts, principles or skills so that one can bring them to bear on new problems and situations, deciding in which ways one's present competencies can suffice and in which ways one may require new skills or knowledge."[20] What is meant by "sufficient grasp" and "bring them to bear"? What do degrees of understanding look like, and what is the relation between accurate knowledge and understanding?

The temptation in light of the quote and questions might then be to try to think of understanding as unitary. But if one asks teachers in a workshop, What are the indicators of naive versus sophisticated understanding? they give revealingly diverse answers. Naive understandings, they say, are brief and undeveloped; they lack a rationale or good reasons; they are simplistic, obvious or without apt qualification, and black and white. They are egocentric or without perspective. Sophisticated understandings are said to be well-supported and innovative, to involve shades of gray, to be made clear through application and derived by reflection. These answers and our common language suggest that the term *understanding* is multi-dimensional, encompassing very different shades of meaning.

Five overlapping and ideally integrated yet separate aspects of understanding emerge from analysis and need to be developed through schooling, hence through ongoing assessment. These facets are related to yet independent of one another. They derive from the different meanings we attach to the word *understand* in all conversation and writing. They may be summarized as follows:

1. *Sophisticated explanation and interpretation.* The ability to develop, offer, and substantiate accurate and coherent theories and stories of what one has learned and encountered. This facet of understanding involves clarity and insight about how things work, what they mean, where they connect, and why they matter. Irrespective of how his or her sophisticated account was obtained, the student with understanding in this sense has internalized and connected ideas, skills, and facts so as to be able to give a good account of things, including novel aspects of the ideas or experience in question. The ideas or experience have meaning that extends beyond the disparate facts and binds them together. The deeper the understanding, the more facts and layers of story and theory are made coherent and insightful.

2. *Contextual performance know-how and sensitivity (savvy).* Understanding how to use and apply knowledge effectively in diverse and even unique situations. To show that we understand something, we demonstrate our ability to use it, adapt it, or customize it. When we must effectively negotiate different constraints, social contexts, purposes, and audiences, understanding is revealed as performance know-how—the ability to accomplish tasks successfully, with grace under pressure, and with tact.

3. *Perspective.* Gained through critical thinking and exploration of points of view. To understand in this sense is to see things from multiple vantage points, including from the vantage point of what is implicit, tacit, or assumed. When we have or can take perspective, we can gain a critical distance from our habitual or immediate beliefs, our feelings, or our surface meanings and appeals in order to see their objective merits. Insight results when we make explicit new

avenues of discovery, expose questionable or unexamined assumptions, or cast old experience in a new light. With perspective we grasp the importance or significance of what we know.

4. *Empathy.* The ability to get inside another person's feelings and worldview, to experience the world as another person experiences it. Empathy is not sympathy. It is a disciplined "walking in someone else's shoes," a strategy of working to find what is plausible, sensible, or meaningful in the ideas and actions of others, even if those ideas and actions are puzzling or off-putting. Empathy can lead us not only to rethink but to experience a change of heart as we come to understand what seemed odd or alien. "To understand is to forgive," as a French saying has it.

5. *Self-knowledge.* The ability to know our own intellectual prejudices and to see how they influence and even determine what and how we understand (or do not understand). Deep understanding is inseparable from what we mean by wisdom. To understand the world we must understand ourselves and vice versa. Through self-knowledge we also understand what we do not understand: "Know thyself," as philosophers from ancient Greece to the present have often said, is the maxim of those who would really understand. Socrates is the patron saint of understanding: he knew he was ignorant when most men did not know that they were.

A key notion implied in the five facets is that understanding involves rethinking—reflecting upon, reconsidering, and perhaps fundamentally revising the meaning of what we have already learned and what we believe to be knowledge or adequate account. An education for understanding involves circling back to revisit old ideas in a new light, digging deeper and making new connections, hence challenges to reveal whether students can make newer, clearer, and better sense of complex data, facts, and experience. Thus students must be asked to rethink constantly the important ideas and theories they have learned or built, and good instruction and assessment entail the design of appropriate problem-laden work. As philosopher and educator John Dewey put it, "no experience is educative that does not tend both to knowledge of more facts and entertaining of more ideas and to a better, a more orderly arrangement of them."[21]

Understanding is not just about coverage of knowledge, then, but about uncoverage—being introduced to new ideas and being asked to think more deeply and more carefully about facts, ideas, experiences, and theories previously encountered and learned. Students' work must ask *them* to uncover insights, questions, assumptions, and conclusions and to justify their knowledge as knowledge, not as received ideas and skills to be unthinkingly used when the students are carefully prompted. Understanding involves the testing of ideas in action, and insight into the implications of those actions—that is, deeper meaning.

A second notion is that all of these facets imply the importance of justification and good judgment in assessment of understanding, and hence greater interactivity in assessment than we now employ. Students must have good reasons for their performance or answers, and they must be adept at anticipating and responding to diverse perspectives, situations, and feedback. That is one reason why Gardner argues that "open-ended clinical interviews or careful observations provide the best way of establishing the degree of understanding . . . attained."[22] But it is clear that even in schools where the possibility of more oral examining would be impeded by schedules, we must design work that does not merely make the student perform with knowledge but enables us to judge intentions (clarity and depth of purpose) and rationales, whether through written logs or by observing their response to the results of their efforts. Questions of validation, criticism, meaning, and importance must be designed into the test.

## Obtaining Evidence of Understanding

What tells us that students have achieved each facet of understanding? The essential assessor questions provided in Chapter Three can guide us: What counts as evidence of understanding? How should we carefully distinguish students who seem to have a deep understanding from those who do not? What student acts and responses are most characteristic of understanding, of lack of understanding, and of misunderstanding?

A student who really understands

1. Demonstrates sophisticated explanatory and interpretive power and insight by

   a. Providing complex, insightful, and credible theories, stories, analogies, metaphors, or models to explain or illuminate an event, fact, text, or idea; providing a systematic account, using helpful and vivid mental models.

   b. Making fine, subtle distinctions and aptly qualifying her opinions; seeing and arguing for what is central—the big ideas, pivotal moments, decisive evidence, key questions, and so on; and making good predictions.

   c. Avoiding or overcoming common misunderstandings and superficial or simplistic views, for example, by avoiding overly simplistic, hackneyed, or disconnected and incoherent theorizing.

d.   Effectively and sensitively interpreting texts, language, and situations, for example, by the ability to read between the lines and offer plausible accounts of the many possible purposes and meanings of any "text" (book, situation, human behavior, and so on).

e.   Showing a personalized, thoughtful, and coherent grasp of a subject, for example, by developing a reflective and systematic integration of what she knows affectively and cognitively. This integration would be based in part on significant and appropriate direct experience of specific ideas or feelings.

f.   Substantiating or justifying her views with sound argument and evidence.

2.   Demonstrates that she can apply knowledge in context and that she has know-how by

a.   Employing her knowledge effectively in diverse, realistic, and "noisy" contexts.

b.   Invariably being sensitive and responsive to feedback and effectively self-adjusting as she performs.

c.   Extending or applying what she knows in a novel and effective way (inventing in the sense of innovating, as Swiss child psychologist Jean Piaget discusses in *To Understand Is to Invent*[23]).

d.   Teaching what she knows.

3.   Demonstrates ability to take perspectives by

a.   Critiquing and justifying something as a point of view, that is, seeing it as a point of view and using skills and dispositions that embody disciplined skepticism and the testing of theories.

b.   Knowing the history of an idea; knowing the questions or problem to which the knowledge or theory studied is an answer or solution.

c.   Knowing the assumptions on which an idea or theory is based.

d.   Knowing the limits as well as the power of an idea.

e.   Seeing through argument or language that is merely persuasive, partisan, or ideological.

    f.  Seeing and explaining the importance or worth of an idea.

    g.  Wisely employing both criticism and belief (an ability summarized by Peter Elbow's maxim that we are likely to understand better if we methodically "believe when others doubt and doubt when others believe"[24]).

4.  Demonstrates empathy by

    a.  Projecting himself into, feeling, and appreciating another's situation, affect, or point of view.

    b.  Operating on the assumption that even an apparently odd or obscure comment, text, person, or set of ideas must contain some important insights that justify working to understand them.

    c.  Recognizing when incomplete or flawed views are plausible, even insightful, though incorrect or outdated.

    d.  Seeing and explaining how an idea or theory can be all-too-easily misunderstood by others.

    e.  Listening—and hearing what others often do not.

5.  Reveals self-knowledge by

    a.  Recognizing his own prejudices and style, and how they color understanding; seeing and getting beyond egocentrism, ethnocentrism, present-centeredness, nostalgia, either/or thinking, and so on.

    b.  Questioning his own convictions; carefully sorting out strong belief from warranted knowledge and thus providing evidence of intellectual honesty; knowing, like Socrates, when to be self-assured and when to be self-doubting; and being happy to admit ignorance.

    c.  Accurately self-assessing.

    d.  Defending his views without defensiveness.

As these suggested avenues of evidence and task design show, the facets of understanding are often in tension psychologically, even if they are connected conceptually. One can have a powerful theory but lack application ability and practical know-how, and vice versa. One can have great empathy for others while lacking the kind of critical distance that calls into question the correctness of their views, and vice versa. One can have an exhaustive analytic theory but lack the self-knowledge to see that the theory is really an elaborate rationalization of beliefs whereby all new data is adapted to the old theory (thus making the theorist impervious to feedback). And one can have enormous insight into one's own and other people's prejudices without knowing how to act on that information in context or construct a theory to explain to others those actions and their causes. Wisdom exists in few people because the challenges of understanding are so demanding of personal strength and call for movement beyond one's preferred learning style.

The five facets of understanding can be paired to highlight a different tension inherent in understanding. No one facet is ever sufficient. Sometimes understanding requires emotional disinterest; other times it requires heartfelt solidarity with another. In some contexts, understanding is highly theoretical; other times it is revealed only in effective contextualized practice. Sometimes we best understand through dispassionate critical analysis; other times we need to give an empathic response. Sometimes it is dependent upon direct experience; other times it is gained through detached reflection. Context, hence judgment, determines understanding or misunderstanding.

We can generalize the pairings in this way: understanding is often directed either to people and actions or to ideas. When we are empathic and sensitive to context, we understand other people and we have tact (in the sense described by William James as sensitivity to the demands of the particular situation, a requirement he felt was central to good teaching[25]). When we are intellectually sophisticated, we grasp complex theories and subtle points of view.

The tensions within and among the facets and the different types of judgment required by life's dilemmas also suggest that student assessment should be routinely designed to test the student's ability to get beyond overly favoring one facet or another. Assessment would then be like what soccer coaches do, namely, work hard to get players beyond favoring their natural foot for shooting. The facets are the learning styles; in other words, individual students may be particularly strong in one type or another, and assessment should expand to allow multiple possibilities. But it is the job of schooling and assessment to help the student develop a more fluent and powerful repertoire, and to see the value in new, if unnatural and difficult, forms of inquiry.

The pairings also suggest that competence in all forms of understanding is as much a question of moral maturity as of intellectual mastery. To think of understanding only in terms of cognition is to risk developing learned but self-centered or bureaucratic adults. We all too easily use facts, procedures, rules, or strategies unthinkingly, almost mechanically, irrespective of whether their use involves good sense or of how they make other people behave and feel. We can "justify" our actions, but we may have lost the ability to distinguish rational account from rationalization and self-deception.

Dewey and Piaget both thought that intellectual and moral thoughtlessness were closely related and derived from an overly authoritarian and drill-based approach to education.[26] The word *thoughtlessness* was used earlier because it implies both the intellectual idling and moral insensitivity (as opposed to intractable ignorance) that these educators believed to be related. It insinuates that we could think but we do not, suggesting in part that our education has not been sufficiently geared toward the discipline of asking questions, making meaning, and grasping the effect of ideas and actions. Thoughtlessness is encouraged when we are allowed by schooling and testing to ignore the consequences of our work, our answers, and our actions on others. I do not think it is too much to suggest, again, that an assessment system unmoored from the aim of understanding and from genuine feedback can unwittingly lead to moral lapses as serious as some of the intellectual ones noted earlier. Because a student can be skilled without being wise, knowledgeable without being effective, technically proficient without possessing insight or tact into what he or she does, thoughtless mastery can be completely hidden from conventional test techniques and subtly rewarded by them, based as they are on simple stimulus-response theory and a content-focused view of learning.

Indeed, all educators have a moral obligation to understand their students, empathically and intellectually. Schooling needs to be better designed to make it less likely than is now the case that teachers will lose their empathy for what it is like to be a novice student (as demonstrated, for example, by the impatience sometimes shown by teachers when students don't quickly understand). As I suggest in Chapter Eleven, our failure to devise a better feedback system for teachers (in the form of ongoing discussion about results in performance appraisal, job descriptions, and clinical supervision systems) has resulted in a good deal of teacher egocentrism that hides the depth of student misunderstanding—the very impediment to our being better teachers.

A term that sums up the balanced moral and intellectual tenor of genuine understanding is *good judgment*. We want students to bring knowledge and skill to bear intelligently and concretely on unique events, to be open to the new even as they bring explanations from past experience. A "good judge," says Dewey, "has a sense of the relative values of the various features of a perplexing situation," has "horse sense," has the capacity to "estimate, appraise and evaluate," and has "tact and discernment." Simply "acquiring information can never develop the power of judgment. Development of judgment is in spite of, not because of, methods of instruction that emphasize simple learning. . . . [The student] cannot get power of judgment excepting as he is continually exercised in forming and testing judgments."[27]

To teach and assess for student understanding thus requires more than rigorous content standards and a willingness to pursue student interests through projects. It requires that we perpetually confront students with unclear tasks, murky problems, situations that are inherently incomplete, and controversies that demand sorting through—problems that have human as well as intellectual implications—in short, dilemmas. (Such a view is central to problem-based learning and the case study method found in medical, law, business, and engineering schools everywhere.) This is not what usually happens, of course. Far from it: schoolwork almost always postpones an inquiry into the limits, worth, or warrant of what is known, in the name of knowledge accumulation and mere technical proficiency. Under such conditions human judgment can atrophy, waiting to be used.

Rather than being grounded in unambiguous and unproblematic questions that test uncontroversial knowledge and skill use, an assessment for understanding must demand thoughtful and qualified answers to sometimes unanswerable questions. We require an assessment system that knows how to judge understanding based on the thoughtful questions a student (as opposed to a test maker) asks. We must find tasks that let us see if students can derive and make increasingly better meaning with (and of) limited knowledge.

## Implications for Assessing Understanding

In short, we must do a better job of teaching and assessing the construction of meaning by the student (rather than testing exclusively the student's recall and use of those meanings presented by the teacher or textbook) and his or her thoughtful use of knowledge and skill in important contexts. Leaving aside the more practical questions of test and task design, what practices are implied if we are to assess for the five facets of understanding validly (in a way that will let us draw accurate inferences about students from the test) and reliably (in a way that will let us treat test scores as accurate representations of students' abilities) for the five facets of understanding?[28]

1. *Design interactive assessments.* Mere answers or products, even in response to demanding questions and problems, are not necessarily adequate evidence of understanding. We need to know *why* students have done what they have done; we need to hear them or see them justify their answers or products in response to targeted questions.

Consider that we require certain advanced learners not only to write a dissertation (typically buttressed by many footnotes) but also to defend it in an oral exam. The thesis is not considered sufficient evidence of mastery. We need to confront the candidate with counterarguments, counterexamples, and requests for comments and critiques on other points of view.

A question-and-answer session after a speaker's presentation often reveals more about the speaker's understanding than the talk itself. I once watched a wonderful oral assessment in a Colorado physics classroom after students had built "Rube Goldberg machines" that were to illustrate a dozen key principles in physics. Most of the machines were wonderfully clever, yet some of the students' answers to pointed questions about the design were shaky.

One need not have one-on-one oral exams to honor this idea. Interactivity can and ought more often to be a function of the task environment (as when a student responds to audience questions), the design of the task itself (for example, a balsa bridge built to a particular theory fails under the weight load and must be rebuilt according to a better theory), or a written element added to a task (for example, write a self-assessment and a justification of the approach taken as a separate part of the assessment).

2.  *Use reiterative core performance tasks to assess whether understanding is becoming more sophisticated.* We need to use recurring tasks to assess sophistication of understanding for the same reason that we assign recurring genres to assess writing skill: to gauge students' progress over time. Apt tasks and prompts are most easily obtained by deriving them from recurring essential questions (see Chapter Nine). In place of one-shot secure test questions, we should use recurring performance tasks that are as well known as the essay test or the soccer game (or, for example, the "Sludge" science task in which students must identify the unknown contents of a beaker). The tasks would be deliberately designed to assess for core ideas, skills, or questions that are at the heart of a subject. One approach that has been use in the districts of South Brunswick, New Jersey, and Edmonton, Alberta, is to use the same writing prompt across many or all grades.

3.  *In light of the inevitability of misconception, use assessment tasks that will best evoke such misunderstandings.* To make tests more like probes, they must contain questions that build on predictable misunderstandings and mistakes. These questions would work similarly to test "distracters" (answers that might sound right but are not) that traditional test designers use, but the aim here is to see if the student can recognize and *overcome* a misconception. (Oddly enough, few people seem to notice that Bloom's *Taxonomy* lists typical errors and misconceptions relating to each level of cognition.)

A simple approach cited by the authors of the article mentioned earlier on the fourth grade class that discussed the cause of heat had the teacher asking students to choose between two theories: a plausible view that heat can come from any object (like a blanket) or the correct view that heat derives mostly from the sun and our bodies. Here, instead of the distracter being used as part of a "Gotcha!" test with no ability to get feedback in a timely manner, it is used to challenge understanding so as to further it—the real meanings, after all, of the words *test* and *prove*.

4.  *Require students to self-assess their previous as well as their present work.* It is only through student self-assessment that we gain the most complete insight into how sophisticated and accurate a student's view is of the tasks, criteria, and standards he or she is to master. A simple strategy is to make the first and last paper assignments of any course the same question, test, or experience and to require students to write a self-assessment postscript describing their sense of progress in understanding.

5.  *Conduct assessment along a novice-expert continuum, using longitudinal rubrics (scoring standards that remain the same over time), not merely task-specific rubrics.* When we use reiterative tasks, we need stable rubrics if we are to gauge sophistication. What is a naive view of the American Revolution? What is a sophisticated view? From novice learners we would expect answers that oversimplify or misconceive. We can predict, for example, that naive thinkers will view the Bill of Rights as a set of clear, unambiguous rules to follow or as unrestricted license; a more sophisticated account will make clear the difference between the spirit and the letter of the law; and an even more sophisticated view will be based on the awareness that in matters of judgment about spirit and letter, conflict over meaning is inevitable but some opinions can genuinely be said to be better supported by analysis and precedent than others.

Few such rubrics exist in adequate form. One gets a sense of what the rubrics need to be from looking at some of the Advanced Placement rubrics found in booklets containing released questions and answers provided by the College Board (a rich source of prompts, anchor papers, and commentary related to performance standards for all teachers, not just Advanced Placement teachers, by the way). The best papers were described as having "a clear, well-developed thesis that deals [with the topic] in a *sophisticated* fashion," while less successful answers "responded superficially" and had "some analysis" and "concrete examples with limited development." Poor answers contained "little or no analysis."[29]

We might use the rubric to infer what we might see if we gave the prompt to students across a range of grade levels. In other words, the rubric may also generalize developmentally (that is, the lower scores may reflect patterns of answers from the better students in lower grade levels) and it could serve as a rough draft for teachers working with middle and high school students. More deliberate research would obviously be needed, but it seems safe to say that more sophisticated answers, regardless of age or experience, tend to be better substantiated, better focused, better developed, and better argued than less sophisticated responses, regardless of topic, as the rubric suggests. Indeed, the simple distinction between analysis and narrative indicates the depth of the problem: even advanced students fail to get beyond a retelling in their papers.

We can generalize here. Figure 4.1 illustrates the rubric suggested by the proposed five facets of understanding.

If we additionally imagine adding bulleted indicators to each descriptor in this rubric (as discussed in Chapters Six and Seven), whereby concrete signs for each level of performance are provided by teachers for the particular topic, the rubric could be used K–12.

6. *Design curricula and build tests around recurring essential questions that give rise to important theories and stories.* To judge growth in the relative sophistication of a student's model, story, or explanation, we need to ask the same or similar questions over and over: Does a particular book necessarily have a moral? Is history only the winners' story? What were the chief causes and implications of the Civil War? What is *Pigman* or Huck Finn about? How does evidence in science and history differ? What is a proof? and so on.[30] In other words, an assessment of understanding invariably involves an assessment of the student's concepts. One reason that *concept webs* or *maps* have become such an interesting tool for assessing as well as instructing is that they require students to visually lay out key ideas and their interconnections.[31] We need to know how the student sees the network of concepts and the depth of his or her conceptual grasp, because having a sophisticated definition of something is not the same as having a complex understanding of it. Moreover, definitions can be learned as mere verbal formulas. Indeed, a major goal of assessment for understanding must be to find out whether a student's definition is a formula or a summary of personal inquiries, uses, and syntheses.

7. *Use assessments that routinely ask whether or not the student sees the big picture.* Can students see the connections between lessons, units, and courses? Do they understand the bearing of current work on past work? We must ask them. A simple device is the one known in higher education as the *one-minute paper.* Students are asked at the end of each lecture to answer two questions: What is the big point you learned in class today? and What is the main unanswered question you leave class with today? Harvard professors have called this technique one of the most effective innovations in their teaching.[32] In

Figure 4.1  Rubric for Assessing Understanding

| Meaningful | Effective | In Perspective | Empathic | Reflective |
|---|---|---|---|---|
| *Sophisticated:* an unusually penetrating, illuminating, elegant, and/or novel account (story, theory, implication, connection, meaning, causal reasoning) | *Masterful:* fluent, flexible, efficient; able to use/adjust understandings well in diverse and difficult contexts | *Insightful and coherent:* a fully justified and qualified viewpoint; effectively critiques. encompasses other plausible views; takes the long and dispassionate critical view | *Mature:* disciplined; disposed, and able to see and feel what others see and feel; unusually open to and willing to seek out the odd, alien, or different | *Wise:* deeply aware of the boundaries of one's own and others' understanding; able to recognize one's own prejudices and projections |
| *In-depth:* an atypical and revealing account, going well beyond what is obvious or what was explicitly taught; sees nuance, more subtle connections and implications; inventive thinking | *Skilled:* competent in using and adapting understandings in a variety of appropriate and demanding contexts | *Thorough:* a fully developed and coordinated critical view, with logically sound support; successfully addresses multiple perspectives; makes apt criticisms, discriminations, and qualifications | *Sensitive:* disposed to see and feel what others see and feel; open to the unfamiliar or different | *Circumspect:* aware of one's ignorance and that of others; aware of one's prejudices |
| *Knowledgeable:* an account that reflects some in-depth and personalized ideas; the student is making the work his/her own, going beyond the given | *Able:* limited but growing ability to be adaptive and innovative in the use of knowledge and skill | *Considered:* a reasonably critical and well-developed point of view, with adequate support; addresses other points of view | *Aware:* knows and feels that others see and feel differently, and is somewhat able to empathize with others | *Thoughtful:* generally aware of what he/she does and does not understand; aware of how prejudice and projection occur without awareness |
| *Viable:* an adequate and apt account, extending and deepening somewhat what was learned, is beginning to "read between the lines"; account is fairly black and white | *Apprentice:* relies on a limited repertoire of routines, able to perform well in only a few familiar or simple contexts | *Sketchy:* aware of different points of view and able to develop a view, but weakness in support and/or considering of other perspectives | *Maturing:* has some capacity and/or self-discipline to "walk in others' shoes," but is still primarily limited to one's own reactions and attitudes; puzzled or put off by different feelings or attitudes | *Unreflective:* generally unaware of his/her specific ignorance; generally unaware of how prejudgments color understanding |
| *Naive:* a superficial, literal, or crude account; more descriptive than analytical or creative; a re-statement of what was taught or read | *Novice:* can perform only with coaching and/or relies on highly scripted, singular "plug in" types of approaches | *Narrowly conceived:* unaware of differing points of view; prone to state facts or cite opinions without being able to support, defend, or explain them; a fragmentary or limited view | *Egocentric:* has little or no empathy, beyond intellectual awareness of others; sees things through his/her own ideas and feelings; ignores or is threatened or puzzled by different feelings, attitudes, views | *Innocent:* completely unaware of the bounds of his/her understanding and of the role of projection and prejudice in opinions and attempts to understand |

my own teaching I require students to bring at least two written questions to class each day. We typically begin class by having them discuss their questions in groups of three, then bring the most important question to the whole class for consideration. Then we look for patterns through a concept web of questions and proposed answers. With a few minutes to go before the end of class, I ask a few students to summarize the conversation and ask everyone to write some notes. These materials can all be assessed, for control over both process and content. (Perkins proposes many other such strategies in *Smart Schools*.[33])

8.  *Use tasks and rubrics that determine whether students have mastered the purpose of skills, knowledge, and performance, not just mastered techniques or formats.* An understanding reveals itself in context when students act more than dutiful or compliant. We judge a student to understand more than another when, regardless of the technical skill or result shown, the student reveals by word and deed that he or she understands what it is he or she is trying to do, why, and whether or not it has been achieved. This is a vital issue because unless we look for this, we will confuse proficiency with understanding; the two are related but are not synonymous.

Too few students understand persuasiveness or effectiveness in context because they are taught merely to follow certain recipes for writing essays and solving problems that are labeled persuasive or effective. The only hope we have of getting students to be persuasive is to get them mindful of purpose—when it happens, when it does not happen, and why. (See Chapters Six and Seven on the importance of "impact" criteria in performance assessment and getting the student to more explicitly focus on the reason behind and the goal of the performance in question.)

9.  *Use simulations or real applications that require students to use knowledge with a purpose and a context in mind.* Even within the context of a blue book exam, we can do more with application than we do now. The following exam question from a Harvard core curriculum course in science (asked as part of a traditional blue book exam) illustrates this kind of realistic application:

> Your government decides it wants to harvest the rare and commercially important snail *Helix memoresus* for its memory-enhancing mucus. The government decides to adopt a fixed quota harvesting policy.
>     As an expert naturalist, explain to the myopic politicians the potential problems of such a policy: What advice would you give about how to set the harvest and why?

10.  *Assess student self-adjustment in response to human or situational feedback.* Only when students can respond intelligently and

effectively to unanticipated effects of their work or of errors they have made can we conclude that they understand the nature, purpose, and quality expected of their work. A regular inability to self-assess personal performance accurately indicates that students—regardless of how well they do on conventional tests—lack understanding of both the task and the standards by which that kind of task is best evaluated.

11. *Use rubrics that measure degree of sufficiency and power of answers, not simply their correctness.* The focus in assessing for understanding must always be on the adequacy (effectiveness, plausibility, thoroughness, and aptness) or evidence, argument, approach, or style—not merely on whether an answer is right or wrong. In effect, the question in scoring students' answers becomes, Does the answer "work" in this context? Is it substantiated? Unlike questions and tasks related to knowledge recall or plugging in skills, questions and tasks here are judged not so much by accuracy but by student justification of answers and approaches. David Perkins summarizes this need with the list of verbs he argues are at the center of "performances for understanding": explaining, exemplifying, applying, justifying, comparing and contrasting, contextualizing, and generalizing.[34]

Perkins's fine account of understanding may cause us to ignore the nouns of understanding as opposed to the verbs, that is, the key insights or intellectual ideas at the heart of a subject versus the means by which understandings of all kinds are revealed. Though I sympathize with his intent to get people to think of understanding as revealed through performance and learned through inquiry, understandings are also revealed through evidence of grasping particular and important ideas that represent accomplishments or milestones in the field and in personal understanding. Some ideas are more important than others, and many of the most important ideas are subtle, opaque, or counterintuitive. For example, we must look to see whether students grasp the difference between a democracy and a republic, a postulate and a hunch, irony and coincidence.

Validity issues are at stake here, too. No matter how elegant the student's analytic writing, if he or she persists in talking about gravitational force as if it were a physical thing that one can directly handle and observe, then the student does not have a sufficiently sophisticated view of gravity. There are surely conceptual benchmarks just as there are performance benchmarks. Conversely, students might reveal their insight that light can be a particle or a wave without being able to provide answers in a discursive way. Their insights may be revealed implicitly in the nature of the lasers they build or the stories they write.

12. *Assess students' ability to be spontaneously self-critical and flexible in perspective taking.* As discussed earlier, students should be able

to look at ideas, skills, and systems learned from new, unanticipated, or odd but revealing points of view. They must see the importance of their knowledge, yet also grasp its limits or possible weaknesses. Assessing students' use of perspective includes asking the following questions:

- *Is the student aware of different ways of knowing, seeing, or proving a specific idea?* Students with understanding know that there are invariably alternate proofs, powerful analogies, and other ways of making meaning of a phenomenon; they are more inclined and able to ask (and answer), Isn't there another way to look at this? Can't both points of view be seen as justifiable?
- *Is the student aware of or can he or she intelligently speculate on an author's or theorist's particular perspective and intent?* It may not be possible to judge a student's understanding of a text adequately if one does not know the author's intent, because the judgment involves knowing whether that particular intent was realized. This is more obvious with fiction and history, perhaps, but nonetheless true in science and, yes, mathematics.
- *Is the student aware of the understandings and misunderstandings of others?* The person who understands is, like Socrates, Freud, or Piaget, aware of many levels and sides of a matter, tolerant of the anxiety caused by realizing how differently people think, and able to grasp fully what more naive people understand (and why their view is reasonable) and do not understand. This result of understanding could be called the inherent irony of genuine perspective and empathy.[35] Those who understand can easily and patiently enter the perspective of the novice. Therefore we might ask students to teach novices what they now claim to understand, as Einstein tested his ideas by imagining how they would have to be presented to audiences of different perspective and knowledge.[36]
- *Is the student aware of the history of the idea or theory he is studying?* Self-assessment and portfolios make a writer document and think about the history, or "biography," of a piece of writing. Similarly, an education for understanding should teach students that each key text or idea they study in a discipline has a history, which too often gets hidden behind the imposing veneer of proofs and formal exposition. Learning this history helps students to realize that experts are no different from them in terms of developing an understanding. Knowledge is a hard-won result, the end point, of disciplined thinking; it is not static ex cathedra pronouncements made by intuitive geniuses.

13. *Assess breadth and accuracy of knowledge independently of depth of understanding.* Students could have a deep, subtle, refined insight into, say, the Opium Wars or the fundamental theorem of calculus,

yet have some, maybe even many, of the details wrong. Students could have an encyclopedic grasp of the chronology of the Wars but have limited insight into their causes and implications. Understanding is composed of both depth and breadth: in the first facet—sophisticated account—there must clearly be both well-supported and well-developed ideas.

We must, therefore, use multiple rubrics or scoring guidelines so that we separately assess control over content, argument, and the impact of the communication. These are separate and often independent traits of performance. (This point is further addressed in the next two chapters.)

14. *Assess for self-knowledge.* Experts who are also wise are quick to state that there is much that they do not understand about a subject (they have Socratic wisdom). Enrico Fermi, the great physicist, the story goes, was reputed to have always assessed doctoral candidates in physics on the accuracy of their self-assessments concerning how much they knew about physics, and he thought it was a flaw to be wrong on either side (to be more cocky or more diffident and unsure than was warranted). At the very least, we should require students to identify the most questionable assumptions, ideas, sources, and lines of argument in their work.

## Conclusion

By its very nature, understanding is personal, and it admits to relative, not absolute, success. Understandings are more or less defensible, sophisticated, and insightful; they are provisional, even for geniuses. Worse, understandings are idiosyncratic: experts can have very different and justifiable understandings of the same phenomena in science, history, and psychology. Thus we need to know why students think what they do, not merely that they know what is believed to be true. This all makes the typical test paradigm, with its binary correct-incorrect structure, ill-suited to an assessment of understanding, especially when no explanation of answers is permitted.

Our goal in teaching and assessing must be to get beneath the surface of pat packages in teacher presentations or textbook summaries, to begin using methods of assessment that require students to regularly rethink what they thought they knew. Moreover, if failing to understand or misunderstanding complex ideas, texts, and experiences is inevitable, we must begin as teachers to try to predict key misunderstandings better (based on observation, research, and our own past assessment results). Our methods and syllabi must be designed to anticipate problems in understanding and overcome them: every textbook and performance assessment should have a troubleshooting guide. We must come to see the naïveté of the view that a good education inoculates students against misunderstanding. We must come to see that much of the energy and self-discipline required to learn further and dig deeper comes from grasping the problems inherent in understanding that lurk behind a seemingly fixed and complete knowledge.

We need an assessment system that lets us know how much progress students are making toward sophisticated understandings, a system that constantly checks that students are hearing what we say and that gives them many opportunities to apply their learning in authentic tasks, get feedback, increase their understanding, and perform again. A system that teaches us to rethink and to understand the need to rethink is the essence of an education for and an assessment of understanding. Bacon said it well: understanding emerges more readily from error than from confusion; the scientific method of (deliberate) trial and (instructive) error that he helped to formulate shows how we can help students discover and reveal understanding.[37] In other words, to develop and assess understanding, we must confront students with feedback and see how well they cope with it.

But perhaps Plato said it best in his allegory of the cave. If that parable is insightful, then what many people think teaching is, is not true—namely, the putting of sight (knowledge) into blind eyes. Rather, it is the act of rousing a mind to reveal to itself what is and is not yet understood. Only in that rousing, in that self-aware and knowledgeable ignorance, can there be true life-long learning—and hence, *philosophia*, the love of wisdom.

# PART TWO

# Designing Assessments

## CHAPTER 5

# Standards and Criteria

Assessment design is like architecture: the architect deals with given constraints, not just opportunities; building codes and design values are informed by functional needs and aesthetics. So too in assessment design: the designer must meet the requirements of content standards, standards for the design of evaluation instruments, and societal and institutional expectations of schooling, while making the challenges intellectually interesting and of value to the clients.

But typical assessment design gets the matter backward. In architecture, the primary aim is to please the client while being mindful of the constraints. In the design of school testing, however, designers too often worry primarily about satisfying their own needs (such as the need for easy-to-test and easy-to score results) or the "building codes" (that is, the technical measurement standards) instead of serving clients' interests. Educative assessment requires assessment designers to right the matter and better honor the students' needs for more engaging and useful work, and the teachers' needs for more direct, useful, and timely information. How, then, should assessment standards be construed to ensure that such aims are met? That is the purpose of this chapter: to lay out a set of design standards and a system of logic for ensuring that educative assessment is more likely to occur.

The goal of assessment design might well be summarized in the old design adage "form follows function." Architectural design decisions about content, scale, and aesthetics (that is, form) are cast in terms of the function, or purpose, of the space: What will happen here? Who will inhabit this building and what will they do in it? What kind of feel, traffic flow, and scale are appropriate for these inhabitants and these activities? What kind of design suits such purposes and audiences?

In assessment, the design insight that form follows function has been too long ignored. The primary function, namely, helping students to know their obligations and meet them, has been co-opted by the secondary purposes of adults (such as program accountability) and by habitual test forms. Our penchant for reducing assessment to testing and reducing tests to easy-to-score "secure" instruments comes about when we have lost sight of our obligations to students.[1] Mere design principles derived from sound ideas are cheap, however, like talk. Habits run too deep, and adult interests will likely always get a better hearing than student interests when those interests diverge (as they do when time and energy are at stake). To improve student assessment, we need design standards that are not only more clear but also more forceful—and that are backed by a more explicit oversight and review system of assessment designs. If we are to avoid ignoring a whole range of student needs and begin fulfilling the educative purpose of assessment, we need to rethink not only the way we design but also they way we supervise the fashioning, using, and reporting of assessments.

This chapter is a guide to beginning such rethinking, based on the insights from previous chapters. It presents the first phase of a performance-based view of design, discussing why we need to build tests mindful of standards and outlines and what those standards might look like. The reader should thus come to see that assessment design is parallel to student performance—accomplished not by plugging in design rules but through intelligent trial and error, using feedback to make incremental progress toward design standards. The elements that the assessment designer must consider are analyzed, and the logic that binds them together in necessary relationships is described and completed in Chapters Six and Seven. The chapter looks at both why we should design our assessments thoughtfully and how we might begin.

## What Is a Standard?

Some introductory words of clarification are in order. By *standard* I do not mean simply high expectations or general goals, and I certainly do not mean minimum competency scores on a test or minimal legal standards of test design. A true standard, whether for student performers or teacher designers, points to and describes a specific and desirable level or degree of exemplary performance—a worthwhile target irrespective of whether most people can or cannot meet it at the moment. Such a target is very different from so-called educational standards or benchmarks, which are really normed, that is, they define a level that we believe a large number of students or teacher designers not only can but ought to meet if they persist and are well taught. (This standard-based view calls for a different approach to the scoring and grading of student work, as we shall see in Chapter Ten.)

Standards are made concrete by criteria. It is a standard that students should leave school able to "write well"; criteria identify what we mean by *well*. We can thus describe good writing as clear, lively, engaging, and insightful; but such criteria are only necessary, not sufficient. To set a standard using such criteria, we need to show just how clear and engaging the writing has to be by using examples, models, or specifications.

Standards differ from criteria in another way. The criteria for, say, the high jump or the persuasive essay are more or less fixed, no matter what the student's age or ability. All successful high jumps must clear the bar; all persuasive essays must effectively use lots of appropriate evidence and argument. But how high should the bar be? And how sophisticated and rigorous should the arguments be? These are performance standard questions. (The need for standards is also why a rubric is only necessary but not sufficient; as we shall see in this chapter and in Chapter Seven, the descriptors in rubrics typically refer only to the generalized criteria, while the anchor papers provided as examples of each score point set the standards, that is, they indicate how well the criteria must be met.)

Given this view, what kinds of standards and criteria for assessment design might help us make assessment more educative as well as technically sound? And how can design standards most effectively honor the student performance standards being promulgated around the county and nationally? The standards presented in this chapter, like the educational performance standards just described, are worthy and informative targets. In certain school settings at present, they may strike readers as unrealistic. But that view misunderstands what a standard is meant to be: the principles embedded in a vision to serve as the model against which all judgments are then made about current practices. As noted in Chapter Three, in other words, a self-correcting system always requires a mix of standards, reality, and feedback to move the system from what is toward what ought to be.

One further clarification of the meaning of *standard* is necessary before proceeding with this chapter's inquiry into design standards: we must make sure that we understand the role that assessment design standards play in the larger realm of educational standards and specific performance standards for students.

## Three Standards for Education_____

There are essentially three different kinds of educational standards:

*Content standards:* What should students know and be able to do?

*Performance standards:* How well must students do their work?

*Task (work-design) standards:* What is worthy and rigorous work? What tasks should students be able to do?

All three types of standards are needed, though most people have never thought through the third type. But the first two standards are also not as self-explanatory as people think. When we say, "Here is what students should know and be able to do as a result of instruction," we may think we are talking about both content and performance standards, but we are really talking only about the content to be covered and some suggested indicators of competence. By using only very general verbs (such as *problem solve* or *communicate*) we offer neither specific performance standards nor the guidance about the specific tasks that are most appropriate for assessing such a standard.

Stating performance standards in specific, measurable terms is therefore necessary to ensure that challenging content is not subverted by low standards and expectations. Knowing what counts as problem solving, and what kinds of specific standards will be used to judge whether a solution is adequate or not, is essential to setting and upholding standards, because then teaching aims toward those specific standards.

Yet content and performance standards are still insufficient. What assessment or work design standards need to ensure is that what is called high-quality performance is really based on credible intellectual work. As assessment currently stands, students can be asked to read difficult literature, for example, but merely have to fill out worksheets and answer multiple-choice test items—to a high performance standard, as reflected in the percentage of right answers—in order to be deemed literate and to have shown mastery of the text—with the negative consequences for understanding cited in the Chapter Four. Similarly, students can be given a demanding physics syllabus but have only to respond well on paper-and-pencil test questions to be deemed in control of physics. (This was a notorious failure of many Mastery Learning programs,[2] in which the operational definition of mastery was scoring 80 percent or more on tests that often were very simplistic.) In too many schools, "high standards" really means tests and assignments that are arbitrary at best and trivial "Gotcha!" tests at worst. Grading on a steep curve and using secretive and picayune test items are neither educative nor defensible; yet in many schools, they pass for rigor.

That is why work design standards are so essential to school reform. It is not enough to demand high scores, given some quality content. We need to test all local tests against standards for task worthiness and aptness, a step that is commonsensical but without precedent in most schools, where much of test and project design is left to individual teachers.

An example from music education will illustrate the need for clear performance and assessment standards to support content standards. We can state the desire that a student be a "well-rounded pianist." That would be a very general goal. We can then specify what the goal means by saying that the student should not merely "know and recognize" musical pieces but "be able to perform" them. This is an achievement target, measurable in a way that the original goal was not. But we have not yet said what counts as a standard of "acceptable performance" and of worthy musical pieces. To do that, we must first specify how well specific musical pieces must be played, and according to what criteria; then we must specify what counts as appropriate music.

This is just what is provided in the New York State School Music Association's (NYSSMA) competition guidelines, for example. Soloists, small groups, ensembles, and full bands and orchestras each have a prescribed list of pieces arranged in six degree-of difficulty categories. The musicians must choose most of their pieces from the appropriate list. Then their performance is scored against a six-point "quality of performance" scale, regardless of degree of difficulty. Thus those at one degree of difficulty are not scored against those at a different degree of difficulty; all are scored only against the rubric for quality of performance.[3]

As this example reveals, setting standards depends on two decisions about what we mean by "excellent performance." Standards must consist of a combination of the right kind of task and the quality of the performance. The NYSSMA music adjudicators have rank ordered the difficulty of specific prescribed pieces, and they have developed a continuum for judging the quality of any performance, regardless of how difficult the piece. It is not enough that a student play the piano "well"; he or she must also play certain pieces from the standard repertory well.

All rubrics and their criterial language are thus insufficient. Knowing only, for example, that the playing of the piece must be "error free" and "fluid" and "graceful" does not tell us *how* fluid and graceful or exactly what counts or does not count as an error. Those decisions can be made only by agreeing on the standard-setting pieces and on the particular rigor with which the quality guidelines are to be applied (such as tolerating fewer mistakes in notes and tone in more advanced flute players). These examples or standards say, in effect, "This is how well you must play on pieces as demanding as these." Whether we are talking about performance testing or conventional testing, a performance standard is established by agreeing on specific, worthy samples of work that meet a valid target (as judged by professionals), irrespective of whether many students can meet such a standard, and by specifying certain criteria by which performance will be judged.[4]

We have yet to tackle in academic classrooms the challenges addressed by these music educators. The problem in education of establishing and clarifying performance standards is considerably worsened by the fact that overall we have yet to agree on standard-setting performance tasks for students. We therefore have no clear sense of what kinds of direct performance tasks are worth mastering or of the most appropriate standards for judging work. We do not even agree yet on the specific types or genres of intellectual tasks that ought to anchor all academic programs. Teachers and test designers at the local level are left pretty much to themselves to try to figure out not only what should count as rigor but also what should count as appropriate work. To go back to the example of assessing musicians, it would be as though those who are trying to develop a well-rounded pianist had no agreed-upon standards for what counts as a worthy musical composer, composition, or recital program—never mind what counts as good piano playing.

Chapters Eight and Nine discuss the role of portfolios of work in providing such work requirement standards, but for now we might observe how the recently framed portfolio requirements of the national New Standards project, led by Lauren Resnick and Marc Tucker (with backing from numerous state departments of education and foundations), work to partially solve this problem. In addition to specifying the content and performance standards and offering national standardized tests for those standards (with a mixture of selected and constructed-response tasks), New Standards schools ask students to collect evidence from assignments and assessments that set a de facto standard for what counts as performance. Figure 5.1 summarizes the portfolio requirements for high school mathematics and English.[5]

Without specific guidelines for what counts as important kinds of work, and without an assessment system that sends the message that such work is mandatory, content and performance standards are moot. New Standards goes further by identifying an *application* standard, with examples of the kinds of tasks and projects that can be done to fulfill it. Even rigorous content standards easily lose all their power and educative value for reform when they are embedded in inappropriate or soft assignments and assessments.

### Figure 5.1 New Standards Portfolio Requirements for High School Mathematics and English

| *Mathematics* | *English* |
|---|---|
| Conceptual Understanding Exhibit | Reading Exhibit (1–2 entries for each item) |
| Number and operations (2 entries) | Literature |
| Geometry and measurement (1–2 entries) | Informational materials |
| Functions and algebra (1–2 entries) | Public documents |
| Probability and statistics (1–2 entries) | Functional documents |
| | Quantity, range, and depth in reading |
| Problem Solving Exhibit (4 entries) | |
| | Writing Exhibit (1 entry for each item) |
| Project Exhibit—1 entry chosen from: | Response to literature |
| Data study | Literary genre |
| Mathematical modeling | Narrative account |
| Management and planning | Report |
| Pure mathematical investigation | Narrative procedure |
| History of a mathematical idea | Persuasive essay |
| | Free choice |
| Skills and Communication Exhibit (additional entries needed only to fill out what is shown in earlier entries) | Control of Writing Conventions (Pick 2 previous entries) |
| Skills | Use of processes and strategies for writing (Pick 1 previous entry) |
| Communication | |
| | Speaking, Listening, and Viewing Exhibit (1 entry for each item) |
| | Information |
| | Influencing and opinion |
| | Viewing opinion (optional) |
| | Reflective Essay Exhibit |
| | Reflective essay (1 entry) |

To shift the analogy from music to athletics in order to illustrate the need for assessment design (work) standards and an example of a solution, imagine what had to happen one hundred years ago when the decathlon was invented for the modern Olympics. Many people claimed to be great all-around athletes, but there was no agreement on what that claim meant or how to measure it. A group of people decided that great all-around athletes were those who could qualify to compete in ten specific tasks that the Olympic founders felt tapped the full range of genuine track and field performance.

This is where we are today in education: with no agreement on what constitutes required work worth mastering, despite the fact that we have clear guidelines for what schools should teach. In every school, district, and state there needs to be agreement on the kinds of performance tasks (if not specific tasks) that would count as the basis for evidence of general intellectual excellence within and across subjects, and these tasks need to be limited to a manageable sample of complex tasks from the whole domain of intellectual performance. These "performance genres" would form a matrix with content standards. Student assessment at the local and state level would be designed to address the intersection of these genres and standards (examples of such genres are provided in Figure 5.7).

Such agreement is essential to a self-correcting system. It is the main reason that athletic and artistic performances improve at all levels while educational performance does not. Clarity about work standards (what counts as good tasks and performance) would lead to more focused teaching and learning. It would undo some of the mystery and arbitrariness inherent in all indirect testing. Coaches know that they and their athletes must engage in widely agreed-upon tasks (games, events, and so on) and that they must meet public performance standards (that is, meet or beat existing records) to improve; architects know they must design buildings that satisfy building codes and client needs to succeed in their occupations. When we can agree on standards for tasks and performance (and agree on supervision of such design work through peer review, as described in Chapter Eleven), like coaches and architects we will have some assurance that the tasks and assessments we design do what we intend them to do. The further challenge is to develop standards and processes that will constantly improve local teacher design of assignments and assessments, as well as student performance, without sacrificing desirable differences and idiosyncrasies in teaching, learning, and assessing.

## Assessment Standards

Let us now turn to the matter of developing standards for an entire local assessment system. In the work my colleagues and I at the Center on Learning, Assessment, and School Structure (CLASS) do with school and district staff, we use the following six criteria to safeguard our core assumption that assessment should improve performance, not just measure it. All assessments should be

1.  Credible to all stakeholders, but especially to teachers, parents, and older students. Credibility depends on

Authenticity of the work

Technical soundness of the measures

Trained and disinterested judging

Justifiable and validated standards, that is, school measures and standards linked to the schools' valued institutional customers or the wider world of performance

2. Useful, meaning user-friendly and helpful to the student performers and their coaches, namely teachers.

3. Balanced in the use of all assessment methods, to provide a rich, defensible, and feasible profile of achievement, but anchored in authentic and complex performance tasks.

4. Honest yet fair—so we report how each student is doing against important standards but do not uselessly rank novices and experts against each other.

5. Intellectually rigorous and thought provoking—focused on core ideas, questions, problems, texts, and knowledge; but also designed to be engaging and stimulating of inquiry and interest in intellectual work.

6. Feasible in terms of resources, logistics, politics, and redeployment of time for collaboratively designing, debugging, using, evaluating, and effectively reporting student work.

Let's consider each criterion in a little more detail.

## Credible

Saying that assessment must be credible is not the same thing as saying that it must be as statistically error-proof as possible. Credible data is information that we trust, data by which we are willing to be held accountable.

A Supreme Court decision is credible. So are the judgments made by major league umpires and judges in gymnastics competitions. The inherent subjectivity of human judgment is not a flaw in assessment, in other words. It is a sad commentary on American education that we so often seek to rid the system of human judgment in the name of statistical perfection. In fact, the judging for most upper-level college exams, doctoral exams and orals, and professional performance appraisal systems are credible though subjective. Even many subjective tests are seen as credible, by educators and noneducators alike. A major part of each Advanced Placement exam is scored by teacher-judges, and a major part of each New York State Regents exam is not only judgment-based but scored by each student's own teacher (with a sample of exams audited by the state).

In fact, the United States is the only country in the world that uses the "objective" multiple-choice test format as the predominant technique in student assessment at the district and state level. All other countries focus on one or another more complex form of evaluation involving judges, and those judges often consist of teams of local or regional teachers.[6] Indeed, both common sense and the highest levels of Bloom's Taxonomy of Educational Objectives reveal that the most intellectually important tasks involve human judgment in both performance and evaluation. And the building of local capacity, through a self-correcting system of collaborative teacher design and scoring, is central to any plan to improve schools.

As the assessment standards just presented illustrate, four factors in particular contribute to credibility: authenticity of the work, technical soundness of the measures, trained and disinterested judging, and justifiable content, task, and performance standards. Chapter Two discussed authenticity as an essential element of assessment tasks. Despite their "messiness," authentic tasks make assessment more credible because these tasks clearly relate to real-world demands; we are assessing what matters to many people in addition to the students. But our overarching commitment to assessment based on authentic tasks that require human judgment does not obviate the need for ensuring the technical soundness of the measures. Grounding judgments in hard data is essential to credibility. Athletic records are trustworthy and enable personal accountability. This is true for many reasons: a pattern of results gets established over long seasons, based on lots of different data and observations; biases are minimized by the use of nonparticipant and trained referees; no outsiders' judgments based on secure or arcane methods are required to determine how many runs or goals were scored; the tasks and criteria are tacitly accepted by all coaches; each team's coach has complete control over strategy; and the resultant data is rich enough to enable self-adjustment by coaches and players alike. Validity and reliability depend on these conditions being met. In other words, we use as much objective data as possible in making subjective judgments about overall performance.

As a result of both the quantity and quality of the information available, no coach gets very far by saying, "We lack adequate talent. All these losses and unending lopsided scores aren't due to my work." Instead, coaches take what they are given and work to make progress over time on a credible and worthy challenge to which there is tacit consent and for which there is lots of data. Even when coaches fret over the raw talent of their opponents, the data generated from the games are credible to them. (This view of credibility is clearly central to any effective system of accountability. In fact, a useful indicator of credibility is that data are credible when we believe that poor results are our responsibility.)

As the examples suggest, credibility in assessment requires known, agreed-upon, apt, and uniform scoring criteria and standards, and the use of an oversight process to ensure that the (occasional) inappropriate score can be overridden. Thus, for the sake of credibility, some standardization in local assessment is essential, especially with respect to performance tasks, criteria, and scoring.

We also need to ask to whom assessment needs to be credible, to whom must standards be justifiable. If assessment is to improve performance, then we certainly must answer to the student and the student's teachers. But they are not the only ones who need assessment information. The methods and results of assessment must be credible to parents, board members, institutions that further educate and employ our graduating students, and representatives of state agencies. It may be that a good portion of our education troubles stem from educators worrying more about what some stakeholders want from assessment than about what our primary clients need and have a right to expect; nevertheless, our assessment reform must be credible to these stakeholders. The argument presented here, of course, is that by using assessment based on clear and excellent standards to improve students' intellectual performance, we can meet both students' and other stakeholders' needs.

Finally, credibility depends on trained and disinterested judging. School outsiders appropriately want more disinterest in local judgment-based assessment than can be provided when the child's teacher makes all key judgments. Disinterested and adequately reliable scoring is central to credibility. If we want local assessment to be credible to outsiders, teachers must have access to standards and, as mentioned earlier, to well-designed tasks and rubrics so that the isolated individual teacher is no longer solitary judge and jury in local student assessment, especially when the teacher-judge has a stake in the results. This issue of local scoring goes to the heart of the problem of credibility.

There is a long, sad history here.[7] District, state, and national standardized tests remain in demand partly because of experiments like those performed by Daniel Starch and Edward Elliot eighty years ago. In their simple studies they asked teachers around the country to grade the same paper, with the student's class, age, and track all known and held constant. The score ranged from the 30s to the 90s on a 100-point scale.[8] We are no freer today from woeful inconsistencies in teacher grading. As long as the parent does not know what a B stands for, and as long as Miss Smith's B and Mr. Jones's B have completely different significance, then we have got a problem. (Throwing out letter grades entirely only exacerbates the problem, as I argue in Chapter Nine.)

## Useful

Assessment must be useful. To whom? The student of course, if we are to honor the core premise of this book.

As noted in previous chapters, useful assessment is a radical idea, even if it seems like common sense, for it means that all assessment designers, be they classroom teachers or commercial test designers, must do a far better job of building educative work and powerful feedback to the student into the assessment from the start. Test designers need to aggressively seek out student and teacher feedback about the quality of student assessment tasks and instructions, and teachers need to do a better job of polling students to determine whether teacher tests and feedback seem fair and helpful. Teachers and commercial testers alike are obligated to survey students and teachers about whether the test was not only fair but helpful in terms of how the results are reported and analyzed. Usefulness implies not only timeliness and intelligibility of the results but also opportunities to use them.

## Balanced in Methods, Anchored in Authentic Performance Tasks

Reform must not be construed as simply throwing out the old and thoughtlessly embracing the new. It is not about choices that exclude one another but about wise use of all available techniques of assessment. We must correct the woeful overuse of simple test exercises and make sure that assessment is always focused on students' effective performance, in which they use their judgment and repertoire of skills, learning, and understanding rather than mainly plugging what they have learned into artificially neat and clean exercises.

Figure 5.2 is the first of two graphs you can use to see the need for better balance and more genuine performance. The x axis has a wide array of assessment strategies at one end and the narrow use of one or two assessment methods—usually involving test items—at the other; the y axis has authentic performance at the top and indirect and out-of-context test items at the bottom.

Overuse of multiple-choice and short-answer tests and underuse of complex tasks hampers our quest for both excellence and engagement in students. As Bloom and his colleagues put it, "Because of the simplicity of teaching and evaluating knowledge, it is frequently emphasized as an educational objective all out of proportion to its usefulness or its relevance to the development of the individual. In effect, the teacher and school tend to look where the light is brightest."[9]

Most traditional forms of testing, especially from fifth grade on, are best termed drill tests or exercises. Consider any complex performance (the soccer game, the sculpture, the trial, the surgery on the

## Figure 5.2 Typical Imbalanced Assessment in Classrooms and Schools

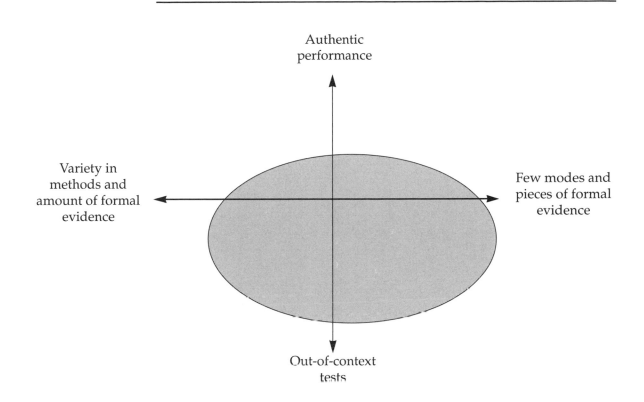

patient): each has a complex set of performance requirements, as well as particular exercises or drills that aid in the development of skills (for playing two-on-one soccer, for building more stable armatures for sculpture, for working on a summation for a trial, or for improving the asking of questions in taking a personal medical history). There is no doubt that if we want to coach people to achieve a good performance on a complex task, we need to use such exercises. But such simplified, highly structured, and out-of-context exercises are not sufficient to cause students to meet complex performance standards.

A conventional test question or item is like a sideline drill in coaching. Though the reader may not call such tests exercises or drills (because drills suggest instruction more than assessment), they remain means to a (performance) end, useful activities though not the real target. They deliberately decontextualize and simplify performance into its elements. They let coaches isolate a bit of performance from the context and work on it with the performer. But the sum of drills is not genuine (flexible, fluid, graceful, responsive, and effective) performance. Drill testing is always necessary but insufficient. In addition, students must practice performing (that is, grappling with relatively unstructured or unscripted demands) and adjusting their performance in light of feedback. To determine whether students are heading toward genuine performance, they must be assessed for their repertoire of skills and for both the ability to apply those skills and the good judgment to know when to do what, in context.

A simple piece of vocabulary catches the difference: to "do" science is very different from and more authentic than replicating scripted demonstrations in a lab, even though the latter is hands-on skill-building work. Similarly, to do history is to gain experience in telling a new or different story about the past—not merely to summarize other people's stories. As discussed in the previous two chapters, understanding is best revealed when students are faced with new application situations. Gardner puts it well in discussing the kinds of assessment that are suited to assessing for performances of understanding. He argues that there is a fundamental difference between "rote, ritualistic or conventional performances" and "genuine" adaptive disciplinary performance. In the latter case, students must apply what they know "flexibly and appropriately in a new, somewhat unanticipated, situation. . . . The test of understanding involves neither repetition of information learned nor performance of practices mastered. Rather, it involves the appropriate application of concepts and principles to questions or problems that are newly posed."[10]

This is not a new or radical idea, as noted earlier. It is sound measurement. Figure 5.3 shows the kind of balance we need, in which assessment is anchored in authentic work and teachers assess achievement and evaluate performance using a variety of modes and a sizable number of pieces of evidence.

The portfolio is an ideal vehicle for determining a practical way of honoring the need for balance in the evidence collected, while nonetheless anchoring assessment in genuine performance tasks and standards. Portfolio design is considered later in this chapter and in Chapters Eight and Nine.

## Honest yet Fair

A learner- and learning-centered assessment system is more than just a technical matter. As noted repeatedly in this book, student interests are easily lost sight of when other adult stakeholders demand our attention. Safeguarding our standards requires that we bring moral considerations into the design picture. What we need is a system that is both honest and fair.

Assessing for excellence requires that we be honest in the sense that we must accurately and unflinchingly give students feedback concerning their levels of achievement against a standard of

Figure 5.3 Exemplary Assessment Balance

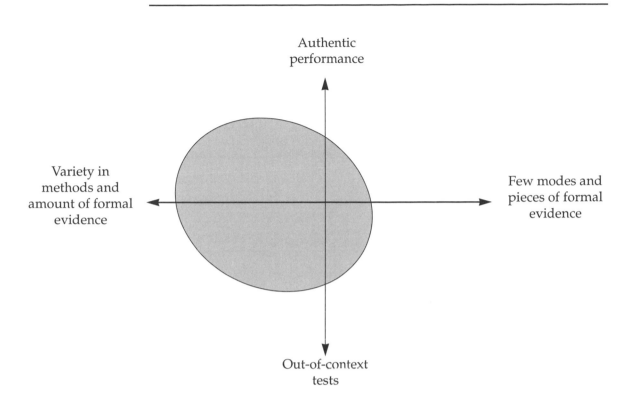

excellence. But we must also be fair in that we must factor in appropriate information about students' prior levels of experience, recent growth, and extenuating circumstances. Out of fairness we should not judge novices and experts with the same expectations. Vagaries of schedules and bureaucratic regulations sometimes plunk a novice and an expert into the same classroom, but this does not mean we should hold them to the same degree of excellence at the same moment in time.

Honesty and fairness also require, however, that we not deceive students who are well below the performance levels of other students into thinking that their work is on par with their classmates' efforts. We must have high standards but reasonable (that is, appropriately differing) expectations, as argued further in Chapter Ten. Conducting our assessment through the use of developmental or longitudinal scoring systems, whereby we place performance levels on a continuum of novice to expert, is the chief way to honor both honesty and fairness, as argued in later chapters of this book: the student knows where he or she stands, but is not obligated to be at a specific spot on the continuum by a particular date. The primary obligation is to make continual progress toward a common and valid ultimate standard of excellence and a minimal exit standard, in which all scores are given in terms of that final standard (as now exists nationwide in Great Britain,[11] unlike the isolated course or grade-level standards we use in our local grading).

Fairness also requires that we think through carefully what is elective and what is mandatory in student assessment. Student interests, strengths, and learning styles differ. Though we should not use that fact as a dishonest excuse to cover up poor performance, we need to be willing to tolerate options in student assessment, despite the hassles this causes the psychometrician (the test designer or administrator), who is fearful of the technical challenge of statistically equating (different) results. If we again go back to credibility issues, we see in many college and professional evaluation situations that the student or client has many options, even on exams. It is quite common, in college as well as in the workplace, to have a say in how and on what work one will be evaluated. This is not only fair but intellectually sound in a diverse democratic world of specialization. Everyone need not know or do the same things, to the same standards, in order to succeed. (It is hypocrisy of the worst sort to expect all students to meet the same high standards across every academic subject when few successful adults at present can do so.)

Decisions about standardization and elective options in testing come down to common sense and analysis of achievement targets and their validity. If we say we want students to be effective communicators, then it is not reasonable that we fail to give a diploma to a student who has not mastered a specific writing genre, like the essay. But if we feel that essay writing is a defensible and worthy performance goal, valued and demanded by our institutional clients (that is, competitive colleges), then we are within our rights to demand that all students master it adequately. Specific standards must be very local matters of school niche, personal aspiration, and standards of the school's clients.

## Intellectually Rigorous and Thought Provoking

It would not seem necessary to have such a standard as intellectually rigorous and thought provoking, but the pressure to revert to simplistic proxy items in testing requires us to counterbalance the tendency. Most school tests are boring and uninspiring.[12] They offer little in the way of intrinsic incentive or intellectual merit, with negative consequences for student motivation and adult teaching. It is vital that academic departments, faculties, and district personnel develop standards for what counts as quality work, as noted earlier. Students deserve better than endless quizzes and worksheets.

## Feasible

What good is a good idea if it cannot happen? The greatest perceived obstacle to all school reforms, including assessment reform, is lack of time to do the work properly. This concern and others related to impediments are taken up in Chapter Twelve, but a few preliminary points are made here.

Demanding that the assessment system be feasible should not be taken to mean that better assessment must somehow fit into our current dysfunctional schedules and school structures. If we insist on viewing our current structures and routines as given, then it is clear that significant change will never occur. On the contrary, a feasible assessment system depends on a more intelligent use of existing time, material, and human resources. The maxim at this chapter's outset that form should follow function is to be true of all school structures, including schedules. At present, in many schools the aphorism is turned on its head: all functions somehow have to adapt themselves to existing forms. We need a strategy, therefore, for making realistic but fundamental changes in how time is used in schools—in particular, how noncontact time is built into a schedule and effectively used for student assessment. Suggestions are offered in Chapter Thirteen.

Time is inseparable from personnel. We need to find creative and cost-effective ways of freeing teachers to assist one another in performance assessment, just as we need to find ways of bringing in credible and appropriate outsiders for assistance in judging student work. Suggestions on how to do this, based on districts that have devised useful and creative solutions, are found in Chapter Twelve.

Feasibility also involves issues related to professional development. A central change in assessment would be not merely to provide *more* professional development but to create an entirely new conception of professional growth as grounded in a different job description for teachers as well as administrators. The true building of capacity requires more than training. It requires a vision, a set of standards, and a set of professional obligations that make high-quality assessment mandatory. (Issues related to descriptions and policies are taken up in greater detail in Chapter Eleven.)

Feasibility also cannot be separated from technology. A daunting part of assessment reform is the lack of availability of models, feedback, and easy ways of sharing work. Needless reinventing of the wheel is happening in schools all over the United States. As I will argue in Chapter Twelve, it is neither feasible nor desirable to have everyone invent every assessment they use. This is as foolish as saying we must each invent our own computer software. In addition, the various Internet and intranet solutions now cropping up in schools and districts everywhere are a vital part of undoing needless isolation and reinvention. A database of approved tasks and rubrics, for use in individual schools and districtwide, is not only a more feasible approach to design but also a more coherent one. While high-technology solutions are not essential for implementing the ideas contained in this book, they clearly offer effective ways of reducing needless inefficiencies.

These assessment standards are the touchstone against which all assessment design should occur. Any use of indirect conventional testing, whether locally designed or externally imposed, must fit comfortably within the context outlined here. How then can we think about the overall assessment design process in light of this standard-based view?

## The Logic of Assessment Design

Assessment that does not merely audit student knowledge but improves student performance requires careful, sound design. At CLASS we have found over the last decade that people new to assessment design invariably make two critical false starts: they think of the process as following a recipe, and they think that activity design is the same as assessment design. These misconceptions lead to failure to check designs adequately for errors and to correct them (debugging), and the failure to constantly judge work in progress against criteria that reflect evidence that the work is valid. Designers of sound assessment must be mindful of the results they seek (in this case, the evidence of student learning), but they must also be aware that they can take many procedural paths to collect it.

The logic of assessment design, like any logic, is not a recipe, not a fixed chronology. Even in the kitchen, though recipes can be "useful things," they can also be "tyrants, leaving even the most well-meaning cook unsure of his own instincts. A slavish devotion to recipes robs people of the kind of experiential knowledge that seeps into the brain. . . . Most chefs are not fettered by formula; they've cooked enough to trust their taste. Today that is the most valuable lesson a chef can teach a cook."[13] In other words, chefs cook on the basis of ideas, standards for taste, and feedback. They constantly taste and adjust as they go. Thus, a logic of action and self-correction is not the same as a recipe, in cooking or education. A taxonomy of educational objectives is not a chronology; a textbook's table of contents is not the same as an effective syllabus; a design flowchart is not a list of steps. As these three brief contrasts suggest, an analytic logic does not necessarily dictate or imply a specific plug-in procedure. Neither does good design, be it in the kitchen or the classroom, involve merely following step-by-step directions. Designing assessments requires attention to standards and to the feedback that occurs when we see how our design decisions play out, which we need to meet those standards. We must always self-assess and self-adjust as we go, in light of the emerging design and how well or poorly it seems to meet our needs. As John Dewey put it so clearly in *How We Think,* logic is the method of testing and communicating results, not a prescription for arriving at good decisions or solutions to problems. We can be obeying such logic even when our thinking is nonlinear and begins in a variety of places, on a variety of timelines, using a variety of methods.

As an example, consider how educators use outcome statements in developing projects. Although these statements of goals precede project design, we do not ever fully understand or explicate our own objectives adequately until we have worked on the project enough to start imagining how it will come out. Then we find we must begin going back and forth through our work, tracing a logical network of interconnections between the parts of our work and our ideas and objectives, and adjusting and recasting both work and objectives until we have a finished project that does want we want it to do.

Similarly, because assessments are designed to gauge desired outcomes, outcome statements must precede assessment design even though, paradoxically, we do not yet know in concrete terms all that the outcome statement implies. For example, we must know in advance that we want students in a mathematics course to be, say, critical thinkers. But it is not until we try to assess for critical thinking that we grasp the concrete implications of that objective and typically come to see that our initial outcome statements need to be recast and rethought.

Asking the key assessor questions right away—What counts as evidence of our meeting or not meeting our goals? How are we now doing with respect to our outcomes? and What kinds of assessment are needed to best assess for these proposed outcomes?—would have greatly improved so-called Outcomes-Based Education, for example.[14] As faculties answered these questions, they would have seen that their original outcome statements were often vague and vacuous, and they might have seen more quickly and in time to avoid needless political backlash that global statements of school purpose do not replace or rank higher than subject-matter unique goals, which ended up missing from most school lists of overall shared goals.

These assessor questions are at the heart of the distinction between assessment tasks and instructional activities. This distinction, mentioned earlier in this chapter and discussed in Chapter Two, is the other critical aspect of education that is overlooked in reform projects. By virtue of both long familiarity with lesson planning and minimal experience in meeting technical measurement standards in assessment, most teachers instinctually build assessments on the foundation of existing classroom activities without scrutinizing those activities for their aptness in measuring specific achievements.

A simple example will suffice to show how common this problem is. A group of third grade teachers sought to develop an assessment of reading. They proposed a performance task in which each student was asked first to choose a book with which they were comfortable (that is, in terms of degree of difficulty), then to read a few pages out loud to the class, and then to share their views as to why the book was worth reading. This is a fine activity, but an invalid and unreliable way to assess a student's reading ability. The confounding variables were the self-selection of the book, the overreliance on oral performance, and the focus on the student's interest in the book rather than on his or her understanding of it. While developing an interest in and comfort with books is surely a worthy achievement target, it was not identified by the teachers as the main thing being assessed. The teachers believed that the activity assessed the students' reading abilities.

What makes this example so important is that it is just this sort of conceptual cloudiness that is so common in thinking about assessment in schools. Teachers choose a favorite activity (such as reading aloud, building a diorama, or conducting a research project) and then look in a very general way for an achievement that might plausibly be related to the task. The proposed reading task is not wholly inappropriate, I stress. It is just that the designers have not stopped to ask, What specifically can we infer and not infer on the basis of the evidence that this activity will yield? Instead, because the activity happens to involve reading and because the task is educative, the designers came to think that such casual correlations were sufficient to make it all work as assessment.

A different way to grasp the import of the assessor's questions comes from asking, Using what indicators, criteria, or evidence will the judges discriminate excellent from average from poor performance? Such discrimination is of course central to any assessment. But oddly enough, few teachers grasp this point at the outset. Not only do some teachers think that such discrimination is to be avoided as harmful, but there is a general failure to see that unless we have rules or guidelines for such discrimination, then in truth there is no assessment at all, because then we lack any standards against which to judge actual performance relative to ideal performance.

In fact, a good deal of assessment design is counterintuitive. We need an explicit logic of design, backed by a process of review and adjustment, precisely because all designers are bound by habits and instincts that undercut good design. Let us look at such a logic to better see what kinds of judgments need to be made as we design so that we might avoid these common mistakes.

Figure 5.4 names eleven elements to be considered in the logic of assessment design, and Figure 5.5 shows how they might be described for an assessment of competency in math. The remainder of this chapter along with Chapters Six through Eight describe the elements listed in Figure 5.4. As I have already emphasized, the logic illustrated by the flowchart represents only the logic of the process, not the many different possible chronologies of work and refinement. The logic is best used to check design work that is in progress. Users should find themselves moving around in the logic freely rather than treating it as a recipe of steps.

## Achievement Target Formulated

All assessment logically begins with a clear, apt, and worthy achievement target. We are assessing for some desired result, which is the capacity we seek in students and therefore that for which we must deliberately measure.

Formulating a fitting achievement target involves taking a (typically) relatively vague teaching goal and casting it broadly in measurable terms, as mentioned earlier in the discussion of standards. "Students should be good thinkers" is a worthy but relatively vague teaching goal. So we need to cast it in more useful and precise terms: for example, "All students, after this unit on reasoning and problem solving, should be able to criticize arguments and claims effectively, construct sound arguments, and solve open-ended problems."

Now we have a general sense of what we need to measure for. We will need some open-ended problems, perhaps some propaganda or questionable arguments and the like as material for students to work with. We must then logically infer, What kind of evidence will enable us to identify critical thinkers? Answering this question requires asking another that we may not usually put to ourselves or others directly: Where shall we look and what shall we look for in distinguishing critical from uncritical thinkers? It is this question that takes us from the target through the rest of the logic. It is this question of discrimination that enables us to move from merely thinking like a goal setter to thinking like an assessor.

Classifying achievement targets helps us to know whether we have framed our targets wisely and usefully. CLASS staff identify five distinct kinds of achievement targets (mentioned previously in Chapter Four):

Figure 5.4 The Logic of Assessment Design: Example

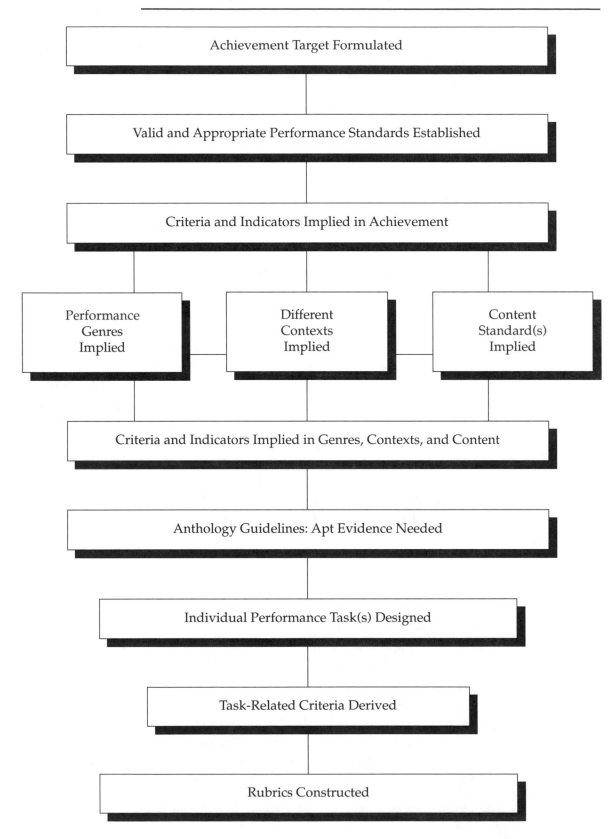

## Figure 5.5 The Logic of Assessment Design: Example

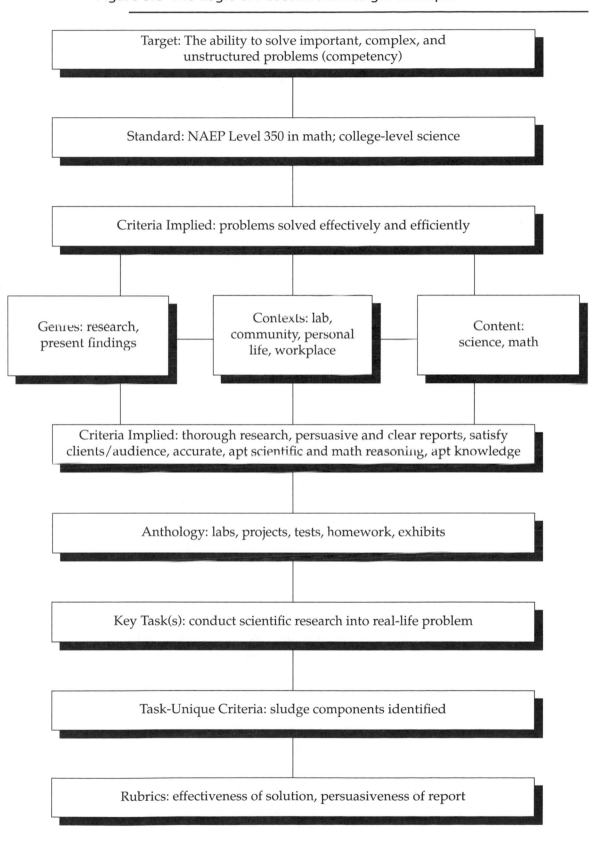

Target: The ability to solve important, complex, and unstructured problems (competency)

Standard: NAEP Level 350 in math; college-level science

Criteria Implied: problems solved effectively and efficiently

Genres: research, present findings

Contexts: lab, community, personal life, workplace

Content: science, math

Criteria Implied: thorough research, persuasive and clear reports, satisfy clients/audience, accurate, apt scientific and math reasoning, apt knowledge

Anthology: labs, projects, tests, homework, exhibits

Key Task(s): conduct scientific research into real-life problem

Task-Unique Criteria: sludge components identified

Rubrics: effectiveness of solution, persuasiveness of report

1.  Accuracy and precision of subject-matter knowledge
2.  Sophistication of subject-matter (and cross-subject-matter) understanding
3.  Effectiveness and efficiency of technical skill
4.  Effectiveness of general performance and production
5.  Mature habits of mind

These distinctions are useful for clarifying just what kinds of evidence (and assessment tasks) are needed. As argued in the discussion of understanding in Chapter Four, knowledge is not the same as understanding. One can have a great deal of technical knowledge and know-how but limited understanding of what it means. To understand is to be able to justify or creatively use what one knows—abilities unnecessary for many straightforward knowledge-related tasks. This has immediate assessment implications, as previously noted: if understanding is our aim, we need to ask students to apply what they have learned. A person could know many complex and important things about physics, but neither fly planes nor prove Bernoulli's principle (a central law in aerodynamics).

Similarly, we can distinguish two varieties of know-how: we apply technical skills within specific subject areas, and we apply our performance and production abilities in broader areas, spanning disciplines as we do research and communicate with others in a multitude of ways. Such general performance and production skills are often independent of technical knowledge. We have all encountered highly competent people who cannot effectively communicate what they know or work with others. And we know facilitators and managers, say in computer or medical companies, who know very little about technical matters but can effectively run design teams in these companies to solve difficult problems or persuasively communicate findings to others. Many writers are poor editors, and many fine editors are not experts in the literature they edit.

Another reason to distinguish between such skills is to make clear that no one teacher ought to have responsibility for developing all of them in their students. Developing performance capacities in particular cries out for a team approach, over many years of learning and assessment. The notion of development over time has a validity implication, too. All students need to have had practice in the specific competencies that make up performance tasks. When we are using students' performance skills in tasks that use such skills as a means to assess students' technical skills and understanding, we need to ensure, on grounds of both fairness and validity, that all students are suitably equipped to take on those tasks. This concern will (properly) cause us to worry and collaborate more, to ensure that students have had sufficient practice and rehearsal of all key performance genres (which are alluded to earlier in this chapter).

Whatever the kind of target, it must logically precede all decisions about specific tests or tasks. Only after we clarify what kind of achievement we are seeking can we with confidence propose performance tasks that are likely to yield the right kind of evidence. And even then we must move back and forth to justify and clarify specific objectives and get an even clearer conception of the specific results we seek from our own teaching and of what that evidence looks like.

## Valid and Appropriate Performance Standards Established

As described in the discussion of education standards, performance standards answer the question, How well must students perform? In assessment design, the performance standard follows logically from the achievement target. Once we know we want students "to be effective problem posers, clarifiers, and solvers" or "to understand the Civil War," the next logical questions are: How effective? How well understood? According to what standard must students solve the problem or exhibit understanding? Against what models or specifications?

Many new assessment designers imagine that such questions do not get answered until a specific task has been identified and rubrics are being built. But again, this is the approach to building teaching activities, whereas designing assessments calls for working backward from larger educational goals under which activities are subsumed and which imply the evidence needed. Depending on how we frame the target and then the performance standard, certain kinds of performance tasks (and instructional activities) may or may not be appropriate; and the particular task is a stand-in for many different tasks of the same type (because the particular tasks used are meant to be samples from a larger domain).

For example, suppose we say that the standard students are to meet in scientific problem solving relates to governmental policy rather than just, say, biology. So the problem to be solved must require students to provide answers that meet standards related to negotiating the dilemmas and politics of public policy (such as cost-benefit analyses, as found in many problem-based learning tasks), in addition to calling for answers deemed acceptable to the scientific community. Meeting standards for publication in a scientific journal on the one hand and standards for successful public policy on the other require students to undertake very different kinds of performance tasks and indirect tests. Such an emphasis has later implications for instructional approaches, sequencing, and materials.

An example from writing shows how the standard can change not only the assessment but the instruction. Suppose the standard we set in writing is that a student must produce some publishable work and get at least one piece published in a periodical, journal, or book. (Some programs actually do this, while allowing great leeway in the nature or location of the publication.) Given this standard, we now know something important about our instructional obligations. Our instructional and assessment tasks must require the students to work from real models and publishing guidelines, to get and use feedback effectively, to learn from real editors how they evaluate manuscripts, and to learn to revise work repeatedly. None of this would likely be built into the curriculum or the assessment if we simply began from the premise that we needed a generic district writing prompt requiring only perfunctory prose and no public exposure.

## Criteria and Indicators Implied in Achievement

The previous points about targets and standards lead logically to identifying the most appropriate criteria and indicators for use in the assessment. As was noted in the description of how criteria make standards more explicit, if the goal is problem solving and the performance standard is "acceptable as public policy," then the criteria to be used must follow logically from them. Thus, acceptable problem solutions (in both science and public policy) will be those that meet such criteria as "thoroughly researched," "persuasively presented to a policy audience," "mindful of budgetary and political realities" (that is, credible to all stakeholders), and the like.

Many novice designers try to go in the other direction. They begin with a task idea and derive criteria only from the idiosyncrasies of that task. But this again misunderstands the purpose of the task and the nature of assessment in a large domain. A single task contains only a small sample of possible challenges in a subject or genre, so we had better design and use each assessment task wisely, mindful of our larger aims. The goal of education is not for students to get good at a small number of idiosyncratic, perhaps enjoyable, but randomly designed activities. The goal is for them to master apt representative tasks through a wise sampling of the larger domain of the subject and all its possible kinds of tasks. The decathlon is not arbitrary. It represents a coherent and valid approach to assessing for criteria—speed, strength, agility, and so on—that relate to well-rounded athleticism.

A criterion is a way of defining success at meeting a target achievement or educational outcome, as noted at the start of the chapter. When criteria are met, then we may conclude not only that the specific performance has been successful—that a lesson has worked—but also that a larger educational goal has been addressed. Criteria are thus always necessary and sufficient: the larger success has not occurred unless the criteria are met, and the criteria apply in all attempted performances of the same type.

Here are some examples of criteria related to performance targets:

*Criteria for a history research paper:* Write an accurate, persuasive, and clear essay.

*Criteria for effective speaking:* engage and inform the audience in the allotted time.

*Criteria for solving problems:* provide accurate, cost-effective, efficient solutions that are acceptable to clients.

Note again that the criteria are more general than any particular research, speaking, or scientific task. They act as a bridge between the broader intellectual achievement target and the idiosyncrasies of a particular task. Regardless of the specific essay prompt, for example, what we really want to know is whether or not the student can routinely write good essays—that is, routinely meet criteria for the essay genre, regardless of topic. Such criteria will specify essay attributes like persuasiveness and clarity—general criteria that should apply to all essays, regardless of the teacher, the program, or the age of the writer.

**Indicators.** In addition to determining the criteria implied by the particular achievement target, we should also determine indicators. An indicator is a behavior or trait that is typical of the particular performance being assessed. It is a concrete sign or symptom of a criterion being met and thus makes assessment and self-assessment easier.

For example, consider assessment of good speaking. When the criterion is "student speaks in an engaging manner," indicators that the student is meeting that criterion might include "makes eye contact," "modulates voice pleasantly," "uses stories and humor appropriate to audience and context," and "handles audience questions gracefully."

An indicator may not always be reliable or appropriate in all contexts; though "asks apt questions" is a good indicator of listening well in a classroom, it is a bad indicator during services in church, mosque, or synagogue. Though the indicators are not always reliable they are nonetheless helpful for teacher-judges and student performers. They provide concrete cues or feedback on whether the standards have been met.[15]

**Criteria Types.**    Several design errors arise from designers' choices of criteria types. Designing quirky and invalid performance tasks and mistaking indicators for criteria will result in poor assessments, and so will criteria that lack coherence and intellectual appropriateness. As discussed in Chapter Two, teachers who are learning assessment design tend to overemphasize criteria that relate to the form and content of performance rather than looking to the purpose of the performance and impact-related criteria. They also tend to produce too few designs that assign appropriate points to each criterion, which thus is not weighted appropriately relative to the achievement target. Most designers make all criteria of equal value, which is simple but rarely an accurate reflection of their value in relation to what the designer wants to know from the assessment.

To address both problems, CLASS staff came up with the following typology of criteria to help people design and edit their assessments. The typology especially helps designers not to overlook impact-related criteria, the focal point of real performance and feedback.

| Criteria Type | Description |
|---|---|
| Impact of performance | The success of performance, given the purposes, goals, and desired results |
| Work quality and craftsmanship | The overall polish, organization, and rigor of the work |
| Adequacy of methods and behaviors | The quality of the procedures and manner of presentation, prior to and during performance |
| Validity of content | The correctness of the ideas, skills, or materials used |
| Degree of expertise | The relative sophistication, complexity, or maturity of the knowledge employed |

Following are some examples of the different types of criteria implied in a specific achievement:

**Criteria for Goal of Building a Habitat**

| | |
|---|---|
| Impact | Animals thrive in the environment, in terms of health and procreation. |
| Methods | The habitat is designed in an efficient and thorough manner. |
| Work quality | The habitat is well designed and well constructed. |

| Content | The habitat reflects accurate knowledge of the animals and their preferred environment. |
| Expertise | The habitat reflects sophisticated understanding of the animals and of the design of habitats. |

Figure 5.6 contains examples of each of the different criteria types that might be implied in an achievement target and used in assessment design.

## Implied or Suggested Genres, Contexts, and Content

The three elements of assessment design just described—achievement targets, performance standards, and implied criteria and indicators—

### Figure 5.6 Examples of Assessment Criteria by Type

| Successful impact is achieved when performance results in | Work is of high quality when it is | Adequate methods and behaviors are found when performers and performances are | Valid content or material is | Knowledge is sophisticated when it is |
|---|---|---|---|---|
| Effective answers | Well designed | Purposeful | Accurate | Deep |
| Satisfied clients | Clear | Efficient | Correct | Expert |
| Solved problems | Well planned | Adaptive | Precise | Insightful |
| Moved audience | Elegant | Self-regulated | Justifiable | Fluent |
| Settled situation | Clever | Persistent | Verified | Rich |
| Informed reader | Graceful | Enterprising | Authentic | Cutting-edge |
| Persuaded reader | Well crafted | (Self-)Critical | Apt | Proficient |
| Work of great value | Organized | Thoughtful | Focused | Skilled |
| Satisfying work | Thorough | Careful | Required | Competent |
| Ethical conduct | Coherent | Responsive | Honors request | Masterful |
| Novel work | Mechanically sound | Inquisitive | Meets rules | |
| Created knowledge | A genuine voice | Methodical | | |
| A championship | Concise | Well researched | | |
| Winning proposal | Polished | Well reasoned | | |
| Winning judgment | Stylish | Collaborative | | |
| | | Facilitative | | |
| | | Cooperative | | |

suggest three things: (1) no single task can ever adequately assess for a complex target; (2) no single context (for example, situation, audience, purpose, or set of constraints) can be adequate for judging a student's broad mastery; and (3) no single kind (or genre) of performance and product yields valid and reliable evidence. All three ideas stem from the same questions: What will give us credible and defensible assessment results? How do we make sure that we have not arbitrarily singled out one or two tasks, contexts, and genres that inappropriately favor students who happen to be comfortable in those areas, or that favor teacher activities that work as instruction but not as assessment?

Again, take reading, the most difficult area of performance achievement to assess because an overreliance on any single task or type of performance will skew results. If we ask students only to write about what they read, then we easily end up assessing writing, not reading. If we have lots of debates and seminar discussions and do little writing, then we may wrongly infer that quiet students lack literacy skills or understanding. In addition, too many complex performances may hide from us knowledge about particular subskills of reading that may not show up enough or be easily lost in fluid complex performances. Thus, a sound assessment of reading breaks down reading into its many components, assesses for them holistically as well as in isolation, and uses multiple means of assessment to ensure that no one method of assessment or mode of performance is overly stressed. Consistent with the earlier athletic analogy, just having students play one complex "game" of reading is rarely enough evidence for sound assessment. We also need other performances and the sideline drill exercises found in such approaches as miscue analysis and the cloze method to help us build a complete profile of performance.

Note too that genuinely competent adults are comfortable across different tasks and situations. They not only go beyond the drill tests to performance, but their performance is fluid and flexible, not narrow and rote. Thus we need to build a diverse set of performance tasks and situations to determine whether students have genuinely mastered a subject or merely mastered a few test questions and procedures.

The public policy achievement target in science, for example, immediately suggests kinds of situations for students to work in, either in simulation or for real, and the kinds of performance genres they might have to negotiate in such situations. For example, such situations as testifying at legislative hearings, addressing town council meetings, meeting with a company's board of directors, proposing a solution to the president's science council, and so on all suggest promising tasks from both the assessment and pedagogical angles.

These situations then also suggest the kinds of performance genres that might be appropriate: doing an oral presentation, gathering field research data, writing up of findings in an article, writing a position paper or proposal, and so forth.

Just as we talk about genres of writing—narrative, essay, poem, autobiography, and so on—so can we talk about other genres of performance in other subjects. And just as students should be proficient in a variety of writing genres, they should also regularly encounter all major performance or production challenges in their learning and assessment and become competent in most or all of them. Districts should agree on a list of these performances and make it the foundation of curriculum guides and software databases. (Performance genres bridge curriculum design and assessment, as discussed in Chapter Nine.)

Mindful of the fact that no one teacher should be held accountable for developing complex performance ability over time, it is wise to standardize all possible task types by establishing a districtwide and schoolwide list of the intellectual performance genres that need to be taught, practiced, and assessed repeatedly throughout a student's career (see Figure 5.7). Such a list ensures that there will adequate rehearsal for and better validity in the assessment.

But a focus on genres is not sufficient. We need to make sure that students encounter a variety of real and simulated contexts to ensure that their education is effective. In designing for authenticity, as discussed in Chapter Two, the context, not just the task, must be authentic and appropriate. Consider the following context variables:

### Figure 5.7 Intellectual Performance Genres

| *Performance Genres* | | | |
|---|---|---|---|
| Oral | Speech | Recitation | Acting |
| | Report | Simulation | Counseling |
| | Proposal | Discussion | Directing |
| | | Debate | |
| Written | Essay/analysis | Description | Poem, song |
| | Letter | Script | Log |
| | Critique | Proposal | Law/policy |
| | Narrative | Report | Plan |
| Displayed | Demonstration | Artistic performance medium | Artistic visual medium |
| | Graph/chart/table | Electronic media | Advertisement |
| | Exhibit | Model | Blueprint |

- Complexity

  Task ambiguity
  Relative control over situation

- Purpose

  Degree of clarity and specificity of desired impact(s)
  Single or multiple audience(s)

- Noise

  Inherent distractions in the real situation
  Feedback quality and availability

- Incentives

  Intrinsic to task situation
  Extrinsic to task situation

As these variables suggest, we need to make sure that contexts are diverse and realistic—much like flight simulators in pilot training or case studies in law and business. For example, we should prepare foreign language students for the reality of slurred speech and impatient native speakers in a foreign country through simulations that make them encounter such situations.

But even language labs and other highly controlled academic performance tests may be too neat and clean as settings for assessment if the targeted achievement is "speaking the foreign language in context." CLASS staff worked with a team of teachers from Mundelein High School in Illinois that developed a wonderful assessment of French oral and written proficiency. It involved a simulation in which an extended family (the class of students) planned to come together from all over France at a family reunion in Paris. This required, for example, phoning simulated travel agencies, hoteliers, maitre d's, and the like while speaking only in French.

We need to honor the messy, distracting, ambiguous, and purpose- and audience-driven ways in which typical adult performance invariably occurs. I once watched a teacher make a presentation on whole language to a school board. She clearly knew a great deal about her topic, but her presentation was completely ineffective: board members revealed in their body language and questioning that they found incredible her comments that invented spelling and reading logs are more important than testing. Yet she failed to pick up on this feedback or tailor her remarks to their predictable skepticism. Instead her report was a testimonial. Like many others I have heard in such settings, she made the tactical error of justifying her approach to teaching by citing anecdotes of student enthusiasm and by sounding too evangelical and insufficiently critical. Savvy performers know that their success in presentations is highly dependent on couching the report in language and argument that is mindful of the listeners' needs and frame of reference. (Application with perspective and empathy!)

Figure 5.8 summarizes a way of assessing for contextual realism and authenticity.

## Criteria Implied in Situations

As we sharpen and refine the list of possible task types and contexts to be used in assessing for our chosen achievement target, we can identify the kinds of context-specific criteria implied in the situations. If, for example, we want the student to perform in a simulated legislative hearing or foreign country, then we have to use criteria suitable to such contexts in judging the work. Such additional criteria in the hearing might be "responsive to questions and mindful of audience," and in the foreign country it might be "adaptive and effective in getting message across, degree of use of target language." Again, however, we must note a dilemma: on the one hand, we want to give the student useful anticipatory guidance and eventual feedback on the disaggregated aspects of performance. On the other hand, the context-specific and task-specific criteria matter less in the long run in terms of the validity and reliability of the overall assessment of achievement.

A solution that we at CLASS have found is to keep the criteria paragraphs sufficiently stable and task independent to ensure their consistency and soundness, and to use BULLETED indicators to assess for task-specific criteria for each unique task. Consider the following example, a description of criteria for sophisticated work in general:

> Shows a sophisticated understanding of the subject matter involved. Concepts, evidence, arguments, qualifications made, questions posed, and/or methods used are expert, going well beyond the grasp of the subject typically found at this level of experience. Grasps the essence of the problem and applies the most powerful insights and tools for solving it. Work shows that the student is able to make subtle and insightful distinctions, and to go beyond the problem/situation to relate the particular challenge to more significant or comprehensive principles and/or models of analysis.

Underneath this deliberately content-free descriptor we can then use highly contextualized bulleted points as indicators—for example, bullets that relate to a seventh grade math task involving building containers:

## Figure 5.8 Assessing for Contextual Realism and Authenticity

| | Authenticity | | |
|---|---|---|---|
| *Context* | *Low* | *Medium* | *High* |
| **Situation** | | | |
| Setting | "Neat and clean"—a decontextualized task found only in schools<br><br>• An "item"— a simplistic drill test | A realistic intellectual challenge, somewhat simplified contextually, but in which performer still must size up and negotiate complex agendas, people<br><br>• A dress rehearsal or scrimmage | Embedded and messy<br><br>• The "doing" of the subject in a rich context, requiring a repertoire and good judgment— tactful and effective understanding |
| Control | No control over resources, negotiation of ends and means. No ability to personalize task<br><br>• A "secure" test | Some ability to modify or personalize task; some control over resources; ability to work with others | Apt control over situation<br><br>• Full access to people and resources, ability to negotiate ends and means |
| **Purpose** | | | |
| Impact | No intrinsic purpose: a school task, judged for form and content | A simulated problem with a simulated need/client | A real challenge—with real consequences to success or failure |
| Audience | No real audience or client | A simulated audience or client | A real audience or client |
| **Noise** | | | |
| Inherent Distractions | No distractions or conflicts built into the task | Some minor distractions built into the task | Distractions inherent in situation, impeding successful performance<br><br>• Such as hostility, anxiety |
| Feedback quality and availability | No helpful feedback permitted | Inadequate feedback available while performing | Ongoing feedback available during performance |
| **Incentives** | | | |
| Intrinsic incentive | No intrinsic incentive | Some intrinsic incentive (such as closure to a puzzle) | Intrinsic incentives related to the task and purpose |
| Extrinsic incentive | A teacher grade | Some consequence of value beyond grade | Significant consequences to success or failure |

- Student uses algebraic or calculus tools to judge the maximum volume and minimum surface area.
- The work grounds empirical investigations in a theoretical framework.
- The student has considered other plausible design approaches and rejected them, with sound evidence and argument.

These indicators will naturally be different for a tenth grade task on the causes of the Civil War. But the general paragraph for each score point stays the same for each general performance criterion across all teachers and programs, giving students the stable frame of reference they need to understand their obligations and master all their work. This is a vital form of standardization, with important room for personalization.

The specifications have now been set. With clear standards and criteria established for assessment building, we now have a better sense of the kinds of tasks, quizzes, and so on that we need to design and the likelihood that no single test—be it authentic or inauthentic—will be sufficient to reveal mastery of the standards and criteria. We now turn to the next phase of the design process—working within the constraints of the standards and criteria established to design for the evidence we need by developing tasks, rubrics, supplementary quizzes, tests, and thought-provoking, engaging, and educative work.

## CHAPTER 6

# Individual Performance Tasks

It is part of the core premise of this book that tests should teach, not just measure. The logic of assessment design assumes that we need to focus reform on worthy and complete achievement targets—enduring knowledge and competence—and that we must anchor our assessments in worthy, authentic performance problems, tasks, and projects that point toward those targets. Our assessments must be concrete manifestations of our intellectual values and goals. These are the kinds of worthy work we expect students to do well. These are the challenges that best exemplify our values and goals. These are the kinds of assessments that best link schools to the wider world of adult performance.

Just as there are standards for the assessment system in general, it is wise and useful for self-assessment and peer review to have design standards for performance tasks.

Performance tasks should be

- *Authentic:* as much as possible, they should address realistic problems, and they should have realistic options, constraints, criteria, and standards, a realistic audience, and a genuine purpose.

- *Credible:* they should be valid and reliable, and they should address rigorous content and performance standards.

- *User-friendly:* they should be feasible, appropriate (given the experience and age of students), enticing and engaging, and rich in feedback; they should have rehearsal and revision built in; they should provide a clear and complete set of instructions, guidelines, and models; and troubleshooting should be available.

Some cautions are in order, however, because authentic assessment has become synonymous in the minds of many with alternative or performance assessment. But tasks can be performance-based without being authentic. Some so-called alternative assessments look an awful lot like traditional test items minus multiple choice and therefore do not even qualify as performance (even if the test maker tries to score some marketing points by calling it a performance assessment). Validity issues complicate things further. Authenticity and validity do not automatically accompany each other. Many educators do not seem to understand that an inauthentic test can nonetheless be valid. The opposite can also be true. Designers therefore should keep the following points in mind if we are to avoid confusion and mere political correctness in reform:

1. *Just because it is a performance task does not mean that it is authentic.* Not all performance tasks are authentic. If students are constrained in unrealistic ways (for example, if students have no access to their own notes and materials) or if there is no guiding purpose in the situation by which performance is focused and adjusted (for example, if the need is merely to please the teacher rather than to stimulate an audience), then the task is inauthentic—even if complex performance genres (such as speaking or writing) are involved.

2. *Just because the task involves hands-on work does not mean that it is authentic.* For example, many science labs involve performance but are not authentic in that they do not involve the methods and procedures of scientific investigation. On the contrary, in many so-called labs, the procedures are given by the text or the teacher, and the answers are already known. The labs amount to practice in the use of equipment and procedures—a hands-on lesson—which is something far different from the test of a design into problematic or unknown matters. Similar cases exist in speeches to the class or team problem solving in which the process and content are given.

3. *Just because it is a constructed-response task does not mean that it is authentic or even a performance task.* Performance or production requires the student to plan and execute a new work from scratch and to use good judgment in choosing apt content and shaping a quality product—a "synthesis" leading to a "unique" creation by the student, in the words of Bloom's Taxonomy. Some constructed-response tasks do not even qualify as performance tasks in this technical or any commonsense use of the term. When what is wanted is really a right answer to a nonproblematic question in sentence or

paragraph form, no genuine performance is at stake, much less an authentic adult one.

In this book, I am thus reserving the word *authentic* for assessment tasks that closely simulate or actually replicate challenges faced by adults or professionals. The set of such tasks is small—much smaller, for example, than the set of all possible academic problems, questions, or tests. Authentic tasks are a subset of performance tasks.

4. *Because a task is authentic, it does not follow that it is valid.* Validity in testing entails the ability to make an inference about performance based on an apt sample of work (just as the Gallup poll samples only a few opinions over the phone to predict national voting performance). Tests are valid if we can infer real performance results for specific standards from test results. Many authentic tasks make this difficult because there are so many simultaneous variables at work. Maybe the student's excellent performance was due more to native intelligence than to mastery of the content—control over the latter being the reason the task was designed.

In fact, many authentic challenges make poor assessment tools, because they do not permit easy isolation of performance into the most salient discrete elements, nor do they allow comparability through standardization.

Equally important to recognize is that validity is not absolute: strictly speaking, it is not the task but the link between the task and a specific standard that is valid or invalid. A highly authentic task can be valid in terms of one standard but invalid in terms of another. The Civil War diorama is highly authentic and valid for students working for a Civil War museum or for students whose knowledge of a particular battle is being assessed. However, as discussed in Chapter Three, the results from that task do not yield valid inferences about whether students have reached the particular achievement target of "understanding the Civil War."

Further, many educators are guilty of a conceptual mistake when they define standardized tests as the opposite of performance assessment. Standardized is *not* synonymous with multiple choice. A test is standardized when the conditions under which it is given and scored are uniform across test takers, such as the New York State hands-on science test for fourth graders or the writing tests in many states. Many inauthentic tasks are not only valid but are excellent pedagogically, such as the best essay prompts or math problem sets.

5. *Just because a task is inauthentic does not mean it is invalid.* This notion naturally follows from the previous points. It may well be that even a highly simplistic test correlates with results we care about. The test items can be very inauthentic, yet they may yield valid results, because their sampling is made accurate through

correlation to credible results. For example, the Advanced Placement exam in U.S. history is built on a number of inauthentic constraints: no access to the students' own research, no access to libraries, no ability to talk with other researchers, and so on. Yet the results of the Advanced Placement history test correlate well with students' history performance in college. Similarly, conventional drill tests that ask for knowledge or skill out of context and give us an idea of breadth of knowledge and skill are inauthentic but may be vital complements to performance tasks in painting a useful and full picture. (This suggests why we should not look to state departments of education to develop an array of authentic tasks and portfolio requirements; authentic tasks are not needed for accountability testing, and indirect testing is less intrusive and more cost-effective.)

There is an irony in these points taken together. For what they reveal is that from an assessment perspective, authenticity is not required to meet most educational aims as currently framed. Many of the current state and district standards can be met by tests that mix open-ended performance prompts and multiple-choice questions, all of which lack authenticity. For example, the Regents exams in New York have mixed selected-response and constructed-response prompts for decades; so, too, have the SAT2 tests for college admissions. And both yield valid results in the narrow sense of correlating with grades in school and college. The importance of genuinely authentic tests of performance stems from their educative power, their instructional necessity.

In an educative assessment system, students (and teachers) come to learn two important things from authentic and valid assessment tasks, projects, and problems: (1) what (enticingly) "big people" really do—in the same way that burgeoning athletes and artists have constantly put before themselves tests that replicate the challenges facing working athletes and artists; and (2) why lessons and traditional tests can be meaningful—how they lead to mastery of more complex and interesting performance tasks. Just as the basketball player or flutist endures the drudgery in shooting endless three-pointers or playing scales with dreams of having it pay off in performance, so too must students come to see, to experience, that testing and teaching pay off in better performance. And if we and our students do not sense that work and assessment are routinely paying off, then we must conclude that our teaching and testing methods are not working. The sample performance tasks presented in Figure 6.1—from Center on Learning, Assessment, and School Structure (CLASS) work in progress—suggest this fact.

We might even qualify the term *authentic task* further for educational benefit. We might coin the term *touchstone task* to signify those

Figure 6.1 Sample Performance Tasks

| | |
|---|---|
| *Towering Trees.* | How can the tech crew backstage best meet scenery needs? Students must determine a linear function relating height and another appropriate variable to construct trees for a stage production. Using that equation, the students must use the most appropriate and cost-effective size of plywood to construct props for the Summer Theater Arts Guild productions. The students must support their findings in an oral presentation and written report to their boss using apt graphics and other support material. |
| *Troubled Waters— Headline News.* | "CONFLICT ON THE COAST—FRIENDLY RIVER BECOMES DEADLY. Major fish kills.... 100,000 fish wash ashore; child returns from swim with hives; seafood harvest plummets; and scientist discovers fish-killing invader!" What is the problem? In this task, students take on the role of the "Riverkeeper," whose job is to maintain healthy rivers. Students will analyze data gathered along the Anywhere River, pinpoint pollution hotspots, and research to determine potential sources. Two letters will be drafted: (1) an informative letter to fishermen, and (2) a letter to an agency, convincing them to address this situation. |
| *True Concessions.* | Students will use data from the previous two years to decide on an amount of food to order for this year's concession stand at the local football stadium. A list of food and amounts of each must be generated and accompanied by a written justification, based on surveys and statistical analysis. |
| *What a Find.* | The student is a professor of literature at a local college. A friend is on the board of the local library, which was just burned. All the records about the library's history were destroyed. In the ruins, the original cornerstone was found. Inside the cornerstone is a collection of literature. The friend feels confident that this collection will be key in determining when the original library was built. The friend asks that the professor identify when the literature was written. In addition, the cornerstone is to be reused in the reconstructed library. The student is asked to suggest a collection of literature to be placed in the cornerstone that best reflects the late twentieth century in American history and letters. |

particular performance challenges or problems that induct the student into or point to the essence of the discipline or subject matter proper. Such touchstone tasks might be said to include doing oral histories and working with primary source documents in history, building a mathematical model of complex phenomena needing analysis, writing successfully for a real audience, communicating effectively to native speakers of a foreign language who speak no English, designing and debugging an original science experiment, and exhibiting original art in a gallery. To generalize: a touchstone task represents those key challenges that are central to the life of the person in a field. We would use these tasks to assess students for the same reasons that professional soccer players and actors are "tested" in their performance skills. This is the heart of the matter, irrespective of the measurement messiness or logistical awkwardness that might arise. In Chapter Nine, where the curricular implications of educative assessment are explored, these issues are analyzed further.

Jerome Bruner is well known among the first modern educators to have brooded on the problem of authenticity in education. He spearheaded a curriculum-reform movement in the 1960s that had as its premise the ideas that "doing" the subject should be the essence of instructional work and that the objective of any curriculum should be "to make the subject your own, to make it part of your thinking."[1] What was less well understood at the time was that Bruner's view required one more careful distinction—the distinction between competence and performance. The goal of school is not to master a fixed set of performances; rather, the goal is intelligence or "intelligent adjustment" in all major fields. Competence is not obtained by training in specific tasks alone. Bruner argued that "what seems at work in a good problem-solving 'performance' is some underlying competence . . . and the performance that emerges from this competence may never be the same on any two occasions. What is learned is competence, not particular performances. Any particular performance, moreover, may become 'stuck' or overdetermined."[2] Bruner was arguing here against the Behaviorists who believed that all learning was reducible to discrete reinforced lessons.

Advocates of mastery learning and performance testing would do well to heed this caution, because in too many current schemes the meeting of standards becomes *de facto* the mastery of a list of tasks. But mastery of tasks is not the same as expertise. The sum of the drills is not performance, and mastery of a few particular performances does not an expert make. Thinking of a favorite sports athlete or team can help us realize that even at the professional level, consistency of excellence at all phases of the game against all opponents is a rare occurrence. Expertise involves the capacity to read situations, respond accordingly to each, and constantly achieve good results. As I pointed out in Chapter Four, this requires good judgment combined with understanding and skill. Such judgment involves, in part, deciding which performance to engage in, why it is called for, how to manage that performance, and how to adjust performance in light of results or requirements. The practical implications are that many tasks are necessitated by different contexts and that more tasks should require the student to modify the task, materials, and situation as needed.

Even if a particular complex performance revealed a student's competence at tasks of a particular type, there might still be a measurement problem—what psychometricians refer to as *generalizability*. A single task in a single genre, no matter how rigorous and complex, is still likely to be a limited slice of the overall domain of the subject. This is obvious in writing, and writing has a very limited domain of content; excellence in poetry does not transfer to essays and vice versa. This is why a portfolio of diverse evidence is typically required to assess for the most important and complex educational standards. Feasibility and efficiency rule out the constant use of complex performance tasks for all assessments, even if in an instructional sense it might be justifiable. As noted, design is always about trade-offs.

## Developing Task-Related Criteria

Having specified the task particulars, the next step is to develop task-specific criteria and indicators to serve as the basis for rubrics. Take the example of one of the tasks mentioned in Figure 6.1, Troubled Waters. Having built a task that meets both content and competency standards for the state syllabus in biology, we are now prepared to link the general criteria of "informative, accurate, and persuasive" to the work of this task. As described in Chapter Five, we can add bulleted indicators to the general descriptors for each criterion that suits this task. Thus, under *informative* we can discuss the particular qualities we seek in the two different letters that have to be written as part of the task requirements. Similarly, we can specify just what we mean by "accurate" data in this context (given the data tables developed and researched as part of the task).

## Constructing Rubrics

Having identified the criteria and indicators appropriate to both the task and the achievement target, the next step is to develop full-fledged rubrics that describe performance along an excellent-to-poor continuum. Decisions about how many rubrics to devise and how big the scoring scale should be are made while keeping in mind need and time constraints. Rubric construction is discussed at length in Chapter Seven.

## Adapting Instructional Activities as Assessment Tasks

As noted elsewhere, teachers often think of turning instructional activities into assessment tasks. The constant caution about the invalidity of many activities should not be construed as a blanket condemnation of their use. With modifications, sometimes minor, a favored activity can be adapted for assessment—if we are clear on what we want and need to assess, and know precisely how the activity does or does not assess for it in its current form. The flow-chart in Figure 6.2 illustrates this process in the light of the logic of assessment design presented in Chapter Five (see Figure 5.3). This particular process, one of many assessment design processes, assumes that a teacher designing an assessment has an educative activity worth adapting as an assessment task. The flowchart walks the designer through a series of questions and criteria that refer back to the logic but that suit this particular process. Once again, the logic is the test to which a design is put. (For an example of how such thinking and peer review can lead to a happy result, refer back to the description on page 33 in Chapter Two of the Russian history debate that was transformed into a sound assessment.)

## Task Template, Peer Assessment, and Self-Assessment

At CLASS, once we familiarize our clients with the logic presented in Chapter Five, we teach them to design assessments toward and through a task template. Figure 6.3 provides a sample of a completed task template that reflects the different logical elements of assessment design for an eighth grade mathematics task described in Figure 2.3 in Chapter Two. The template serves two functions. First, it teaches the criteria for a good assessment task and illustrates what good tasks look like, so it can be used as a model of an assessment design and task that meet design standards. Second, it illustrates the structure that could be used to set up a searchable district database in which district teachers could find tasks they could use or modify as needed. Why needlessly reinvent the wheel in each classroom? At CLASS we have made our template available at our World Wide Web site, and readers are invited to go to www.classnj.org to see for themselves how such a system could work.

To self-assess and self-adjust as they design assessments and performance tasks and projects, teachers need feedback. Figure 6.4 is a rating criteria checklist that teachers can use to get peer reviews of their assessment designs, and Figure 6.5 is a self-assessment checklist.

# Figure 6.2 Process for Adapting an Activity for Assessment

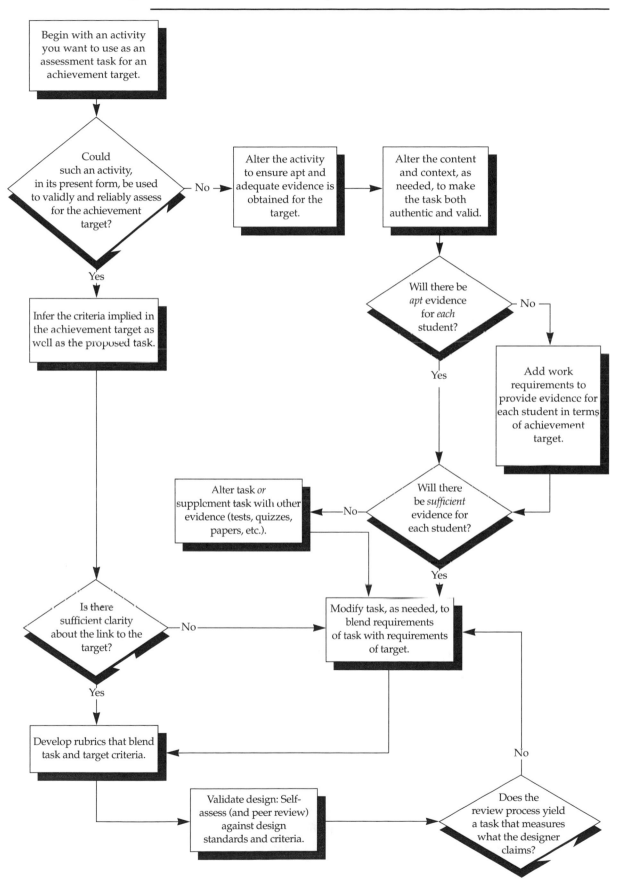

Figure 6.3  Sample Performance Task Template

| | |
|---|---|
| Task Designer(s): | North Carolina Design Team |
| School/District/Organization: | |
| Unit/Course Title/Grade Level: | U.S. History |

*Your task:*

You are a research assistant to a United States Supreme Court Justice. A case involving questions about possible Constitutional violations has come before the Court.

Federal legislation has been passed requiring states to make passage of a drug test by any teenager a precondition for getting a driver's license. If states do not enact this requirement, they will lose all federal funding for highways. A nineteen-year-old teenager refused to take the drug test. When the state denied the driver's license, the teenager brought suit, charging that the action violated the rights or protections guaranteed by the Constitution.

The case has worked its way up to the United States Supreme Court. The national media has focused on this case at each level of appeal. Keenly sensitive to the issues involved, the Justice you work for has assigned you the responsibility of preparing a bench brief.

A bench brief includes the following components:

- Identification of the issues in this case. The issues you will deal with are 1. due process (equal protection under the law), 2. state's rights, and 3. unreasonable search and seizure.
- For each issue, the relevant facts in this case.
- For each issue, the relevant parts of the law.
- The case law (as revealed in the attached court decisions).
- A clear statement of which precedents support the teenage plaintiff's position and which support the state and federal governments' actions, and why.

The Justice has told you that your brief must be *informative, clear,* and *justifiable.* By justifiable, the Justice means that the information in the brief must be *accurate, focused,* and *relevant.*

*Achievement Target(s):*

    Performance competencies:                 Content standard(s):
        Processing information                  U.S. Constitution, Bill of Rights
        Problem solving
        Communication

*Criteria to Be Used in Assessing Performance:*

    Impact:                           Work quality:
        Informative                      Clear
    Content:
        Justifiable (accurate, focused,
        relevant, supported)

*Mode(s) and Genre(s):*

    Written report

*Rubric to Be Used:* (check one from each list)

| | | |
|---|---|---|
| ❐ Holistic | ❐ Task specific | ❐ Event |
| ☑ Multiple (analytical trait) | ❐ Genre specific | ❐ Longitudinal |
| | ❐ Generic (mode specific) | |

### Figure 6.3 Continued

*Feedback to Be Given to Students:*

- ☑ Score(s)
- ☑ Rubrics to explain scores
- ☑ Models, samples

- ☑ Personalized written account(s)
- ☐ Personalized oral comment(s)
- ☐ Other_____

*Performance Standard: Justification/Validation*

- ☐ National, state, or regional exemplars/samples
- ☐ Local exemplars/anchors used
- ☐ Equated with credible external standard
- ☑ Validated by expert outsiders
- ☑ Validated through internal peer review
- ☐ Other_____

*Person(s) Assessing Product/Performance:*

*Task Title:* "Clear Justice"

*A Brief Task Description:*

   (focusing on what students must do and the performance/product(s) that will result)

The students are asked to write a bench brief for a Supreme Court Justice, reviewing case law in an important Constitutional law case.

The requirements of successful performance:

1. Each student will examine and read court decisions that deal with the issues of due process (equal protection under the law), state's rights, and unreasonable search and seizure.
2. Each student will prepare a bench brief (summary) of the case law and indicate which precedents support which side of the arguments in the case.

*Evidence to Be Collected to Ensure Reliability and Validity of Assessment:*

   (quizzes, observations, logs, notes, etc.)

1. All students will receive a copy of the task assignment within one week of the introduction of the unit of instruction. They may keep the assignment.
2. All writing will take place in school. Students may talk about the assignment at home and in school, but all writing will be done independently and in school.
3. Students may word process their reports, although this is not required. All students may use a dictionary and a thesaurus. The rule of thumb is, if research assistants would use the strategy or tool, the students may. The students should not, however, be reminded that they can or should use any specific tool or strategy.
4. The task may *not* be modified in any way.
5. The teachers must remember that during the completion of this task, they are assessors, not instructors/coaches. What you are interested in is finding out what the students can do independently.

*Performance Task Administrator Guidelines*

Curricular Context:

   (prior lessons/units, the content and skills that have been taught and practiced)

As a focusing unit in a study of the Bill of Rights

### Figure 6.3 Continued

*Resources Required by Students for Successful Task Performance:*

Supreme Court decisions          Bench briefs          Bill of Rights

*Approximate Number of Days Required for Task:*     1 week

*Guidelines on How Best to Use the Time Allotted:*

*Task Background:*

☑ Known in advance     ☐ One-day in-class only     ☐ Standardized: district

☐ Secure     ☐ Multiday in-class only     ☐ Standardized: school

☑ In and out of class     ☑ Standardized: classroom

☐ Student able to modify task, methods, media

*Protocol* (dos and don'ts to ensure fairness, validity, and reliability):

1. Allow team research but require individual writing.

*Key Trouble Spots and Troubleshooting Tips:*

1. Students must be taught an understanding of relevant parts of the Constitution. They0

must be taught how to read and interpret Court decisions. They must understand the concepts of case law and precedent.

2. Students must be taught the meaning of the criteria: informative, clear, and justifiable.

3. Students need to be taught the skill of self-assessing and adjusting the quality of their work based on the criteria that defines excellence in this assessment.

4. Students should be given the opportunity to practice, at least orally, the construction of a bench brief as it would be done regarding court cases they have already studied.

*Other Grade Levels, Courses, Programs Where Task Might Be Used, with Minor Modifications:*

*Information Regarding Task Piloting:*
(course, grade level, number of students, date(s) of pilot)

Piloted in five North Carolina districts in spring of 1996.

*Source:* Center on Learning, Assessment, and School Structure, ©1996.

### Figure 6.4 Assessment Design Rating Checklist for Peer Review

*Check the appropriate box, then circle your rating for each of the three criteria.*

*Credible*           OVERALL RATING:   1    2    3    4

❐ Yes   ❐ No    Does it measure what it says it measures? Is this a valid assessment of the targeted achievement?

❐ Yes   ❐ No    Are the scoring criteria and rubrics clear, descriptive, and explicitly related to district goals and standards?

❐ Yes   ❐ No    Is the scoring system based on genuine standards and criteria, derived from analysis of credible models?

❐ Yes   ❐ No    Does the task require a sophisticated understanding of required content?

❐ Yes   ❐ No    Does the task require a high degree of intellectual skill and performance quality?

❐ Yes   ❐ No    Does the task simulate authentic, real-world challenges, contexts, and constraints faced by adult professionals, consumers, or citizens?

❐ Yes   ❐ No    Does the scoring system enable a reliable yet adequately fine discrimination of degree of quality?

*Instructionally Worthy*     OVERALL RATING:   1    2    3    4

❐ Yes   ❐ No    Does the task require learnings at the heart of the curriculum?

❐ Yes   ❐ No    Is the task worthy of the time and energy required to complete it well?

❐ Yes   ❐ No    Is the task challenging—an apt "stretch" for students?

❐ Yes   ❐ No    Will the feedback to students en route enable them to self-assess and self-adjust?

❐ Yes   ❐ No    Will the students likely be able to verify resultant scores and use feedback to improve later performance?

*User Friendly*        OVERALL RATING:   1    2    3    4

❐ Yes   ❐ No    Is the task an engaging one for students?

❐ Yes   ❐ No    Does the task permit an *appropriate* latitude in style and approach necessary for the student to display her/his own strength?

❐ Yes   ❐ No    Are the directions to the student and teacher clear and thorough but concise?

❐ Yes   ❐ No    Are the responsibilities of the student/teacher/assessor self-evident and well integrated?

❐ Yes   ❐ No    Will teachers likely gain useful feedback about instruction from the overall results?

*Source:* Center on Learning, Assessment, and School Structure, ©1996.

### Figure 6.5 Assessment Design Self-Assessment Checklist

*Apply this checklist to the task you designed.*

❑    It is clear which desired achievements are being measured.

❑    The criteria and indicators are the right ones for this task and for the achievement being assessed.

❑    Content standards are addressed explicitly in the design: successful task performance requires mastery of the content standards.

❑    The genre(s) of performance/production are important and appropriate for the achievements being assessed.

❑    Standards have been established that go beyond the local norms of the school to credible outside standards, or have been established by internal or external oversight.

❑    The students will have ample and appropriate guidelines for understanding their performance obligations.

❑    The task will provide the students and teachers with ample feedback for self-assessment and self-adjustment both during and after its completion.

*Source:* Center on Learning, Assessment, and School Structure, ©1996.

## CHAPTER 7

# Scoring Rubrics

One of the most basic tools in the performance assessor's kit is the rubric.[1] It tells potential performers and judges just what elements of performance matter most and how the work to be judged will be distinguished in terms of relative quality.

Questions abound among educators about rubric design and use. The previous chapters have given some examples of appropriate rubrics for various assessment tasks and have suggested that the central role of sound rubrics in assessment is improvement of performance through performer self-adjustment. This chapter delves further into such questions as

Should rubrics be generic or task specific? Holistic (focused on an overall impression) or trait-analytic (focused on a single criterion)?

To whom are rubrics addressed—the novice performer or the veteran judge?

Can a rubric yield reliable scoring without yielding valid inferences?

Does a rubric stifle creativity even as it helps the student know what is wanted?

How does an assessor go about constructing a rubric?

## What Is a Rubric?

The word *rubric* derives from *ruber*, the Latin word for red. In medieval times a rubric was a set of instructions or a commentary attached to a law or liturgical service and typically written in red. Thus *rubric* came to mean something that authoritatively instructs people.

In student assessment, a rubric is a set of scoring guidelines for evaluating students' work. Rubrics answer the following questions:

By what criteria should performance be judged?

Where should we look and what should we look for to judge performance success?

What does the range in the quality of performance look like?

How do we determine validly, reliably, and fairly what score should be given and what that score means?

How should the different levels of quality be described and distinguished from one another?

Typically, a rubric contains a *scale* of possible points to be assigned in scoring work on a continuum of quality. High numbers usually are assigned to the best performances. Scales typically use 4, 5, or 6 as the top score, and 1 or 0 as the lowest score.

A rubric provides *descriptors* for each level of performance, to enable more reliable and unbiased scoring. Sometimes *indicators* are used in or under a descriptor to provide examples or concrete telltale signs of each level, as noted in Chapter Five. Because descriptors contain criteria and also often refer to standards, a good rubric makes possible valid and reliable—that is, criterion-referenced—discrimination of performances. Figure 7.1 illustrates the use of criteria, descriptors, and indicators in a rubric for assessing a high school senior essay.[2]

The criteria are the conditions that any performance must meet to be successful; they define what meeting the task requirements means. For an intellectual task such as "effectively listen," for example, we perhaps decide on two criteria: comprehend (or take apt steps to comprehend) the message, and make the speaker feel heard. Citing indicators, or specific behaviors that indicate whether or not the criteria have been met, would give more specific guidance. Indicators that a student has taken steps to comprehend what they've heard, for example, include taking notes, asking apt questions, paraphrasing the message, looking attentive, and so on.

The reason that we do not build rubrics out of indicators, which may look more concrete and helpful to students and judges alike, is that indicators are not infallible. Criteria *must* be met for success;

Figure 7.1  Rubric for Heritage High School, Littleton, Colorado, Senior Essay

9–8   The upper-range responses satisfy the following criteria:

    a.  *Summary.* <u>The summary should identify the main idea</u> [of the reading].

    b.  *Focus of agreement.* Agreement and/or disagreement may be complete or partial but <u>writer must make clear what he/she is agreeing/disagreeing with</u>. Specifically, 9–8 papers must address author's thesis, not substance abuse in general.

    c.  *Support for agreement/disagreement.* Support should provide an analysis of argument and/or relevant and concrete examples.

    d.  *Style and coherence.* These papers demonstrate clear style, overall organization, and consecutiveness of thought. They contain few repeated errors in usage, grammar, or mechanics.

    [The four phrases in italics represent the dimensions being scored. Two of the criteria are underlined.]

7   This grade is used for papers that fulfill basic requirements for the 9–8 grade but have less development, support, or analysis.

6–5   Middle range papers omit or are deficient in one of these four criteria:

    a.  *Summary.* Summary is absent or incomplete, listing only author's thesis.

    b.  *Focus of agreement/disagreement.* What the writer is agreeing/disagreeing with is not clear or is unrelated to author's proposals. Example: writer doesn't use enough phrasing like "on the one hand . . . on the other hand . . ." [an indicator].

    c.  *Support.* Writer only counterasserts; examples are highly generalized or not distinguishable from examples in the article. Analysis may be specious, irrelevant, or thin.

    d.  *Style and coherence.* These papers are loosely organized or contain noticeable errors in usage, grammar, or mechanics.

4   This grade is used for papers that are slightly weaker than the 6–5 papers. Also, a student who writes his/her own parallel essay in a competent style should receive a 4.

3–2   These papers are deficient in *two* or more of the criteria. Typically they weakly paraphrase the article *or* they have serious organization/coherence problems. Papers with serious, repeated errors in usage, grammar, or mechanics must be placed in this range. [This whole paragraph, like all the previous ones, is a descriptor for this point on the scale.]

indicators are helpful, but a student might meet the criteria without meeting the particular indicators described. An indicator tells assessors where they might look and what to look for in judging successful performance. But no indicator is 100 percent reliable. For example, the apparently attentive student listener may not be trying hard to understand what is being said, while the student who looks away from the speaker and does not take notes may nonetheless be listening intently.

Many rubrics make the mistake of relying on indicators that are easy to see but unreliable. We must be careful to ensure that the criteria we choose are *necessary* and, as a set, *sufficient* for meeting the targeted achievement. Educators' first attempts at rubrics often overlook the more difficult-to-see but more valid ways of measuring the achievement.

## Rubrics and Standards

A rubric also depends on standards. A standard specifies how well criteria must be met. For example, a standard for the high jump specifies precisely how high that jump must be to be considered excellent. How well did the student succeed in meeting the criterion of clearing the bar? That is the standards question. Merely getting over the bar—the criterion—is not enough if the bar is very low and the student wants to jump competitively. A high jump standard is typically established in terms of specific heights that either need to be jumped to qualify for a championship or have been jumped by the best jumpers in the past; thus the standard is based on patterns of actual performance and instances of exemplary performance.

## Absolute Standards and Developmental Standards

As noted in the Chapter Five discussion on task design logic, performance standards are set once the achievement target is clear and appropriate criteria have been established in relation to that target. Criteria are *inferred* from the goal, but standards are *selected* to represent excellence in performance, using appropriate exemplary performances or specifications.

The high jump example illustrates only a yes/no assessment system. Cooking supplies an example that is still simple but closer to the multiple levels of academic assessment. Criteria for making pasta primavera, for example, will probably relate to things like good taste and appearance, but we might decide that healthfulness in the form of fat and cholesterol content matters, too. From these three criteria—taste, appearance, and healthfulness—we could develop three separate rubrics for judging the pasta dish. Now suppose the spaghetti and vegetables are neatly piled on a plate (good appearance) and partially covered by a circle of low-fat but tasty sauce (healthy and good tasting). We have met the criteria.

Suppose further that our dish has met the "local" standards of our spouse and children. But perhaps these local standards are not high enough. How would a restaurateur judge the dish? Or a restaurant critic? The critic rightfully will use more demanding standards for judging the three criteria than will most families judging a parent's cooking. When the spaghetti is cooked but not really al dente, when the presentation is neat but not exceptionally interesting, and so on, the dish may meet or even exceed family expectations but be deemed totally unsatisfactory in a four-star restaurant. The relative importance of each criterion might also change when we shift *contexts* from family dinner to restaurant meal: appearance matters greatly in a good restaurant but is less important at a family meal.

Now consider a writing assessment. The criteria to be met typically involve clear prose, effective voice, insightful analysis, and the like, and there are concrete indicators for these criteria, such as no jargon, vivid images and analogies, minimal use of the passive voice, and so on. However, as in the spaghetti example, there are also degrees of meeting these criteria. Students meet or fail to meet the criteria on a continuum or scale from fully to incompletely. The differences in their achievements constitute different levels of performance, the points on the scale. These levels of performance can be judged against two kinds of standards and against expectations.

*Absolute standards* (the kind I have been focusing on so far, such as models and exemplars) are established de facto through the description of the top score on the rubric and therefore through the specific work samples chosen to anchor the rubric to an excellent or best standard. We typically need to qualify the absolute standards to arrive at another set of standards that deal with *developmental* realities. Thus, in athletics, in addition to the best performance models that everyone looks to, there are standards for the Olympics, for college, for high school varsity and junior varsity, and so on. Each of these latter standards notes what excellent performance is for the *best* of the cohort. The standard for a high school track meet, for example, based on current patterns of performance, is that a high jumper needs to clear well over six feet to be considered excellent.

An *expectation* is another matter. Instead of looking at the best of the cohort, it looks at the pattern of overall past performance of an individual or group—that is, the norms. A student might be *expected* to jump five feet or more or to write a 4-level paper or better because historically people of his or her level of experience and ability have done so.

Results that refer to norms and expectations differ in significance from results that refer to standards and criteria. *Students can exceed norms and expectations but still not perform up to standard.* For example, students in the 89th percentile on a norm-referenced test can be said to have performed poorly as judged against a standard. This is why many educators mistrust norm-referenced testing: it hides how students and teachers are doing when judged against worthy standards.

It is critical to remain aware of the differences between these terms, not only in order to design effective assessment tasks and rubrics, but also to make feedback as clear as possible. We need to know when we are talking about the best models or standards, when we are talking about developmental standards, and when we are talking about expectations. When we say "up to standard" do we mean "acceptable" or "exemplary" at a particular grade or cohort level? Are we also looking at developmental standards across grades or cohorts so we can assess students' progress from novice to expert? In writing, for example, there are world-class professional standards set by published authors, there are exit-level high school standards (including minimum standards of acceptability), and there are grade-level standards. In each case, no matter how small or large the frame of reference, the absolute standard is set by the best performances—the exemplars. This may be easier to see when we look at standards set by specifications. For example, "zero defects per million parts" is an engineering standard that perhaps is never met, but it is still the goal. The best current performance, the exemplar, in the automobile industry is approximately six defects per million.

Absolute standards and criteria stay the same; developmental standards vary by level of experience and context. So we might say that to be judged coherent, *all* papers must meet the top criterion of "overall organization and consecutiveness of thought." Some rubrics do enable us to judge the top score as synonymous with standard-setting performance. If the top score is described as "a paper of quality suitable for publication in a journal," for example, then the standard is specified in the descriptor. In day-to-day school performance the language of rubrics is usually more ambiguous. The best papers have to be "persuasive," "organized," and "mechanically sound." But those phrases do not imply or point toward a specific standard.

That is where work samples enter the picture. The rubric is necessary but insufficient for good assessment and good feedback. To know what the rubric's language really means, both the student and the judge need to see examples of work considered persuasive or organized. Why? Because the performer's view of what it means to meet these criteria and the standard may be way off the mark.

Why do we need to sort out absolute standards, developmental standards, and expectations instead of just continuing to do what we have always done—give grades or scores based on our judgments about excellence? Because local norms and patterns are not reliable as standards. Maybe the best work a teacher typically sees from kids is mediocre when compared to work from around the region or state. So how do we ensure that local standards are valid? How can we protect the student by ensuring that high-scoring local papers—the local standards—are truly excellent? We cannot unless we can relate local standards (through samples or correlations) to regional, state, and national standards. The rubric criteria must always be met for students' work to be considered acceptable. Writing should always be organized, clear, and insightful, no matter who is doing it or in what context. But the standards question is different: when meeting these criteria, how good is good enough—not only in the local context but in other schools and in the adult workplace?

A concrete example of the difference between criteria and the different kinds of standards appears in the rubric in Figure 7.2.[3] Can you tell from its criteria whether it should be used to judge problem-solving work by calculus students or work by fifth graders using arithmetic?

As this rubric illustrates, the criteria for assessment of mathematics will remain pretty much the same across the grades, but the developmental standards and our expectations will appropriately vary. If we used sophisticated calculus papers as the only standard, then no arithmetic student is likely to get a score above 1 (not because they do not know calculus but because their problem-solving skills will likely be relatively crude and limited by comparison), even though the criterion remains the same: solve the problem with clear and appropriate logic and substantiation. Conversely, if we say that excellent fifth grade papers are the sole standard, then all but a few very incompetent or careless calculus students will get a 6 or a 5.

So we need developmental standards but we also need absolute standards to *educate students about real excellence,* just as the work of young athletes and musicians is ultimately judged against standards (models or samples) set by professionals. Even an assessment of first grade students' audiotaped reading of books may usefully employ a professional sample as the absolute standard even though we do not expect first graders to produce professional products.

The value of the anchoring of work in absolute quality and feasibility is easy to see when the rubrics are longitudinal, or developmental, and rubric criteria are blended with developmental standards, as in the sample developmental writing rubric in Figure 7.3.[4] Obviously there is no failure in being at a lower level on a developmental rubric if the student is a novice; however, if the student has years of experience but is still performing like a novice, she or he can be expected to do better. For example, it does not make sense to say that novices in Spanish I or German I must all get poor grades because they are not as fluent as students in Spanish IV or German IV. (This idea is central to the argument for not translating performance scores into letter grades, as argued in Chapter Nine.)

## Figure 7.2 Rubric for Open-Ended Mathematical Problems

|  | *Demonstrated Competence* |
| --- | --- |
| Exemplary Response:<br>Rating = 6 | Gives a complete response with a clear, coherent, unambiguous, and elegant explanation; includes a clear and simplified diagram; communicates effectively to the identified audience; shows understanding of the problem's mathematical ideas and processes; identifies all the important elements of the problem; may include examples and counterexamples; presents strong supporting arguments. |
| Competent Response:<br>Rating = 5 | Gives a fairly complete response with reasonably clear explanations; may include an appropriate diagram; communicates effectively to the identified audience; shows understanding of the problem's ideas and processes; identifies most important elements of the problem; presents solid supporting arguments. |

|  | *Satisfactory Response* |
| --- | --- |
| Minor Flaws But<br>Satisfactory:<br>Rating = 4 | Completes the problem satisfactorily, but the explanation may be muddled; argumentation may be incomplete; diagram may be inappropriate or unclear; understands the underlying mathematical ideas; uses ideas effectively. |
| Serious Flaws But<br>Nearly Satisfactory:<br>Rating = 3 | Begins the problem appropriately but may fail to complete or may omit significant parts of the problem; may fail to show full understanding of mathematical ideas and processes; may make major computational errors; may misuse or fail to use mathematical terms; response may reflect an inappropriate strategy for solving the problem. |

|  | *Inadequate Response* |
| --- | --- |
| Begins, But Fails to<br>Complete Problem:<br>Rating = 2 | Explanation is not understandable; diagram may be unclear; shows no understanding of the problem situation; may make major computational errors. |
| Unable to Begin<br>Effectively:<br>Rating = 1 | Words used do not reflect the problem; drawings misrepresent the problem situation; fails to indicate which information is appropriate. |
| No Attempt<br>Rating = 0 |  |

## Designing Rubrics

Designing a good rubric has much in common with designing a performance task, as described in Chapter Five. There is logic, and there is chronology. In the latter case, we want to know the best chronology of events in the design process; in the former case, we want to know the overall criteria against which our rubric should be evaluated and modified.

The best rubrics will follow a logic. This means that even though there is no set recipe for constructing rubrics, we need a useful

### Figure 7.3 K–12 Developmental Rubric for Levels of Writing Ability

| Level | Pupils should be able to: |
|---|---|
| 1 | Use pictures, symbols, or isolated letters, words, or phrases to communicate meaning. |
| 2 | Produce, independently, pieces of writing using complete sentences, some of them demarcated with capital letters, periods, or question marks.<br><br>Structure sequences of real or imagined events coherently in chronological accounts.<br><br>Write stories showing an understanding of the rudiments of story structure by establishing an opening, characters, and one or more events.<br><br>Produce simple, coherent, nonchronological writing. |
| 3 | Produce, independently, pieces of writing using complete sentences, mainly demarcated with capitals, periods, and question marks.<br><br>Shape chronological writing by beginning to use a wider range of sentence connectives than *and* and *then*.<br><br>Write more complex stories with detail beyond simple events and with a defined ending.<br><br>Begin to revise and redraft in consultation with the teacher or other children in the class, paying attention to meaning and clarity as well as checking for things such as correct use of tenses and pronouns. |
| 4 | Produce pieces of writing in which there is a rudimentary attempt to present subject matter in a structured way (e.g., title, paragraphs, verses), in which punctuation is generally accurate, and in which evidence exists of ability to make meaning clear to readers.<br><br>Write stories that have an opening, a setting, characters, a series of events, and a resolution.<br><br>Organize nonchronological writings in orderly ways.<br><br>Begin to use some sentence structures that are different from those most characteristic of speech (e.g., subordinate clauses).<br><br>Attempt independent revising of their own writing and talk about the changes made. |
| 5 | Write in a variety of forms (e.g., notes, letters, instructions, stories, poems), for a range of purposes (e.g., to plan, inform, explain, entertain, express attitudes or emotions).<br><br>Produce pieces of writing in which there is a more successful attempt to present simple subject matter in a structured way, e.g., by layout, headings, paragraphing; in which sentence punctuation is almost accurately used; and in which simple uses of the comma are handled successfully.<br><br>Write in standard English (except in contexts where nonstandard forms are appropriate) and show an increasing differentiation between speech and writing, e.g., by using constructions that decrease repetition.<br><br>Assemble ideas on paper... and show some ability to produce a draft from them and to redraft or revise as necessary. |

Figure 7.3 Continued

| Level | Pupils should be able to: |
|-------|---------------------------|
| 6 | Write in a variety of forms for a range of purposes, showing some ability to present subject matter differently for different specified audiences. |
| | Make use of literary stylistic features, such as alteration of word order for emphasis or the deliberate repetition of words or sentence patterns. |
| | Show some ability to recognize when planning, drafting, redrafting, and revising are appropriate and to carry these processes out. |
| 7 | Produce well-structured pieces of writing, some of which handle more demanding subject-matter, e.g., going beyond first-hand experience. |
| | Make a more assured and selective use of a wider range of grammatical and lexical features appropriate for topic and audience. |
| | Show an increased awareness that a first draft is malleable, e.g., by changing form in which writing is cast (from story to play), or by altering sentence structure and placement. |
| 8 | Write, at appropriate length, in a wide variety of forms, with assured sense of purpose and audience. |
| | Organize complex subject matter clearly and effectively. Produce well-structured pieces in which relationships between successive paragraphs are helpfully signaled. |
| | Make an assured, selective, and appropriate use of a wide range of grammatical constructions and of an extensive vocabulary. Sustain the chosen style consistently. Achieve felicitous or striking effects, showing evidence of a personal style. |

(though not rigid) method and guidelines; most important, we need criteria for constant use in judging the effectiveness of the design work that is under way. The design guidelines are like a traveler's itinerary; the criteria are like the conditions the traveler must meet to have a worthwhile journey. In educational terms, the guidelines are like the instructions given to students for doing a task, and the criteria are like a rubric given to students by the teacher for self-assessing and self-adjusting en route.

Rubrics make student self-assessment easier. But self-assessment is a means—to what end? Self-adjustment and eventual expertise. No performance can be mastered simply by following rules, itineraries, or recipes. All complex performance mastery occurs through feedback in relation to criteria and standards. The question, Did we get to our destination? is very different from asking, Did we try to have a nice trip? Learning requires ongoing feedback (through assessment and self-assessment) to ensure that the student derives from the journey the impact intended by the tour director–teacher.

Similarly, the rubric designed to score student performance needs to be designed in relation to criteria and standards, and ongoing self-assessment and self-adjustment.

In designing rubrics we need to consider the types of rubrics available to us. Rubrics may be either *holistic* or *trait-analytic*. If holistic, a rubric has only one general descriptor for performance as a whole. If analytic, it has multiple rubrics corresponding to each dimension of performance being scored. For example, we might have separate rubrics for "syntax," "focus," and "voice" in writing, and for "precision of calculations" and "understanding of scientific method" in science. Rubrics may also be generic, or they may be genre, subject, or task specific. If a rubric is generic, it judges a very broad criterion, such as "persuasive" or "accurate." If it is genre specific, it applies to a specific performance genre within the broad performance category (for example, essay, speech, or narrative, or graphs and charts). If subject specific, its criteria refer to content-related skills or knowledge (for example, oral history report or mathematical reasoning). Task-specific rubrics refer to unique or highly specific criteria derived from a particular task. Finally, a rubric may be focused on an event or it may be longitudinal. If it is focused on an event, performance is described in terms of the particulars of that task, content, and context. If it is longitudinal (or developmental), it measures progress over time toward more general mastery of educational objectives (for example, literacy or fluency); performance is assessed on a novice-expert continuum and gains are measured in terms of sophistication or level of performance over time.

How do we ensure rubric validity? How can we distinguish such things as useful behavior and guidelines from useful criteria? What should criteria contain? And how can we design rubrics for new assessment tasks?

## Ensuring Rubric Validity

Recall that validity is a matter of determining what is permissible to infer from scores. Suppose that students are given a task in story writing and the rubric for judging this task places exclusive emphasis on spelling and grammatical accuracy. The scores would likely be highly reliable—because it is easy to count such errors—but they would yield invalid inferences about students' ability to write stories effectively. It is not likely that spelling accuracy correlates with the ability to write an engaging, vivid, and coherent story, which is the intended outcome of the task; so the rubric would be measuring something accurately, but not what we wanted it to measure.

Rubric design, therefore, should consider not just the appropriateness and validity of the performance *task* (as discussed in Chapters

Two and Five) but the appropriateness and validity of the *criteria* and *descriptors for discrimination* in relation to that task. Given the valid task and the capacities on which it draws, does the rubric focus on criteria that will assess those capacities? Have the most important and revealing dimensions of performance been identified, given the criteria that are most appropriate for the achievement target?

Does the rubric provide an authentic and effective way of discriminating between levels of performance? Are the descriptors for each level of performance sufficiently grounded in actual samples of performance of different quality? These and other questions lie at the heart of valid rubric construction.

## Holistic and Analytic-Trait Rubrics

The ability to design a valid rubric thus depends a great deal on how criteria are defined. To begin with, how many criteria might be needed to describe the traits central to successful task performance? Criteria tell us what to look for in distinguishing achievement from nonachievement; traits tell us where to look.

For example, "weight" and "cholesterol count" are personal traits; "healthy weight" and "low cholesterol" are criteria for health. Criteria place a value beyond merely describing all possible manifestations of the trait: there are minimum and maximum body weight ranges for healthfulness, and there are numbers above which a person is deemed to have a dangerously high cholesterol count. (But change the criterion to "happy eating," and the value of the cholesterol trait might change.) To meet the criterion of being healthy, I must at least meet the criteria established for these two traits of my health profile. Similarly, voice, focus, organization, and mechanics are common traits assessed in writing. "Personal and vivid" might be a criterion for voice. What it takes to do well on each criterion is described by the top-level descriptor within the rubric for that criterion.

An analytic-trait rubric isolates each major trait into a separate rubric with its own criteria. The reverse, a holistic rubric, yields a single score based on an overall impression. But feasibility typically requires that analytic-trait rubrics combine different traits according to feasibility. For example, voice, organization, focus, sentence structure, word choice, coherence, content accuracy, aptness of resources and references, and persuasiveness are apt criteria for judging essays, but using ten rubrics with their accompanying criteria would overtax even the rubric devotee. For convenience's sake, the ten criteria might be collapsed into three rubrics: quality of the ideas and argument, quality of the writing, and quality of the research, for example. Or in certain instances they might be collapsed into one criterion and rubric: Was the paper persuasive (because defects in mechanics and logic will render the paper unpersuasive)? In the latter case, the diverse criteria under each of the three headings might now serve as indicators.

The holistic approach may seem simpler, but it may also compromise validity, reliability, and the quality of the feedback to the student in the name of efficiency. Go back to the dinner criteria for an example. Appearance is independent of tastefulness is independent of healthfulness, and they must each be assessed separately if we are to make valid inferences from the results. It is rare that the quality of the content, the organization, and the mechanics rise or fall together. Consider the misleading feedback that results from a holistic rubric of complex performance. Two papers are deemed equally unpersuasive, but their defects are quite different. One paper is a mess mechanically but filled with wonderful arguments. The other paper is clear but superficial and based on inaccurate facts. A holistic rubric would require the same score for both papers. In fact, however, performance criteria are often independent of one another. Validity and quality of feedback demand that we use analytic-trait scoring.

Sometimes it is unclear how to give any score in a holistic scheme. The oral assessment rubric in Figure 7.4 illustrates the problem. What should we do if a student makes great eye contact but fails to make a clear case for the importance of his or her subject? The rubric would have us believe that making contact with the audience and arguing for the importance of a topic always go together. But logic and experience suggest otherwise.

Given its track record, why should we ever bother with holistic scoring? It is quick, easy, and often reliable enough when used to assess a generic skill like writing (though not for assessing specific genres of writing, for which the criteria that should be assessed vary, appropriately, from genre to genre). Nevertheless, choosing holistic scoring over analytic-trait scoring always requires a trade-off.

Reliability is also threatened when different judges unwittingly apply different criteria as they form an impressionistic whole judgment using a vague holistic rubric. This is what happens when Johnny and Suzy both get a B for the year but for vastly different reasons: in one case, the B might be the result of inconsistent test scores; in the other, poor homework quality. Yet no one knows this but the teacher—and certainly not the reader of the student's transcript. The same teacher might give the same students different grades at different times for varying reasons or criteria. Explicit rubrics based on clear, distinct, and aptly weighted criteria, however, keep the scoring process consistent and stable—across students and across judges.

Figure 7.5 shows analytic-trait scoring that contains a set of four rubrics for assessing scientific research and problem solving.[5]

### Figure 7.4 Holistic Oral Presentation Rubric

| | |
|---|---|
| 5 – Excellent | The student clearly describes the question studied and provides strong reasons for its importance. Specific information is given to support the conclusions that are drawn and described. The delivery is engaging and sentence structure is consistently correct. Eye contact is made and sustained throughout the presentation. There is strong evidence of preparation, organization, and enthusiasm for the topic. The visual aid is used to make the presentation more effective. Questions from the audience are clearly answered with specific and appropriate information. |
| 4 – Very Good | The student describes the question studied and provides reasons for its importance. An adequate amount of information is given to support the conclusions that are drawn and described. The delivery and sentence structure are generally correct. There is evidence of preparation, organization, and enthusiasm for the topic. The visual aid is mentioned and used. Questions from the audience are answered clearly. |
| 3 – Good | The student describes the question studied and conclusions are stated, but supporting information is not as strong as a 4 or 5. The delivery and sentence structure are generally correct. There is some indication of preparation and organization. The visual aid is mentioned. Questions from the audience are answered. |
| 2 – Limited | The student states the question studied but fails to describe it fully. No conclusions are given to answer the question. The delivery and sentence structure are understandable, but with some errors. Evidence of preparation and organization is lacking. The visual aid may or may not be mentioned. Questions from the audience are answered with only the most basic response. |
| 1 – Poor | The student makes a presentation without stating the question or its importance. The topic is unclear and no adequate conclusions are stated. The delivery is difficult to follow. There is no indication of preparation or organization. Questions from the audience receive only the most basic or no response. |
| 0 | No oral presentation is attempted. |

Breaking out the traits not only makes assessment more accurate but also actually teaches students about the desired results. A parallel set of rubrics for students, in kid language, tells students about the purpose of the performance task and how the skills relate to the purpose.

## Selecting Criteria

Many rubrics focus on obvious successes or failures that may be incidental to whether the overall result or purpose was achieved. Judges of math problem solving, for example, tend to focus too much on obvious computational errors; judges of writing tend to focus too much on mechanics and not enough on the power of the writing. We do not want to score the strengths and weaknesses that are easy to see and count. We want to use criteria that relate most directly to the purpose and nature of the task.

One simple test of criteria is negative: Can you imagine someone meeting all your proposed criteria but not being able to perform well

### Figure 7.5 Analytic-Trait Rubrics for Fifth Grade Science Experiments

| *Experiment Design* | | *Scientific Results* | |
|---|---|---|---|
| 4 | Design shows student has analyzed the problem and has independently designed and conducted a thoughtful experiment. | 4 | Pamphlet explained with convincing clarity the solution to the problem. Information from other sources or other experiments was used in explaining. |
| 3 | Design shows student grasps the basic idea of the scientific process by conducting experiment that controlled obvious variables. | 3 | Pamphlet showed that student understands the results and knows how to explain them. |
| 2 | Design shows student grasps basic idea of scientific process but needs some help in controlling obvious variables. | 2 | Pamphlet showed results of experiment. Conclusions reached were incomplete or were explained only after questioning. |
| 1 | Design shows student can conduct an experiment when given considerable help by the teacher. | 1 | Pamphlet showed results of the experiment. Conclusions drawn were lacking, incomplete, or confused. |
| *Data Collection* | | *Verbal Expression* | |
| 4 | Data were collected and recorded in an orderly manner that accurately reflects the results of the experiment. | 4 | Speech presented a clearly defined point of view that can be supported by research. Audience interest was considered as were gestures, voice, and eye contact. |
| 3 | Data were recorded in a manner that probably represents the results of the experiment. | 3 | Speech was prepared with some adult help but uses experiment's result. Speech was logical and used gestures, voice, and eye contact to clarify meaning. |
| 2 | Data were recorded in a disorganized manner or only with teacher assistance. | 2 | Speech was given after active instruction from an adult. Some consideration was given to gestures, voice, and eye contact. |
| 1 | Data were recorded in an incomplete, haphazard manner or only after considerable teacher assistance. | 1 | Speech was given only after active instruction from an adult. |

*Note:* There is a parallel set of rubrics for students in "kid language" not shown here.

at the task? Then you have the wrong criteria. Formal and mechanical aspects of writing, for example, do matter; but as rubric criteria they do not get at the point of writing. What is the writer's intent? What is the purpose of any writing? It should "work," or yield a certain effect on the reader. *Huckleberry Finn* works even though the narrator's speech is ungrammatical. The real criteria for assessing writing will be found in an analysis of the answers to questions about purpose. If we are assessing analytic writing, we should presumably be assessing something like the insight, novelty, clarity, and compelling nature of the analysis. Notice that these last four dimensions implicitly contain the more formal mechanical dimensions: a paper is not likely to be compelling and thorough if it lacks organization and clarity. The descriptor for the lower levels of performance can address these matters as deficiencies that impede clarity or persuasiveness.

It is helpful here to recall that all criteria can be divided into five categories, as noted in Chapter Five. There are criteria that relate to the impact, the craftsmanship, the methods, the content, and the sophistication of the performance. But not every performance must be assessed against all five types. For example, in many performance-based assessments involving public performance (music, painting, athletics), the judges pay no attention to the methods used in preparation and training; they just judge impact. In a debate or other spontaneous performance, we might not judge craftsmanship or polish too greatly because performers have so little time to consider and polish them. And for teaching purposes we might deliberately focus on only one type of criterion if we feel that students needed practice and feedback on, say, their methods of beginning their papers, or on developing a researchable question and hypothesis. But in general, complex performance involves most or all types of criteria.

The challenge is to make sure that we have a feasible set of the right criteria, and that we have distinguished between genuine criteria and mere indicators or useful behaviors. Take speaking: many good speakers make eye contact and vary their pitch. But these are not the ultimate criteria of good speaking; they are merely useful behaviors or techniques in trying to achieve a desired effect or impact. Impact criteria themselves relate to the purpose of the speaking—namely, the desired effects of a student's speech: Was she understood? Was she engaging? Was she persuasive or moving? Whatever the student's intent, was it realized? We should say to students, "The purpose is to engage an audience. That's a criterion. And there are certain strategies, useful behaviors, that tend to work. But there may be others. The proof is in the pudding, the reaction of the audience, given your goal."

Students are too often led to think that performance is merely following recipes or rules rather than doing what has to be done to achieve a result. Current rubrics tend to overvalue specific methods and formats while undervaluing the result. That tells the student that obeying instructions is more important than succeeding.

Such rule following and its opposite—aimlessness—typically involve a failure to make the purpose of performance clear. Consider class discussion. All teachers want to improve it, yet few formally assess it. And many students fail to adequately grasp their role and goal in participating in it. What is the purpose of discussion? Whatever the teacher's answer, the aim is not merely to talk a lot and share opinions, as many students believe. The goal is collaborative and insightful inquiry into texts and ideas, a purpose that has a dilemma built into it: sometimes some participants' quest for the truth of a text is hampered by the confused and confusing ideas of others; sometimes participants lose sight of the issue of the truth of the text or the participants' contributions and get taken up only with the collaborative conversation.

Consider the assessment rubrics for the *Socratic seminar*, provided in Figure 7.6, which were developed to show how assessment devices can teach students about performance purpose and improvement. The figure presents the summary form of the rubrics; students receive an elaborated set that contains indicators for each descriptor. These rubrics tell them what different levels of performance look like so they can know how they will be assessed and so they can self-assess and improve their performance as the seminar progresses.

As the rubrics in the figure make clear, an emphasis on purpose does not obviate the need for assessment of discrete processes and behaviors. In fact, the best rubrics make clear how process and product go together and with what degree of priority by means of a weighting factor for each trait. Thus, in a Socratic seminar, we might treat "Conduct" as worth double all the other traits (especially where there is a great diversity in reading and writing ability in the class). And such weighting of criteria relative to one another can vary over time, as teacher purposes and student needs dictate. For example, in beginning archery a coach might aptly desire to score stance, technique with the bow, and accuracy. Stance matters. Conversely, the ultimate value of the performance surely relates to its accuracy. In practice that means we can justifiably score for a process, but we should not overvalue process so that it appears that results really do not matter much.

The point is that we often arbitrarily weigh processes and results equally in rubrics, distorting the results. And beyond that, we need to be aware that weighting can vary over time: accuracy may be

Figure 7.6 Rubrics for a Socratic Seminar

| | Conduct | Leadership | Reasoning | Listening | Reading |
|---|---|---|---|---|---|
| Excellent | Demonstrates respect, enthusiasm, and skill for the purpose of seminar: insight into important texts and ideas gained through the interplay of collaborative and personal inquiry into a text. Demonstrates in speech and manner a habitual respect for the text, reasoned discussion, and shared inquiry. Effectively contributes to deepening and broadening the conversation, revealing exemplary habits of mind. | Takes clear responsibility for the seminar's progress or lack of it. Takes stock of the overall direction and effectiveness of the discussion, and takes apt steps to refocus or redirect conversation and/or to cause others to rethink previous statements. Offers apt feedback and effective guidance to others. Takes steps to involve reticent participants and to ensure that unnoticed points are attended to. | Arguments are reasonable, apt, logical and substantiated with evidence from the text so as to consistently move the conversation forward and deepen the inquiry. The analyses made are helpful in clarifying complex ideas. Criticisms made are never ad hominem. | Listens unusually well. Takes steps routinely to comprehend what is said, is consistently attentive (as reflected in direct and indirect evidence). Later responses (actions, comments, and writings) indicate accurate and perceptive recall of what was said and by whom. | Conduct and written work indicate student has read the text carefully, is thoroughly familiar with the text's main ideas, can offer insightful interpretations and evaluations of it, is respectful of the text while also reading it critically, and has come prepared with thoughtful questions and reactions. |
| Good | Demonstrates in speech and manner an overall respect for and understanding of the goals, processes, and norms of reasoned discussion and shared inquiry. Participates to advance conversation and displays mature habits of mind, but may sometimes be ineffective in sharing insights, advancing inquiry, or working with others. | Is generally willing to take on facilitative roles and responsibilities. Either makes regular efforts to be helpful (in moving the conversation forward and/or including others in it) but is sometimes ineffective in doing so; or does not typically take a leadership role but is effective when does so. | Arguments are generally reasonable, apt, and logical. There may be some minor flaws in reasoning, evidence, or aptness of remarks, but the ideas contribute to an understanding of the text or of comments made by others. Criticisms are rarely ad hominem. | Listens well. Takes steps to comprehend what is said. Generally pays attention and/or responds appropriately to ideas and questions offered by other participants. Later responses involve accurate recall of what was said and by whom. | Conduct and written work generally indicate student has read the text carefully, grasps the main ideas, can offer reasonable (if sometimes incomplete or surface) interpretations, and has come with apt questions and ideas regarding the text. |

Figure 7.6 Continued

| | Conduct | Leadership | Reasoning | Listening | Reading |
|---|---|---|---|---|---|
| Fair | Speech and manner suggest that the student misunderstands the purpose of the discussion and/or is undisciplined concerning seminar practices and habits of mind. May contribute, even frequently, to conversation but is ineffective due to opinionated, unclear, and/or inadequately explicit views. | Takes on facilitative roles and responsibilities infrequently and/or ineffectively. When taking on a leadership role, may misconstrue the responsibility by lobbying for favored opinions or speakers only, and/or by trying to close off discussion of diverse and unresolved views in favor of neat-and-clean premature closure. | Unsubstantiated or undeveloped opinions are offered more than sound arguments. Comments suggest that the student has some difficulty in moving beyond mere reactions to more thorough arguments, or difficulty in following the complex arguments of others (as reflected in questions asked and/or non sequiturs). Student may sometimes resort to ad hominem attacks instead of focusing on the critique of claims and arguments. | Does not regularly listen very well and/or is not always attentive, as reflected in comments and body language. Verbal reactions reflect an earlier difficulty or failure to listen carefully to what was said. Behavior may signify either that the student lacks effective note-taking strategies and/or does not grasp the importance of listening to different points of view and reflecting on them. | Comments indicate that the student may have read the text but has either misunderstood it (due either to difficulties in reading and/or assuming a stance that is too egocentric or present-centered) or has not put enough disciplined and focused effort into preparing for the seminar. Varying patterns of participation also suggest that the student's preparation is inconsistent. |
| Unsatisfactory | Speech and manner display little respect for and/or understanding of the seminar process. Student appears to lack essential habits of mind: is either routinely argumentative, distracting, and/or obstinate, or is disengaged—extremely reluctant to participate, even when called upon (to the point of making others feel the detachment). | Plays no active facilitation role of any kind, or actions are consistently counter-productive in that role. | Comments suggest that student has great difficulty with analytical requirements of seminar. Remarks routinely appear to be non sequiturs and/or so illogical or without substantiation as to be not followable by others. Student may often resort to ad hominem comments to text author and other students. | Does not listen adequately, as reflected in later questions or comments (for example, non sequiturs and repetition of earlier points as if they hadn't been spoken) and/or body language that is very suggestive of inattentiveness. | Student either is generally unable to make adequate meaning of texts or has generally come to class unprepared. The student may be unable to read complex texts and/or may not know or use disciplined strategies for understanding and taking notes on such texts. |

worth only 25 percent when scoring a novice but 100 percent when scoring an expert in competition.

## Assessing Through Comparisons

Many rubrics also rely heavily on comparative (and evaluative) language to distinguish among performance levels. For example, a score of 6 may be given to thorough or clear or accurate work, and a 5 to work defined as less thorough, less clear, or less accurate than a 6. Reliance on comparative language stems from a failure to seek the unique features of performance in different levels of students' work. Maybe the quality of performances differ simply because one group has less of what another group has. But usually, with sufficient effort, we can find qualities, empirical descriptors, that are unique to each level of work.

More to the point of this book's main argument, that assessment should improve performance, the student is left with rather weak feedback when rubrics rely heavily on phrases like "less than a 5" or "a fairly complete performance." This is not much different than getting back a paper with a letter grade on it. Ideally a rubric will focus on discernible and useful empirical differences in performance; that way the assessment is educative, not just measurement. Too many rubrics based on comparative criteria end up as norm-referenced tests in disguise. But mere reliability of results is not enough: we want a system that can improve performance through feedback.

Compare the excerpts from the guidelines of the American Council on the Teaching of Foreign Language (ACTFL), contained in Figure 7.7, to those from a social studies rubric, contained in Figure 7.8. The ACTFL rubric is rich in descriptive language that provides insight into each level and its uniqueness.[6] The social studies rubric never gets much beyond repetitive comparative language in describing the dimensions to be assessed.[7]

Although it may be necessary to use considerable comparative language on a first rubric (as discussed later), be aware that it is never valid to confuse comparative qualitative differences with often-arbitrary quantitative differences in discriminating between performances. There is considerable temptation to construct descriptors based on quantities instead of qualities, because of course they are simpler to score. Although a "less clear" paper is obviously less desirable than a "clear" paper (even though such a description does not say much about what clarity or its absence looks like), it is almost never valid to say that a good paper has more facts or more footnotes or more arguments than a worse paper. A paper is never worse because it has fewer footnotes; it is worse because the sources cited are somehow less appropriate or illumi-

### Figure 7.7 Excerpt From ACTFL Spanish Proficiency Guidelines

| Novice–High | Able to satisfy partially the requirements of basic communicative exchanges by relying heavily on learned utterances but occasionally expanding these through simple recombinations of their elements. Can ask questions or make statements involving learned material. Shows signs of spontaneity although this falls short of real autonomy of expression. Speech continues to consist of learned utterances rather than of personalized, situationally adapted ones. Vocabulary centers on areas such as basic objects, places, and most common kinship terms. Pronunciation may still be strongly influenced by first language. Errors are frequent and, in spite of repetition, some Novice–High speakers will have difficulty being understood even by sympathetic interlocutors. |
|---|---|
| Intermediate–High | Able to handle successfully most uncomplicated communicative tasks and social situations. Can initiate, sustain, and close a general conversation with a number of strategies appropriate to a range of circumstances and topics, but errors are evident. Limited vocabulary still necessitates hesitation and may bring about slightly unexpected circumlocution. There is emerging evidence of connected discourse, particularly for simple narration and/or description. The Intermediate–High speaker can generally be understood even by interlocutors not accustomed to dealing with speakers at this level, but repetition may still be required. |
| Superior | Able to speak the language with sufficient accuracy to participate effectively in most formal and informal conversations on practical, social, professional, and abstract topics. Can discuss special fields of competence and interest with ease. Can support opinions and hypothesize, but may not be able to tailor language to audience or discuss in depth highly abstract or unfamiliar topics. Usually the Superior level speaker is only partially familiar with regional or other dialectical variants. The Superior level speaker commands a wide variety of interactive strategies and shows good awareness of discourse strategies. The latter involves the ability to distinguish main ideas from supporting information through syntactic, lexical and suprasegmental features (pitch, stress, intonation). Sporadic errors may occur, particularly in low-frequency structures and some complex high-frequency structures more common to formal writing, but no patterns of error are evident. Errors do not disturb the native speaker or interfere with communication. |

nating. A paper is not good because it is long but because it has something to say and says so thoroughly.

A rubric should always describe "better" and "worse" in tangible qualitative terms in each descriptor: What specifically makes this argument or proof better than another one? Therefore, when using comparative language to differentiate quality, make sure that what is being compared is relative quality, not relative arbitrary quantity.

Figure 7.8 Excerpt from a Canadian Social Studies Essay Exam Rubric

| Score | Scoring Descriptors |
|---|---|
| 5 – Exceptional | The examples or case studies selected are relevant, accurate, and comprehensively developed, revealing a *mature and insightful* understanding of social studies content. |
| 4 – Proficient | The examples or case studies selected are relevant, accurate, and clearly developed, revealing a *solid* understanding of social studies content. |
| 3 – Satisfactory | The examples or case studies selected are relevant and adequately developed but may contain some factual errors. The development of the case studies/examples reveals an *adequate* understanding of social studies content. |
| 2 – Limited | The examples or cases selected, while relevant, are vaguely or incompletely developed, and/or they contain inaccuracies. A *restricted* understanding of social studies is revealed. |
| 1 – Poor | The examples are relevant, but a minimal attempt has been made to develop them, and/or the examples contain major errors revealing a lack of understanding of content. |

## Indirect Descriptors

Rubric criteria should seek both strengths and errors. Errors are often hallmarks of all lower levels of performance. Look back at the ACTFL foreign language proficiency levels in Figure 7.7. They identify the features that are most characteristic of each level, including the most telling errors.

Moreover, sometimes perfectly valid rubrics do not use descriptors that strike observers as the essence of a level of performance. The purpose of judging is to validly and reliably discriminate between levels of performance, and assessors may learn over time that identifying certain features of performance makes this discrimination easier, even though these features may not strike others as the most important. For example, after some experience we may well find that the central differences between the most persuasive essays and the somewhat less persuasive essays at the next level have less to do with the quality of the argument than with the cropping up of minor errors that distract from the argument in the next best essays. Sometimes the basis of a sound discrimination does not directly address the essence of a performance result; instead it correlates with that result. (In the ACTFL guidelines, for example, specific sets of frequent errors are used to assess abilities we might more commonly think of simply as, say, fluency and comprehension.)

This raises an immediate question, however: Isn't it tougher for students and teachers to learn from rubrics and to prepare properly for performance if the rubrics (and the judges who use them) do not routinely look at essential points of difference? This is of course one of the things that makes traditional standardized multiple-choice tests so problematic. When these tests are properly designed, their results do correlate with results on authentic tests of performance. For example, vocabulary tests are good predictors of college success. But that does not help the test taker and the teacher understand and practice for the ultimate challenge, the criterion performance.

Here as elsewhere we must ask, For whom are we assessing? For whom are we writing the rubric? Sophisticated and experienced judges require very different descriptors than do novice performers who are looking for ways to self-assess and self-adjust as they make their learning and performances more and more like adult learning and performances. That is why some schools rewrite rubrics for teacher-judges in language that students will understand and can apply to their work.

## Rubrics for Content Mastery

Today it appears that most educators have chosen to focus on the assessment of generic skills instead of on specific subject matter understandings (as discussed in Chapter Four). It is certainly easier to assess general academic skills, and the results are usually easily generalized: speaking is speaking, after all, even if the content of the speech varies. Whereas understanding $F = ma$ has nothing to do with understanding Boyle's law or the concept of dramatic irony. So understanding needs to be assessed separately for each concept taught. More importantly, few teachers or assessors have sufficiently explored the question, for example, What counts as evidence of understanding $F = ma$ as opposed to having thoughtless control over the formula and plugging it into typical textbook problems? How should we distinguish between crude and sophisticated understandings?

Typically, all that is assessed is knowledge and application of a formula. But it is possible to distinguish between levels of understanding, as we do between levels of skill, by following the basic rule outlined here: if we have samples of work that represent a range of performance, then we can develop rubrics.

Of course, to do this well we need to get over our traditional tendency to think in terms of right or wrong answers when dealing with subject-matter content. It is easy to think of assessment of students' control of content in terms of accuracy of facts and application. However, once we consider that understanding develops over time and begin to use terms like "depth of insight," we can then talk about gradual differences in understanding. We can chart a student's progressive insight on a scale that has "deep and sophisticated insight" at one end and "crude and superficial understanding" at the other.

## Task-Specific Versus Generic Rubrics

We face many choices in designing rubrics and descriptors and one of them is whether to use task-specific or generic rubrics. Reliability is no doubt served by using a rubric that is unique to a task and to the samples of performance that relate to that task. However, we also have a feasibility problem: it is too prohibitive in time and energy to design a rubric for every task. And we may have lost sight of our larger goal, the target for which the task was designed, as discussed in Chapter Five.

Sound assessment thus argues in favor of using a general set of analytic-trait rubrics. The criteria by which we judge performance are more important than (and logically prior to) the design of any particular task. And the criteria relate to the overall achievement target, which tends to be broader than any particular task that we use in an assessment. It is preferable, then, to use across tasks rubrics that focus on key criteria related to key targets. For example, a rubric for evaluating a student's ability to "argue persuasively" and "master the core understandings of a text" is suitable for use across paper topics and oral exams—particularly if the same important outcomes (such as "argue persuasively") are viewed as the main things to be assessed.

If a general rubric applied to a specific task clearly sacrifices the specificity of the feedback to the student performer, we can employ the compromise discussed earlier: use general criteria that do not vary across tasks, and use unique indicators to further define the criteria as the changing tasks require. These indicators can be attached by individual teachers for individual tasks or by program leaders in support of particular program goals.

## Criteria and Subjectivity

From the vantage point of the logic described in Chapter Five, criteria result from analysis of assessment purpose and intended performance impact. Thus they are not essentially matters of value or taste. If my purpose is to solve problems or write stories, then, a logical analysis can show me that some criteria for success are apt and others are not. "Persuasiveness" is not a highly useful criterion in technical writing, but "accuracy" and "clarity" are essential. This is as objective as saying that in baseball having two men on the same base is inappropriate. That is not a subjective aesthetic or moral judgment but a logical one; the rules and purpose of the game do not permit it. Deriving criteria analytically does not mean that assessors will not disagree, of course, about a complex analysis of implications. But appropriate criteria can be agreed to if we are clear about purpose.

In other words, choice of *purposes* is a matter of values, but the identification of *criteria*—given a clear purpose, audience, and standard—follows logically: we search for criteria that fit and make the most sense. We may disagree about the value of story writing, but we should be able to agree to the criteria for distinguishing good from not-so-good story writing once we agree on what a story is meant to be and on what samples are exemplary. We find these criteria by asking: What is the essence of the good stories we hold up as exemplary? When stories work most, what do they do?

What if I think the stories of Hemingway work and you think they do not? If we can agree on samples of exemplary writing, that the criterion of impact surely matters, and on the use of criteria derived from an analysis of the chosen samples, then it should be relatively easy for both of us to discern impact in a work (even if we disagree on its effect on us or disagree about other traits, such as development or style).

Everett Kline, my senior associate at the Center on Learning, Assessment, and School Structure (CLASS), lays out in workshops the following simple strategy for getting beyond contentious value-based disputes:

1.  Pilot a task and get back a large sample of student work.

2.  Agree in advance to score the work using a few criteria.

3.  For each criterion, have everyone do a quick read-through of the papers, ensuring that at least three people read each paper and assessing each paper on a six-point scale.

4.  Have readers put their scores on Post-its on the back of each paper, not visible to the next reader.

5.  When all papers have been read, identify all those papers that all readers agreed should receive the same scores.

6.  Set aside all those papers about which there were disputes: Why argue if we now have agreed-upon anchor papers for all the score points?

At CLASS we find that most disagreements about work quality stem from readers not having made explicit the criteria they use and then disagreeing about the merits of the paper based on their different criteria and weighting of criteria. This is needless talking at cross-purposes.

Teacher-judges are most likely to disagree about taste and to confuse it with impact. You say that Shakespeare's sonnets are exemplary poems; I say that the songs of Bob Dylan are. You say that Dylan's work is doggerel; I say that Shakespeare's is ponderous. We disagree. Now what? We can reach agreement only by working toward common criteria in which we define the form *poem*. It is usually the case that the old guard thinks the new forms are dangerous and base precisely when their impact is significant and the change in methods or language is shocking. So we should be able to agree that there is an impact even if we continue to disagree about whether or not we like that impact. Most disagreements are not about criteria, but about weighting them (Should engaging count twice as much as developed?) and applying them to borderline cases. In addition, once we begin seeking criteria on which we agree, we may find the works of Dylan and Shakespeare have some traits in common that are important but not obvious through superficial inquiry. This ability to find the criteria that matter is one reason why we say good judges are expert—they typically see shades and details of performance that novice observers cannot. Nevertheless, agreeing on criteria can be hard, messy work, with no recipes.

We can even devise criteria and rubrics for creativity and open-mindedness if we can agree on samples of exemplary creativity and open-mindedness in performance or conduct, analyze what it is that makes some work more creative, and describe those qualities. If creativity means casting things in a new, revealing, and powerful light or developing new forms for timeless ideas, then Dylan's "Subterranean Homesick Blues" was creative and Ohio Express's "Yummy, Yummy, Yummy" was not—despite the greater commercial success of the Ohio Express and the "unmusical" nasal delivery of Bob Dylan. It is noteworthy that whether we consider the controversy over Impressionism, or Dylan getting booed for plugging in his guitar, in both cases it was the rejection of orthodox form in the service of greater (threatening to some) impact that fueled the artist's direction.

I would go so far as to say that if we value a certain quality and recognize it when we see it, then we can assess it with adequate precision. (Think of wine tasting or the artistic elements of figure skating in the Olympics.) Conversely, we stifle creativity when we use inappropriate criteria and a single anchor performance as a model for students. Under those conditions, we simply encourage students to mimic a particular approach. And once again, the more we highlight the approach or format and not the criteria for the accomplishment, the more we encourage mere mimicry. It is with samples of *diverse* excellence that we encourage the performer to consider novel, maybe even unorthodox, means of achieving the end.

Figure 7.9 lists criteria that are used for scoring a story as part of the portfolio assessment of the National Assessment of Educational Progress (NAEP), and illustrates criteria that constrain performer imagination.[8] This rubric does not assess creativity, only technique. A student could write the most boring and psychologically uninteresting story in the world and still get a 6 if the story fit the formula wanted by the rubric. Large-scale testing seems destined to produce bland or stifling rubrics, perhaps because the designers are often more interested in reliability than validity, and are anxious to avoid contentious debates about criteria.

Figure 7.9 NAEP Criteria for Scoring a Story

| 1 – Event Description | Paper is a list of sentences minimally related or a list of sentences that all describe a single event. |
| --- | --- |
| 2 – Undeveloped Story | Paper is a listing of related events. More than one event is described, but with few details about setting, characters, or the events. (Usually there is no more than one sentence telling about each event.) |
| 3 – Basic Story | Paper describes a series of events, giving details (in at least two or three sentences) about some aspect of the story (the events, the characters' goals, or problems to be solved). But the story lacks cohesion because of problems with syntax, sequencing, events missing, or an undeveloped ending. |
| 4 – Extended Story | Paper describes a sequence of episodes, including details about most story elements (i.e., setting, episodes, characters' goals, problems to be solved). But the stories are confusing or incomplete (i.e., at the end the characters' goals are ignored or problems inadequately resolved; the beginning does not match the rest of the story; the internal logic or plausibility of characters' actions is not maintained). |
| 5 – Developed Story | Paper describes a sequence of episodes in which almost all story elements are clearly developed (i.e., setting, episodes, characters' goals, or problems to be solved) with a simple resolution of these goals or problems at the end. May have one or two problems or include too much detail. |
| 6 – Elaborated Story | Paper describes a sequence of episodes in which almost all story elements are well developed (i.e., setting, episodes, characters' goals, or problems to be solved). The resolution of the goals or problems at the end are elaborated. The events are presented and elaborated in a cohesive way. |

Compare the NAEP approach to the one implied in an advertisement for the J. Walter Thompson advertising agency that appeared in *The New York Times* a few years ago. The ad gave eight clever performance tests to would-be copywriters (for example: "You are a writer for Walletsize Books. Describe the history of the United States in one hundred words or less.") And it supplied the following criteria for judging: "If you want to get our attention and a job, you're going to have to show us *fresh, fearless,* and *more or less brilliant* stuff." Wouldn't these criteria do a better job of spurring creativity than typical criteria related to format, development, and mechanics? Do they seem any more subjective than the criteria "well developed"?

Furthermore, we may be more productive if we do not try to assess directly such value-laden matters as creativity or sensitivity to others. Rather, it may be wiser to sometimes design tasks that can only be completed if the student shows some imagination or some sensitivity to other group members or groups. As noted previously in Chapter Two, I like to call this "intellectual Outward Bound." As in Outward Bound, we can observe and document a great deal of behavior about, say, cooperation, in large part because getting from point A to point B is not doable unless there is cooperation.

Many educators have experienced the difficulties that arise when they ask students to display a certain character (personality trait) that is up to a certain standard and then try to measure that character directly. It is better to make it clear that there are certain very important intellectual tasks that demand character, and to offer a description of the way a student performs in these demanding situations. That way, different specific, worthy, and authentic tasks can be designed to demand different specific virtues. (This is a situation in which group grading may be reasonable. When parents object to group grading as a general policy, they are right; that is not how evaluation of adults' work goes on all the time. But on tasks where sensitivity to and efficient teamwork with others defines success, it makes perfect sense.)

We never want to build rubrics that restrict the methods or formats to orthodox or conventionally formal work or conduct. As mentioned earlier, history offers many examples of creative performance defined in terms of meeting certain approved or official criteria. The French Academy of Painting and Sculpture thought that Manet and his fellow Impressionists were not meeting the criteria that defined art. In effect, the leaders of the academy had defined art and its purpose in such a way that Impressionism was ruled out as an appropriate result. The paintings had impact but not as works of art, they said.

We should avoid such mandating of process, format, method, or approach. Rubrics do not inherently stifle innovation; only bad rubrics do, and these are the result when we forget about or shy away from assessing impact and purpose. A rubric does not require us to set out a recipe that people must follow. Many science teachers, for example, design problem-solving rubrics that require students to use the five-step procedure taught in their science classes. John Dewey warned against this years ago in *How We Think*. He repeatedly urged readers to think of the five stages of reflective thinking not as a series of invariant steps but as a set of criteria. His admonition has not prevented countless researchers from ossifying his criteria into rules of procedure.[9]

Methods are judgment-based means to ends. Rubrics should highlight the appropriate result or end. If the goal is to build a working roller coaster or a debate position, then we do not need to specify the method; we need to specify the traits of the successful roller coaster or the winning debate. Creativity is then heightened, not impeded: unorthodox approaches will yield high scores if they work, that is, if they yield the results sought. Yes, artists and critics may well argue forever about whether a piece works, and there may well be continued controversy over whether the artist's intention or lack of intention has anything to do with art, but creative work will always be recognizable by its impact and avant garde nature.

A basic method for avoiding the problem of rigid formalism is as follows: first, scoring is anchored with diverse, even divergent models of excellence: samples of Shakespeare, W. H. Auden, and e. e. cummings for poetry; videotapes of Jesse Jackson and Ronald Reagan for public speaking; and so on. We thus make it clear that there is no one method, style, or approach to meeting an objective. Instead we ask, What were these exemplars trying and able to accomplish as poets and speakers? This focuses on purpose and impact, and makes it more likely, not less, that students will invent perhaps unorthodox and novel approaches to a task. As has been said throughout this book, rubrics depend on standards and purposes. Change the purpose, change the standards, and you must change the rubrics.

Maybe what we should say is that tastes do influence judgment, but what limits performance is orthodoxy about criteria when the criteria are derived from taste instead of analyzed from the achievement target. Take music: the creators of jazz, rock, and now rap found innovative ways to achieve impact. Melody and formal structure became downplayed in favor of rhythm, realism in lyrics, and the importance of apparent spontaneity. At first only a few people, looking to the purposes of music, acknowledged the new music's effect as in fact a musical impact; many listeners, relying on orthodox taste to define the impact, saw it as unmusical and even dangerous. Now of course these forms of music have come to be mainstream and are piped into shopping malls, because the threat from their newness is gone and people have learned to like the effect of the music.

We should always be open to new ways of working and new definitions of success or impact. The bottom line is that in authentic work, if not always in art, the performer has a purpose and works within a context. The work can always be judged in terms of purposes and contexts. There may well be times when the performer's and the audience's purposes, hence their judgments, diverge. But even here, agreement about assessment criteria can still be reached, making clear in advance what the judges are looking for, given their purposes.

My hunch is that if we are clear about performance and the accomplishing of goals, we will keep adjusting our criteria and standards as we go. That seems to happen in all healthy performance systems. For example, as society focuses more on health issues, we naturally direct our attention to food preparation differently. New criteria (such as low fat content) emerge naturally as we try out new purposes and gain clarity about what they imply. So it goes in human affairs. Change in values, styles, or tastes is no excuse for throwing up our hands and declaring performance unassessable. Our students deserve better guidance than that. A good deal of intellectual performance is noncontroversial and amenable to formal evaluation, as the long history of Advanced Placement exams shows.

## Developmental Rubrics

As we construct rubrics and criteria, we need to keep in mind the difference between event-related rubrics and developmental or longitudinal rubrics. Doing well or poorly on an event, a specific performance of a task, does not tell us much about a student's overall intellectual progress or place. Maybe the task was too hard for him. Maybe the task was already familiar to her. Validity requires that we not make rash generalizations based on one or two complex performances.

The ACTFL rubric in Figure 7.7 allows us to chart progress toward fluency over time. But would we use that rubric to assess a novice's ability to parse a sentence? No, we would assess the parsing event with its own context-sensitive (and content-sensitive) rubric so that we could look at just the quality of the parsing performance. On another occasion we would want to take all the event results and make a more general determination of the level of performance.

Similarly, when assessing beginning readers we do not want merely to say that Joe "cannot read well" because he cannot handle the task we gave him. Joe may be behind his peers in development, but that does not mean he is a bad reader in terms of his speed and sophistication.

A related problem is that we do a poor job of distinguishing between the quality of a performance and its sophistication. Recall the description in Chapter Five of how the New York State School Music Association deliberately distinguishes between the difficulty of the pieces played and the quality of the playing. Similarly, in diving and gymnastics we build in weighting factors because we understand that complex dives or moves are more likely to have errors than simple ones. So for fairness and validity we multiply the quality points by a degree of difficulty factor.

The same distinctions need to apply in schooling. Very bright and able students who are tackling unusually complex work can nonetheless be careless and sloppy in the quality of that work. The reverse is also true. Many students who are "behind" their classroom peers are nonetheless doing high-quality error-free work in the tasks given to them. We need a better way of assessing and reporting these distinctions.[10]

## Developing First Rubrics—and Beyond

Rubrics are not designed through mere imagination and discussion. They are derived from standards and from an analysis of existing samples of performance of different quality. A rubric should reflect the most tangible and appropriate differences of quality between performances. How else could we do assessment and validate it? After all, presumably observable differences in quality came first, and analytic description of those differences, generalized in the rubric descriptors, comes second. Otherwise, we are just guessing at criteria, and we fail to validate our work.

As Supreme Court Justice Potter Stewart said about pornography, we know it when we see it, even if we cannot define it. Similarly, we can and do sort student work into piles of decreasing quality. But it is only when we stop to look at how the piles differ and to carefully explain the differences that we begin to get a clear sense of what the descriptors need to be for each pile.

But what do we do in year one? We just have to do the best we can, basing our rubric on our overall experience of differences in this type of performance, of any pilot tasks we did, and of any samples we have of performance on similar challenges in the past. Yes, in the beginning of our work we may need to lean on comparative and evaluative language. For a first rubric, being clear about the highest level of performance and then using comparative language to describe the progressive weakness of other levels of performance may be just fine. But we need to refine the rubric as soon as we have more performances to analyze—because a rubric is only as a good as the breadth and depth of our sample of performances, and as our powers of generalizing the results of sorting student work. Each year brings a more diverse and revealing sample of possible performances, and hence deeper insight into the most salient differences in performance levels and the surprising diversity of work possible within each level.

This means that we must have some faith that our samples of (agreed-upon) exemplary performances really are exemplary, and that our criteria derive from an analysis of excellence, not just from abstract ideas about excellence. This distinction strikes at the heart of the difference between norms and standards. If we rely only on samples of products that are the best our kids are capable of doing but not the best that are possible for other people to do, we will be building rubrics out of an analysis of mediocrity—describing indicators for merely acceptable performance while claiming they are for the highest level of performance. Imagine for example if we derived the criteria of exemplary musicianship from the best performances of relative novices and you will see the problem we face when we begin assessment with a poor range of work from our students.

The best rubrics depend on a clear and uncontroversial definition of exemplary performance, as gained from exemplary samples, and then we work down the scale from there.

## Summing Up Rubrics

The best rubrics are those that

1. *Are sufficiently generic to relate to general goals* beyond an individual performance task, but specific enough to enable useful and sound inferences about the task.

2. *Discriminate among performances validly*, not arbitrarily, by assessing the central features of performance, not those that are easiest to see, count, or score.

3. *Do not combine independent criteria in one rubric.*

4. *Are based on analysis of many work samples* and on the widest possible range of work samples, including valid exemplars.

5. *Rely on descriptive language* (what quality or its absence looks like) as opposed to merely comparative or evaluative language, such as "not as thorough as" or "excellent product," to make a discrimination.

6. *Provide useful and apt discrimination* that enables sufficiently fine judgments, but do not use so many points on the scale (typically more than six) that reliability is threatened.

7. *Use descriptors that are sufficiently rich* to enable student performers to verify their scores, accurately self-assess, and self-correct. (Use of indicators makes description less ambiguous, hence more reliable, by providing examples of what to recognize in each level of performance. However, even though indicators are useful, concrete signs of criteria being met, specific indicators may not be reliable or appropriate in every context.)

8. *Highlight judging the impact of performance* (the effect, given the purpose) rather than overreward processes, formats, content, or the good-faith effort made.

Rubrics that meet technical requirements are

1. *Continuous.* The change in quality from score point to score point is equal: the degree of difference between a 5 and a 4 is the same as between a 2 and a 1. The descriptors reflect this continuity.

2. *Parallel.* Each descriptor parallels all the others in terms of the criteria language used in each sentence.

3. *Coherent.* The rubric focuses on the same criteria throughout. Although the descriptor for each scale point is different from the ones before and after, the changes concern variance of quality for the (fixed) criteria, not language that explicitly or implicitly introduces new criteria or shifts the importance of the various criteria.

4. *Aptly weighted.* When multiple rubrics are used to assess one event, there is an apt, not arbitrary, weighting of each criterion in reference to the others.

5. *Valid.* The rubric permits valid inferences about performance to the degree that what is scored is what is central to performance, not what is merely easy to see and score. The proposed differences in quality should reflect task analysis and be based on samples of work across the full range of performance; describe qualitative, not quantitative, differences in performance; and not confuse merely correlative behaviors with actual authentic criteria.

6. *Reliable.* The rubric enables consistent scoring across judges and time. Rubrics allow reliable scoring to the degree that evaluative language ("excellent," "poor") and comparative language ("better than," "worse than") is transformed into highly descriptive language that helps judges to recognize the salient and distinctive features of each level of performance.

# PART THREE

# Applications and Implications

# CHAPTER 8

# Portfolio as Evidence

Portfolios have become a common feature in many schools and districts. And a few states, such as Vermont, have implemented or are planning to use portfolios as part of their formal assessments. In light of what has been said so far in this book, it is easy to understand their popularity. With a system built on diverse evidence and anchored in student work, teachers find such assessment more credible, and students can be more effectively invited into the self-assessment process than in a system dependent on traditional testing. Portfolios serve as an illuminating focal point for teacher-parent conferences and teacher-student conferences alike.

But just what is a portfolio? Uncertainty abounds about just what should go in a student portfolio, who really should own it (the student or the teacher), and what value, if any, there is in passing portfolios along to the next teacher or school. This confusion stems in part from a failure to think through the purposes of the portfolio—a problem I have noted throughout the book. This problem is ironic in the case of portfolios, because they are most widely assigned in language arts and English classes, where the two basic writing process questions—Who is the audience? and What is the purpose?—dominate instructional guidance and shape feedback to students about their writing. In too many classrooms, schools, districts, and states, however, educators are not asking and thoroughly answering the two key questions about their own work with portfolios.

In fact, there are very different possible purposes for and uses of portfolios, with different implications for contents and scoring, as a few examples will make clear. Consider these possible uses:

- As a showcase for the student's best work, as chosen by the student
- As a showcase for the student's best work, as chosen by the teacher
- As a showcase for the student's interests
- As a showcase for the student's growth
- As evidence of self-assessment and self-adjustment
- As evidence enabling professional assessment of student performance, based on a technically sound sample of work
- As a complete collection of student work for documentation and archiving
- As a constantly changing sample of work chosen by the student, reflecting different job applications and exhibitions over time

We can identify a few basic implications in these examples. Portfolios can primarily serve instruction or assessment; they can be focused primarily on documentation or evaluation; their contents can be defined by the student or by the teacher; they can be seen as a résumé, as a representative sample of overall performance (good and bad), or as a constantly changing exhibit. Too few teachers and administrators have thought through these purposes and their implications. As a result, many portfolio programs are ineffectual and cumbersome, and they lack credibility as a method of assessment.

Consider the difference between an instructional versus an assessment perspective. Depending on what the teacher has in mind, the student may or may not be permitted to choose the categories for submission, the criteria for submission under the category, or the specific products. By *categories,* I mean the kinds of work submitted, such as the examples cited in Chapter Two from New Standards. By *criteria,* I mean the guidelines for deciding what work fits into which categories, and, especially, who makes the decision. For example, if the category is "best work," the criterion might be "highest scores" or it might be "most satisfying." The judge of whether the criteria are met might be the teacher or the student. By *specific products,* I mean the actual samples chosen to meet the categories and criteria. Teachers might specify categories and criteria, but they might ask students to make the specific choices. Or teachers might choose the samples to ensure that they are truly representative of the students' overall performance. There might also be requirements about the inclusion of specific products or standardized performance tests for all students.

Some portfolios blur the boundaries in a useful way. Categories might be specified by adults to include "free pick" and "most and least satisfying work." Other school systems, especially large ones, specify the categories and criteria but provide great leeway in the choice of samples. In almost all systems, student self-assessment is made a central feature, because the portfolio provides a unique opportunity to take stock of performance over a longer time frame than that represented by single tests.

Whether broadly or narrowly framed, a portfolio can be assembled to prove very different things, thus it can yield potentially diverse and rich categories, criteria, and contents. A portfolio designed to show evidence that a particular performance standard has been reached is very different from a portfolio designed to show progress over time—from novice to expert—and is very different from a portfolio designed to show the student's interests and abilities as judged by the student. In each case, we would expect to see very different samples of work.

But in all cases, far fewer samples are needed than people typically imagine. A huge collection of student work is not necessary to show that a particular standard has been reached or that a particular interest exists and has been developed. A few papers, projects, and tests are likely to be sufficient to certify that a student is now advanced or is talented. A portfolio is fundamentally a sample of work, regardless of its purpose. It is not a file cabinet or exhaustive collection of artifacts.

Even a portfolio designed to chart progress over time with a strong emphasis on self-assessment need not include all or most work, particularly if our longitudinal rubrics summarize the key indicators of progress and the most salient features of next-level work. Of course, we need to document more than just the current level of performance, but a careful pruning of the portfolio based on specific rubrics will likely result in a far smaller but telling collection of artifacts than many teachers commonly deal with.

Thus, the distressed cry of "Where and how do we keep this massive amount of stuff?!" is indicative of some muddled thinking about purpose. If the portfolio is a valid sample, then it will shed evidence happily all along the way, and when this evidence is no longer needed, the portfolio can be returned to the student. Thus, once two teachers have certified that Susie can write at the intermediate level, based on six samples of writing in the fourth grade, they no longer need more than one or two representative pieces of work as backup to the judgment in the event of a future dispute. In fact, there need not be a portfolio at all, just a collection of scores or comments linked to credible samples and standards of anchor performances and products, as we find, for example, in such areas as diving, figure skating, chess, and karate. I am puzzled, therefore, why so many portfolio projects are founded on the often overwhelming idea that the entire collection of student work should be passed on from teacher to teacher. This onerous burden is unnecessary for most assessment and evaluation purposes. Tellingly, when I interview the teacher-recipients in districts that pass on all this work, they often sheepishly admit that they rarely study the material carefully. This proves that such a complicated collection is of no real value except in some abstract romantic sense.

## The Portfolio as Sound Evidence

If we assume that good assessment—as opposed to interesting documentation—requires a valid and reliable sample of work, and if we further assume that this is to be a formal assessment of performance against program standards, then it follows that the guidelines for what goes in the portfolio must be dictated by the demands of sound evidence, not by the desires, standards, and interests of the student. Because the student is not an expert in assessment or in the field of study, and because the teacher will likely want to compare the portfolio against standards (that is, against specifications and sample portfolios), adults must frame the demands. Except under rare circumstances—for example, in which program goals coincide with students' personal goals, as happens in some arts, vocational, and graduate programs—the professionals must determine the categories and criteria of evidence in a portfolio designed as assessment. The assessment portfolio belongs to the adults, even if it is the student's to maintain.

When the portfolio is further intended as a means of evaluation, still greater care and control in framing the guidelines for content are required of the adults. An assessment need not require evaluation; the terms are not synonymous as I use them. In assessment I *describe*; in evaluation I make a *value judgment,* as the term suggests. In assessment, I place the student's performance on a continuum; for example, I might describe the performance as novice and the work as strong on voice but inconsistent on organization, as judged against performance standards. An evaluation adds another layer of judgment, which can be posed as a question: Given where the student is as determined by the assessment, is that where he or she should be? Is it acceptable or unacceptable performance to be at that level at this point in the student's career? Assessment alone is more of a clinical look at performance, its characteristics, its strengths and weaknesses.

However, in an evaluation we make a further judgment as to whether such a profile is good or bad in light of institutional or personal expectations. The practical point is that in evaluation we fix passing scores or establish criteria for when performance is good enough. In assessment, the student may earn a score, but in the final report card the teacher will likely state the meaning of the score in value language, that is, the teacher will grade the student's performance, whether or not letter grades are used. (This point is further explained, with examples, in Chapter Ten.) When evaluation is highlighted, a good deal of standardization in portfolio contents and grading may also be required to ensure fair and credible comparisons of performance.

In an instructional or personal portfolio, educators need not worry about either professional standards of evidence or making an evaluation. The usual goal is simply to provide students with a vehicle to develop a profile based on interests and abilities and/or to provide an opportunity for self-assessment and self-adjustment. Standardization in categories, criteria, and contents is usually unnecessary, or is even intrusive in instructional portfolios. Under the broad banner of "This is my work," the student is typically free in an instructional portfolio to determine not only the contents but many of the categories and criteria. Thus in many classrooms, some students might include their best work, others might put in their most interesting work, and still others might put in a representative sample of work showing their progress. Even if we specify such categories as "best work," students are typically permitted to be the judge as to what pieces meet the criterion. Students may think their most interesting pieces are their best work, even if they received lower grades on those pieces than on other work they found less interesting. Even if the teacher judges the piece not to have been the "best work," the student may feel that it is and might be allowed the final say, usually in the name of self-assessment and the development of style, voice, and interest.

On pedagogical and empowerment grounds this eclecticism is all highly desirable. In large-scale assessment, however, it is a potential disaster. As many readers are no doubt aware, there was a highly publicized, critical report from the Rand Corporation of Vermont's first years of portfolio use in the language arts, which cited serious problems with the validity and reliability of scores.[1] The problems stemmed from a fatal flaw: Vermont had instituted the system as an accountability measure, but teachers were encouraged to treat the portfolio as the student's property in the service of learning. Many fourth-grade students put "best work" in their portfolios, but it was not their best work as judged by teachers. Sometimes the students chose work that reflected a complete misunderstanding of the criteria, yet their decisions counted. And thus their school's language arts programs were judged on the results. (The report also cited inadequacies of training and oversight in scoring consistency.)

My point is not to blame the designers of the system. My point is to alert readers to the dangers that lurk in a failure to think through the purposes of this method. It is tempting to be politically correct in giving students a full voice about what goes into their portfolios. But it is a misguided if well-intentioned idea if the results are intended to be used in a formal assessment of performance against standards.

In this chapter, I deliberately focus on the purpose of formal assessment of student performance against standards. In so doing, I do not mean to devalue or argue against the importance of instructional or personal portfolios. On the contrary, effective learning depends on methods such as this one, and the student self-adjustment based on self-assessment described throughout the book can only be well developed if some such teaching and learning system is used. But a portfolio designed by and for the adult educators, based on professional standards for evidence, must exist if our aim is credible and useful assessment. In the rest of this chapter, I assume that as the purpose under discussion. I leave open the question of evaluation here, as that involves highly contextual judgments about what is or is not acceptable work. Furthermore, the act of setting a passing score for portfolios is no different than the act of setting a valid passing score on a test or assignment.

## The Anthology

To better distinguish the assessment portfolio from the instructional portfolio, we at CLASS have coined a new word to capture what we mean: we refer to a deliberately designed-to-be-valid sample of student work as an *anthology*. In what follows, I will describe how such an anthology might be conceived and implemented, based on my experience in schools, districts, and, especially, in developing a portfolio system for the North Carolina Commission on Standards and Accountability. Use of the word *anthology* is not critical; however, at CLASS we find it useful in distinguishing instructional from assessment portfolios in conversations with clients.

In our ongoing work for the State of North Carolina we have developed guidelines for such anthologies, honoring the standards for assessment described in Chapter Five and requiring evidence anchored in authentic performance tasks but rich in variety and in assessment techniques.[2] These guidelines are also deliberately designed to be used at the district and school levels.

According to these guidelines, the student anthology would be composed of the following three different types of work evidence:

1.  *Tasks:* scored work from elective and on-demand approved performance tasks

2.  *Prompts:* evaluated work from local and state constructed-response assignments

3.  *Tests and quizzes:* scores from local, district, state, and national tests

*Tasks.* These would be integrated performance tasks. They would be deliberately designed to require students to produce authentic work using core content and skills. Each task would have at least two scoring rubrics associated with it. These tasks and rubrics would be approved (by educators at the site or district level), available to all teachers, and where possible, available on an intranet or from the existing CLASS database available on the World Wide Web. The tasks would be designed based on the CLASS template and design standards discussed in this book. The CLASS peer review process would be used to validate tasks for use in the database.

The task database would be nonsecure in the sense that all tasks in the database would be visible and available for downloading and use at all times. This rids the system of inappropriate secrecy and makes ongoing reliable assessment of the student's competency against common high standards more possible at the local level.

The tasks would be standardized in the sense that modifications in scoring or administration would not be allowed without prior permission from the appropriate overseer.

These official performance tasks would be available on demand in one important way. Each year, one or two on-demand performance tasks would be required of all students. Though required, they would be made public prior to their use. Teachers would have a window of time—typically a month—during which the tasks would need to be given and completed. The main reason for such a required task is to improve teacher scoring reliability across the system, and thus to calibrate teacher grading continuously.

The remaining tasks in the portfolio would be elective in the sense that no other particular tasks would be required of all students. Rather, teachers would select any of the approved tasks that suited their instructional plans and calendars, and the credit needs of their students. Each student would have to accrue a minimum number of performance credits for each of the agreed-upon competency areas, using only approved tasks. (Figure 8.1 contains a sample of a student's competency credits gained over the course of a year.[3]) It is expected that over the course of three years the student will have typically completed six or seven of these tasks.

Tasks would be designed by teachers and approved by appropriate oversight persons or groups. Resulting tasks would be judged against the specific criteria: authentic, credible, and user-friendly. Central to each task would be the existence of high-quality models and requirements that the student self-assess and self-adjust based on preliminary trials and feedback.

Clearly there would be an incentive for each teacher to design tasks and have them approved, because the requirements could then be met by their own work. (This parallels the system used in Germany for the rigorous abitur exams, where teachers design their own exam for the state test and have those tests approved by the state examination board.)

*Prompts.*   These would be like conventional open-ended writing questions, as typically found on state performance tests, advanced placement exams, and many school and college final exams, where constructed-response questions are common. These challenges would be developed locally as well as available from a database. Along with tasks, they would be categorized in terms of performance genres.

### Figure 8.1  Sample Anthology Scoring

| | | Student: John Doe | | | |
|---|---|---|---|---|---|
| Competency | Credits Required | Tasks | Tests | Challenges | Number of Credits |
| Communication | 25 | 9 | 4 | 12 | 25 |
| Using Numbers | 20 | 7 | 7 | 7 | 21 |
| Processing Information | 20 | 10 | 8 | 2 | 20 |
| Teamwork | 10 | 8 | | 2 | 10 |
| Problem Solving | 15 | 11 | 4 | 4 | 19 |
| Using Technology | 15 | 6 | 4 | 5 | 15 |
| **Credits: Subtotal** | | **51** | **27** | **32** | **110** |
| Portfolio Validity | 5 | | | | 5 |
| **Credits: Total** | | | | | **115** |
| Range Required | | 45–55 | 20–27 | 25–35 | |
| Total Required | 110 | | | | 110 |

*Tests and quizzes.*   These would include district and state tests, which would be a balanced mixture of multiple-choice and performance items, and locally designed and scored tests.

The goal of this approach to portfolios is to base important decisions about student competence, promotion, and graduation on a collection of credible work that is representative of that student's performance with key knowledge, skill, in the most important intellectual performance genres. The anthology thus would require, in addition to work grounded in authentic performance tasks, that teachers also collect and factor into their judgments results from traditional tests, assignments used by the teacher, and test results from any district, state, or national tests. This triangulation of information would make the anthology more valid, reliable, and credible. The primary role of the district supervisors, then, would be to oversee the quality of site-based assessment. Local control with quality control would be the motto.

## Anthology Review

The anthology would consist of previously scored and evaluated work. This collection would be assessed annually as a whole, in the fall, by a team of two or more educators. One of the reviewers would be the student's new teacher. The other would be an educator, identified by the school or district, who has not taught the student. This review schedule and double scoring would ensure that the receiving teacher gets the feedback when it is most useful, near the beginning of the year of instruction. It would ensure the higher credibility that is achieved through scoring by two relatively disinterested parties. And it would ensure that student progress toward competency would be regularly and knowledgeably tracked so that no surprise would occur in the more formal audit of the benchmark years: fourth, eighth, tenth, and twelfth grades.

The purpose of official review of anthologies would be to certify that the credits and scores assigned previously to each task were warranted. That is, formal anthology scoring would involve explicitly validating or not validating the local claim that scores for previously evaluated tasks, tests, and assignments are accurate and valid, that the total number of performance credits is accurate, and that the judgments made about the student's meeting or failing to meet the benchmark are valid and appropriate.

A student's performance would be considered to have met the benchmark for the appropriate grade level when the anthology credits and scores meet or surpass the minimums set for each category of work and for the anthology as a whole.

## Performance Credits

A student would earn performance credit when a task, test, or prompt meets state standards for a valid task, test, or challenge, and when the student's performance is of an acceptable quality. The credits that each task permits for each of the six competencies would be assigned by the state. For example, a task might offer two credits in communication, one in problem solving, and two in technology.

Similarly, the credits granted through the state's tests and for the challenges in the database would be assigned by the state. Credits for local tests and challenges would be assigned at the district level. A small random sample of these modes of assessment would be collected and reviewed across all districts to ensure validity.

In addition, a minimum number of credits would be needed for each competency: a required range of points in each of the three modes of assessment (task, test, and challenge) and a minimum number of total credits needed for meeting the benchmark. This system would thus be similar to the approach used in diving, gymnastics, and musical competitions, in which achievement is assessed by an accrual of points earned in the performance of both required and elective tasks. This permits appropriate variations in student proficiency while still requiring high levels of performance.

Credits would also be dependent on performing in an array of required genres. A literary genre, for example, is an accepted and distinct form of writing. When handed a play or asked to write one, we know to read it or write it differently than a novel, short story, or letter. One special credit would have to be earned by the student making a formal presentation of the whole anthology: he or she would have to include both a written and an oral self-assessment of the anthology. The presentation would be made to a panel, at a parent conference, to a group of teachers and students, and/or to a group of community members. This credit would be earned prior to the validation of the anthology.

## Scoring of Individual Works

Each task or prompt would have to receive at least two scores, which would be given for two *dimensions* of work: the degree of *expertise* shown (the sophistication of the reasoning, methods, style, and content), and the *quality* (accuracy, organization, craftsmanship, and impact) of the products and/or performances. These two dimensions would need to be kept separate, because a student with great expertise can produce flawed or careless work, and a student with unsophisticated skill can produce highly polished work that is still simple. (All during instruction, the teacher would likely use rubrics corresponding to all relevant traits of performance, as suggested by the criteria typology discussed in Chapters Three and Seven.) A student would have to achieve the minimum required score on both scales before credit could be earned for the work or before it could be placed in the anthology.

Given that the proposed anthology system is open and continuous, the most important interventions would occur en route, in a timely fashion, before the formal benchmark readings and validations. That is why the windows of opportunity for the use of approved performance tasks and the collaborative scoring of anthologies would occur in the fall. The system was deliberately designed so that teachers and administrators will monitor progress along the way and make apt decisions about adjustment in instruction and assessment based on emerging performance difficulties—before it is too late. Administrators would thus find it in their interest to seek regular updates from teachers, teams, and departments on student progress toward passing credits in each and all competency areas, and to hold discussions on how to adjust program and instruction if the data suggest that some students will not meet their credit requirements at the current rate.

Figure 8.2 summarizes the performance-based approach to assessment design and anthologies by suggesting competency-specific guidelines for the evidence that needs to be collected over a student's career. Figure 8.3 more specifically summarizes four types of work and tasks that we ask students to do. Of course problems and questions, performance tasks, and extended projects must be designed to highlight authentic tasks.

Regardless of the type of anthology teachers choose to design work around, they must make a series of thoughtful decisions about what will go in the record, to ensure that the approach they choose serves its purposes. CLASS staff use the matrices shown in Figures 8.4 and 8.5 to help educators make these decisions. Figure 8.4 shows questions and answers that teachers can use to determine what student work will document the four purposes listed on the left-hand side of the matrix. Figure 8.5 shows questions and answers for looking at how the anthology will be used to assess these same four purposes.

Figure 8.2 Summary of Performance Evidence Required in Achievement Anthologies

| Competency | Evidence | | | |
|---|---|---|---|---|
| | *All work types represented: exercises, test results, prompts, performance tasks, and projects* | *All performance genres represented in tasks and projects (oral, written, displayed)* | *All performance criteria types represented: impact, craftsmanship, apt methods, valid content, sophistication* | *Examples of the variety of performance prompts, tasks, and projects* |
| Communication | Local tests and exercises<br><br>State tests<br><br>National tests<br><br>Performance tasks and projects | Report, essay, narrative, critique, recitation, listening | Persuasive, clear, informative, engaging, organized, etc. | Giving directions, Socratic seminar, formal speech, research paper, ad campaign |
| Team Work | Local tests<br><br>Performance tasks and projects (on-demand and local options) | Plan, proposal, blueprint, report | Efficient, effective, inclusive, thorough, informed, etc. | Business plan, skit, team research |
| Problem Solving | Local tests<br><br>State tests<br><br>National tests<br><br>Performance tasks and projects (on-demand and local options) | Discuss, direct, construct model, exhibit, graph, use electronic media | Effective, careful, methodical, novel, responsive, skilled, etc. | Solve a community problem, identify river pollutants, build cheapest sturdy bridge |
| Information Processing | Local tests<br><br>State tests<br><br>National tests<br><br>Performance tasks and projects (on-demand and local options) | Analysis, report, debate, listening, discussion, acting | Efficient, self-regulated, critical, logical, accurate, thorough, etc. | Assess propaganda, do position paper, review books, collect data and report findings |
| Use of Numbers and Data | Local tests<br><br>State tests<br><br>National tests<br><br>Performance tasks and projects (on-demand and local options) | Demonstration, graph, electronic media, model | Skilled, precise, accurate, reasonable, powerful, etc. | "Best fit" data analysis, creation of family travel itinerary and budget, foreign policy expense analysis |
| Use of Technology | Local tests<br><br>State tests<br><br>National tests<br><br>Performance tasks and projects (on-demand and local options) | Electronic media, model, multimedia display | Effective, skilled, sophisticated, etc. | Multimedia presentation, use of graphing calculators, use of spreadsheet in business plan |

### Figure 8.3 Four Types of Student Work

| Work Type | Definition | Examples |
|---|---|---|
| Quiz | A highly structured challenge having a right answer, targeting a particular skill or understanding out of context—like the sideline drill in athletics. Typically involves constrained and unproblematic application—the plugging in of a fact, formula, method, theory. | State or national test items<br><br>Objective local quizzes and tests<br><br>End-of-chapter homework questions<br><br>Worksheet drill questions |
| Prompt | A discrete question, puzzle, or issue requiring a constructed response, with no single answer or approach. The setting tends to be examlike and the work tends to be paper and pencil. No real audience or purpose beyond the suggestion of it in the prompt. | Questions such as: "How big a mortgage can you afford (given data)?" "Must a story have a moral?" "What is this 'sludge' chemically composed of?"<br><br>Academic problems and writing prompts, such as debugging software; meal menus when there are health, cultural, and taste issues; First Amendment concerns and the Internet; hazing and bullying in the school. |
| Performance task | A complex challenge culminating in a product or performance—in which knowledge must be skillfully and gracefully used and the result must be well crafted. Real or simulated audiences and purposes. Preparation and refinement are demanded and expected. | Museum exhibit, community problem, formal debate, science lab, formal dramatic reading, writing of a poem, job interview, oral history interview, design of a new tuna can to maximize volume, etc. |
| Project | A multistaged and multifaceted set of interlocking tasks, culminating in one or more complex products, performances, or exhibits (typically requiring cross-content knowledge, skills, and collaboration). | Designing and building a museum, science fair project, art anthology and exhibition, civic reform, mock trial, model United Nations, video documentary, etc. |

Figure 8.4 Questions and Answers for Documentation of Student Work

| Purposes | What is documented? | Who determines what is documented? | *Documentation* What degree of student choice? | What degree of teacher choice? | Uniform assignments required? |
|---|---|---|---|---|---|
| Profile of Achievement | A valid and reliable sample of work across the program domain | Teachers | Limited to work within prescribed genres, topics, program goals | Some | Some, to obtain more credible and comparable assessment |
| Record of Progress/ Growth | A valid and reliable sample of work across iterative and ongoing program goals | Teachers and supervisors of a program | Limited to specific pieces within recurring tasks and topics | Significant, as long as the choices suit program goals | Some, especially key skill tasks used as ongoing pre/post measures of progress |
| Student Talents and Interests | Work that reflects student talents and interests | Teacher and student | Significant | Some, through conferences with student where "what is in the student's interest" gets clarified | No |
| Program Accountability | Samples of work showing achievement levels for program goals | Supervisors, teachers, school boards, state officials, etc. | Limited or none | Limited to data that is viewed as credible by overseers | Yes, to make possible comparable results |

Figure 8.5 Questions and Answers for Assessment of Student Work

| Purposes | Assessment | | | | | |
| --- | --- | --- | --- | --- | --- | --- |
| | *What is assessed?* | *By whom? (for credibility)* | *Scope or sample size?* | *Evaluation essential?* | *Source and nature of standards and criteria?* | *Performance expectation (minimum score) required?* |
| Profile of Achievement | Levels of achievement against national standards | Disinterested insiders and/or outsiders | Depth and breadth of subject-matter domain; valid and reliable samples of work from all students | Yes | Valid wider-world standards and criteria | Yes |
| Record of Progress/ Growth | Rate or degree of progress | Teacher(s) and supervisors of a program | A sample of student work, from all students | No, but reporting of norms for progress is useful for establishing the meaning of the trend | Wider-world and local norms of performance over time | Optional: recommended range of progress rate, based on data about eventual exit performance |
| Student Talents and Interests | Work quality, depth, and breadth of talent and interest | Teacher(s) and student | A sample of student work, from all students | No | Standards based on goals and self-assessment | No |
| Program Accountability | Extent to which program goals and standards were met | Teachers other than the classroom teacher, external assessors | A sample of student work from a sample of students | Yes | National and local subject-area and program standards | Yes, but in terms of cohort scores relating to mean, range |

## CHAPTER 9

# Curriculum and Instruction

If we are to teach for understanding as well as knowledge and skills, and if we are to give students ongoing authentic assessment tasks and scoring rubrics that have been thoughtfully designed to give them feedback that will improve their performance, we clearly need to change more than our assessment practices.[1] When we no longer assume that assessment is what we design and do *after* curriculum writing, teaching, and learning are over but instead make assessment a central part of our teaching and a way for students to achieve progressive understanding, then the very way we think about curriculum, teaching, and learning must change.

Once we move to performance-based assessment, we soon see that most of what we currently call curriculum writing is a waste of time, inappropriate in *form* more than content. Effective learning and school improvement are possible only when we grasp that curricula must be built backward from authentic assessment tasks, the latter providing a rationale and a basis for selecting content, skills, modes of instruction, and sequence. Only when we grasp the logic required by a focus on student *understanding* and *performance* as opposed to the logic of content will we see how nonpurposeful and ineffective traditional curricula have been.

Students should encounter content as an obvious and helpful means to known and concrete intellectual performance ends. This way of putting the matter may seem obvious to some, but the implications require wholesale changes in our habits and curricular frameworks. This view requires that we design courses, not just assessments, "backward" from the standards and their particular demands (representing the broader core achievement targets), not "forward" from a logic based on the arrangement of a textbook or other analytical topic arrangements. The organization should be in the *learning,* not in the abstract order of the topics. In traditional courses, content leads nowhere, from the learner's point of view, except toward more content.

In a curriculum designed to achieve improved performance, the organizing principle refers to a movement toward known performance goals, and a back and forth movement between means and ends—movement that feels natural to the learner. With clarity about the *purpose* of content in the pursuit of the intended performance results, teachers and students will be able to grasp and adjust their efforts in light of their priorities from day one. The practical implication is that courses lead to work anthologies, where overarching questions and performance tasks are known by the student from the beginning.

Jerome Bruner once said that it was an "epistemological mystery why traditional education has so often emphasized extensiveness and coverage over intensiveness and depth."[2] But when teachers are taught to think egocentrically about course design (What should I teach? What would I like to teach?), when tests are based on asking students to give back a sample of the content taught, and when education systems and teaching and testing materials encourage teachers to think that "coverage" is the best approach because it maximizes teaching and test performance (versus learning and competence), the mystery disappears. This chapter explains more about why we have the curricula we do, and it points toward a new world of learning-centered curriculum design, including some examples of design templates and design assessment rubrics used at the Center on Learning, Assessment, and School Structure (CLASS).

## Backward Design: Deriving Curriculum and Instruction from Targets and Assessments

As noted in Chapter Five, so-called backward design in assessment requires that we derive the appropriate assessment evidence from the standards and criteria for which we are aiming. Instead of jumping to any old task or test idea, we must ask: What kind of task should we design in light of the evidence we need? and Where should we look and what should we look for in light of the target?

We now expand the logic of backward design to show how instructional design derives from the previous answers. The logic can be summarized in five steps. (Note that the logic discussed in

Chapter Five is contained in the first two steps; the instructional implications follow in the remaining three steps.)

1. Identify desired results (standards).

    - What should students understand, know, and be able to do?

2. Specify apt evidence of results (assessments).

    - How will we know if students have achieved the desired results?

    - What will we accept as evidence of student understanding and proficiency?

3. Specify enabling knowledge and skills.

    - What "enabling knowledge" (facts, concepts, principles) will students need in order to achieve the desired results and master the specified tasks?

    - What "enabling skills" (procedures, strategies, methods) will students need to perform effectively?

4. Design appropriate sequence of enabling work (activities and experiences).

    - What "enabling activities" will develop the targeted enabling understanding and skills?

    - What design approach will make the work most engaging and responsive to student interests, needs, and abilities?

    - How will the design provide opportunities for students to dig deeper, revise their thinking, and polish their performance?

5. Specify the needed teaching and coaching.

    - What will I need to teach and coach to ensure effective performance?

    - What materials need to be assembled or provided to ensure maximal performance?

This approach is backward because teachers must establish with specificity the standards and measures before determining what will be taught, how to teach it, and in what order to teach it. At the heart of such design is the idea that content knowledge and skills should be framed by and chosen in reference to complex performances that embody curricular standards. In selecting and ordering content, the questions become: What knowledge will equip and enable students to do worthy work by the course's end? and How should we design the work to enable us to equip students with apt knowledge and skill while addressing questions, topics, and texts we care about? The consequence of such design is that students encounter content as the obvious and helpful means to known and overarching intellectual performance ends. They grasp that their job is to master tasks and grapple with questions that require integrated content and skill, not just to learn content in isolation.

A course of study may thus be construed as a set of work-focused units that address the overarching program goals and targets in the form of complex performance tasks. Each unit is organized around work requirements that are designed to provide apt assessment evidence. The set of complex tasks acts as a bridge between the overarching standards of the course and program and the specifics of teaching. Again, consider the decathlon analogy. The ten events give specific meaning to the goal of overall athlete. The specificity and primacy of the events then focus training, coaching, and learning.

The necessary link between assessment design and curriculum design can be usefully thought of as coherence between assessment and curriculum. At its most basic, the word *coherence* implies a sensible organization. As the *Oxford English Dictionary* puts it, coherence is "logical connexion or relation; congruity, consistency."[3] There should be a clear relation of the parts to the whole and to one another; there should be an apparent unity.

But apparent to *whom?* Coherent from *whose* point of view? As this book has argued throughout, the answer is the performer, not (just) the designer. This requires that worthy and educative assessment tasks be the anchors of curricular design—just as in all sports, the arts, and other genuinely performance-based endeavors. The game or recital does not come only *after* teaching and learning. Its demands are what focus learning, lesson design, and midcourse adjustment in light of feedback. The complex performances we want students eventually to master are what *prioritize decisions* about content, materials and activities, and textbook outlines. We thus come to think of knowledge as enabling tools, not as inert and directionless stuff.

Note especially that interdisciplinary courses, although popularly believed to be a way of increasing coherence and student involvement in content, are not the answer to the problem of incoherent and purposeless learning. They do not produce curricula designed to improve performance. Most courses of this type merely present an arrangement of more diverse content than is found in the typical course, not a new logic of organization based on a clearer goal. Directionless courses are not rendered coherent by bringing in related subject matter. On the contrary, they can easily seem more fractured than before if they focus on content divorced from performance.

Similarly, what has been called measurement-driven instruction or mastery learning does not produce genuinely educative and performance-driven curricula. Instead, mastery learning projects have been bedeviled by simplistic testing designed only to show whether discrete facts and skills that were taught were learned. Such a view easily leads to teaching and measuring what is easy to measure and produces a reductionist and anti-intellectual kind of teaching.

## Overarching Questions and Tasks

The cultivation of reflectiveness is one of the great problems one faces in devising curricula: how to lead children to discover the powers and pleasures that await the exercise of retrospection.

Let me suggest one answer that grew from what we have done. It is the use of the organizing conjecture. They serve two functions, one of them obvious: putting perspective back into the particulars. The second is less obvious and more surprising. The questions often seemed to serve as criteria for determining where they were getting and how well they were understanding.[4]

For students to perceive a relation of parts to a whole in their work they must be aware of specific recurring overarching objectives and performance standards (whether or not the course crosses subject-area boundary lines). "Why are we doing this?" and "What is its value?" are questions that any curriculum should explicitly address, and a student should rarely need to ask. The answers should be evident. Two strategies in curriculum writing make this more possible: organizing all work and chronology around essential questions and pointing inquiry toward final tasks and other work requirements. Knowing the overarching questions and standards that inform and justify the choice of content provides students with guiding insight as they work. Knowing the final tasks and performance obligations further clarifies students' priorities.

For example, in my teaching over a decade ago, all my courses were organized around "essential questions" that determined the texts rather than around texts that determined the questions.[5] Thus, in an upper-level English elective one of the units was entitled "Who Has Vision?" In light of this question we read *Oedipus Rex*, Plato's allegory of the cave, an excerpt from Helen Keller's autobiography, and biographies of various artists, scientists, and innovators. The assessment products involved two writings (a culminating essay on the overarching question, known to the students on day one of the unit; and a journal of reflections on each reading). Each student also gave a talk to the class on his or her answer to the question. Although there was nothing particularly innovative about these final performance tasks, the virtue for the students was in knowing their obligations up front as well as being clear about the rationale for the assignments. The students' reading had far greater focus and purpose than typically occurs in secondary school, where students often have no clear idea of why a particular book is assigned, what questions will be pursued in class, or what will be expected of them at unit's end. It is extraordinarily difficult to read a complex text when one has no clear inclusive objective and is not sure what ideas have priority. Teachers who resist such directed reading should try to experience it from the students' point of view: not knowing the objectives and priorities makes study needlessly difficult and too much like "Gotcha!" testing. Moreover, it is disingenuous to claim that the direction provided by a guiding question somehow interferes with the students' reading interests: after all, the teacher teaches and tests from a point of view about what is important to note and why.

Let us explore the idea of essential questions further. As I noted in Chapter Four, understanding requires rethinking. Therefore, more than assessments should recur. The key questions at the heart of each subject should recur, and curriculum should be organized around these recurring and important questions. Indeed, essential questions provide the optimal framework for the design of instruction and assessment. If knowledge is made up of answers, then what are the questions? Too often students leave school never realizing that knowledge is produced and refined in response to inquiry and debate. Too often, as a result, standards are experienced in intellectually sterile ways, as if learning was mere imitation and ingestion and instruction was mere didactic teaching. And too often the design of a course precludes students from asking and pursuing penetrating questions as they arise in the unfolding work, which leads to less engagement.

As I have argued throughout the book, intelligent use of knowledge is at the heart of each subject discipline—what Bruner called the blend of competence and performance, as noted in Chapter Six. Shouldn't we try to make coursework more authentic, in the sense that it should reveal how all adult knowledge is pursued, shaped, and eventually systematized through questioning? And thus, shouldn't we help the student simulate or recreate some of the processes by which the knowledge was created?

Think of curriculum, then, as involving not only the learning of what we know but as helping the student learn how we know it, how we came to know it, and what makes it knowledge instead of a hunch. Put as an instructional goal, a carefully designed recreation of how knowledge came to be knowledge (out of questions and competing theories) is one key to developing genuine understanding in students.[6] Our aim as teachers then becomes one of not merely coverage but of *un*coverage. (This also inevitably makes important room for student questions that now seem important, not "stupid" or off topic.)

The following curricular unit—an award-winning one from a CLASS-sponsored design competition—shows how understanding can be developed in a questions-focused, iterative, and performance-based way. In Daniel Beaupré's unit on ancient civilizations (shown in its complete form in Figure 9.1), he asks students to think like an archaeologist. Students are confronted first with the key questions "What is a civilization?" and "What are its signs?" The work really begins with a rehearsal for a real archaeological analysis. Students are asked to analyze a penny as an introduction to the problem of making sense of artifacts (and the danger of projecting present-day or culture-bound ideas onto ancient artifacts). The students conclude by analyzing a famous artifact, the Standard of Ur, and then critiquing the analysis of the archaeologist who found it, staying mindful of the problems they encountered in the earlier exercise. The work culminates in a revisiting of the questions that began the unit.

Here is another illustration of using question-focused and performance-based logic to provide purpose (meaningful goals that supplant comparatively aimless coverage deriving from the logic of a textbook-driven syllabus), this time in a mathematics course. Consider a typical high school course in geometry. The curriculum is usually dictated by the textbook and its many topics and exercises. Though the course is organized by topics and by the logic of proofs derived from axioms, it cannot usually be said to have a purpose other than covering a certain number of facts and formulas. But imagine a unit of such a course on the Pythagorean theorem that is designed to cause mastery of the following tasks and questions (which would be known by the students as the unit starts):

1. Provide two pieces of work based on research that show interesting and insightful real-world applications of the Pythagorean theorem. One of those pieces might involve alternative proofs of the theorem.

2. Does the Pythagorean theorem still work when the figures drawn on the legs are not squares? Investigate.

3. Be prepared to discuss and write on the question "Was the Pythagorean theorem true before the Greeks discovered the proof?"

Three additional overarching questions would dominate the course:

1. Using your knowledge of geometry thus far, address the question "Was geometry invented or discovered?" (This

## Figure 9.1  Unit Design for the Standard of Ur

1.  Introduce the unit using the essential questions: What is civilization? How do we know what we know? Have students write a brief definition of civilization. An additional activity can be based on having students bring in an object they believe symbolizes a civilization.

2.  In class the U.S. penny is examined. Students make observations and make a list of observable facts. They will be called "near facts." There is a sharing of facts and near facts so students accumulate as many as possible. Magnifying glasses and microscopes can be used to closely observe the penny. After each student selects facts and near facts, they copy each one onto a small card. Facts are pink, and near facts are blue.

3.  Students will arrange the layers of facts and near facts at the bottom of a pyramidal tower. By arranging and rearranging the cards they combine facts and near facts to make knowledge claims. The knowledge claims are written on yellow cards.

4.  After sharing knowledge claims with each other, each student makes a final interpretation of the penny. This is done at home. The final interpretation is written on a green card. Some students will make one interpretation for each side of the artifact, in which case they will make a final interpretation on another card of a different color. They write a journal entry on the strengths and weaknesses of the interpretation.

5.  Interpretations are shared.

6.  In partnerships, students accumulate facts and near facts based on a close observation of the "Standard of Ur." The name of the artifact is not shared with the students because it may influence their interpretation. The same color coding is used.

7.  At home, individual students make knowledge claims and a final interpretation of the artifact. Lines are drawn. For organization purposes students should arrange all the facts, near facts, and knowledge claims based on each side of the artifact in separate sections of the tower.

8.  Students present their finished inductive towers to the class. Classmates are encouraged to question the validity of each interpretation.

9.  The published interpretation of Sir Leonard Woolley is read. At home, students deconstruct his and their own interpretations.

10. Students write another definition of civilization with the intention of making a more sophisticated definition based on what they have learned in the inductive process.

11. Last, students write a journal entry on the strengths and weaknesses of the inductive method based on their experiences with the penny, the Standard of Ur, and Woolley's interpretation. A discussion entitled "How Do We Know What We Know" ends the unit.

question will be asked twice again in the course.) For example, if axioms are given, how are they given and by whom? In what sense are they true? In what sense are they arbitrary? Why did Euclid distinguish between axioms and postulates? In light of your answers, how should we best describe or justify the particular postulates?

2.  Complete the stem "You can't really be said to understand Euclidean geometry unless you can . . ."

3. Conduct at least one investigation of the history or application of nonEuclidean geometries to address the question "What are the strengths and weaknesses of the Euclidean model of space?"

Now the course goes somewhere: the student must use the fruits of the many specific subskills and notions of the course to address more sweeping and substantive questions and challenges. Merely following the textbook through its chapters and end-of-chapter problems is far less likely now that there are integrative tasks to be mastered, requiring a logic of efficiency and larger effectiveness. Known and required portfolio tasks ensure that teacher and students will keep these tasks in view in the beginning, middle, and end of their studies. The teacher's job now is to use the textbook as a reference book, not as a syllabus outline. Practically speaking, it would now be unwise to build assessment exclusively out of the problems at the end of each chapter. Coherence between curriculum and assessment will improve when the course is purposeful in this way.

In Victoria, Australia, this method of curriculum design has already been adopted, so the curricular frameworks for high school courses are built around "work requirements." Here is an outline of the work requirements for chemistry:[7]

### Victoria, Australia, High School Chemistry Work Requirements

Modelling Structures

- Construct models to represent continuous lattices, molecules
- Inspect and evaluate models of atom, polymers, ceramics, alloys
- Discuss strengths and weaknesses of models

Investigation of Waste Materials

- Experiments on properties of waste materials
- Design and perform experiment on how to treat a waste sample, e.g. contaminated water
- Identify waste materials generated during production of a useful material, strategies used for dealing with waste
- Discuss advantages and disadvantages of methods used in waste treatment and their implications for continued use of material

Investigation of Oxidation-Reduction Reactions

- Perform a range of experiments to observe oxidation reactions, demonstrate electron transfer nature by constructing simple galvanic cells

- Design and perform an experiment which relates to metal reactivity and corrosion protection, evaluate the design

Other Work Requirement Categories

- Media File
- Record of Reactions
- Investigation of an Instrument
- Changing Models of the Atom
- Investigation of Useful Materials
- Investigation of a Chemical of Local Importance
- Product Analysis
- Investigation of Equilibrium
- Investigation of Periodic Table
- Investigation of Properties of Water

(The similarity between these requirements and the New Standards portfolio guidelines listed in Chapter Four is due to the fact that Ann Borthwick, who directed the Victoria work, now works for New Standards.)

## Criteria for Essential Questions_____

Generalizing from the examples given earlier, here are some standards for overarching questions.

1. *Overarching questions go to the heart of a discipline.* They can be found in the most historically important (and controversial) problems and topics in the sciences: What is adequate proof in each field of inquiry? What does federalism or states' rights imply? Is our society more advanced than those of the past? Is light a particle or a wave? Are mathematical concepts inventions or discoveries? Does the fossil record support Darwinian theory? Must history tell a story, or does it falsify history by doing so? Each course and program can be designed to explicitly address the essential questions; textbooks, lectures, exercises, and other resources and assignments can serve as the means to address these questions. Lessons can involve a bridge between the larger questions and the specific questions that arise from specific books, topics, or skills (just as criteria in tasks derive from the standards but must include the specific criteria appropriate to the chosen task).

2. *Overarching questions have no one obvious right answer.* Essential answers are not self-evident. Even if there are principles, truths, and laws in a discipline, the student must come to know that

there are other plausible theses and hypotheses to be considered and sorted through along with the sanctioned views. The essential stories and theories are thus seen as better and justifiable explanations, not just givens or the only possible accounts. Thus a question with a known, uncontroversial answer—no matter how important the topic—is not an essential question.

3. *Overarching questions are "higher-order," in Bloom's sense—always matters of analysis, synthesis, and evaluative judgment.* The student is always asked to "go beyond the information given."[8] Such questions require constant rethinking; they admit not so much of correct answers as justified and plausible answers.

4. *Overarching questions recur; they are raised naturally rather than asked throughout one's learning.* Really essential questions arise and re-arise. Our answers should become increasingly sophisticated. Consider the question of nature versus nurture as the guiding influence in human development, which has arisen anew three or four different times in the last forty years, as behaviorism, sociobiology, biochemical views about mental illness and addiction, and evolutionary biology have gained credibility.

5. *Overarching questions are framed to provoke and sustain student interest.* Essential questions work best when the questions are edited to be thought-provoking, generative of interesting inquiries, and able to accommodate diverse interests and learning styles. A real question provides opportunities for enterprising and creative approaches; there is not one way to do things or to prove that mastery of the question—as opposed to an answer—has been achieved. It's one thing to ask "Did Gorbachev fulfill or undermine the promise of the Russian Revolution?" It is another to ask "Who blew it?" The latter question clearly works better for working with adolescents than the former, even if their purpose is the same.

6. *Overarching questions link to other essential questions.* Good questions engender other good questions. It is therefore useful to think of a family of related questions as anchoring a course and a unit and also to make clear to students that the questions that arise naturally for them are part of clarifying the essential questions.

Here are some examples of essential questions:

- Must a story have a moral? A beginning, middle, and end? Heroes and villains?

- Is geometry more like mapmaking and using a map or more like inventing and playing games like chess? Were theorems invented or discovered?

- Is our history a history of progress?
- Can novels reveal inner life without falsifying it?
- Is light a particle or a wave?
- Do statistics lie?
- "War is diplomacy by other means." Is this true? Is it immoral if we believe it?
- Are some aspects of language and culture not understandable by people from other cultures?
- Is terrorism wrong? Do revolutionaries differ from terrorists? Or from criminals? Were our country's founders terrorists?
- Is gravity a fact or a theory? Is evolution a fact or a theory?
- Do mathematical models conceal as much as they reveal?
- In what ways are animals human? In what ways are humans animals?
- Must a biography have a plot?
- Were our country's founders hypocrites for terming slaves *partial people?*
- Who really has vision? Oedipus? Teiresias? Helen Keller? Van Gogh?
- What makes a liberal a liberal and a conservative a conservative?
- Is biology destiny?
- Who is authentic? Who are phonies? What makes people be phony? (Why does it matter to Holden Caufield?)

Many teachers fear that complex projects or performance tasks will cut too deeply into their overall content-related goals—that breadth (and sometimes rigor) will be sacrificed for depth. The fear is understandable but unfounded. The tasks and projects are deliberately designed to require teaching of the core content now being taught more didactically and piecemeal, as the following example shows.

The following list is a summary of an approach to teaching and assessing the New York Regents course in global studies, which I presented to the Regents almost a decade ago. These tasks were developed backward from an analysis of typical patterns of test questions and the major ideas outlined in the syllabus. They thus map the major elements of the required core content in the syllabus into tasks that require control over those elements.

1.   Design a tour of the world's most holy sites.
2.   Write an International Bill of Rights.

3. Report to the Secretary of State with a policy analysis and background report on a Latin American country.

4. Collect and analyze media reports from other countries on U.S. policies in the Middle East.

5. Conduct an oral history on a topical but historically interesting issue of global significance.

6. Design a museum exhibit using artifacts and facsimiles.

7. Write and deliver on videotape two speeches: one by the visiting head of an African country on the history of U.S.–African relations, and the other a response by the U.S. President's spokesman.

8. Take part in a formal debate on a controversial issue of global significance, for example, aid to Russian republics, the U.S. role in the fall of communism, and so on.

9. Conduct a model United Nations, with groups of two to three students representing a country; address a new Security Council resolution on terrorism and a resolution on aid to Bosnia.

10. Write a textbook chapter for middle school students on the topic "People, Ideas, Events, or Economic Conditions." Which are the primary causes of revolution? Were the most important revolutions revolutionary or evolutionary?

11. Write and research a position paper for your school administration on how to handle the diversity of viewpoints on the proper celebration and recognition of religious holidays in the school.

12. Take additional tests and quizzes on content and skill.

Whatever (inevitable!) delays and diversions occur during the school day, whatever asides and deliberate following of student interests occur in the classroom, all parties know that the work requirements, those defined and known core tasks, must be mastered. And now the teacher must rethink traditional chronology and textbook chapters to ask, What kinds of instruction will build toward and enable such performance? Further, as with any other coaching, the teacher will have to make sure that students have ample opportunity to work on weaknesses of performance as they arise in "rehearsal."

There is no attempt to establish a new orthodoxy here. Each unit need not culminate in an authentic task. Rather, as occurs in performance coaching in the arts and athletics, and as suggested by the decathlon metaphor used in other chapters, the goal is to make curriculum design responsive to performance requirements. This book has said throughout that the assessment (and now the curriculum) should be anchored in core tasks based on core genres and applications of key ideas, but that there remains a vital role for traditional tests and quizzes as complements and building blocks. And as noted in the architecture analogy used in Chapter Five, the designer must always worry about the givens that obligate teachers and students, such as state frameworks and/or tests. But within those frameworks there are great opportunities for innovation, as suggested by the global studies portfolio framework just presented.

The Central Park East Secondary School, the extraordinary school founded by Deborah Meier in New York, has taken the idea of coherence derived from performance requirements to the next level: the last two years of schooling are defined by performance requirements; the teaching must adapt to the learner, not the learner to the teaching. After two years of required courses, the student enters the Senior Institute, where the final performance requirements (Figure 9.2) determine everything about the student's direction, schedule, and timetable.[9] The following guidelines are given for the final portfolio: "Portfolio items are evaluated for quality and demonstrated mastery using a grid that reflects five major criteria: a viewpoint that encompasses wide knowledge and deep understanding; an ability to draw connections among information and ideas; appropriate use of evidence; an engaging voice and awareness of audience; and use of proper conventions."[10] In such a system (whether for assessing mathematics, history, or graduation requirements), the learner's experience becomes more logical to the learner because there are performance requirements—goals—that cause teachers and students to plan and adjust teaching and learning in light of the tasks, criteria, and standards connected to those goals.

This way of thinking about curriculum design, as framed and determined by measurable objectives, is not new. It was most clearly and concisely formulated by Ralph Tyler almost fifty years ago in his book *Basic Principles of Curriculum and Instruction.* Tyler argued that a logical and effective curriculum was possible only when clear and explicit purposes guided all choices of lessons, texts, and tests. Moreover, teacher intentions are not to be confused with these educational purposes; instead, Tyler insisted, curricular objectives need to be stated in terms of the learner's actions, not the teacher's. "Since the real purpose of education is not to have the instructor perform certain activities but to bring about significant changes in the students' patterns of behavior, it becomes important to recognize that any statement of the objectives . . . should be a statement of changes to take place in the student."[11]

Figure 9.2
Central Park East Secondary School Graduation Requirements

| | |
|---|---|
| 1. Postgraduate plan | Each student outlines his or her purpose for earning a diploma. This section includes long- and short-range career and life goals, financial concerns, living arrangements, and indicators of progress such as examinations, interviews, and letters of reference. |
| 2. Autobiography | This reflective project may examine family history, special events or relationships, values, or beliefs in any of a variety of forms. |
| 3. School/ community service and internship | Opportunities for working and serving others are part of student experiences starting in seventh grade. Students develop a formal resume of their work experiences along with a project demonstrating what they have learned from one or more of them; this may include essays, videos, work samples, reference letters, and the like. |
| 4. Ethics and social issues | Students demonstrate their capacity to see multiple perspectives, weigh and use evidence, and reason about social and moral issues by staging a debate, writing an editorial, discussing important issues raised by a novel or film, or another project. |
| 5. Fine arts and aesthetics | Creative expression and creative appreciation are both evaluated. Student must create a hands-on exhibition of performance in any of the arts and also show understanding or knowledge of an aesthetic area by studying or critiquing a work, an artist, or a field of artistic expression. |
| 6. Mass media | Through a project or activity that includes a relevant bibliography, students must demonstrate understanding of how different forms of media work and how they affect people and their thinking. |
| 7. Practical skills | Students must show evidence of working knowledge in a number of areas (health and medical care, employment, citizenship, independent living, computers and technology, legal rights) in a variety of ways (securing a driver's license, registering to vote, operating a computer). |
| 8. Geography | A teacher-made test and a student-designed performance are used to evaluate geographical knowledge and the ability to use geographical tools such as maps and globes. |
| 9. Second language and/or dual language | Students must demonstrate competence in a language other than English as a speaker, listener, reader, and writer. (This can be done via the New York State language proficiency exam or a College Board exam.) In addition, all students must describe their personal experience with dual language issues and be prepared to discuss a key social or cultural issue associated with language use. |
| 10. Science and technology | Students must demonstrate knowledge in traditional ways—a summary of the work they have completed in high school and passage of a teacher-made or state competency test—as well as in performances that demonstrate use of scientific methodology (e.g., conducting and documenting an experiment) and awareness of how science is used in the modern world (e.g., by staging a debate or conducting research on a scientific development analyzing social costs and benefits). |

Figure 9.2 Continued

| 11. Mathematics | Students must demonstrate knowledge by passing a state competency test and a teacher-made test. In addition, they must demonstrate higher-order thinking abilities by developing a project using mathematics for political, civic, or consumer purposes (e.g., social science statistics or polling; architectural blueprints) and either scientific or "pure" mathematics (e.g., using mathematics in a scientific application and/or studying a theoretical problem). |
|---|---|
| 12. Literature | Students prepare a list of texts they have read in a wide range of genres to serve as the basis for discussion with the graduation committee. They also submit samples of their own essays about literary works or figures, demonstrating their capacity to reflect on and communicate effectively about literary products and ideas. |
| 13. History | In addition to passing a state competency test in history, students must prepare an overview of the areas of history they have studied in secondary school and a timeline of major significant events and persons. They must also demonstrate understanding of historical work by conducting historical research using primary and secondary sources and developing a bibliography. Their work must draw connections between and among past and present events, weigh and use evidence, speculate on other possibilities, and evaluate how history is used or abused in current debates. |
| 14. Physical challenge | Students demonstrate and/or document their participation and proficiency in any team or individual sport or activity over the past four years. The goal is to encourage the development of lifelong health habits and attitudes of independence, interdependence, personal responsibility, and sportsmanship. |

*A more extensive final **senior project** is also required in an area of particular interest to the student, which may be one of the portfolio items explored in greater depth.*

## Beyond the Egocentrism of Coverage

Our outdated view of what it means to write curriculum and teach it thus rests on a basic misunderstanding. A curriculum is not merely an abstract sketch of ideas, designed for the teacher's benefit only, to be justified in broad intellectual terms ("covered" and "logical" to the designer). It is more like a blueprint designed for subcontractors to yield work that meets building codes and contracts. The question we then ask in judging design is, Do the student products—like finished buildings—honor the contract, and do the products and the knowledge they reflect "hang together in harmonious connexion"?[12] Are the effects of our plans coherent—or do they only *seem* coherent? Does the student—the building contractor—understand what we want her or him to produce? From this vantage point, coherence is measured by the results of instruction, not by the intentions of the teacher (just as was true in the logic of assessment design). The student is not the "product"; the students' work products are the product of our work—as if we were chief contractors and they our subcontractors.

Alas, when I ask teachers to state the student performance goals implied in their written curriculum—what students should be able to do and see when the teaching is over that they could not do before—many describe instead what they intend to teach and what they intend students to know: "I want them to read Salinger to understand what it's like to be an alienated adolescent," or "I want them to solve problems of multiple variables." These statements are preludes to the answer; they are not themselves the answer. Because until the teacher explains what kinds of work (to what standards and criteria) serve as evidence of the desired skill and insight, there is no actual goal against which progress can be measured by both performer and coach. It is as if a baseball coach said that the purpose of the program was to "understand the game and develop baseball skills" and left it at that, devoting most of his time to didactic teaching about the game. When I describe the kinds of evidence requirements that might focus a course, many teachers argue that they "can't do such intensive work because it takes time away from the content." But that is like a coach saying that there is no time for games because there is so much baseball content to teach. Such a view also makes it possible to rationalize almost any instruction, because no specific results on specific tasks are targeted.

When the goal of teaching is improved performance, teacher intention and action are not going to get us very far. Neither is knowing the calendar by which the teacher is going to lay out her or his adult knowledge. We need to know what equipping and enabling work will occur, leading toward what counts as valid evidence that students have understood what is to be learned; and we need to know whether the teacher knows how to change the plans and the schedule in light of ongoing results. We want to know how the teacher will ensure the best possible performance. Those questions can be answered only by a teacher who is thinking like an assessor, as noted in Chapter Five, who is stating up front, for herself or himself and for the students, what counts as evidence of understanding and skill—the final tasks, scoring criteria, and justifiable standards—given the aims.

This discussion is really about changing our view of the teaching job. Remember the old chestnut, "I taught it, so they must have learned it"? This is what I call the educator's egocentric fallacy, and many of us are still acting on it. This fallacy—that it is teaching that causes learning—is the reverse of the view that has been emphasized throughout this book.

Learning comes from the successive approximations taken by the student to accomplish the learning. Those successive approximations involve slowly mastering, sometimes by trial and error, core intellectual tasks—tasks that can be done well only by those with understanding and skill. As already described, such understandings are not taught, in the old sense of that word, but derived from mastery of understanding performances and learner self-assessment using teacher designs and guidance. In the new view, teaching is coaching targeted instruction in support of performance needs and emerging problems—much like what the coach does in response to game performance at half-time and for the next practice. Thus the goal in curriculum design should be, first, to help the learner see that knowledge has value for performance and how seemingly isolated facts and skills in fact cohere, and then to determine what will tell us that the student has in fact understood the knowledge and skills and can apply them.

The illusion of thoroughness derived from considering only one's own lesson plans and not their impact means that teachers can go a lifetime without conducting research into their own practice, without asking the assessor's kinds of questions: How is performance on these overarching tasks optimized? How are we doing? What do my current results reveal? How might the coaching, rehearsals, and sequencing be improved? Which poor results were due to the incoherence of my design and methods, and which were due to the givens of my students? The defenders of the overly didactic syllabus have typically never done the experiments that follow from these questions. Rather, they usually rationalize their own habits—and blame students for poor performance. Consequently, coverage of content is sustained as a habit. The thinking is that by telling, explaining, and testing, the teacher maximizes learning; that by assigning lots of pages and "demanding" results, the teacher is absolved of responsibility for the predictably wide range of results. What this approach fails to consider is whether teacher performing and demanding is maximizing learning.

A focus on coverage of content also encourages the teacher to overlook the implications of the fact that any curriculum is a sample of a much larger domain of subject matter. A brief overview of a subject can seem complete to the teacher even though it seems sketchy and random to the learner and superficial or incomplete to the expert. When curricula are textbook driven, the appearance of coherence is even greater: texts are typically written to provide the illusion of thorough coverage of a subject, but in fact they often provide only encyclopedia-like synopses of ideas and facts. Textbook-driven courses also implicitly suggest that everything covered is important or it would not have been selected. Thus the student's only job is to learn all of what is in the text.

But if everything is important, then nothing is important. Importance, to be understood as such, must be verified by the student through inquiry and performance. It depends on the student rethinking what he or she has learned through reiterative performance. Important ideas emerge as such only when their value is repeatedly observed in numerous attempts, revisions of work, and connections across works. Any curriculum, then, is best judged on its ability to enable students to gain sophisticated and graceful control of a few worthy and generative tasks that both require and reveal deep understanding.[13] It takes an iterative, not a linear, curriculum to ultimately address the problem that Bruner identified, of why "traditional education has so often emphasized extensiveness and coverage over intensiveness and depth,"[14]—not merely more performance-based assessment grafted onto traditional syllabi.

## Toward a Results Focus in Curriculum: Organized Adjustment

Naively calling our coverage plans a curriculum also means we tacitly assume that learners will have no impact on our plans. One of the most extraordinary facts about most curricula and syllabi (especially at the secondary and college level) is that they are designed to be impervious to learners. If it is Tuesday, April 11, then we must be teaching World War I or the quadratic formula. This abstract curriculum sticks close to its schedule, despite such realities of school keeping as fire drills, snowstorms, stomach flu, early dismissal for football away games, and students with varying and sometimes inadequate preparation.

Unforeseeable interruptions, serendipitous teachable moments, student mobility, and diverse learning rates dominate the reality of curriculum users, but too often curricula are written and syllabi followed as if these problems did not exist. How telling it is, for example, that most teachers do not use a pre-test/post-test approach to better gauge what students bring to a subject. In contrast, a results-based curriculum is sensitive to emerging learner struggle and misunderstanding, to learner's unanticipatable difficulties, detours, epiphanies, and emergent interests. Learners appropriately alter the curriculum and its outcome by these unanticipatable responses.

There is thus an inevitable tension to resolve in any curriculum design. We want students to learn and to learn to do certain things, but students may or may not learn on our timetable or in response to our methods. We then have a stark choice: either design a curriculum that can be responsive and flexible without losing sight of its goals, or continue teaching the coverage curriculum as if nothing had happened. In most schools, the latter practice still predominates.

The only way we can stay on the course that improves learners' performance is to know our specific destination (have a performance-related purpose) and to have a compass and sextant (final performance tasks and standards, and troubleshooting guides). Curriculum guides must become more like a map and troubleshooting guide for intelligent teacher performance, not a mere list of preordained sites to visit on an itinerary. There must be feedback indicators and advice about whether we are on or off course when en route, in the face of various unpredictable adventures and detours. Our flexibility and ability to adjust depends on knowing in advance the bottom-line results expected from any trip we take.

There must therefore be a built-in set of criteria (found in the final tasks) for troubleshooting a syllabus when time (inevitably) falls short of our plans and wishes. An effective curriculum must be fluid while being focused, built on feedback loops in relation to fixed operational performance goals—where we are versus where we need to be eventually. The learner's idiosyncratic and unpredictable responses to our teaching toward goals must cause the curriculum to adjust; the learner's emerging performance and needs ultimately determine how the curriculum unfolds; but the curriculum must enable students to meet preestablished targets.

The problem therefore lies primarily in our conception of what a curriculum is—its form, not its content. A syllabus organized around knowledge and skills to be covered can never provide a criterion for learner success or safeguard against ineffective and (from the students' viewpoint) aimless teaching. Grounding the syllabus in student performance obligations based on knowledge and skill can.

Once again, look at athletics. When a soccer team is 0–6 halfway through the campaign (as mine was in my third season of coaching junior varsity soccer), the coaching plans, no matter how well thought out or coherent in the abstract, are clearly not working. Those carefully crafted August plans suddenly look foolish or inadequate. So what does a coach do? Adjust the plans (and his or her performance) in light of the results and the feedback from student performance. Is the team weak on corner kicks and offside traps, despite the fact that the logically organized plan "covered" them in sets of drills for two weeks? Then the coach has the team do lots more corner kick and offside drills than he or she had planned; the curriculum is altered to respond to evident need—need established by the coach's performance goals for the team (play the game well) and by student performance (weak this year in corner kicks and offside plays). Feedback about performance becomes central to teacher adjustment, just as earlier chapters argued for a similar self-adjustment experience for students to be designed into the assessment process.

How frequently, however, do we see a teacher, or especially an entire faculty, think and act like an effective soccer coach once the curriculum is under way but before the "season's end"? Teachers in special education and performance-based courses in the arts do this, but how often do others do it? How frequently do we see a syllabus or program altered en route in light of the effectiveness—or ineffectiveness—of the planned syllabus? How frequently do we hear at a staff meeting, "We're 0–6 in reading. Let's completely rethink the rest of the syllabus this year"? Even the most successful programmatic adjustments in instruction, such as in Reading Recovery (the outstanding literary remediation program from Australia and New Zealand), call for an external intervention in the form of an additional syllabus and teacher, not an overhaul of traditional approaches to reading instruction. Our addiction to coverage—to teaching in spite of results—can sustain itself only in a world where the curriculum designer's intent is viewed as more important than the performance results. This also reminds us why, as discussed in Chapter Two, many ongoing, or formative, assessments against final (exit) tasks and standards are so important, if we and our students are to adjust (and know when and where to adjust) in a timely way.

No one has perhaps made this point about classroom coaching more clearly than educational researcher and writing teacher Peter Elbow. In his essay "Trying to Teach While Thinking About the End," Elbow sums up the benefits (and problems) in teaching toward known competencies embodied in performance tasks. Pointing out that this approach to teaching causes more material to be effectively learned, he notes that teachers feel more obligated and able to help students who are having difficulty. Why? Because students' problems are more understandable now that they are cast in tangible performance-deficit terms rather than in terms that tend toward analysis of students' intellect and character as causes for failure to learn what is intended to be taught. Elbow adds that "the teachers that thrive in these programs often seem to have been bothered in the past by the large number of students who passed courses without really attaining the given knowledge or competence. They are exhilarated at finally having an approach which ensures that their students will learn. I talked to a whole range of teachers who were initially skeptical about a competence approach, but when they finally saw the results on the learning of their own students, they became enthusiastic supporters."[15]

When we teach for competence, for performance that shows evidence of understanding, we end up teaching more, as judged according to the aggregate learning of all students. However, such teaching for competence requires a curriculum that can stay focused on the hoped-for learner accomplishments—not only on the knowledge but also on the "rehearsals" and feedback that go into achieving them.

## Toward a New Logic: Dusting Off a Lost Deweyan Idea_____

To describe this new approach to curriculum design as results-based still does not fully reveal how we must change our thinking about the form in which we should write curriculum.

We can begin to understand this change by considering the common phrase used to summarize the logic of curriculum: *scope and sequence.* Today it means parceling out the content in a way that is logical from the perspective of the subject, and then adapting it to grade levels, mindful of developmental issues. But this is an ironic dilution of its original meaning. Hollis Caswell, the inventor of the phrase, originally meant to capture a melding of the expert's concerns and the learner's needs: thus *scope* referred to "the major functions of social life," and *sequence* referred to the "centers of interest" in students' lives. In this view, the proper ordering of topics—the logic of the syllabus—was to derive from developmentally appropriate areas of focus.[16] This progressive philosophy may now strike us as naive, but its instinct about curriculum design was sound: the unfolding of work should seem as natural as possible to the learner.[17]

The change in meaning of scope and sequence reveals that the logic of schoolwork is not a given. We can have different views of it. We can and should ask, Which logic? Which logic should apply when we design curriculum? Today the logic of almost all course curricula derives from the logic of completed knowledge analyzed into its logical parts, not the logic of gaining insight into and mastery of expert performances. Which logic supports the learner's attempts to understand and as a result perform effectively with knowledge?

Consider one last time how difficult mastery of a performance—a mock trial, say—would be if the performances involved had to be learned through a syllabus based on the logic of the laws as codified in legislative archives, by a methodical paper-and-pencil study of the great past trials in chronological order, and by a logic of drill that went from the opening to the closing—without ever involving students in complete preparation and execution of a trial plan. Mastery of legal defense, as well as of English, math, social studies, and science, works differently: students learn from constant involvement in the target performance, from successive approximations, and from a movement in and out of performance for coaching and drill through feedback loops (learn-try-see results-adjust). In performance-based teaching, we never front-load all possible information about the subject and performance requirements, and we move back and forth from the whole complex performance to discrete lessons.

John Dewey provided the classic formulation of the problem: the logic required to master inquiry is different than the logic of a textbook; the logic of efficient learning is quite different than the logic of completed knowledge. A manual or textbook is orderly in the same way that the dictionary or encyclopedia is orderly: it analyzes a complex subject into its elements. It does not follow, however, that one should teach the dictionary or encyclopedia from start to finish, page by page—even though there is a kind of coherence within a text organized alphabetically, analytically, or chronologically. As Dewey put it: "Logical forms do not pretend to tell how we think or even how we should think. . . . In short, these forms apply not to arriving at beliefs and knowledge, but to the most effective way in which to set forth what has already been concluded."[18]

Dewey's arguments suggest that a different logic to the organization of material is required, one in which "specific properties" are taught only as an outgrowth of a logic of problems arising in or about to arise in upcoming performance: "Every subject in the curriculum has passed through—or remains in—what may be called the phase of 'anatomical' method: the stage in which understanding the subject is thought to consist of multiplying distinctions . . . and attaching some name to each distinguished element. In normal growth, specific properties are emphasized and so individualized only when they serve to clear up a present difficulty."[19]

Alas, our habits run deep. We teach knowledge as finalized, and we pay the price: "There is a strong temptation to assume that presenting subject matter in its perfected form provides a royal road to learning." The sad outcome "is written large in the history of education. . . . Technical concepts, with their definitions, are introduced at the outset. Laws are introduced at a very early stage. . . . The necessary consequence is an isolation [of the work and its unfolding] from significant experience."[20]

Instead of this practice, students must be given problems that cause them to use (and want to use) texts and materials to help them conduct inquiry, fashion arguments, and develop quality products: "A painter is disciplined in his art to the degree in which he can manage and use effectively all the elements that enter into his art. . . . Practice, exercise, are involved in the acquisition of power, but they do not take the form of meaningless drill, but of practicing the art. They occur as part of the operation of attaining a desired end. . . . All genuine education terminates in discipline, but it proceeds by engaging the mind in activities worthwhile for their own sake."[21]

The *discipline* of a discipline is achieved as the result of guided and effective practice focused on touchstone tasks and questions. It is noteworthy that in areas like skiing and computer use (where clarity about the ultimate challenges exist for coach and performer alike), curricular designers made this leap quickly. Ski classes no longer require the learner to learn snowplows, stem christies, and other overly abstract analytical approaches to building up performance; instead the learner starts to parallel ski quickly, using short skis. Similarly, software manufacturers now provide tutorials and usage ideas in separate, brief manuals, in addition to the complete reference manuals that are organized analytically. With the brief manuals, we can get right to simple performance uses of the software to solve the problems that led us to buy the product in the first place.

Yet our history, science, and mathematics textbooks still universally make the mistake of organizing their content around the analytic logic of completed results or linear chronology.[22] Postulates, axioms, theorems, and historical principles are rarely revisited in light of later understandings; no overarching questions and problems inform the choice of subject matter and student work. Instead of helping teachers to frame overarching performance objectives, questions, and tasks that would make the content useful, the texts (especially in the sciences) present definitions, principles, postulates, and elementary theorems first, more complex laws and theorems later—with exercises in between. I believe that this approach to text design (which then shapes our syllabi) to be a major cause of our failure to get more students to understand and appreciate the sciences. With no overarching and clear performance task requirements akin to "fluency in software use" or "mature skiing ability" (that is, with no agreement on what doing science and mathematics means), we fall back on organizing the knowledge—rather than organizing the work by the strategies and criteria that produce knowledge and reveal its meaning—so that the student thinks science is a catechism of fixed results.

This is an ironic problem. We thus are teaching physics as if it were dogmatic metaphysics. As argued earlier, no matter how precise and well ordered the proposed lessons and exercises are, a student cannot be said to understand the importance or nature of the postulates in geometry or the laws in physics without grasping their justification, their uncertainties, and their history—how they were needed and derived to enable geometers and physicists to prove what they wanted to prove. The student misunderstandings discussed by Howard Gardner and highlighted in Chapter Four are due to, more than any other cause, a curricular logic and textbook blandness that induce one-shot coverage as opposed to rethinking by teachers and students in light of performance results and inevitable problems and questions.

This concern with the logic and implied purpose of curriculum is not a new lament. Mathematicians and philosophers have complained about this problem in pedagogy for centuries. The father of modern analytic geometry, René Descartes, was one of many who argued that learning geometry in logical order from the systematized results of theorems (the "synthetic" treatment, in his terms) impedes understanding. Such an approach hides the fact that the results were derived by completely different (analytic) methods—methods far simpler to use than is suggested by studying the resultant theorems in logical order. This recognition led Descartes to a cynical conclusion: "Indeed, I could readily believe that this mathematics was suppressed by [the Greek mathematicians] with a certain pernicious craftiness, just as we know many inventors have suppressed their discoveries, being very much afraid that to publish their method, since it is quite easy and simple, would make it seem worthless. And I believe they preferred to show us in its place, as the product of their art, certain barren truths which they cleverly demonstrate deductively so that we should admire them."[23] The philosopher Hegel, a clear influence on Dewey, remarked about the typical teaching of geometry that "the instruction to draw precisely these lines when infinitely many others could be drawn must be blindly obeyed without our knowing anything," and that we cannot gain understanding this way because our "insight is an activity external to the thing."[24] More recently, Jean Piaget argued that the student must verify or "discover" the key truths encountered, not just receive them and play them back unthinkingly as part of a formal framework: "Formalization should be kept for a later moment as a type of systematization of the notions already acquired. This certainly means the use of intuition before axiomatization."[25]

How can we present questions and tasks so that they naturally lead students from novice understanding to expert insight into a subject? How then might texts be differently used (if not differently structured) to honor the needs of performance learning and eventual mastery?

It was Bruner's stark postulate that "any subject can be taught effectively in some intellectually honest form to any child at any stage of development."[26] Such teaching requires a new curriculum, and Bruner popularized the idea of the curriculum as a spiral of continual discovery and refinement. From the outset of education and all along the way, the "young learner should be given the chance to solve problems, to conjecture, to quarrel as these are done at the heart of a discipline."[27] The ultimate coherence of a curriculum can thus be said to depend on the student's having repeated opportunities to experience directly not just adult ideas and products but the work of producing or validating such products in context—the challenges and dilemmas at the heart of a profession, or knowledge in use.[28]

Such a curriculum for understanding requires the student to constantly revisit the relevant postulates and laws through doing ever more complex problems and getting counterintuitive results, to see that these postulates and laws are neither arbitrary nor unproblematic givens. As Bruner put it, we need coursework that enables students to "sense an emphasis upon ratiocination with a view toward redefining what has been encountered, reshaping it, reordering it."[29] Can a student be said to understand geometry or physics without doing work and encountering problems that make this clear? I do not believe so. Without revisiting, without the occasional counterintuitive result, most students will come away from the typical geometry lesson with a quasi-Platonic view of the postulates as somehow God-given and self-evident—never mind their confusion over how terms can be undefined yet pictured in a familiar way.[30]

Though Bruner gets credit for popularizing the idea of the spiral curriculum, Dewey in fact already used the metaphor to describe how subject matter ought to be organized to move naturally from one deliberately designed performance problem to the next, thus yielding increasingly sophisticated and self-refined ideas. Facts and ideas "become the ground for further experiences in which new problems are presented. The process is a continual spiral."[31] Otherwise, "knowledge" is inert and meaningless, perpetually "isolated from the needs and purposes of the learner. . . . Only in education, never in the life of farmer, sailor, merchant, physician or scientist does knowledge mean primarily a store of information."[32]

The teacher's task is to construct a genuinely educative experience out of problems as they arise in performance—the ultimate result being, as it is for the scholar, the production of new ideas. Dewey believed that students should apprentice to performing in the same way that the professional performs when the aim is the production, criticism, entrepreneurial use, and extension of knowledge.

Whether or not we agree with Dewey about the purpose of schooling, he presented us with a challenge that remains inadequately explored: how to organize experiences so that the learner is never puzzled by what is to happen next and sees each part of the curriculum as part of a larger whole and a natural outgrowth of what came before, even when the learner is a novice. The unfolding of a curriculum will appear logical to the student only when new work arises out of current work and future obligations. This is truly learning in students' interest (rather than according to what students may like at the moment or what linear coverage may suggest).

It is useful here to recall Fred Newmann and colleagues' general standards for authentic tasks: they must demand construction of knowledge, disciplined inquiry, and value beyond school. Higher-order thinking is tapped by designs that involve "students in manipulating information and ideas by synthesizing, explaining, hypothesizing, or arriving at conclusions that produce new meanings and understandings."[33] Deep knowledge depends on instruction that "addresses central ideas of a topic with enough thoroughness to explore connections and relationships and to produce relatively complex understandings," and on work that elicits and requires "substantive conversation."[34] These standards have rubrics attached to them whereby the teacher or observers can judge whether authentic work is predominant or not.

In short, all design must negotiate dilemmas. Any unit or syllabus must be

Authentic *but* meaningful

Meaningful *but* rigorous

Rigorous *but* engaging

Engaging *but* coherent

Coherent *but* responsive

Responsive *but* effective

Effective *but* feasible

To better honor these criteria and strike the right balance, we will need a more helpful template than we now have for teachers who are preparing to write curriculum or to do lesson plans.

## A Curriculum Template

A template should serve as an intelligent tool in design. By filling it in step-by-step, we are indirectly taught about good design and helped to avoid unhelpful habits, especially the habit of merely specifying inputs (that is, what the teacher will cover). If curriculum is to be reconceived as shaped by evidence and work requirements rather than as the content to be covered, then we will need a template that focuses designers on results and assessments and from which apt teaching and activities are derived. Five major categories of information—corresponding to the backward design discussed earlier in the chapter—form the structure of the new template: after a summary of the unit, we would find information on standards, assessment, knowledge (content standards), work and sequence, and teaching chronology. Each unit would specify all the assessments (tasks, prompts, and quizzes as discussed in Chapters Five and Eight), and each assessment task or prompt would have specific rubrics attached to it. Figure 9.3 shows a unit written in a curricular template that honors these ideas.

The teaching chronology (lesson plan) comes last because decisions about how to teach, what to teach, and in what order to teach it are derived from the (performance and content) standards and assessments and the enabling knowledge and proficiency required for the tasks—not from the textbook's table of contents. Note also that by such a structure, activities cannot be arbitrarily strung together—for example, without any overarching performance purpose—as is now too often the case. Activities are derived from the complex tasks and ideas to be mastered and the overarching questions and standards that anchor the overall design and each unit.

Thus the whole course of study is thought of as an anthology (or a portfolio) of such units. If all teachers in a school or district design in this way, then it also becomes possible to share and modify course and unit designs through a database. This not only makes design more appropriately public (hence, more likely better than current design and more likely to be constantly improved), but it makes it easier to train new teachers and help teachers whose design skills are weak to improve. Teachers, like students, need models.[35]

Figure 9.4 contains a checklist that teachers can use to self-assess their own curriculum designs and to have peers review the curricula for whether the design is sound and will in fact lead students to the achievement target through the tasks assigned. It allows adjustment of the curriculum if necessary before it is put into use.

The logic of the curriculum design described is derived from the learner's perspective and is based on a movement toward a performance goal, through iterative lessons and successive approximations of masterful performances by the student. Content is a means in this kind of curriculum; it both raises and solves problems, raises a question, and provides some answers. The designer's question about the overall syllabus structure then is, What is a useful sequence of (recurring and logically prior) intellectual challenges around which core content can be ordered? What is the most efficient movement from the students' incomplete and necessarily crude grasp of the whole of a subject matter to their sophisticated and systematic view of it? That movement is feasible only when we have identified key questions and performance understandings that represent the authentic doing of a subject, and have organized lessons around them.

### Figure 9.3  Unit Design for *The Catcher in the Rye*

| | | | | | | |
|---|---|---|---|---|---|---|
| Unit Title | *The Catcher in the Rye* | | | | | |
| Designer: | David Grant | Grade(s): | 8-10 | | School: | Class |
| Subject Area: | English | Time frame: | 6 days | | District: | |
| Course: | 9th Grade English | Topic: | *The Catcher in the Rye* | | | |
| Unit summary: | Unit title: *The Catcher in the Rye* | | | | | |

At the end of a close reading of *The Catcher in the Rye*, students act as part of a peer case-review committee at the hospital from which Holden is telling his story. With access to the transcript of Holden's own words plus selected related materials, they write a diagnostic report for the hospital and a prescriptive letter to Holden's parents.

Quizzes and a writing exercise in which student's describe Holden from the perspective of another character act as prompts to understanding. At the end of the unit, students analyze their own evolving understanding of the novel, as chronicled in their daily journals.

| | |
|---|---|
| *Content standards* | • Understand the novel beyond the oversimplification of "Holden's Excellent Adventure." |
| | • Introduce students to frameworks of understanding in psychology that have bearing on Holden's story: Freud, Kübler-Ross, etc. |
| *Performance standards* | • Develop a well-reasoned hypothesis through a close reading of a text. |
| | • Work collaboratively to produce and defend a product. |
| | • Demonstrate ability to "think about thinking," specifically to recognize their own misunderstandings as they move toward a rich understanding of the novel. |
| *Overarching "Essential Questions"* | • What is the relationship between "fiction" and "truth?" |
| | • Why do writers write and readers read? What's in it for them? What's in it for me? |
| | • Who are the "heroes" in American literature? |
| | • What insights do we gain into American history and contemporary culture through heroic characters? |
| *Unit-specific questions* | • Who is a phony? Who isn't? Why does it matter to Holden? |
| | • Is something the matter with Holden? |
| | • Is Holden a hero? Is he a tragic figure? |

*Performance tasks and projects*

• What's wrong with Holden?

Students serve on an advisory committee to the hospital where Holden Caulfield is telling his story. After a close reading and discussion of Holden's account of the events of the preceding December, the committee will produce: a report for the hospital and a letter to Holden's parents. Finally, they will appear before a panel to explain and justify their conclusions and recommendations.

*Prompts*

• Daily journal

The students respond at the end of each reading assignment to two questions: What is the most important thing you learned about Holden in this section of the novel? and What is the most important unanswered question about Holden at this point in the novel?

### Figure 9.3 Continued

A third question comes with each reading assignment:

1. Chapters 1–4:      What observations do you have about Holden's use of language?
2. Chapters 5–9:      What observations do you have about Holden's fight with Stradlater?
3. Chapters 10–14:   On p. 87, Holden says, "The Navy guy and I said we were glad to've met each other. Which always kills me. I'm always saying 'Glad to've met you' to somebody I'm not at all glad I met. If you want to stay alive, you have to say that stuff, though." Based on your own life and experiences, do you think this last observation is true? Be specific.

- Description of Holden

  For the use of the committee at the hospital, write a one-page letter/description of Holden from the point of view of another character in the novel.

  Each member of the committees of four will write from the perspective of a different character. One letter/description must come from a member of Holden's family, one from a teacher, and two from a friend/peer.

- Analysis of journal

  The final piece of written work in this unit is an analysis of your own journal, written with an eye toward "understanding understanding."

  In a 2–3 page essay, analyze your own evolving understanding of the novel. Please address the following questions: What changed for you in the way you saw Holden as this book went along? and If, as some people claim, "misunderstanding is inevitable" when you encounter new material, what were your misunderstandings at any point during this unit and how did you correct them? Finally, reflect upon this question, If you were to teach this novel to next year's students, what would you do to ensure they understand the novel as opposed to know it?

*Enabling knowledge*
- Salinger's novel *The Catcher in the Rye*
- Excerpts from Kübler-Ross's, *On Death and Dying*; essay on Freud
- Burns's poem, "Comin' Thro' the Rye"

*Enabling skills*
- Strategies used in reading and analyzing literature
- Collaboration in a small group
- Writing a coherent, persuasive report
- Oral defense

*Context and purpose of the unit*

The unit gives students the chance to practice core skills of the course: reading and analyzing literature, discussion, collaboration, writing, and speaking.

Thematic connections will depend on the other literature read in the course. In the context of an American literature course, for example, there will be obvious connections with *Huck Finn*. In the context of a thematic course on "Identity" or "Comedy and Tragedy" or "Coming of Age," other connections will be made.

Reading *The Catcher in the Rye* in any context allows adolescents to consider vital questions in their lives in the relative safety of literary distance and, one hopes, a supportive classroom environment. It will be important for each teacher to assess that level of safety and trust while gauging how far to pursue questions about "phoniness," including discussions about social conventions and hypocrisies, adolescent sexuality, family dynamics, and dealing with death.

Figure 9.3  Continued

---

*Instructional chronology: Day-by-day teacher and student work*

*Unit title*: *The Catcher in the Rye*

At the end of a close reading of *The Catcher in the Rye*, students act as part of a peer case-review committee at the hospital from which Holden is telling his story. With access to the transcript of Holden's own words plus selected related materials, they write a diagnostic report for the hospital and a prescriptive letter to Holden's parents.

Quizzes and a writing exercise in which students describe Holden from the perspective of another character act as prompts to understanding. At the end the unit, students analyze their own evolving understanding of the novel, as chronicled in their daily journals.

Day One: Prologue/Introduction. It is best to talk about *The Catcher in the Rye* in class before the first homework reading assignment. Read aloud at least the first two paragraphs. What do the students notice? Who is speaking? What are the circumstances? What about language? The key is to be sure all the students know from the start that Holden is telling his story from a rest home or psychiatric hospital in California and to compare notes as a class on "What sort of guy is this?" Right from the start, set the tone of a puzzle to be solved—a character and a situation that will be revealed to us gradually.

The other important job in this first class is to launch the journal. (Unless it is already a standard part of the course, in which case it just needs to be customized for this novel.) Ask the students to respond in the journal at the end of each reading assignment and before the next class to two questions: (1) *What is the most important thing you learned about Holden in this section of the novel?* and (2) *What is the most important unanswered question about Holden at this point in the novel?* Student responses to these questions will begin and end daily class discussions. In addition, the students are asked to address in writing a third question with each assignment.

The novel is divided into six reading assignments. The teacher may adjust, of course, to fit local circumstances. The assignments are as follows (using the Little, Brown and Company paperback edition), along with suggested third journal question:

Reading assignment #1. Chapters 1–4 (pp. 1–35):
What observations do you have about Holden's use of language?

Reading assignment #2. Chapters 5–9 (pp. 35–66):
What observations do you have about Holden's fight with Stradlater?

Reading assignment #3. Chapters 10–14 (pp. 66–104):
On p. 87 Holden says, "The Navy guy and I said we were glad to've met each other. Which always kills me. I'm always saying 'Glad to've met you' to somebody I'm not at all glad I met. If you want to stay alive, you have to say that stuff, though." Based on you own life and experiences, do you think this last observation is true? Be specific.

Reading assignment #4. Chapters 15–16 (pp. 105–141):
Look at the conversation between Holden and Sally on pp. 130–134. What do you think is most important about it in regards to understanding Holden?

Reading assignment #5. Chapters 19–23 (pp. 141–180):
What do you think is the most revealing moment in the long scene in D.B.'s bedroom between Holden and Phoebe? Why?

Reading assignment #6. Chapters 24–26 (pp. 180–214):
How do you interpret Mr. Antolini's behavior and Holden's reaction to it, at the time and later?

or

What do you make of the line on p.198: "Allie, don't let me disappear"? What scene early in the book does this remind you of?

or

What is the significance of Holden's reactions to the obscenities he sees written at Phoebe's school and at the museum?

Figure 9.3 Continued

*Back to the chronology:*

Day Two: Holden is at his funniest in these early chapters describing Pencey Prep, but even here students will notice how he uses language and humor to distance and protect himself. In discussing student answers to the three journal questions, the following may come up; if not, it is a good idea to remind students to watch for, and write down as they go along in their reading:

1. Any details about Holden's family

2. Things Holden says "depress him"

It is also useful to introduce students to the concept of the "unreliable narrator," if they are not yet familiar with it. What are we supposed to make of a narrator who tells us he lies? Where do his words and his actions seem to be at odds?

Two of the "unanswered questions" about Holden will almost assuredly be "What's wrong with him? and Why is he in the hospital?" This is the time to introduce the "Performance Task" coming up at the end of the reading. The teacher does not have to put the students in groups yet, but they should know by the end of this first full discussion of the book about the three dimensions of the task ahead: the report to the hospital, the letter to Holden's parents, and the oral defense of both to the hospital panel.

Day Three: Give Quiz #1. Class discussion in response to quiz questions and journal writing. Make list of characters on board in preparation for later writing exercise (written from the perspective of one of them). Ask students about their experience with their journals: Is it working? What problems are they having, if any? The use of the word "phony" will have come up in both days two and three. Use this as introduction to the additional journal question accompanying the next reading assignment, which asks them to apply Holden's experience and reactions to their own lives. Tell them that tomorrow they will have some time to meet in their committees of four.

Day Four: Discuss reading assignment #3 using journal responses. Present the full assignment for the performance task "What's wrong with Holden?" Put students in their teams of four and let them do some preliminary talking and planning on the "diagnostic" part of their assignment—the report to the hospital. Remind them of previous work on collaboration using rubric(s) if necessary. Urge them to be specific in their small groups about what they will be looking for in the second half of the book.

Day Five: Discuss assignment #4. Give time for groups of four to meet. Ask them to consider what criteria and standards they will apply to the second half of their assignment—the letter to Holden's parents. Ask each group "What don't you understand yet?" and have each group report back on their answers.

Day Six: Give Quiz #2. Discuss quiz and journal responses to assignment #5. Use text of Burns's poem if time allows; at least point out that it is available to them on their reserve shelf of readings. Last part of class spent in the teams of four.

Day Seven: First discussion of end of book. Give prompt #2 as homework assignment: each student will write a one-page letter/description about Holden from the point of view of another character in the novel. The four students working together as a team would each write from the perspective of a different character, with one writing as a member of Holden's family, one as one of his teachers, and two as his friends/peers.

Day Eight: As a whole class, read excerpts from homework assignments. Collect the assignments. Rest of time spent in small groups outlining responses to the performance task and assigning specific duties.

Days Nine to Eleven (or Twelve): Scheduling of the last days of the unit will depend on the size of class, length of meeting time, flexibility in the daily schedule, and ability of teams to meet together outside of class time. The goal is that during this time students will accomplish the following: (1) for the performance task—written responses to the two parts of the assignment and

### Figure 9.3 Continued

an oral report to the panel followed by a chance to revise their products before turning them in and (2) an analysis of their own journal, with a focus on "understanding understanding." Guide questions are: (1) What changed for you in the way you saw Holden as this book went along? (2) If, as some people claim, "misunderstanding is inevitable" when you encounter new material, what were *your* misunderstandings at any point during this unit? (3) Given your experience as reflected in your journal, if you were to teach this novel to next year's students, what would you do to ensure they *understand* the novel as opposed to know it?

Students will not necessarily hear all of the other groups report to the panel, though they should hear at least one other. The journal will be turned in to the teacher along with the analysis of it.

Teacher resources

*Barron's Educational Series: The Catcher in the Rye*. World Library, Inc. 1993.

Belcher, William F., and Lee, James W., eds., *J. D. Salinger and the Critics*, Belmont, CA: Wadsworth, 1962.

French, Warren. *J. D. Salinger*. New York: Twayne, 1963.

Grunwald, Henry A., ed. *Salinger: A Critical and Personal Portrait*. New York: HarperCollins, 1962.

Rosen, Gerald. *Zen in the Art of J. D. Salinger*. New York: Odyssey, 1963.

Internet resources.

Student resources

Salinger, J. D. *The Catcher in the Rye*, Boston: Little, Brown.

Packet of excerpts.

Internet resources, e.g. question and answer exchange at http://killdevelhill.com/salingerchat/www.board.html

As we develop such curricula, we will accelerate our need for longitudinal and developmental assessment. We will need to chart performance gains of the novice on the continuum that ends in expert performance; we will therefore always design our curricula backward from expert and fluent performances and genres that we wish novices to master. This will affect curriculum design even in the earliest grades and will help us to choose simplified scaffolded versions of the final performances for novices instead of the simplistic decontextualized lessons they frequently get now.

To establish such curricula in our schools we need to teach their value not only to educators but to the public. Consider, for example, public reaction to the Whole Language movement, which is based on the importance of giving students practice at tasks and allows, for example, naive spelling as part of getting younger students to do constant writing. This and other movements have fostered a strong backlash because most laypersons (and many educators) have

### Figure 9.4  Peer Review and Self-Assessment Checklist

| | | Wow! | Good | Refine | Redo |
|---|---|:---:|:---:|:---:|:---:|
| Authentic: | A contextually faithful encounter with the "doing" of a subject. | ❐ | ❐ | ❐ | ❐ |
| | • The work engages students in experiences and challenges that replicate or simulate the tasks, demands, and situations encountered "in the field." | ❐ | ❐ | ❐ | ❐ |
| | • The performance and production challenges are genuine. They assess whether students can fashion a quality product or performance in ways that adults are "tested" (e.g., oral reports, conducting an experiment, juried exhibits of artwork, judging the adequacy of a design, developing policy, etc.). | ❐ | ❐ | ❐ | ❐ |
| | • The tasks involve real problems, not (merely) drills or exercises. (If a novice-level course, some of the work is authentic in that it is scaffolded performance or apprenticeship.) | ❐ | ❐ | ❐ | ❐ |
| | • Primary sources and/or first-hand research are expected. | ❐ | ❐ | ❐ | ❐ |
| Meaningful: | The work will be appropriate to the intellectual interests, prior experience, and levels of (diverse) students. | ❐ | ❐ | ❐ | ❐ |
| | • The design results in genuine intellectual challenges that are nonetheless accessible to students. | ❐ | ❐ | ❐ | ❐ |
| | • The work is aptly scaffolded, simplified, or adjusted for the developmental needs of students. | ❐ | ❐ | ❐ | ❐ |
| Rigorous: Likely to Yield Under-standing | Content, competency, work design, and performance standards are high. | ❐ | ❐ | ❐ | ❐ |
| | • The materials used and ideas focused on are challenging; and the lessons, assignments, and assessments demand quality work from students. | ❐ | ❐ | ❐ | ❐ |
| | • The work of the unit/course focuses on worthy topics, issues, texts, problems—big ideas, essential questions. | ❐ | ❐ | ❐ | ❐ |
| Responsive: | The design allows room for diverse abilities, interests, and unanticipatable reactions, and for emerging student interests. | ❐ | ❐ | ❐ | ❐ |
| | • The design of the work leaves room for adjustment, by both teacher and students, based on emerging performance difficulties. | ❐ | ❐ | ❐ | ❐ |
| | • The work can be done by students with diverse learning styles and talents without compromising rigor. | ❐ | ❐ | ❐ | ❐ |
| | • The calendar leaves ample room for students to follow up on questions, interests, problems, etc. that emerge from the work requirements and performance. | ❐ | ❐ | ❐ | ❐ |

## Figure 9.4 Continued

| | | Wow! | Good | Refine | Redo |
|---|---|---|---|---|---|
| Coherent: | The unit or course has a clear and obvious logic to the *student*. | ☐ | ☐ | ☐ | ☐ |
| | • Assignments and assessment tasks lead "naturally" to others. The work of the unit(s) builds, from the simple to the complex—not just as activities, texts, or lessons strung together. | ☐ | ☐ | ☐ | ☐ |
| | • Despite surprises, twists, and turns about how the work will ultimately play out, the student is never confused about where the work is headed in terms of overarching focus on final work requirements. (In narrative terms, students sense the movement toward a resolution of *known* purposes, issues, and tensions at work in the syllabus "story-line"). | ☐ | ☐ | ☐ | ☐ |
| Engaging: | The work requirements, experiences, and lessons are thought provoking and generative of deepening interest and quality work. | ☐ | ☐ | ☐ | ☐ |
| | • The activities pique student curiosity; they take the student beyond merely enjoyable actions and opinion-offering to inquiries and performance demands that cause depth of thought and the desire to do tasks well. | ☐ | ☐ | ☐ | ☐ |
| | • The work is rich enough and accommodating of levels enough that it will likely engage all students, not just the most able, the most dutiful, or only those able to delay gratification. | ☐ | ☐ | ☐ | ☐ |
| Effective: | The work requirements and incentives are such that we should expect atypically good performance results based on this design. | ☐ | ☐ | ☐ | ☐ |
| | • The assessment tasks and standards are so clearly spelled out (while challenging), and the design so effectively builds toward them that we can expect across-the-board fine performance, if students attend to the requirements. | ☐ | ☐ | ☐ | ☐ |
| | • Modeling and feedback opportunities are part of the design. | ☐ | ☐ | ☐ | ☐ |
| Feasible: | The work requirements are such that the unit will *work* in the time/syllabus/grade level proposed and is not dependent upon an unrealistically ideal school context. | ☐ | ☐ | ☐ | ☐ |
| | • The unit will work in the time/syllabus/grade level allotted. | ☐ | ☐ | ☐ | ☐ |
| | • The unit can be successful without impossibly unrealistic school conditions (though some structural changes may be required in scheduling, interdisciplinary courses, etc.). | ☐ | ☐ | ☐ | ☐ |
| Efficient: | The work requirements are such that the unit takes up the right amount of time and energy, given the overall course and program priorities and objectives. | ☐ | ☐ | ☐ | ☐ |

difficulty imagining educational success from a strategy that tolerates inevitable performance mistakes in the interest of enabling the novice to practice and mimic eventual performance. Leaving aside the fact that some so-called Whole Language programs avoid making rigorous reading demands on students, what many critics do not see is that expertise is never just the sum of simple drills done perfectly. We tolerate mistakes from students of music, athletics, and drama because error in complex performance is inevitable. Who in fact really learns anything of importance from unending, simplified drill work? Who learns software, for example, by reading through the manual page by page and doing only simple tutorial exercises? The adult who wants children to learn from drills seems to forget that he or she personally rarely learns by studying bits of knowledge and skill in an unending precise and "logical" order—because this does not yield thoughtful and effective performance.

There should be no mystery or controversy about this approach, if really done properly: the Little Leaguer gets to play baseball right from the beginning. So do the musician, the dancer, and the actor get to practice their crafts. We know how to design the curricula that will allow our students to reach understanding through practice of chemistry, history, mathematics, and other disciplines. It is time for us, too, to apply what we know.

## CHAPTER 10

# Grading and Reporting

New and more complex forms of assessment clearly demand new forms of reporting. Rich information based on new kinds of tasks and content standards, and on performance standards that are broken down by categories and criteria, cry out for a more sophisticated system of communication with parents and other clients, such as colleges and employers. And the clear recent national interest in report card reform stems in part from pent-up demand caused by assessment reform.[1] This chapter examines how we can achieve reports that are standard-based, honest yet fair, rich in context, and user-friendly. Five possible approaches are suggested that could give parents, students, and others useful, educative information, and some samples of report card reform are presented.

Reform is not always welcome, however. There has been a backlash among parents to many proposed report card reforms. I often hear from frustrated faculties that have redone their letter-grade report card to provide more helpful and detailed information to students and parents alike and to play down the harmful crude comparisons of students. They might have developed narrative-based reporting systems, introduced a new symbol system, or broken out new sub-categories of performance (such as computation, problem-solving, and communication of ideas in mathematics). These efforts cost many faculty hours, but they seem well worth the effort. Yet in many cases, at the first parent conference parents ask, "OK, but how is she doing?" This question and the intent behind it demand everyone's attention.

Revision of report cards is best not construed as a matter of teachers coming up with new designs and grading systems based on their own interests. Better reports require that we ask a radical question (in radical's original meaning of "going to the root"), indeed the same writing process question we use in our classrooms: Who is the audience and what is the purpose of the writing? The only sensible answer is the parents (and later, the student, too). The purpose of the report is to enable parents and student to understand the student's performance to this point and to know what is required for future progress and mastery. This seems straightforward enough. Yet many well-intentioned faculties are inventing reporting systems based more on their own interests than on those of students, parents, school boards, and receiving institutions or teachers. Reports typically offer either too little data or overly selective data that are opaque to an outsider. Instead, reports must summarize what the student has accomplished, in terms that any reader outside the classroom can understand. This requires educators to provide a frame of reference—including standards and expectations—whereby outsiders can see the student's performance in some wider context.

Parental backlash is more easily understood when one attends more carefully to how some educators describe their report reforms. Some faculties clearly do not want to report how the student is "really" doing, thinking this information inappropriate or harmful. Indeed, teachers in some schools where narrative report cards are used are instructed never to make negative statements or comparisons of any kind, to focus only on what the student does well. Some report card changes, in other words, seem motivated less by a goal of providing more accurate feedback than by a goal of casting the student's performance in the best possible light, even if teachers have to lie by omission. A report must do more than highlight some positive or unique accomplishments of a student if the report is to have meaning, and much of the current public backlash to assessment and report card reform can be seen as an understandable concern that reform means weakening or blurring standards and reports in the name of students' self-esteem.

This chapter, indeed this book as a whole, takes a far different view. More information, not less, is desirable: more data grounded in valid standards and more accuracy, not less. We need to make reference to valid and agreed-upon standards in support of value judgments, and data in support of generalizations. When necessary, we need to be able to show "triangulation" of data, in the scientific sense of squaring (inevitable) discrepancies or anomalies between local, regional, state, and national assessment results (as discussed in Chapter Five). In short, reports must analyze all available assessment results so as to present a rich and accurate intellectual profile of students' major strengths and weaknesses.

Successful redesign therefore depends on an ongoing tension: we must report what is of interest to parents and students as we also report what we know is in their long-term interest (even if they have yet to realize it and we are squeamish about reporting it).

## Standards and Criteria for Designing and Judging Reports

Here, too, we need standards based on purpose. For student report cards to be as educative as the assessment described in this book, they must be thought through in the same way as performance criteria. Design must focus on desired impact: What should the report yield? How would we judge the report's ultimate success or failure? What do we expect the reader to be able to know and do as a result of what is reported? Surely at the very least the answer must be that the report should paint a clear and credible picture of the student's profile within the context of standards. We are prone to give information that is often too decontextualized, too linked to local norms only, or sometimes too sugarcoated for the reader to understand how the grades were computed and earned.

Three general conditions can help guarantee clear and credible reports:

1.  A stable, known, and credible basis for comparing the student's performance to some standards, grade-level expectations, cohort norms, or a combination of standards and norms must be clear.

2.  The relative weight attached to the diverse factors that make up grades—achievement, progress, habits, attitudes, and conduct—must be made explicit and kept uniform across students, time, and teachers.

3.  Any summary judgments made in the report must be supported by data. The ideal report card enables readers to see grades, scores, and comments as justified, based on documentation.

### Honesty and Fairness

But how should we judge what is the right kind of information to purvey, the right tone to strike, and the right mix of data and teacher judgment? By what criteria do we determine if we are framing the descriptions and judgments properly? Two core values should underlie all reporting of performance: it should be *honest* yet *fair*. Our reports must be honest in communicating how the student is "really doing" against credible standards or empirically derived norms of development. But reports must also be fair in appropriately taking into consideration facts and factors that lead to apt teacher judgments based on reasonable expectations for the individual child. This chapter therefore proposes that letter grades be retained but narrowed to function as a fair summary of individual progress. Such grades would be complemented, not replaced, by performance scores that would be standard based.

Regardless of what reporting symbols or language we choose, the point remains the same: everyone's interests, including those of the students, are served by truthfulness, by more not less information from different perspectives, and by reports that balance the celebration of student idiosyncrasies and strengths with data about student performance against common worthy standards. As stated throughout this book, we need to provide more useful feedback that makes self-adjustment possible. Neither simplistic grades nor narrative comments on past achievements alone can accomplish that aim.

The advent of a wealth of new performance data, the use of multiple rubrics and portfolios, and the existence of numerous performance genres all tied to complex content standards makes striking a careful balance even more complicated. Our new reports will have to be more comprehensive as befits our new assessments, yet also more clear and helpful than most current reports. Let us then add two other criteria to honest and fair—*rich in detail* yet *user-friendly*. How should reports look to honor these criteria? First the problem of context must be considered: the report reader can only know how the student is "really" doing when the frame of reference is enlarged. After a discussion of the appropriate and inappropriate roles played by standards and norms in reporting, we will consider how multiple grades might be used to give more information and might still be understood by parents. The full context should be provided, and grades should be used that give more information but that can still be understood by parents. Thorough justification of judgments should be made available, but should not be overwhelming.

## Toward More Context in Reporting: Standards and Norms

As the opening story implies, an isolated narrative, no matter how caring or rich, is never quite honest enough. By itself it can never tell the client whether laudatory or critical language in the report represents absolute, relative, or idiosyncratic achievement. Maybe all students "work hard," have made "great progress," and also "do well on multivariable math problems," as Susan's narrative says of her; who knows other than the teacher? Maybe the teacher has set different standards for each student. Maybe Susan's progress is relative; maybe she has fallen behind all other students. Or maybe Susan has improved relative to everyone in her class, but what is considered good performance in Susan's class is mediocre in the school as a whole and poor in the region. How will we know without some information about the performance context and the basis of judgment?

Comparisons provide one such frame of reference, as the parents' query suggests. OK, but how is she doing? might mean, How is my child doing vis-à-vis district or national norms? Or it might mean, How is she doing compared with other kids in the class? Or it might imply a subtle challenge: Regardless of how she or anyone else is doing in terms of your personal grading system, how does her performance compare to a valid standard? The parent (or any other outsider) cannot make sense of the narrative without some such information. It is always legitimate to ask for meaning in terms of comparison to something. A description of only what and how a child did leaves parents with no meaningful judgment. The parent has a right to an evaluation, not just a description. The parent has a right to know if the described performance is on track, acceptable, indicative of later success, and so on. (The teacher, of course, knows this larger context and deliberately teaches and reports with this context in mind.)

Consider the following simple illustrations of lack of context in reporting. Suppose Rico is described as successful 93 percent of the time. Sounds like a fine job until we find out that Rico is a typist or a pilot. Or suppose Joe is described in highly specific terms as "working very hard" and "successful on his performance tasks one-third of the time." That certainly seems to an outsider like a poor achievement record, regardless of what praise might accompany that report. But not if Joe is a major league outfielder batting .300, and not if the person getting the information is a knowledgeable fan who understands that historical norms reveal this to be an excellent performance, batting at the level of the best hitters in the game. Then again, if Joe were in Little League, his .300 batting performance would probably be only average. Context matters even when we purvey objective, quantitative data. Honest yet fair reports do not shy away from helpful data comparisons such as historical performance levels of similar students. Knowing percentiles or stanines on nationally normed tests has great appeal to parents because it gives them just such comparative information, even when the test in our view as educators does not reveal much useful information about students.

Comparisons can certainly be invidious and misleading. Merely comparing all the students at the same grade level can be misleading at best and hurtfully unfair at worst (especially when chronological ages vary significantly or when the ranking hides the fact that quality of the performances varies only slightly from best to worst). To give a single low grade as the course grade to a recently mainstreamed student simply because her recent performance was not as good as that of her classmates, to fail a third grader for what amounts to being years behind his peers in at-home literacy experience, to give a B+ to a student for merely being the most experienced student in an otherwise novice-filled class, to give A's to our best students even though they are performing in the 20th percentile on nationally normed tests, or to grade on a curve in the most demanding schools and thus give C's to students who would get A's if judged on their level of achievement—all such decisions are unfair and misleading. Honesty requires that we report comparative data. Fairness demands that we factor in relevant personal and extenuating circumstances when giving grades and, thus, ensure valid and useful comparisons.

Current reports often err on one side or the other. They typically either consist of glib judgments and misleading letter-grade comparisons, or they offer euphemistic comments that sugarcoat bad news and couch everything in terms relative only to the student's individual growth.

Comparisons best serve the performer and the school clients when what is compared is performance against known standards or credible developmental norms (now often called *benchmarks*). These are the comparisons that parents are really asking for (even when that request is couched as apparent support for multiple-choice tests). Just what did the student actually do or not do, and how do those achievements relate to wider world standards or patterns of performance? How do school evaluations relate to meaningful real-world performance benchmarks? Without such a set of comparisons, any judgment made is capricious or opaque.

Standard-referenced information is helpful even when—especially when—the news is bad. When students are scoring very low in absolute terms, it is in their (and their parents') interest to know how low and whether such low scores are worrisome, that is, what has been the typical pattern of development (the norms) and future success or failure academically for this kind of student at this point in a career? Knowledge of standards and students' relation to them gives all parties a chance to help all students meet worthy standards, helps teachers avoid inappropriately low or capricious expectations, and ensures that student performance is judged wisely by the public.

And once again, simply providing more accurate and credible data grounded in valid standards does not necessarily mean better information. Beyond sound data, clients need the translations and evidence that explain grades, scores, and comments and enable clients to verify the judgments made—or challenge them! (The single-letter grade presented by itself, as argued later, hides the data and makes verification or criticism difficult if not impossible for the reader.) Even if we grant that there will be more hassle in reporting more openly and thoroughly, we must recognize the value to students' ongoing education of getting accurate and useful information to the student and parents. By supplying clients with an adequate context, with anchor papers or performance samples, rubrics, teacher commentaries on the sample products, and the like, our report would describe, judge, and substantiate our teacher judgments—a highly desirable outcome.

## Better Letter Grades and Grading Categories: Usefulness

Thus the problem we need to solve is not the use of letter grades per se. It is the habit of using a single grade, with no clear, agreed-upon, and stable meaning to summarize all aspects of complex performance, that is at the core of our present difficulties. We need more defined grades, and we need more types of grades, not fewer.

A report card is designed to summarize students' school performance. Grades or numbers, like all symbols, offer efficient ways of doing this summarizing. Because parents cannot be expected to wade through all the student's work and draw key meanings and judgments, the educator's job is to make meaning of the performances and to present facts, judgments, diagnoses, and prescriptions in a user-friendly summary form, supported by documentation available on request.

A common criticism of general symbols and rankings is that they lead the student to worry more about grades than about learning. But sixty years ago President Lowell of Harvard University wisely argued the case for working for good grades when the grades stand for something of clear value and validity: "To chide a tennis player for training himself with a view to winning the match, instead of acquiring skill in the game, would be absurd. . . . If marks are not an adequate measure of what the course is intended to impart, then the examination is defective."[2] The message throughout this book has been assess what you value; value what you assess. This extends to reporting. If a grade summarizes the results of performance with known and apt criteria (as in skating figures or rating wine), then motivation to earn that grade is neither extrinsic nor corrupted. Student grade grubbing stems from capricious and mysterious grading, not from grades themselves.

What critics of letter grading must therefore come to understand is that the symbol is not the problem. The lack of stable and clear points of reference in using symbols is the problem. Trying to get rid of familiar letter grades gets the matter backward and also leads to needless political battles—tampering with a symbol system as sacred as that of letter grades can be fraught with peril and backlash. We need more and better data from grading, not less. Parents have reason to be suspicious of us when we want to reduce the amount of available data and get rid of a hundred-year-old system that parents think they understand—even though we know that traditional grades are often inadequate or misleading feedback.

Symbols are not inherently misleading, after all. There is nothing ambiguous about a black belt in karate, an 8.5 in diving, or a score of 800 on the SAT exam. Grades are clear when specific and stable standards and criteria are used in assigning them. Grades are unclear when they represent murky intellectual values inconsistently rated across teachers.

The specific problem with letter grades that must be solved before they can usefully represent standards and criteria is that we use too few grades to accomplish too many and too many different kinds of reporting tasks. Effort, achievement, progress; class participation; quality of papers; the consistency with which homework was done—How can a single grade make sense of these distinct variables? (Recall the criticism of holistic rubrics in Chapter Seven, namely, that combining independent variables in the same rubric makes it more likely that students will get the same score for different performances and that teachers will disagree about the scores.) This problem is compounded when the weighting of those different factors varies not only across teachers but even with the same teacher over time, and when considering different students. Too often, therefore, our current use of letter grades amounts to shifting praise and blame, based on rarely shared and sometimes unjustified personal values. The use of the standard curve for giving grades only exacerbates matters further. A grade on a curve is an artifact that bears no clear relation to valid standards, and indeed is psychometrically indefensible at the classroom level, as Bloom, Madaus, and Hastings argued years ago.[3]

## More Grades and More Types of Grades

A single grade hides more than it reveals. We would not feel comfortable giving each teacher only a single-letter grade in a district performance appraisal system. Why do we allow it for students? Giving more grades, in the form of separate grades for performances in subtopics and skills within subject areas, is in everyone's interest. It is better measurement, it provides more helpful data, and it is both more honest and fair.

The previous baseball statistics analogy is quite revealing here. Suppose some mathematician came up with a way to combine all the data—runs batted in, hits, home runs, strike outs, and so on—into a single statistic using a complex formula known only to the mathematician. How would this be useful to everyone else? A single aggregate statistic, like a single-letter grade, can be highly misleading. Why? Because the many possible statistics (data) are independent of one another. A player may hit for a low average and strike out a lot, but when he hits, he may hit home runs and drive in lots of runs. In contrast a so-called singles hitter may get on base a lot and hit for a higher average, but not be productive in terms of runs batted in. When we call each kind of data independent, we mean simply that to isolate a single statistic and grade on the basis of it would be pointless and bad feedback. It would hide more than it would reveal. It would make it appear as though two very different performances were the same—invalid assessment, by definition.

Such independence of diverse variables is true not only in baseball; it is also true, and much more complex, in such domains as language arts and science. Joey is great with poetry, poor on essays; strong with fiction reading, weak on literary criticism. Nani is the reverse. Should they get the same B– grade simply because that is how the math comes out when we average grades in the grade book? How can that be useful feedback? Susan is thorough and accurate at laboratory work, though weak on tests; she is very conscientious and accurate in her homework problems. Jamie's lab work is spotty but indicative of understanding; he does extremely well on tests, and his homework, when done, is excellent—but it is not always turned in on time, and careless mistakes are made in it. Why give them both the same B? Leaving aside the more insidious problems of inconsistent grading across teachers and grade inflation, we hide and distort the real meaning of performance when we report in this way.

For a model of the type of report that summarizes performance data efficiently in many categories as it also offers a brief narrative judgment about that data's meaning, think of the baseball cards that fans buy. Each player's card gives the fan a brief description of the player's previous year's performance through data highlighting the many subdimensions of that performance over time, and it gives a brief narrative on the player's highlights. The card for one batter reports that he hits for a low average but drives in many runs. And though he struck out a lot, he led his team in home runs. The card for another batter presents a very different profile: high batting average but few extra base hits and few runs driven in. The performance is nowhere reduced to a single grade with, worse, the data hidden in the report. Instead, the disaggregation of data personalizes the report by doing a better job of showing specific and often unique strengths and weaknesses. Allowance is even made for developmental factors: the cards of the new players report their minor league statistics, which often show that their performance falls off as they enter the Major Leagues.

We might therefore build our student reports out of various performance subcategories, standards, and benchmarks using the national content and performance standards now developed for most subjects.[4] In the National Council of Teachers of Mathematics standards, for example, mathematical performance is divided into mathematical power, dispositions, problem solving, communication, and so forth.[5] In addition, the document provides major content categories (for example, synthetic geometry and analytic geometry), with subskills and concepts implied in each. Why not encourage all math teachers to disaggregate their letter grade into these separate categories, with rubrics for each standard? Why not make sure that English teachers report each student's performance on different genres of writing and literature, because as many large-scale assessments have shown, performance across genres is not constant? I am not saying that there is no value in a single composite grade or score. But as in diving or figure skating (where such composite scores are given), there needs to be a transparency that allows us to know all the scores and weightings that went into the final score. If there must be a composite single score, let there also be endless public discussion about the relative weight of factors that make it up. Let there be a consistency across teacher-judges once we have come to some understanding—whether we are talking about individual teachers or entire school systems. And let the report show the sub-grades making up the total grade (and by implication, the formula whereby different traits and performance types are weighted and combined). Only an ongoing public debate about what should go into the overall grade will lead to a rational system.

The psychological danger of the single-letter grade, unmoored from the supporting data and rules of translation, is its artificial solidity. Its unitary nature suggests a kind of finality and objectivity, which hides the diverse data and typically private (and often unconscious) judgments that led to it. As noted earlier, sports fans perpetually argue about who was the best hitter or passer because there are always multiple data and contexts they can use to support their competing judgments. This is true in all performance, and is thus true of academic performance, though that fact is a huge inconvenience. It was once, to the great comfort of many teachers, covered up for us by single-letter grading. But we cannot have it both ways: if we want the kinds of reform argued for earlier in this book, then we have to realize how judgment-based the whole education enterprise really is and find the best ways to live with the consequences. A performance-based system is a judgment-based system. Our goal should not be to develop a grading system that silences would-be arguers, but to invite them into a conversation about credible data and professional judgments. Invariably there will be disagreements.

That is why there must be oversight, as there is in sports and in the judicial system. The single-letter grade lets the teacher present a seemingly definitive result, but it hides an array of judgments that ought to be more public, debated, and warranted—and thereby refined and improved over time.

## The Arbitrariness of Averaging

A glib reduction of all results to a single grade on a report card is doubly wrong if there has been no attempt to validly weight one statistic to another, so that habit or laziness leads us to average it all. Consider baseball again. Players accumulate runs, runs batted in, hits, strikeouts, and home runs—factors that are of clear value by themselves but of unclear and arguable worth relative to one another. That is why fans perpetually argue about excellence! Why would we just total up the numbers and divide by the number of categories? It is arbitrary to average different traits into a single score unless some valid reason or correlation can be given to justify it. We saw the same arbitrariness in Chapter Seven in the way people sometimes handle analytic-trait rubrics, by simply adding scores for separate traits together and dividing by the number of traits to yield a single final score. If such averaging is arbitrary and misleading even in baseball, where all the data are quantitative, think how little warranted it is in school subjects.

Similarly, it is an unwarranted move to average individual grades over time to come up with "the" grade, as we have always done. There are many different types of performance. Maybe the work is harder now; maybe it is easier now. Maybe a new student enters the classroom at midyear and shows enormous gains by year's end. Averaging distorts progress (or lack thereof) and completely hides the range of performance, something that we are presumably interested in reporting.

Averaging makes even less sense once students enter a learning system framed by objective exit standards of performance, and thus move along on a novice-expert continuum. Why average at all under such long-term circumstances? When the student starts out in a class as a novice and ends up the year as an advanced student, is there any use to rating him intermediate at the end by averaging his work across the novice-expert range? In a standard-based assessment system, the use of averages over long periods of time has no pedagogical justification, although it may be an unfortunate expedient for harried teacher-judges. We should rather do as coaches do in sports and arts: agree on different tasks' level of difficulty and chart each student's progress in learning to handle more difficult tasks well. This depends on the development of longitudinal reporting systems, which are discussed later in the chapter.

If more diverse data are desirable—and they are, even at the risk of lowering current parent comfort levels—then reducing all data to A, B, and INC (Incomplete) is heading in the wrong direction. This curtailed system, championed for years by advocates of Mastery Learning and outcomes-based education, cannot be sensible if the goal is better feedback. Getting rid of grades lower than B makes as little sense as not reporting batting averages under .300. More important, it conflates valid standards with unfair expectations. Students may "not yet" meet our expectations, but few will ever meet the highest performance standards (for example, a four-minute mile or perfect scores on national achievement tests). Grade inflation is almost always set in motion by such a system. And the reduction of complex assessment to simplistic tests has been another common feature of Mastery Learning approaches. Thus it is not unfair to students to write more data-driven standard-referenced reports. On the contrary, such reporting supplies feedback that is the key to future progress and eventual mastery.

## Distinguishing Standard-Referenced and Expectation-Referenced Reports

The criteria of honesty and fairness also suggest the need for different kinds of judgments, not just more data. We must make explicit allowance for the two very different kinds of grading that invariably get the grade giver into trouble: performance measured against standards and performance measured against reasonable expectations. (Reasonable expectations can be divided into expectations based on historical norms and expectations based on the individual student's abilities and potential.)

There are thus two basic kinds of questions that a report should address: How did each child do given authentic, valid, and fixed standards? And how did each child do given reasonable expectations for performance gains during the period? To safeguard the conceptual difference, I propose that we reserve the term *scores* for answering the former question and the term *grades* (meaning letter grades) for answering the latter.

How do scores differ from grades (as they have just been defined)? Think of scores as pure performance data, such as the results of performance tests in writing, mathematics, typing, diving, or music, and the results of standardized criterion-referenced achievement tests (for example, the College Board Achievement Tests, the National Assessment of Educational Progress [NAEP] subject-area tests, and the Degrees of Reading Power Test). Scores are given in terms of performance standards. These absolute standards are set by exemplary performers or perfect performance. A standard is a standard whether or not anyone in the school can meet it.

Scoring in this sense, whether by human judge or machine, must be disinterested or "blind" to be valid and credible. The judge considers no mitigating or extenuating factors, such as age, history, or character. The judge simply scores the performance in reference to uniform criteria and standards, through rubrics and exemplars, anchors, or specifications (for example, one hundred words per minute in typing, a raw Degrees of Reading Power score of 68, a score of four out of six on a state writing assessment that is anchored by papers from around the state, and so on). Any performance test (not just multiple-choice tests) should yield valid and reliable—that is, comparable—scores. We are scoring performances, not performers.

Grades, conversely, represent a judgment about a unique performer's overall record in context—the meaning and value of those scores in context. The teacher appraises the value of a student's scores, taking into consideration what it is reasonable to expect from such a performer. Circumstances now appropriately influence our judgment: How good a performance is this for a student at this stage in a career? How good a performance is this for this particular student? We take the scores and translate them in various ways for report readers as we consider each of these questions. When it comes time to grade the performance, we are thus asking: To what extent did the student meet reasonable expectations? And the answer will always amount to, "Well, it depends." A 4.5 diving score may well be a good performance or a poor one, depending on the diver, her prior experience, our sense of whether she worked to capacity, and our sense of the norms for her stage of development.

This is why it is always technically and pedagogically wrong to compute letter grades mechanically on the basis of scores. To translate rubric scores directly into grades—for example, turning a 6 into an A, a 5 into a B, and so forth, as some teachers and districts now do with performance assessments—confuses criterion-referenced scoring with norm-referenced grading. This is as unwarranted as turning the diver's 4.5 into a D, irrespective of the diver's age, experience, and level of competition, simply because a 4.5 computes into a 45 in a 100-point grading system and, by convention, a poor grade. The translation of scores into grades requires not *computation* using neat but arbitrary mathematics but *interpretation* that is mindful of the different natures of the standards and expectations. Expectations properly vary from student to student and over time for the same student.

Some basic questions are often not asked by report card reformers when local grades are at issue: Whose expectations are the grades based on? Against which norms? In what overall credible context? Part of the parental concern with and backlash against changes in local grading systems stems from nagging doubts about teacher expectations based on local, versus national or state, norms. Nothing disturbs a parent more than to learn that a student who has received straight A's in mathematics for three years scores in the 36th percentile on a national mathematics test. Regardless of educators' opinions of the quality of such tests, parents must be granted the right to their concern. What kind of a grading system is it that seemingly hides from students and parents the truth of the quality of performance as viewed in the wider context of national norms? The local report should reflect national norms or standards somewhere; such surprise is indefensible. Many of the earlier proposals in the book for assessment reform relate here, too: teachers should ensure, through collaborative grading and benchmark setting, that local tasks and grades link to some credible wider world norms and standards.

The following chart summarizes the differences between scores and grades (standard-referenced versus norm-referenced reporting):

| *Performance Scores* | *Letter Grades* |
| --- | --- |
| Are absolute (judged against fixed exemplars, hence linked to standards). | Are typically relative (to the individual's best work or to the norms of local cohorts, hence linked to expectations). |
| Are criterion referenced (dependent upon adherence to criteria and a disinterested scoring process focused on achievement only). | Are related to attitude and effort, not just achievement. |
| Are standard referenced (scores refer to validated exemplars; score ranges are unpredictable). | Are norm referenced and individual referenced (scores are based on past patterns for cohorts and the individual). |
| Are not age or experience dependent. | Are context dependent. |

Two kinds of expectations have been mentioned here and they must also be distinguished in reports: expectations relative to the larger context of the student's peer group (often cast in terms of grade level, development, or course level) and expectations relative to each student's personal circumstances. In the former sense, we typically refer to or infer from local norms: "You earned a B in English this term because you met pretty well my general expectations for students in ninth grade English." Such grading against a local norm is the de facto meaning of a letter grade in many schools. The other kind of expectation-based grade is more personalized: "You earned an A, given your improvement vis-à-vis my expectations of you personally, based on your individual record and level of experience." We can refer to the former as a *normed grade* and to the latter as a *growth grade*. A normed grade is based on empirically defensible expectations of a cohort, presumably linked to valid developmental data. A growth grade represents a rough assessment of whether personal potential was realized. Too often teachers now seem to merge these two meanings of expectation as they assign single-letter grades.

Normed and growth grades should be kept separate because they represent distinctly different ideas. Relative to your classmates, you may be doing poorly (made plain by data and rankings for which no grade need even be given). Relative to your previous performance and students with similar past experience, you may be doing extraordinarily well. Being in the 40th percentile when your colleagues are experts is not so bad, but being in the 90th percentile when your colleagues are rank novices and less experienced than you warrants no automatic praise or grade of A. For example, reports often do a poor job of communicating the lack of growth of good students. I have often felt that coaches are far better at communicating this than teachers: coaches will bench the best players for "dogging it," whereas on a classroom report card, the student who achieves at high levels is often made to look inappropriately flawless simply by virtue of their relatively superior achievement on tests and assignments.

Yet, growth is also different from effort. Growth compares projected gains to actual gains and thus yields the grade. A high achiever who makes little effort may still grow as reflected in results. The reverse can also be true: a student might make great efforts but show little growth as measured in changes in achievement. Maybe great intentions can yield poor results, and hard work can be ineffectual. These distinctions are rarely made despite the fact that they are critical for understanding a student's record. Further, a student could grow a great deal but make relatively little absolute progress against standards. She may have moved from 1 to 2 on a scale of 10— great growth for her but still a long way from the standard and well behind her peers. This kind of contextual fact needs to be reported. (This point about progress against standards is discussed further in the later section on longitudinal assessing and reporting.)

## Criteria and Guidelines for Report Card Reform_____

The following introductory ideas suggest some practical implications for building better student performance reports. The first point demands that we answer the question, What were the student's actual achievements, irrespective of capacity, effort, and attitude? But the second point demands that we also ask and answer, Were reasonable expectations set and met for this (and every) child? Have we detailed the unique strengths, weaknesses, and gains of this child in a context that casts them most fairly?

The following five complementary approaches, based on the criteria of honesty, fairness, thoroughness, and usefulness, should lead toward more educative reports:

1. *Report many more subscores of performance in summarizing performance data.* Math or reading is not one unitary performance but many. The performance report should be organized in categories that highlight the many key curricular goals and performance factors used to analyze complex performance (such as those identified for mathematics in the National Council of Teachers of Mathematics's *Curriculum and Evaluation Standards for School Mathematics*, and for science in the American Association for the Advancement of Science's *Benchmarks for Science Literacy*, or Project 2061).[6]

2. *Distinguish explicitly between achievement data and expectation-based evaluation, symbolized as scores and grades, respectively.* Scores would refer to performance measured against valid performance standards; grades would refer to the judgments made by teachers about performance measured against expectations.

3. *Report both kinds of expectation-referenced grades.* Expectations measured by benchmarks for each student's cohort (age-group, class, developmental level, experience level) would be separated from expectations measured by the teacher's judgment of each individual's expected growth versus actual growth. The former grade would be termed *normed* and the latter would be termed *individual growth*. Both would be reported but with different symbols. When the reports are narratives, the symbols would be woven into the discussion of results.

4. *Analyze students' academic achievements through three kinds of data: level of achievement, quality of work, and progress against standards.* Achievement levels refer to achievement against exit-level standards of performance sophistication. Work quality refers to the caliber of the products produced, at any level. (Using both achievement and work quality allows us to make the kind of apt distinction made in arts and athletics competitions between "degree of difficulty" and

"quality" points). Progress refers to absolute gains toward exit standards (not to be confused with growth, which is measured as change in the individual). Progress would be charted along multiyear continua or rubrics, so that a third grader would know how she was doing against fifth grade and (sometimes) twelfth grade standards—again, just as in performance areas like chess, diving, soccer, and band. Comparatively sound judgments could be made on this longitudinal data about whether a student was on course to meet exit-level standards.

5. *Evaluate the student's intellectual character—habits of mind and work—based on established patterns over long periods of time in performance and products.* The report would highlight teacher judgments concerning the dispositions essential to higher-level work success and routinely sought in college reference forms and personnel records (such as persistence, ability to work independently and with others, attention to detail, open-mindedness, and the like).

As these ideas suggest, our reports will only be as good as the quality of local assessment. Too often, crudeness of report card letter grades simply reflects crudeness of testing and averaging. Rarely are grades rationalized and tested for cross-teacher consistency. Even less rarely are grades tied to valid external standards for content, work design, and performance. The key to report card change, then, is for us to make sure that grades, scores, comments, and any shorthand symbol system can be translated by parents into achievements and levels that they can understand as stable and worthy. This requires far more authentic and detailed assessment than we now do; it requires the ongoing educative assessment described in the previous chapters.

## Sample Reports

Let us now turn from these formal considerations of possible standards, criteria, and reporting categories to examples of both real and proposed reports. What are districts now doing in the name of reform? Which of the problems described here do they seem most willing and able to tackle? Have they avoided the mistakes that lead to parent or community backlash?

For example, in West Windsor–Plainsboro schools in New Jersey, educators explicitly report growth against norms and also disaggregate literacy into many different sub-elements, each separately graded. To report on literacy behaviors (for example, "uses appropriate comprehension strategies," "writes effective responses to literature," and "participates successfully in sustained short reading"), the report uses these categories: CO ("consistently demonstrates this behavior"), DE ("is developing this behavior as expected"), DD ("is experiencing difficulty developing this behavior"), and NC ("is not currently demonstrating this behavior"). Teachers thus can hold expectations constant across the students in a particular class.

A suburban Texas district offers a visual record of individual performance compared to both norms and developmental criteria over the course of the year. The graph in Figure 10.1 is used six times and shows the gains made during the year toward grade-level expectations. Figure 10.2 shows a continuum of communication achievements for a kindergartner.[7]

Figures 10.1 and 10.2 represent good reports—pictures—literally as well as figuratively—of the student's growth over time. However, we lack a clear picture of what progress should look like—what exit standards inform Kindergarten benchmarks—and how the student's growth compares with the growth of his or her classmates. Noticeably absent here is any comparative frame of reference as the child's performance unfolds. Whereas parents get a helpful picture of movement toward the benchmarks, the touchstone question still is: But how is he doing (as compared to other students of similar age and type at this point in time)? Though it is convenient bureaucratically to treat all kindergartners as the same type of student, such a view flies in the face of reality. At this age, the youngest and oldest students may be light years apart either developmentally or experientially. Fairness requires that we look at whether the individual student is in the same place developmentally as her peers. That is why we need a growth report in addition to a normed report such as the graph in Figure 10.1.

How might Figure 10.1 be modified to accommodate the idea of progress? First, it might be extended to report beyond kindergarten (as in South Brunswick's report system described later in this section). Second, genuine performance standards might be explicitly equated with the local expectations found on the graph.

## Honesty Requires Standard-Referenced Reports

Local norms and clear, common expectations are not enough, however, to produce fully honest reports. The client needs not only data on local norms but a justification of local norms as, well, normal. Thus we should at least report local performance against credible norms, against an empirically validated wider-world set of data about performance that is considered normal for this type of cohort. That may mean national norms or state norms, but in a good suburban district with high local norms these will be absurd points of comparison. Until recently, New York State suburban districts trumpeted the fact that 99 percent of their students were above the state passing

Figure 10.1 Round Rock Independent School District Graph of Individual Performance

Intellectual Development

| | Communication | | | | Science/Social Science | | | Mathematics | | | Physical Development | | | Aesthetic Development | | | |
|---|---|---|---|---|---|---|---|---|---|---|---|---|---|---|---|---|---|
| | Listening | Speaking | Writing | Pre-Reading | Observes Identifies Predicts | Sequence and Order | Compare Contrast Classify | Observes Identifies Predicts | Sequence and Order | Compare Contrast Classify | Motor and Perceptual Awareness | Wellness | Fine Motor | Singing Concepts | Comparatives and Listening | Rhythm Movement Expression | Visual Arts |
| 6 Performances Beyond K Level | | | | | | | | | | | | | | | | | |
| 5 | | | | | | | | | | | | | | | | | |
| 4 | | | | | | | | | | | | | | | | | |
| 3 Exit Expectations | | | | | | | | | | | | | | | | | |
| 2 Performance at K Level | | | | | | | | | | | | | | | | | |
| 1 Entry Level | | | | | | | | | | | | | | | | | |

Figure 10.2 Continuum of Communication Achievements for a Kindergartner

WRITING

- Expresses ideas through drawing and painting
- Uses writing materials
- Random scribbles

- Expresses ideas through drawing, painting, and dictating
- Shows appropriate use of writing materials to communicate
- Scribbles with meaning

- Expresses ideas using letter-like shapes
- Demonstrates some knowledge of the alphabet
- Associates print with the spoken language
- Shows awareness of left to right, top to bottom

- Expresses ideas and recognizes that experiences and stories can be written about
- Uses letters to represent sound in words with some reversals
- Understands that print conveys message

- Uses temporary spelling to write ideas (some reversals)
- Uses some conventions of capitalization and punctuation
- Shows awareness of spaces between words
- Works left to right, top to bottom
- Begins to revise and edit work

- Attends to purpose while writing
- Extends and elaborates ideas
- Applies many conventions: capitalization, punctuation spacing
- Demonstrates readiness for more direct spelling instruction

PRE-READING/READING

- Develops an awareness of printed materials and pictures

- Displays interest in print
- Spends time looking at books and likes to have stories read

- Recognizes that print conveys meaning
- Retells stories from pictures
- Recognizes concepts of print
- Displays developing fluency of language

- Follows print left to right
- Identifies and connects sounds with letters
- Recognizes some high frequency words or names in and out of context
- Shows signs of becoming a beginning reader
- Actively participates in shared reading

- Participates comfortably in reading activities
- Follows print with 1-1 correspondence
- Begins to use phonics, pictures, and language structure to read for meaning

- Reads for meaning, information
- Uses reading strategies automatically
- Is comfortable with a variety of literature

score in reading—but this passing score is set terribly low to deal with the much weaker performances in the state's five urban districts. The suburban districts would have served themselves and their community better had they done something like what the Educational Record Bureau (ERB) does. ERB reports test results in its writing assessment using three different kinds of percentile scores: national norms, suburban norms, and private school norms. Even quite renowned public school districts stop looking flawless when compared to good private schools. That is useful reporting because it gets even teachers in good districts working to be better.[8]

Chapter Three presented parts of a rubric for eighth grade oral presentations from Toronto's Benchmarks program. To illustrate the use of credible standards and valid norms, Figure 10.3 shows the complete rubric, this time accompanied by summary data that show the percentage of Toronto eighth graders who received each score in the first year of the assessment. The rubric makes clear that what is considered normal is not acceptable: to be performing at Levels One and Two is not good in absolute terms, even if many students are now there. Such criterion-referenced reports make clear the distance to be covered to meet truly high standards. To report such percentages or normed letter grades without the rubric might make it appear as if being at Levels Two or Three were satisfactory. (In addition, in this particular case the anchor performances are eighth grade ones derived from local assessment, making these results less standard referenced and more normed than they could be. Using validated exemplars from the best Canadian eighth graders or from adult professional life would no doubt lower the scores, but it would improve the credibility and usefulness of the results to clients.)[9]

Yet fairness again requires that we judge these scores in context. These results were the very first recorded for the oral assessment. For a new complex performance task never encountered before by students we should expect low scores in both the normed grades and the growth grades. Further, we need to factor in that more than half of Toronto's students have non-English-speaking parents. That fact alone makes it unlikely that most students would do well in early rounds of this oral testing. These observations are not excuses but needed perspective: by reporting scores and percentages, in addition to giving personalized grades, we paint an honest yet fair picture, and we set the stage for later gains.

## Longitudinal Assessing and Reporting

Because growth is not the same as progress, normed grades and standard-referenced scores should be combined in reports. Regardless of growth, are Johnny and Denise making sufficient gains over

### Figure 10.3 Percentage of Students Earning Each Score on Eighth Grade Oral Performance

| | | |
|---|---|---|
| Level Five | 8% | The student is aware of the importance of both content and delivery in giving a talk. The content is powerfully focused and informative. The issue is clearly defined, and detail is judiciously selected to support the issue. The talk is delivered in a style that interests and persuades the audience. Questions, eye contact, facial expressions, and gesture engage the audience. The student displays evidence of social, moral, and political responsibility, and offers creative solutions. Causes and effects are elaborated. The second version of the talk reveals significant changes based on revision after viewing. The student may make effective use of cue cards. The student is confident and takes risks. |
| Level Four | 20% | The student is aware of the importance of both content and delivery in giving a talk. The student's talk is well shaped and supported with pertinent information. The student supports conclusions with facts, and makes connections between cause and effect. The talk is delivered in a style that may interest and persuade the audience. Questions, eye contact, facial expressions, and gesture are used occasionally to engage the audience. Delivery is improved after viewing the first draft of the talk. The student is fairly confident and can self-evaluate. |
| Level Three | 28% | The student is aware of the importance of both content and delivery in giving a talk. The talk displays a noticeable order and some organization primarily through lists. The student includes some specific information, some of which supports or focuses on the topic. The conclusion may be weak. The student may show personal involvement with the topic and concern about the consequences of not dealing with the issues. There is evidence of revision as a result of viewing the first version of the talk. The student is fairly confident and can self-evaluate. |
| Level Two | 22% | The student's talk contains some specific information with some attempt at organization. The main idea is unclear and facts are disjointed. Some paraphrasing of text is evident. The student uses no persuasive devices, has little eye contact or voice inflection, and does not take a clear stand on the issue. The delivery is hesitant and incoherent. Little improvement is shown in the talk after watching the first version. The student demonstrates little confidence. |
| Level One | 22% | The student chooses one or two details to talk about but the talk lacks coherence. The talk is confused and illogical. There may be no response. |

time toward exit-level goals? Even if they are meeting our current eighth grade expectations in oral proficiency, are they on track to meet a real-world standard by graduation? If there are no shared and validated scoring scales across grade levels, how will we know for sure whether each grade level's narrowly framed expectations align with valid benchmarks? To measure progress accurately requires a new approach to reporting, one that places key student performances on a standard-anchored continuum and supplies a new kind of grade with which teachers judge the likelihood of the student's meeting exit standards at the current rate of progress.

We see the value of such reports clearly in the few areas where they now exist: the Proficiency Scales of the American Council on the Teaching of Foreign Language, the Degrees of Reading Power Test, and such scoring systems as tennis ladders, chess master ratings, cross-country running times, karate belts, and computer game levels.

The following material from the American Literacy Profiles reveals how we can combine individual growth and progress reports in a larger context of norms and standards. Recall the Texas report card mentioned earlier, in which growth and progress were visually reported in a graph designed to show movement over time toward the standard. Look what happens when we overlay information about the whole class's performance (Figure 10.4) on writing.[10] The A to I continuum represents the fullest range of performance over the K–8 period, measured against an exit-level standard. The gray areas represent the range of performance in the class, and the black area represents the student's current level of performance.

Now notice what we learn when we do a longitudinal analysis using the so-called box and whisker method of plotting data, illustrated in Figure 10.5.[11] We gain an instant sense of what personal and normed growth look like. In this example, we see that the student is closing the gap with peers after starting far below them: significant growth has occurred. Still better progress is needed, however, to reach benchmarks for the remaining two years and the exit standard.

No one is deceived or likely to be put off by such a report. On the contrary, the less able student sees tangible gains of the kind typically obscured by letter-grade reporting systems linked to classroom norms. (Consider what it would be like for cross-country runners or swimmers not to see their finishing times but to learn only about their place at finish. That's what grades without scores are like.)

Longitudinal rubrics of this type can serve double duty: they can enable teachers to have a stable and useful framework for judging student work and designing valid tasks, and they can serve nicely as reporting systems to students and parents. This is how the ten-year-old national assessment system works in Great Britain.[12] Figure 10.6 shows a rubric currently in use in Great Britain in mathematics.[13]

The need for such scales in academic areas and for caution about framing benchmarks only in terms of a grade level are made clear by national test data and grade inflation. Consider the scale for charting mathematics progress used a few years ago by NAEP (Figure 10.7).[14] According to NAEP data, only 6 percent of U.S. students can perform at the highest levels—despite the fact that these levels

Figure 10.4 Writing Profile Rocket

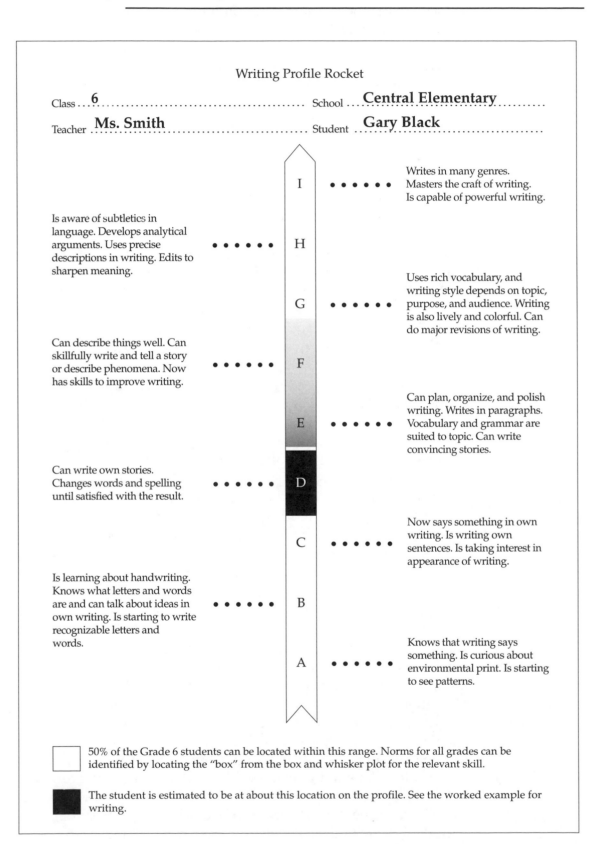

Writing Profile Rocket

Class . . **6** . . . . . . . . . . . . . . . . . . . . . . . . . . . School . . . **Central Elementary** . . . . . . .

Teacher . . **Ms. Smith** . . . . . . . . . . . . . . . . . . . . Student . . **Gary Black** . . . . . . . . . . . . . . .

I • • • • • • Writes in many genres. Masters the craft of writing. Is capable of powerful writing.

Is aware of subtletics in language. Develops analytical arguments. Uses precise descriptions in writing. Edits to sharpen meaning. • • • • • • H

G • • • • • • Uses rich vocabulary, and writing style depends on topic, purpose, and audience. Writing is also lively and colorful. Can do major revisions of writing.

Can describe things well. Can skillfully write and tell a story or describe phenomena. Now has skills to improve writing. • • • • • • F

E • • • • • • Can plan, organize, and polish writing. Writes in paragraphs. Vocabulary and grammar are suited to topic. Can write convincing stories.

Can write own stories. Changes words and spelling until satisfied with the result. • • • • • • D

C • • • • • • Now says something in own writing. Is writing own sentences. Is taking interest in appearance of writing.

Is learning about handwriting. Knows what letters and words are and can talk about ideas in own writing. Is starting to write recognizable letters and words. • • • • • • B

A • • • • • • Knows that writing says something. Is curious about environmental print. Is starting to see patterns.

☐ 50% of the Grade 6 students can be located within this range. Norms for all grades can be identified by locating the "box" from the box and whisker plot for the relevant skill.

■ The student is estimated to be at about this location on the profile. See the worked example for writing.

Figure 10.5 Box and Whisker Method

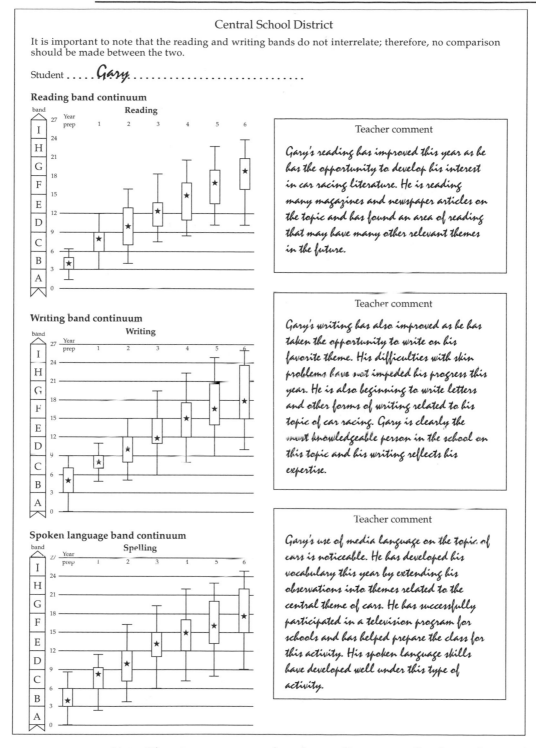

*Note:* The stars correspond to the median scores for the entire grade-level cohort. The top of the box corresponds to the 75th percentile and the bottom of the box represents the 25th percentile. The "whiskers" extend up to the 90th and down to the 10th percentiles.

### Figure 10.6 Attainment Target 2: Number and Algebra

| | |
|---|---|
| Level 3 | Pupils show understanding of place value in numbers up to 1000 and use this to make approximations. They have begun to use decimal notation and to recognize negative numbers, in contexts such as money, temperature, and calculator displays. Pupils use mental recall of addition and subtraction facts to 20 in solving problems involving larger numbers. They use mental recall of the 2, 5, and 10 multiplication tables, and others up to $5 \times 5$, in solving whole-number problems involving multiplication or division, including those that give rise to remainders. Pupils use calculator methods where numbers include several digits. They have begun to develop mental strategies, and use them to find methods for adding and subtracting numbers with at least two digits. |
| Level 4 | Pupils use their understanding of place value to multiply and divide whole numbers by 10 or 100. In solving number problems, pupils use a range of mental and written methods of computation with the four operations, including mental recall of multiplication facts up to $10 \times 10$. They add and subtract decimals to two places. In solving problems with or without a calculator, pupils check the reasonableness of their results by reference to their knowledge of the context or to the size of the numbers. They recognize approximate proportions of a whole and use simple fractions and percentages to describe these. Pupils explore and describe number patterns, and relationships including multiple, factor, and square. They have begun to use simple formulae expressed in words. Pupils use and interpret coordinates in the first quadrant. |
| Level 5 | Pupils use their understanding of place value to multiply and divide whole numbers and decimals by 10, 100, and 1000. They order, add, and subtract negative numbers in context. They use all four operations with decimals to two places. They calculate fractional or percentage parts of quantities and measurements, using a calculator where appropriate. Pupils understand and use an appropriate noncalculator method for solving problems that involve multiplying and dividing any three-digit by any two-digit number. They check their solutions by applying inverse operations or estimating using approximations. They construct, express in symbolic form, and use simple formulae involving one or two operations. |
| Level 6 | Pupils order and approximate decimals when solving numerical problems and equations such as $x^2 = 20$, using trial-and-improvement methods. Pupils are aware of which number to consider as 100 percent, or a whole, in problems involving comparisons, and use this to evaluate one number as a fraction or percentage of another. They understand and use the equivalences between fractions, decimals, and percentages, and calculate using ratios in appropriate situations. When exploring number patterns, pupils find and describe in words the rule for the next term or $n$th term of a sequence where the rule is linear. They formulate and solve linear equations with whole number coefficients. They represent mappings expressed algebraically, interpreting general features and using graphical representation in four quadrants where appropriate. |
| Level 7 | In making estimates, pupils round to one significant figure and multiply and divide mentally. They understand the effects of multiplying and dividing by numbers between 0 and 1. Pupils solve numerical problems involving multiplication and division with numbers of any size, using a calculator efficiently |

Figure 10.6 Continued

| | |
|---|---|
| | and appropriately. They understand and use proportional changes. Pupils find and describe in symbols the next term or *n*th term of a sequence where the rule is quadratic. Pupils use algebraic and graphical methods to solve simultaneous linear equations in two variables. They solve simple inequalities. |
| Level 8 | Pupils solve problems involving calculating with powers, roots, and numbers expressed in standard form, checking for correct order of magnitude. They choose to use fractions or percentages to solve problems involving repeated proportional changes or the calculation of the original quantity given the result of a proportional change. They evaluate algebraic formulae, substituting fractions, decimals, and negative numbers. They calculate one variable, given the others, in formulae such as $V = \pi^2 h$. Pupils manipulate algebraic formulae, equations, and expressions, finding common factors and multiplying two linear expressions. They solve inequalities in two variables. Pupils sketch and interpret graphs of linear, quadratic, cubic, and reciprocal functions, and graphs that model real situations. |
| Exceptional performance | Pupils understand and use rational and irrational numbers. They determine the bounds of intervals. Pupils understand and use direct and inverse proportion. In simplifying algebraic expressions, they use rules of indices for negative and fractional values. In finding formulae that approximately connect data, pupils express general laws in symbolic form. They solve problems using intersections and gradients of graphs. |

correspond to the content of algebra classes in which more than half of American eighteen-year olds will have earned passing grades.[15] Local grading and reporting of math thus needs to offer clearer links to credible national standards. (Such links are often found in other countries where state or national test scores must be factored into local teacher grades—which can be as high as 50 percent of the grade, for example, in Alberta, Canada.)

The progress this scale measures differs from the two kinds of growth because, as described earlier, progress is measured backward from a desired final destination: What percentage of a trip has been completed? How close is the student to the goal from his starting point? How far forward has he traveled, and what would such a trend extrapolate to in terms of reaching his goal? Is his progress normal, optimal, or worrisome? These questions are only answerable if we score backward from a valid performance standard.

Measuring progress also requires us to make a judgment. In reporting progress data over time, we are objectively charting a trend (parallel to reporting norms) that answers the questions, What is the graph of student progress over time along the same continuum? and How does that graph compare to the cohort's graph and

### Figure 10.7 Developmental Rubric for Levels of Mathematics Proficiency

**Level 150—Simple Arithmetic Facts**

Learners at this level know some basic addition and subtraction facts, and most can add two-digit numbers without regrouping. They recognize simple situations in which addition and subtraction apply. They also are developing rudimentary classification skills.

**Level 200—Beginning Skills and Understanding**

Learners at this level have considerable understanding of two-digit numbers. They can add two-digit numbers, but are still developing an ability to regroup in subtraction. They know some basic multiplication and division facts, recognize relations among coins, can read information from charts and graphs, and use simple measurement instruments. They are developing some reasoning skills.

**Level 250—Basic Operations and Beginning Problem Solving**

Learners at this level have initial understanding of the four basic operations. They are able to apply whole number addition and subtraction skills to one-step word problems and money situations. In multiplication, they can find the product of a two-digit and a one-digit number. They can also compare information from graphs and charts, and are developing an ability to analyze simple logical relations.

**Level 300—Moderately Complex Procedures and Reasoning**

Learners at this level are developing an understanding of number systems. They can compute with decimals, simple fractions, and commonly encountered percents. They can identify geometric figures, measure lengths and angles, and calculate areas of rectangles. These students are also able to interpret simple inequalities, evaluate formulas, and solve simple linear equations. They can find averages, make decisions on information drawn from graphs, and use logical reasoning to solve problems. They are developing the skills to operate with signed numbers, exponents, and square roots.

**Level 350—Multistep Problem Solving and Algebra**

Learners at this level can apply a range of reasoning skills to solve multistep problems. They can solve routine problems involving fractions and percents, recognize properties of basic geometric figures, and work with exponents and square roots. They can solve a variety of two-step problems using variables, identify equivalent algebraic expressions, and solve linear equations and inequalities. They are developing an understanding of functions and coordinate systems.

to historical patterns of many cohorts over time? But a judgment must then be made for the client. The progress data should be evaluated as "exemplary," "on course," and "grounds for concern," or the like. These progress reports should be professional predictions based on trend data, not unanchored value judgments. (We often talk about "developmentally appropriate assessment," but until we have done our research on norms and trend data we have little right to make such claims.)

Distinguishing better between growth and progress would benefit our reports in several ways. We would see when growth did not involve adequate progress, when a group of students may have grown a great deal over the years but still not be on track to meet exit standards. Here is where current reports are most deficient. Parents and other clients outside the school typically cannot tell from reports in the early grades the severity of the student's performance progress because the grades are typically linked to grade-level norms, and each grade level has typically not justified its own tests and grades against exit-level standards. In addition to seeing progress difficulties early, we would reveal when students of great abilities (who are thus able to get perfectly fine scores and make progress) are underachieving.

Many educators (especially those worried about the fate of minority children) fear that greater judgment-based assessment about expectations will be derived from bias or prejudice, not from data. The fear is that such a system will only formalize and dignify the establishing of lower expectations for students according to ethnicity, race, gender, class, and so forth. Reporting progress rates and norms of performance (including norms and progress rates for subpopulations) should help prevent such abuses, but ultimately the remedy is an accountability system that requires staff to track progress and intervene when progress for a group slows or stops. A faculty's job, after all, is to maximize the performance of the entire cohort and investigate any discrepancies in performance by any subgroups. (Routinely scoring student work blindly and collaboratively also prevents such abuses.) Credible and effective local assessment demands that these steps be taken.

The longitudinal system needed to measure progress is also more likely to provide incentives for less able learners. Just as runners begin to worry less about their place in finishing the race and more about their times and "personal bests," so too can students of all kinds gain motivational power from ongoing reports of steady gains. Students can be "slow" learners yet see sufficient personal progress over time. As argued elsewhere, a standard-referenced system used over the student's career is feasible, as has been proven in other countries, even though U.S. educators are not used to such an approach.[16]

This too is hardly a new idea. Edward Thorndike, one of the fathers of modern educational measurement, eighty years ago called for scores that "redirect [the incentive of] rivalry into tendencies to go higher on an objective scale of absolute achievement, to surpass one's own past performance." The vice of the letter-grade system was its "relativity and indefiniteness, the fact that a given mark did not mean any defined amount of knowledge or power or skill." Competing against "one's own past" or an "accepted standard," observed Thorndike, yields consistently greater motivation: "To be 17th instead of 18th does not approach in moving force the zeal to beat one's own record, to see one's practice curve rise week by week, and to get up to the standard which permits one to advance to a new feat."[17]

An example from the Cherry Creek, Colorado, schools shows how this measurement of progress can look and how normative data can also be charted (see Figure 10.8). (Note that in this example the standards refer to elementary school exit-level standards.) Similar information is reported on science performance, and normed information is given on a host of intellectual habits of mind and social conduct. Content standards are not lost or forgotten: the full report describes the books read, specific performance tasks mastered, and course-specific major assignments completed.[18]

The staff at Polton Community Elementary School, who devised the Cherry Creek reporting system, found that the story told at the beginning of this chapter, about the parents' question ("OK, but how is she doing?"), was not apocryphal. In an early draft of the report card, the only thing staff were going to report was the achievement level noted on each continuum. I suggested that they needed to think through both the issue of performance quality versus work sophistication, and the issue of norms. Sure enough, the parents demanded the latter: the box that closes the language arts section of the progress report, where the child's performance is compared to that of the class, was recently added to respond to parental feedback.

The descriptors on this progress report, or report card—basic, proficient, and advanced—are helpful but ultimately too broad for use over multiple years. Finer distinctions in performance levels are needed to get a clear sense of just what the child can and cannot do—though without overwhelming parents with data. Consider for example the report used in South Brunswick, New Jersey, to chart progress toward sophisticated literacy in reading in the early school years (Figure 10.9).[19]

The developmental portfolio and assessment system used in South Brunswick includes an approach to spelling assessment and reporting that honors the idea of reporting progress backward from a standard. Rather than simply recording that words on spelling tests are spelled correctly or incorrectly, the teachers in the district (with help from Ted Chittenden at the Educational Testing Services) learned to chart students' progress toward correct spelling over the K–2 grades, using a *word awareness writing activity* (WAWA).[20] Empirically grounded criteria (derived from research on spelling acquisition and naive or invented spelling)

### Figure 10.8 Cherry Creek School District, Polton Community Elementary School Progress Report

Student Name _____ Grade 3 _____ 4 _____

Teacher_____ School Year _____

Performance-based graduation requirements focus on student mastery of the proficiencies. The curriculum and written progress report are geared toward preparing students for this task. A date (e.g., 11/93) indicates where a student is performing on a continuum of progress based on the fifth grade exit standards.

Name          Grade 3          4

Language Arts      Listens, interpreting verbal and nonverbal cues to construct meaning.
Proficiency 1

| Basic | Proficient | Advanced |
|---|---|---|
| Actively listens, demonstrates understanding, and clarifies with questions and paraphrasing. | Actively listens for purpose, demonstrates understanding, and clarifies with questions and paraphrasing. | Actively listens for purpose, demonstrates understanding, clarifies with questions and paraphrasing, and classifies, analyzes, and applies information. |

Language Arts      Conveys meaning clearly and coherently through speech in both formal and
Proficiency 2      informal situations.

| Basic | Proficient | Advanced |
|---|---|---|
| Appropriately speaks to inform, explain, demonstrate, or persuade. Organizes a speech and uses vocabulary to convey a message. | Appropriately speaks to inform, explain, demonstrate, or persuade. Organizes a formal speech and uses vocabulary to convey a message. | Appropriately speaks to inform, explain, demonstrate, or persuade. Organizes a formal speech with details and transitions, adapting subject and vocabulary. Uses eye contact, gestures, suitable expression for audience and topic. |

Language Arts      Reads to construct meaning by interacting with the text, by recognizing the
Proficiency 3      different requirements of a variety of printed materials, and by using
appropriate strategies to increase comprehension.

| Basic | Proficient | Advanced |
|---|---|---|
| Reads varied material, comprehends at a literal level. Recalls and builds knowledge through related information. Begins to use strategies to develop fluency, adjusting rate when reading different material. | Reads varied material, comprehends and draws inferences, recalls and builds knowledge through related information. Applies strategies to increase fluency, adjusting rate when reading different material. | Reads varied material, comprehends literally and interpretively. Synthesizes and explores information, drawing inferences. Critiques author's intent, analyzes material for meaning and value. Applies strategies to increase fluency, adjusting rate. |

*(continued next page)*

### Figure 10.8 Continued

Language Arts
Proficiency 4

Produces writing that conveys purpose and meaning, uses effective writing strategies, and incorporates the conventions of written language to communicate clearly.

| Basic | Proficient | Advanced |
|---|---|---|
| Appropriately writes on assigned or self-selected topics. Clear main ideas, few details. Weak elements in the beginning, middle, end. Sentence structure lacks variety and contains errors. | Appropriately writes on assigned or self-selected topics. Clear main ideas, interesting details, clear organization, sequencing, varied sentence structure, and edits to reduce errors. Appropriate voice and word choice. | Appropriately writes on assigned, self-selected topics. Connects opinions, details, and examples. Effective organization and sequencing, meaningful sentence structure, edits to eliminate most errors. Appropriate voice and word choice. |

As compared to their class in the area of Language Arts, your child

|  | 1 | 2 | 3 |
|---|---|---|---|
| Displays strong performance |  |  |  |
| Demonstrates appropriate development |  |  |  |
| Needs practice and support |  |  |  |

Name _____ Grade 3 _____ 4 _____

Math
Proficiency 1

Uses **numbers** and **number relationships** to solve mathematical problems of increasing complexity and communicates results.

| Basic | Proficient | Advanced |
|---|---|---|
| Demonstrates a basic understanding of number relationships by performing simple mathematical operations. | Demonstrates a comprehensive understanding of number relationships by selecting and using computation and reasoning skills to solve problems. | Demonstrates an advanced understanding of number relationships by applying number theory concepts to make predictions. |

Math
Proficiency 2

Uses **geometry** and **measurement** to solve problems of increasing complexity and communicates results.

| Basic | Proficient | Advanced |
|---|---|---|
| Identifies simple shapes and demonstrates simple measurement skills. | Analyzes properties of various shapes and measures using different units and mathematical calculations. | Uses geometric shapes, calculations, and dates to solve problems logically. |

Math
Proficiency 3

Uses **probability**, **statistics**, and **data analysis** to solve mathematical problems of increasing complexity and communicates results.

| Basic | Proficient | Advanced |
|---|---|---|
| Demonstrates a basic understanding of chance, graphs, and tables. | Uses the fundamentals of probability and data analysis to predict outcomes. | Demonstrates an advanced understanding of probability and data analysis to solve problems logically. |

Figure 10.8 Continued

| Math<br>Proficiency 4 | Uses the recognition and construction of **patterns** and **relationships** to solve mathematical problems of increasing complexity and communicates results. |
|---|---|

| Basic | Proficient | Advanced |
|---|---|---|
| With teacher guidance, recognizes, creates, and extends simple patterns using shapes and numbers. | Uses drawing and number sentences to demonstrate understanding that patterns are symbolically represented. | Demonstrates an advanced understanding of patterns by using them to solve problems. |

| Math<br>Proficiency 5 | Uses **algebra** to solve mathematical problems of increasing complexity. |
|---|---|

| Basic | Proficient | Advanced |
|---|---|---|
| Demonstrates a basic understanding of mathematical sentences. | Demonstrates reasoning abilities when solving simple problems with one unknown variable. | Demonstrates an advanced understanding of algebraic methods used to solve problems by independently constructing formal equations. |

allow levels of sophistication in spelling hunches to be catalogued. A sample of these levels of spelling ability is shown in Figure 10.10, along with some teacher guidelines for analyzing spelling levels.[21]

Readers of the spelling report see this chart as an example and have a clear and verifiable perspective on the student's spelling; and charting of scores over time clearly highlights progress toward the standards of correct spelling. Again I would argue that we gain insight by also reporting the local norms (which South Brunswick does not now report to parents): Where are the student's peers on the same scale at this point? And to be fair I would also report growth, with a letter grade summarizing the teacher's evaluation of the progress in light of reasonable expectations for that student. (South Brunswick does not give such grades.) Note that these assessments against a standard do not favor or undercut any particular teaching philosophy or program philosophy. There is nothing inherently at odds, for example, with a literature-based and process-writing approach to instruction and such developmental scoring scales, as too many educators mistakenly believe.

In all of the examples presented thus far, there is an omission: the crucial distinction between type and frequency of behavior-at-a-level and quality of performance is overlooked. A student could be consistently performing at a high level, but her work could be sloppy. Performance can be crude or sophisticated; students can be novices or advanced performers. In either case, these descriptive terms tell us nothing about the quality of their work. Years ago, Deborah

## Figure 10.9 South Brunswick K–2 Reading/Writing Report

| | |
|---|---|
| 1 – Early Emergent | Displays an awareness of some conventions of reading, such as front/back of books, distinctions between print and pictures. Sees the construction of meaning from text as "magical" or exterior to the print. While the child may be interested in the contents of books, there is as yet little apparent attention to turning written marks into language. Is beginning to notice environmental print. |
| 2 – Advanced Emergent | Engages in pretend reading and writing. Uses reading-like ways that clearly approximate book language. Demonstrates a sense of the story being "read," using picture clues and recall of story line. May draw upon predictable language patterns in anticipating (and recalling) the story. Attempts to use letters in writing, sometimes in random or scribble fashion. |
| 3 – Early Beginning Reader | Attempts to "really read." Indicates beginning sense of one-to-one correspondence and concept of word. Predicts actively in new material, using syntax and story line. Small stable sight vocabulary is becoming established. Evidence of initial awareness of beginning and ending sounds, especially in invented spelling. |
| 4 – Advanced Beginning Reader | Starts to draw on major cue systems: self-corrects or identifies words through use of letter-sound patterns, sense of story, or syntax. Reading may be laborious, especially new material, requiring considerable effort and some support. Writing and spelling reveal awareness of letter patterns. Conventions of writing such as capitalization and full stops are beginning to appear. |
| 5 – Early Independent Reader | Handles familiar material on own, but still needs some support with unfamiliar material. Figures out words and self-corrects by drawing on a combination of letter-sound relationships, word structure, story line, or syntax. Strategies of re-reading or of guessing from larger chunks of text are becoming well established. Has a large stable sight vocabulary. Conventions of writing are understood. |
| 6 – Advanced Independent Reader | Reads independently, using multiple strategies flexibly. Monitors and self-corrects for meaning. Can read and understand most material when the content is appropriate. Conventions of writing and spelling are—for the most part—under control. |

*Note 1:*   *The scale focuses on development of children's strategies for making sense of print. Evidence concerning children's strategies and knowledge about print may be revealed in both their reading and writing activities.*

*Note 2:*   *The scale does not attempt to rate children's interest or attitudes regarding reading, nor does it attempt to summarize what literature may mean to the child. Such aspects of children's literacy development are summarized in other forms.*

*Note:* Rating scale developed by South Brunswick, New Jersey, teachers and Educational Testing Service staff, January 1991.

## Figure 10.10 South Brunswick Spelling Assessment Rubric

A scoring chart is provided below to help you analyze the spelling. Before going further, think about the features that you will look for at each developmental level:

1. Precommunicative spelling is the "babbling" stage of spelling. Children use letters for writing words but the letters are strung together randomly. The letters in precommunicative spelling do correspond to sounds.

2. Semiphonetic spellers know that letters represent sounds. They represent sounds with letters. Spellings are often abbreviated, representing initial and/or final sounds. Example: E = eagle; A = eighty.

3. Phonetic spellers spell words like they sound. The speller perceives and represents all of the phonemes in a word, though spellings may be unconventional. Example: EGL = eagle; ATE = eighty.

4. Transitional spellers think about how words appear visually; a visual memory of spelling patterns is apparent. Spellings exhibit conventions of English orthography like vowels in every syllable and vowel diagram patterns, correctly spelled inflection endings, and frequent English letter sequences. Example: EGUL = eagle; EIGHTEE = eighty.

5. Correct spellers develop over years of word study and writing. Correct spelling can be categorized by instruction levels; for example, correct spelling for a body of words that can be spelled, the average fourth grader would be fourth-grade level correct spelling.

Look at the child's list. Were most of the child's spellings precommunicative, semiphonetic, phonetic, transitional, or correct? This is the child's probable developmental level. You might feel that a child truly falls between two of the categories, but try to put in just one check mark per child

| | 1 | 2 | 3 | 4 | 5 |
| Words | Precommunicative | Semiphonetic | Phonetic | Transitional | Correct |
|---|---|---|---|---|---|
| bed | random | b | bd | behd | bed |
| truck | random | tk | trk | truhk | truck |
| letter | random | lt | ldr | ledder | letter |
| bumpy | random | bp | bmp | bumpee | bumpy |
| dress | random | js | jrs | dres | dress |
| jail | random | jl | gal | jale | jail |
| feet | random | ft | fet | fete | feet |
| shopping | random | sp | spen | shoping | shopping |
| monster | random | m | mnstr | monstur | monster |
| raced | random | r | rast | raist | raced |
| boat | random | b | bot | bote | boat |
| hide | random | hi | hid | hied | hide |

Meier, head of the Central Park East schools and a MacArthur Fellow, observed that "when people say, 'Joe is two grades below grade level,' they usually don't make clear whether or not he's doing A work at that lower level. They typically mean it negatively, in fact:

i.e., he's not doing well for someone at that lower level either."[22] Her comment shows the rationale for honoring the quality-sophistication distinction in progress reports. Slow, for example, does not mean incompetent. We need to better distinguish the slowly developing yet adequate reader from the sophisticated but sloppy reader. Honesty and fairness demand it.

A closer look at the limits to the language of the NAEP or South Brunswick descriptors (Figures 10.7 and 10.9) shows how much we need indications of quality. The differences in levels in Figure 10.9 relate only to the sophistication and scope of the reading strategies employed, not to the accuracy or effectiveness with which they are employed. And both these rubrics hide the fact that increased sophistication does not correlate directly with a decrease in mistakes. On the contrary, the arithmetic student may make many fewer mistakes than the algebra student, and the precocious student may be more careless and sloppy than the slow but thorough student. Similarly the American Council on the Teaching of Foreign Language's Spanish proficiency guidelines (Figure 7.7) distinguish between novice and native speakers but cannot show which students are careful novices or ungrammatical native speakers.

Chapter Five described the New York State School Music Association's assessment process that allows a student or group to choose a level of difficulty and then be assessed in terms of various qualities of performance while performing pieces of music at that level. Novices may play low-level pieces well, and experts may play complicated pieces with mistakes. The teacher's expectations help parents to interpret the judge's scores and help the teacher to know whether or not the piece was too easy or difficult for the student. Scores in piece difficulty are appropriately expected to increase over time, while quality scores might vary as students tackle a new level of difficulty. Similarly, maybe a speller or writer is more sophisticated than her peers but prone to careless mistakes; and maybe a boy who is "slow" produces excellent work for his level of development or amount of prior experience.

The Rialto, California, school system recently developed a new report card, shown in Figure 10.11, that incorporates many of these distinctions.[23] Note that it reports not only the student's performance level but also the quality of work against normed expectations at each level in question, three times each year, using letter grades. Some parents objected to the initial version of the Rialto report system because it seemed to finesse the issue of content standards and grade-level expectations. Those concerns and my feedback led district officials to add the modification shown in Figure 10.12 to the longitudinal rubrics.[24] (Alas, the report failed to meet our other criterion of user-friendliness, and the district has since dropped it.)

## Figure 10.11  Rialto Unified School District Pupil Progress Report K–6

Name:_____

Guardian:_____

Birthdate:_____

Teacher:_____

School/Year:_____

Grade:_____

| | Days Enrolled: | | | |
| --- | --- | --- | --- | --- |
| | Days Absent: | | | |
| | Days Tardy: | | | |

❑  SARB Date:_____

*Keys to Success:*

This Pupil Progress Report (PPR) is one form of communication between school and home. Although growth occurs in a very predictable sequence, each child will have a very different profile that reflects his or her uniqueness. A parent should not feel that all children must show the same progress in each category to be successful. Developmental learning is affected by the age and maturity level of the child, his or her out-of-school experiences, as well as classroom learning.

Rialto Unified School District strives for all students to be responsible learners. A responsible learner exhibits the following behaviors:

• listens attentively • controls talking • follows directions • works independently • completes assignments on time • returns homework • works cooperatively with others • contributes positively to classroom discussions • demonstrates a positive attitude • produces accurate/legible work • demonstrates organizational skills • uses a range of critical thinking skills • enhances work with technology, resources, and/or creativity • respects others • follows classroom and school rules • takes care of school materials • practices the "A.R.T." of communication (i.e., Appreciation, Respect, and Trust).

*Student Services*

❑ Title 1

❑ Resource specialist program

❑ LEP (Level-Fall_____ Level-Spring_____

❑ Adapted P.E.

❑ Special day class

❑ Speech/Language

❑ GATE (Gifted/Talented Ed.)

❑ SST Dates_____

*Student Goals*

Identify areas of focus or concentrated study during the next trimester. Special attention could be needed to further refine a skill area where success is experienced by your student or to apply extra effort to improve growth in an area of concern. (Use extra paper if necessary.)

*Agreements:*

(Date and initials of teacher, parent, and student for each goal set.)

*Teacher Comments:*

(Dated for each reporting period.)

Figure 10.11 Continued

| | Reading | Writing | Communication Skills | Math | Science | History/Social Science | Physical Education |
|---|---|---|---|---|---|---|---|
| 1 | ONLY with individual adult support! Looks at pictures in books. Demonstrates an interest in books or stories. | Uses pictures to create meaning. Orally assigns meaning to their own pictures. | Listens to stories for a short time. Follows a single direction. Responds or reacts using simple words and phrases. | Develops number sense using objects. Counts 1 through 20. Accurately counts set of 5 or more objects. Using a variety of materials, explores basic concepts of +/−, and sharing (÷). geometric shapes, figures, and patterns. Identifies basic colors and shapes. | Observes daily science through all senses. Draws and talks about science. | Identifies self as a member of a family/class/group. Retells one event from a personal time line. | Hops and gallops on preferred foot. Moves in large group without bumping into others or falling. Explores bouncing, throwing, and catching with many objects. Jumps long rope turned by others. |
| 2 | With guidance: Listens to books. Uses pictures to predict a story. Begins to look at words and letters. Knows some or all letters in isolation. | Orally assigns meaning to their own writing. May use letter-like forms, random letters, Spells some high frequency words in isolation. May copy print without comprehension. | Listens for short periods when adults are speaking. Listens for enjoyment. Follows more than one oral direction. Expresses ideas using simple words and phrases. | Expands concepts of basic operations (+ 10, count to 100, − as the reverse of +, multiplication as repeated +, and + as sharing equally). Counts by 10s, 5s, 2s. Uses nonstandard measurement. Identifies geometric shapes in world. Collects and organizes data. Solves everyday problems using +/−. | Communicates orally about science ideas. Compares and orders scientific information. Attempts to use science vocabulary. | Understands/acknowledges need for rules. Expresses own thoughts/ideas. Recognizes ideological and cultural differences. Draws simple map of home/class/school. | Hops and gallops on non-preferred foot, marches, and slides. Travels and changes directions quickly in response to a signal. Performs underhand toss; bounce and catch with two hands; stationary kick; and rolls a ball to objects or classmates. |
| 3 | Independently shows reading behavior with 1 to 1 correspondence. Independently uses pictures to gain meaning from reading material. Memorizes reading material to re-read. Knows some letter/sound relationships. | Writes words in a left to right, top/bottom progression. Reads own writing sequentially and logically. Begins to use book language in their writing. Uses sound/symbol relationships to invent spellings. | Listens for short periods while peers/classmates are speaking. Listens for information. Participates in group discussion upon request. | Developing number operation skills, i.e., +/− facts, +/− zero, × and +. Developing number concepts, particularly the role of zero. Developing place value concepts in three digit numbers. Has basic spatial and measurement sense. Begins to self-select problem solving strategies. | Uses simple oral/written communication to convey science ideas. Accurately uses scientific vocabulary to categorize and label scientific information. | Understands people live/work in communities for mutual benefit. Begins to describe basic elements of culture. Identifies physical characteristics of local region. Produces simple written reports. | Skips, hops, gallops, and slides at various speeds/directions. Jumps self-turned rope repeatedly. Throws overhand with side orientation and opposition. Catches after one bounce (solo and with partner). |
| 4 | Reads with instruction. Describes and predicts story sequence. Begins to self-correct to make sense of reading material. Recognizes frequently used words. Uses letter/sound relationships. | Writes with confidence and enthusiasm. Reads writing to others. Begins to use conventions of print capital letters, spaces between words, and punctuation. | Listens attentively and makes relevant responses. Contributes in a group setting. Expresses ideas using simple sentences in language appropriate to the situation. | Estimates quantities and measures accurately. Selects and uses appropriate computational methods. Uses calculator for complex computations. Uses variables to express relationships. Applies problem solving strategies accurately. Has basic understanding of whole numbers. Developing basic understanding of fractional quantities using manipulatives. | Communicates about science concepts orally and/or in writing. Sequences and organizes scientific information. | Identifies geographic/economic factors influencing location of settlements. Reads and creates compass rose, street map, and physical map. Reads graph/interprets single grid chart to explain data. | Uses movement skills appropriately in tag and relay games. Performs sequential movements in rhythmic activities. Throws accurately from short distances, catches bounced and aerial balls, and dribbles a ball continuously (hands or feet). |

Figure 10.11 Continued

| Reading | Writing | Speaking/Listening | Mathematics | Science | Social Studies | Physical Education |
|---|---|---|---|---|---|---|
| Reads grade level texts with minimal assistance. Understands reading material. Self-corrects to make sense of reading material. Recognizes frequently used words. | Continues to invent spelling with closer approximations. Many commonly used words spelled correctly in writing. Regularly uses punctuation, mechanics, and appropriate grammar. Includes details and expands thoughts in writing. | Listens to others without interrupting. Participates in discussion using language appropriate to the situation. Speaks confidently and effectively. Delivers simple oral presentations with sequence. | Demonstrates understanding of fractions, decimals, and percents. Uses measurement and geometry ideas throughout the curriculum. Demonstrates understanding of chance orally and in writing. Able to determine which operations(s) to use in multistep problem solving. | Understands and articulates concepts of big ideas: change in earth, physical, and life sciences. | Understands and articulates concept of cultural diversity. Describes economics of local community. Understands and explains government levels. Reads political map, longitude/latitude and uses landmarks to create own maps with legend. | Able to jump and land for height and distance. Recognizes fundamental strategies in simple games. Improved accuracy in throwing and catching, striking with body parts and objects, and controls hand and foot dribbling. |
| Reads grade level texts independently. Predicts and summarizes reading material. Self-corrects consistently to make sense of reading material. Uses a variety of strategies to read new words. | Most words are spelled correctly. Writing reflects logical sequence and meaning. Has control of expanded punctuation/mechanics. Includes details and expands thoughts in writing with consistency. Uses a variety of resources to enhance the written product. | Listens and confidently expresses meaningful ideas that further communication. Voluntarily begins to make relevant contributions to class discussions. | Pursues open-ended and extended problem-solving projects. Discusses and writes about math clearly for audience. Explores concepts involving integers. Understands variables, expressions, and equations of algebra. | Draws conclusions and inferences from science lessons and can communicate them to an audience clearly. | Interprets cause/effect and consequences of communities. Understands basic elements of democratic/constitutional rule. Locates information from sources and creates more than one type of communication to report data, including timetables and diagrams. | Able to start, stop, dodge, and pivot by maintaining body control. Performs well in games with emphasis on more than two skills. Throws a variety of objects for accuracy and speed. |
| Reads independently. Has insights about reading material. Questions, predicts, summarizes, and draws conclusions from reading. Reads and understands a variety of increasingly difficult materials. | Uses a variety of writing styles accurately. Writes with examples to support topic. Writer's voice is appropriate to the written task. Uses an expanded vocabulary in writing. | Adjusts speaking style to meet the needs of a situation. Analyzes and applies verbal information. Consistently makes meaningful contributions to class discussions. | Investigates and formulates questions from problem situations. Uses a variety of methods to solve linear equations in algebra. Uses statistical methods to describe, analyze, evaluate, and make decisions. | Shares accurate scientific understanding with others consistently. Communicates abstract ideas of science accurately using writing/multimedia resources. | Makes reasonable hypotheses and predictions regarding societal change (future). Uses compromise to resolve conflicts. | Proficient in performance of all types of movement skills. Able to combine sequences of movements in complex skills. Throws a variety of objects for accuracy and distance. |
| Reads independently for a variety of purposes. Has in-depth insights about and multiple perspectives on advanced reading material. Independent control of the first reading of unseen text. | Consistently uses correct mechanics and grammar. Consistently includes relevant reasons or concrete examples to support topic. The target audience is always clear. Uses specialized vocabulary with fluency. | Listens interactively with the focus on the speaker. Uses different oratorical styles appropriately. Uses complex speech structures (idioms, inference) to communicate. | Represents situations verbally, numerically, graphically, geometrically, or symbolically. Creates and defends models for situations involving probabilities. | Sets up experiments based on validity and laws of science. Accurately records scientific experiences through written observations and mathematical constructs. | Analyzes arguments/data to detect influence of bias and social/class injustices on course of history. Independently creates/analyzes/interprets multigrid charts, graphs, models using multimedia/library resources. | Demonstrates excellent skills in individual and team sports. With minimal instruction, reasons how to perform new skills. Able to design basic offensive/defensive strategies in games designed to keep objects away from others. |

Figure 10.11 Continued

Trimesters:

## GRADE LEVEL STANDARDS

### LANGUAGE ARTS

| | 1 | 2 | 3 |
|---|---|---|---|
| Advanced | | | |
| Proficient | | | |
| Partially Proficient | | | |

### MATHEMATICS

| | 1 | 2 | 3 |
|---|---|---|---|
| Advanced | | | |
| Proficient | | | |
| Partially Proficient | | | |

TEACHER COMMENTS (Dated for Each Reporting Period):

## RESPONSIBLE LEARNING BEHAVIOR

| ✓ Student Strength(s) | 1 | 2 | 3 |
|---|---|---|---|
| Returns homework | | | |
| Follows directions | | | |
| Works independently | | | |
| Completes assignments on time | | | |
| Demonstrates organizational skills | | | |
| Follows school/class rules | | | |
| Respects others | | | |
| Listens attentively | | | |
| Controls talking | | | |

## INDICATE FORMAL INSTRUCTION
### Per Trimester

| HEALTH | 1 | 2 | 3 |
|---|---|---|---|
| Personal health and nutrition | | | |
| Injury prevention and safety | | | |
| Individual growth and development | | | |
| Environmental health | | | |
| Consumer and community health | | | |
| Diseases | | | |
| Tobacco, alcohol, and other drugs | | | |

| PERFORMING ARTS | 1 | 2 | 3 |
|---|---|---|---|
| Theatre | | | |
| Dance | | | |
| Choral music | | | |
| Instrumental music | | | |
| Performances | | | |

| VISUAL ARTS | 1 | 2 | 3 |
|---|---|---|---|
| Design | | | |
| Draw | | | |
| Sketch | | | |
| Painting | | | |
| Graphics/printing | | | |
| Sculpture | | | |
| Architecture | | | |

Special Talents/Skills and Awards

☐ Optional page used.

### Figure 10.12 Modification to Longitudinal Rubrics for Rialto Unified School District Pupil Progress Report K–6

*Appropriate Stages of Development*

Student growth and development in academic and behavioral areas occurs in stages. In elementary school, students pass through stages of development. Each stage represents a cluster of skills that are linked to each other such that level 1 must be learned before level 2, level 2 before level 3, and so on. Stages are not the same as grade levels but, rather, overlap a span of grades. Progress is measured by movement through stages, not grade levels.

Stages of Development

| G | K | | | | | | | |
|---|---|---|---|---|---|---|---|---|
| R | 1 | | | | | | | |
| A | 2 | 1 | 2 | 3 | 4 | | | |
| D | 3 | | 2 | 3 | 4 | 5 | | |
| E | 4 | | | 3 | 4 | 5 | 6 | |
|   | 5 | | | | 4 | 5 | 6 | 7 |
|   | 6 | | | | | 5 | 6 | 7 | 8 |

*Grade Level Standards* have been established that

1. Specify what children are expected to know and be able to do
2. Contain coherent and rigorous content
3. Encourage the teaching of advanced skills

*Assessment Marking System*

K–3 Students: Number in trimester box indicates in which stage of development a child is *currently working.*

Example:

(Primary student is working in stage 2 in first and second trimesters, stage 3 in third trimester.)

4–6 students: Number in trimester box indicates in which stage of development a child is currently working and "A, B, C, M" indicates quality of work within that stage.

Example:

(Intermediate student is regularly producing above average work within stage 4 first trimester, producing same quality work within stage 5 second trimester, and is consistently producing outstanding work within stage 5 third trimester.)

| A | = | consistently produces outstanding quality of work within stage |
|---|---|---|
| B | = | regularly produces above average work within stage |
| C | = | occasionally produces quality work within stage |
| M | = | more quality needed within stage |

But even the addition does not go far enough to capture the difference between level of performance and quality of work. Again a student could be performing at high levels but producing sloppy or inconsistent work, or a student could be "slow" but thoughtful, careful, and thorough. Reports must be able to capture such differences. The scoring system for student portfolios that the Center on Learning, Assessment, and School Structure (CLASS) proposed for North Carolina (see Chapter Eight) honors the difference by calling for each performance task and the portfolio as a whole to receive two scores: one for expertise and one for work quality.

Too often we try to factor these distinctions between sophistication and craftsmanship into our placement system only, and not into our assessing and reporting. This is fine in theory but unfair and misleading in practice. Bureaucratic thinking causes us to treat students as all the same once they have been assigned to the same room, even when they differ greatly in experience and aptitude. Assuming that their work is of acceptable quality, why flunk some students in French I, for example, merely for being behind their class cohort? What is gained? Why not simply report where they began and where they ended on a continuum, along with normative information?

A distinction between degree of sophistication and degree of work quality therefore allows us to treat a performance level as distinct from a course title or classroom grade level—just as has always happened in one-room schoolhouses and multi-age classrooms. In fact, in the nineteenth century a grade level was completely standard referenced and had nothing to do with chronological age: as in diving, playing baseball, or playing the piano today, you advanced to a higher level when your performance level showed you were ready. This is of course what special education and vocational teachers have done for years. We can learn from their reporting systems.

A legacy of the lack of distinction between sophistication and quality is found in the troubled attempts to establish letter-grade uniform weighting systems that depend on the track of the course. I know of one high school where there are four different academic tracks and the weighting system multiplies each grade on a 100–point scale by 1.00, 1.10, 1.25, and 1.50, depending on the track. We may appreciate the intent, but the result is capricious. Is the English I course that is taught in one track in fact more difficult by the specific weighting factor than the course in the next track up? Who has actually run the experiment, using student papers taken from all tracks and graded blind, to validate the system, to show that the scores in the better class are half again as good on average as those in the lower-level class? Must not the expectations stay the same across tracks even if the standards differ? How is that assessed? What role do varying content standards play in grading?

Insofar as a weighting system lacks clear principles or procedures for asking and answering such questions—and for enforcing the system that results—how can it be fair or credible? In theory, weighted grades are fair; in practice, most schools lack the governance structures and oversight policies to ensure that the system works.

## Habits of Mind

Even knowing what a student knows and can do as measured on a continuum of performance progress does not tell us what we should be valuing in the long run about his educational progress: his habits of mind. Despite the typical fuss about Scholastic Achievement Test (SAT) scores and transcripts, college admissions officers and employers are more interested in students' dispositions as learners: Do they persist with difficult work? Can they clarify a task and organize an agenda? Do they ferret out unstated or unexamined assumptions? Are they tolerant of ambiguity? Can they shift perspective and consider different points of view? These capacities are the hard-won fruits of a good education. As noted in Chapter Five, skill in assigned performances should not be confused with intellectual competence and maturity.

By definition, a mature habit of mind is developed only over a long time. Our past penchant for simplistic class ranks and for the one-shot short-answer tests that support these ranks is thus antithetical to a quest for information about habits across time and context. A student may have lots of knowledge and quickly put down right answers, but the assessors have learned nothing about her ability to ferret out possible solutions to murky complex problems or whether she is capable of inquiring effectively into what she does not fully know or understand. Surely in the long run students' capacities to be self-critical, self-motivated, and effective in gathering research or in seeking help are more important to their later intellectual life than whether they can produce pat answers on cue.

That is another reason that we must institute the kinds of assessment reforms suggested in this book. We need to design assessment tasks that can be done well only by students who have such habits of mind. Mature habits of mind are crucial achievement targets that are often left out of assessment designs that focus on short-term knowledge.

These habits of mind clearly matter in the college admissions process. Consider, for example, the rating sheet in Figure 10.13, which is to be filled out by a student's teachers as part of the admissions packet used by more than one hundred private liberal arts colleges nationally.[25] This rating sheet is a useful model not only for

### Figure 10.13 Form Used by Colleges to Rate Students Seeking Admission

Please feel free to write whatever you think is important about the applicant, including a description of academic and personal characteristics. We are particularly interested in the candidate's intellectual purpose, motivation, relative maturity, integrity, independence, originality, leadership potential, capacity for growth, special talents, and enthusiasm. We welcome information that will help us to differentiate this student from others.

*Ratings*

| *No Basis* | *Academic Skills and Potential* | *Below Average* | *Average* | *Good* | *Very Good* | *One of the Top Few Encountered in My Career* |
|---|---|---|---|---|---|---|
| | Creative, original thought | | | | | |
| | Motivation | | | | | |
| | Independence, initiative | | | | | |
| | Intellectual ability | | | | | |
| | Academic achievement | | | | | |
| | Written expression of ideas | | | | | |
| | Effective class discussion | | | | | |
| | Disciplined work habits | | | | | |
| | Potential for growth | | | | | |
| | SUMMARY | | | | | |
| | EVALUATION | | | | | |

designing local school reports but also for asking what sorts of habits of mind need to be designed into our assessment tasks. It also has some flaws, however, that by now we should recognize. Teachers are not asked to justify or defend their rating. And note that the instructions ask for local norm-referenced data, not criterion-referenced data. Maybe "one of the top few encountered in my career" is pretty mediocre in the grand scheme of competitive colleges. By what criteria and indicators are these judgments to be made? The colleges should provide better guidance, as well as some sample data or student profiles that fit each category.

In fact, CLASS is now embarking on a multiyear research study on a common cross-school grading system and transcript. Such a system promises benefits for all parties: students could be confident that the grades have a clear, stable, and valid meaning; teachers could have their own local assessment become more credible, thereby lessening the importance (and dampening effect on teaching) of college admissions tests; and admissions officers could have greater confidence in the scores reported on the transcript than they can have on traditional letter grades.

## Verifying the Report: Providing Models

If we are going to provide more information of different kinds, there will be a pressing need for making it all intelligible and useful to relatively untutored readers, such as parents, few of whom understand assessment reform, why it is needed, and how it fits with traditional testing and reporting. A simple way to help them understand its nature and benefits is to give them one of the kinds of feedback for students described in Chapter Three: provide them with models and rubrics. Parents need to know what counts as exemplary performance, what it actually looks like, if they are to understand scores and grades. If parents are to find reports helpful and credible, we must give them the right interpretive tools—the anchor products and scoring guidelines.

CLASS staff have worked with a few districts to develop document-backed reporting systems, using as a guide the fine work done over the years by the Carleton School District in Ontario, Canada (and similar models found in the booklets published for Advanced Placement teachers). Carleton publishes "exemplar booklets" that provide students, parents, and teachers with the operational standards of assessment: samples of the range of papers, teacher commentaries on those papers, and the rubrics used to score them.[26] Parents are then in a position to verify the grades given (or to challenge them, in the worst-case—but also fair—scenario). The report card then actually informs and educates the parents. It helps turn them into the school's educational partners because they will understand the aims of the school and any gap between student intent and effect.[27]

We have also developed a mockup of a page from a parent report that provides most of the kinds of data considered here. This report would have a page for each aspect of literacy (reading, writing, speaking/listening) as well as separate reports for math, science, and social studies. This report card assumes district use of the American Literacy Profiles, mentioned earlier in this chapter. Figure 10.14 provides excerpts from the literacy profiles scoring system for writing.[28]

The CLASS report card (Figure 10.15) assumes that the parent has received the background documentation for writing, a booklet that describes each of the literacy "bands" (with A through I symbolized only with a letter on the report card), and samples of assignments and student work that correspond to each level.[29]

## Figure 10.14  Excerpt from American Literacy Profiles Scoring System for Writing

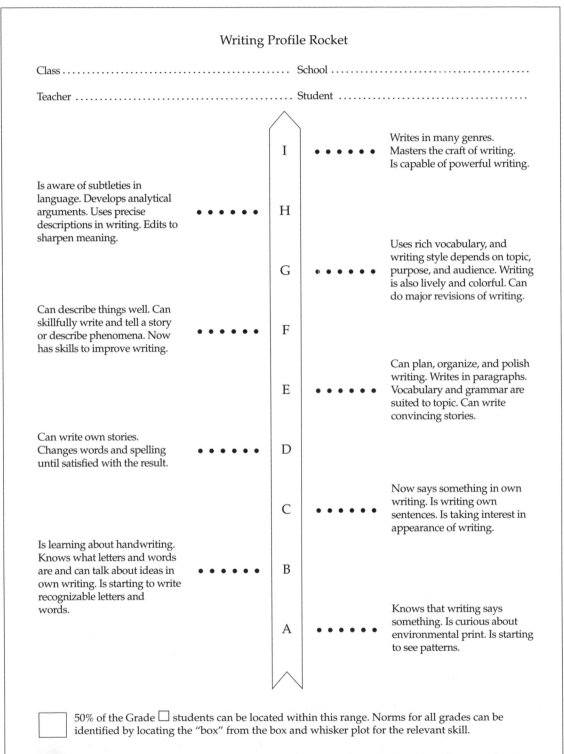

Writing Profile Rocket

Class ............................................... School ...........................................

Teacher ............................................ Student .......................................

I •••••• Writes in many genres. Masters the craft of writing. Is capable of powerful writing.

Is aware of subtleties in language. Develops analytical arguments. Uses precise descriptions in writing. Edits to sharpen meaning. •••••• H

G •••••• Uses rich vocabulary, and writing style depends on topic, purpose, and audience. Writing is also lively and colorful. Can do major revisions of writing.

Can describe things well. Can skillfully write and tell a story or describe phenomena. Now has skills to improve writing. •••••• F

E •••••• Can plan, organize, and polish writing. Writes in paragraphs. Vocabulary and grammar are suited to topic. Can write convincing stories.

Can write own stories. Changes words and spelling until satisfied with the result. •••••• D

C •••••• Now says something in own writing. Is writing own sentences. Is taking interest in appearance of writing.

Is learning about handwriting. Knows what letters and words are and can talk about ideas in own writing. Is starting to write recognizable letters and words. •••••• B

A •••••• Knows that writing says something. Is curious about environmental print. Is starting to see patterns.

☐  50% of the Grade ☐ students can be located within this range. Norms for all grades can be identified by locating the "box" from the box and whisker plot for the relevant skill.

■  The student is estimated to be at about this location on the profile. See the worked example for writing.

Figure 10.15  CLASS Report Card

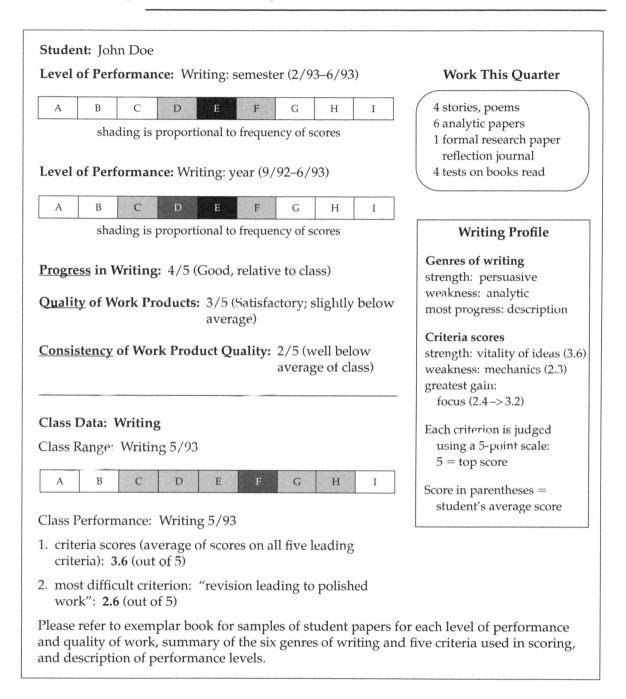

**Student:** John Doe

**Level of Performance:** Writing: semester (2/93–6/93)

| A | B | C | D | E | F | G | H | I |
|---|---|---|---|---|---|---|---|---|

shading is proportional to frequency of scores

**Level of Performance:** Writing: year (9/92–6/93)

| A | B | C | D | E | F | G | H | I |
|---|---|---|---|---|---|---|---|---|

shading is proportional to frequency of scores

**Progress in Writing:** 4/5 (Good, relative to class)

**Quality of Work Products:** 3/5 (Satisfactory; slightly below average)

**Consistency of Work Product Quality:** 2/5 (well below average of class)

**Work This Quarter**

4 stories, poems
6 analytic papers
1 formal research paper
  reflection journal
4 tests on books read

**Writing Profile**

**Genres of writing**
strength: persuasive
weakness: analytic
most progress: description

**Criteria scores**
strength: vitality of ideas (3.6)
weakness: mechanics (2.3)
greatest gain:
  focus (2.4 –> 3.2)

Each criterion is judged
  using a 5-point scale:
  5 = top score

Score in parentheses =
  student's average score

**Class Data: Writing**

Class Range: Writing 5/93

| A | B | C | D | E | F | G | H | I |
|---|---|---|---|---|---|---|---|---|

Class Performance: Writing 5/93

1. criteria scores (average of scores on all five leading criteria): **3.6** (out of 5)

2. most difficult criterion: "revision leading to polished work": **2.6** (out of 5)

Please refer to exemplar book for samples of student papers for each level of performance and quality of work, summary of the six genres of writing and five criteria used in scoring, and description of performance levels.

## Conclusion: Back to Basics

Today, few principals or administrators devote energy, meeting time, and the political gumption to rationalizing the grading and reporting procedure or to leading and cajoling faculty to solve these problems collectively. Teachers are typically left to sort out grading in private. For most teachers, the giving of a single grade is always a hard and sometimes ugly compromise—all the more so as classes become more heterogeneous through mainstreaming and detracking. Without agreed-upon program goals, assessment procedures, and performance standards, there is little the individual teacher can do beyond muddling through, even though it means continued unfairness and well-meaning dishonesty in reports.

Honoring the core premise of this book—building assessment to improve performance, not just to audit it—requires that grades and reports reflect our values and provide apt feedback. Indeed, the whole idea of Total Quality Management (the quality control method used extensively in business and industry) is predicated on the assumption that all workers need to judge products in a sound and consistent fashion if timely and effective adjustments are to be made.

Fundamentally, parents and students have a right to more helpful information than they get now, and they have a right to have a say in what kind of information they get and in what form. The following saying sums up the problems and a good deal of the solution (although it might be distasteful to some readers): the client for the information, not the purveyor, is invariably right about the quality of the information.

## CHAPTER 11

# Teaching and Accountability

Let me begin this look at teacher performance with a bold claim: *no teacher can succeed unless he or she is held accountable.*[1] This of course sounds ominous and untrue, because accountability invariably conjures up images of stern-faced board members thumping tables, assistant superintendents looking for trouble, or rows of young test takers with furrowed brows gnawing on number two pencils while teachers look on gloomily. In other words, in education accountability is usually thought of as a distracting burden, a task for solving someone *else's* needs, not something genuinely good for kids and teachers.

But let's shed the political overtones of the idea for a moment. Look up the word in a dictionary: to be accountable is to be responsible for one's work and responsive to its (sometimes unintended) effects. That means we must attend to results. We are properly responsible for our impact or lack of one, not merely for our good-faith efforts.

## Why We Need Accountability

"Fair enough," you might say, "but that hardly makes me want to *embrace* accountability." Then let me state it more provocatively: *any hope we have of ever being excellent teachers depends on accountability,* because at the heart of accountability—not the arbitrarily imposed accountability you may have experienced but true accountability as I hope to make you see it—is an idea that is also at the heart of this book: that feedback and self-adjustment play a crucial role in any performance. Performers—including teachers—learn and improve from feedback, as has been said throughout the book. No teaching is ever polished and fully effective the first or even the fourth time around, any more than are concert recitals or public speeches. Indeed, as argued in Chapter Four, students are likely to misunderstand the important ideas we intend to teach them or to not see them as valuable. Our eventual success depends on our ferreting out student responses and adjusting our performance, not just theirs, in light of results. True accountability thus involves the obligation of teachers to learn from assessment of student performance (teacher results) in the broadest possible sense (Are we achieving our goals?) and to act on that learning in a timely and effective way.

If the idea that excellent teaching depends on accountability is not yet clear, consider that teaching is liable to be an *egocentric* profession by its very nature of pairing adults with children, in the sense in which Jean Piaget used the term: we find it difficult to see when our teaching is not clear or adequate.[2] It is not easy to imagine how what is so obvious and important to *us* cannot be so to students. Because we have a difficult time understanding (or even predicting) the inevitable misunderstandings and mistakes of novices, and because we have a strong desire to cause learning and to seek evidence of success, we are prone to selective perception or self-deception.

This problem is nicely illustrated in a book on conceptions and misconceptions in science called *Learning in Science: The Implications of Children's Science*. In describing an interview process to be used in exploring a student's perspective on work at hand, which the authors stress is not easy to discern, the book notes how easily we hear what we want and need to hear in a student's answer or question. Our own agenda takes over, even when we are meant to listen: "Teachers and ex-teachers have a particular problem when it comes to the neutrality [in the method]. When teachers interact with students individually, they often almost unconsciously lead them through a series of questions which are aimed at developing a new conception. This is the exact opposite of the procedure. It is not the interviewer's conceptions that we are trying to get into the child's head but the child's conception that we are trying to get into the interviewer's head."[3]

Students play a role in our egocentrism, too. They are "adept at fastening on small cues to find what is expected of them." Thus, "effective probing of children's real ideas requires a conscious value-free approach which is not at all easy for teachers to maintain—but maintain we must if we are to get the information we need. . . .

[Otherwise students perceive that the interviewer] is an examiner, not interested in their personal view."[4]

In short, when we teach we often do not listen very well. This is the unfortunate consequence of trying hard, and for the right reasons, to get people to understand and value what we understand and value. It then often does not occur to us that students are trying equally hard to *appear* knowledgeable. Both facts make assessment far harder.

In other words, we, just like our students, badly need genuine feedback to improve our work; but our fear of it—because of the unknowns that have surrounded it, the absence of any objective record of our teaching that we could study, and the desire of our young charges to *seem* educated or please us—often conspires to keep us in the dark.

I once had a conversation with Stanford professor Lee Shulman about his then-new research for the National Board for Professional Teaching Standards. I asked him what he was finding in terms of one or two revealing indicators of really good teachers, and he said that I would probably find his answer unexciting: the best teachers can accurately describe what takes place in their classroom. I was delighted by his remark because it confirmed a view that I have been describing here: that we need the ability and the resources to self-assess correctly if we are to be excellent teachers. In fact, not two weeks before our conversation I had witnessed firsthand how even good teachers can fail at assessing their effect in the classroom. A high school teacher, reputed to be one of the best in the district and certainly capable of engaging and inspiring her charges, misrepresented two interactions with students. First, after giving some attention to two girls who were having difficulty, she proclaimed delight that they had been able to get beyond their misunderstanding of the group task so easily; but the girls' tentative language in the interaction was obvious to me, the outside observer, and as the teacher left, both girls moved their eyes skyward and threw up their hands in despair about her "help." She also consistently overrated the amount and degree of student participation in the full-class discussion that ensued.

## Learning to Think Like an Assessor About Ourselves

If we had a way of dispassionately assessing our students' views and competence apart from our own agendas, we would have a better view of the actual effects of our teaching. However, our legacy of defining assessing as testing rather than as performance improvement has also worked to prevent us from understanding student understanding.

Thus when I said that we cannot be good teachers without being accountable I meant something far different than "we need to live in a world of imposed, simplistic tests." I meant that we cannot ever be truly effective teachers until and unless each one of us is more flinty-eyed and skeptical about his or her own effect. We must become good assessors, in other words, of our own performance. We must be able to provide answers to the question How did we do?—given the students and given the standards. We must learn to get outside our own inevitably distorted perceptions of what has been achieved, of what has not been achieved, and most important, of what short-comings were our, not our students', responsibilities. External testing is one way, but often not the best way, to accomplish such a disinterested review.

I do not mean anything bureaucratic here. I am not necessarily referring to "formal performance appraisal" or "program evaluation." I do not even mean that we must enlist everyone in regular peer review of the kind described later in this chapter. Instead I am talking about a school life and culture that requires us to be more receptive and responsive to the information available to us about the gap that almost always exists between intent and effect but is typically unsought or unseen. I am talking about our learning to do routinely what we should also be expecting our students to do, as described in Chapters Two and Three.

Let me offer a simple personal example of soliciting and using feedback about teaching. In my fourth year of teaching I decided to videotape my tenth grade class, which focused on what is called the Socratic Seminar (see Chapter Four and Figure 4.2). I reviewed the tape after class by myself. What did I learn? I discovered to my horror, but also to my enlightenment, that far fewer students appeared engaged than had seemed the case to me in class, and that in retrospect even students who had said interesting things about the text appeared to have less understanding than I had thought.

While teaching I was prone only to hear evidence in support of my goals and lesson plans. I heard confirming evidence while subtly ignoring disconfirming evidence that was there to be heard and seen on the tape. I also heard myself using verbalisms that were quite unfortunate, such as using the word *obvious* eleven times in twenty minutes (while working with novices who are naturally tentative about their grasp of complex and very unobvious-to-them texts and ideas). No praise, no blame, just data from the tape: evidence of the need to adjust my performance based on a clear standard (derived from my undergraduate years of seminar work at St. John's College).

The telling and sad postscript to this story of one teacher's struggle to become better is that the audiovisual aide told me afterwards that I was the only teacher who had ever asked to have a class videotaped. In fact, even after I reported to the faculty on my effort, no one pursued it. This fear of or resistance to feedback unfortunately is common, as I have since discovered in school reform and peer review work. And it sets our profession back.

A different yet easy and personal approach to gathering useful feedback is to seek it from clients. Consider a simple approach to client-centered accountability that is still used by a former colleague of mine. Duane hands out index cards each Friday and asks students to fill out one side with the answer to "What worked for you this week?" and the other side with the answer to "What didn't work for you this week?" (Note the language: not "what you liked" but "what worked.") He was always surprised by some of the answers, and he always adjusted his instruction in light of the answers.

Such an invitation to students to give ongoing written feedback is exceedingly rare. Almost all formal course or program evaluations occur, like final exams, during the last days or hours, so students have little sense that the feedback is useful or likely to be used. Yet, when you think about it, how odd it seems that we do not happily and willingly attempt to find out if our work is causing the effects we intend. This is the first crucial step in accountability: to ask, How am I doing? and What might I do better or differently?

The regular collection of such data is what matters. We have historically underassessed our on-going impact on the client (as measured by survey data). We rarely seek routine feedback from students and parents about whether what we do serves their needs and interest. Worse, a sizable minority of teachers I speak with on this subject bristle at the mention of students as clients, as if students have no right to comment on the impact school has on them and no power to call for adjustments when things are not working for them. Few schools survey their former students, which makes very little sense given that the fear for face-to-face disagreement is removed and that there is obvious value in knowing whether our preparation is apt and adequate.

Consider the survey presented in Figure 11.1—a more comprehensive version of my former colleague's two questions—which is designed to provide a teacher with data on all major aspects of the classroom experience from the student's point of view.

How could we object to such a survey if we are interested in knowing how we are doing and how we might do better? Why does it seem odd or frightening to conduct surveys such as this one? In every business, this kind of assessment and analysis is the norm.

### Figure 11.1 Student Survey

| *In this class I feel:* | | | | | | |
|---|---|---|---|---|---|---|
| Important | 1 | 2 | 3 | 4 | 5 | Ignored |
| Comfortable | 1 | 2 | 3 | 4 | 5 | Uncomfortable |
| Involved in the lessons | 1 | 2 | 3 | 4 | 5 | Restless, bored |
| Part of a team | 1 | 2 | 3 | 4 | 5 | Alone |
| Good about my work | 1 | 2 | 3 | 4 | 5 | Bad about my work |
| Sure of where I stand | 1 | 2 | 3 | 4 | 5 | Not sure where I stand |

| *The teacher has been:* | | | | | | |
|---|---|---|---|---|---|---|
| Prepared | 1 | 2 | 3 | 4 | 5 | Unprepared |
| Fair | 1 | 2 | 3 | 4 | 5 | Unfair |
| Helpful | 1 | 2 | 3 | 4 | 5 | Unhelpful |
| Well-organized | 1 | 2 | 3 | 4 | 5 | Lacking organization |
| Clear about what's expected | 1 | 2 | 3 | 4 | 5 | Unclear about what's expected |
| Sensitive to my needs | 1 | 2 | 3 | 4 | 5 | Insensitive to my needs |
| Fully engaged and excited | 1 | 2 | 3 | 4 | 5 | Seemingly bored |
| Knowledgeable | 1 | 2 | 3 | 4 | 5 | Not on top of the subject |
| Able to make difficult ideas accessible and interesting | 1 | 2 | 3 | 4 | 5 | Over our heads |

| *Our work has generally been:* | | | | | | |
|---|---|---|---|---|---|---|
| Thought provoking | 1 | 2 | 3 | 4 | 5 | Dull |
| Effective in helping me learn | 1 | 2 | 3 | 4 | 5 | Ineffective in helping me learn |
| Too fast | 1 | 2 | 3 | 4 | 5 | Too slow |
| Too easy | 1 | 2 | 3 | 4 | 5 | Too hard |
| Too much the same | 1 | 2 | 3 | 4 | 5 | Too unpredictable |
| Too abstract | 1 | 2 | 3 | 4 | 5 | Too simplistic |
| Too little | 1 | 2 | 3 | 4 | 5 | Too much |

Why do educators so often sidestep or resist it? Leaving aside the understandable reluctance to solicit what might be unpleasant news, the point is that such information will help us be better teachers.

Just as this book was going to press, Adam Urbanski, long-time head of the Rochester, New York, Teachers' Association and noted innovator, announced that Rochester teachers would be subject to parental review under one of four criteria (home involvement) in their overall performance appraisal. An excerpt of the evaluation form that will be sent home to parents is shown in Figure 11.2. As reported in *Education Week,* the form will be part of the evidence used in supervisory conversations. Eighty-nine percent of the Rochester teachers supported the survey as part of their new contract.[5] Surely this is a step in the right direction.

This first step is useless, however, without a second step. We have to be responsive to the feedback. We have to follow through and act

**Figure 11.2  Excerpt from the Rochester, New York, Teacher-Evaluation Form**

My child's teacher is accessible and responsive to me when I call or want to meet.

❏ Usually     ❏ Sometimes     ❏ Rarely     ❏ Don't know     ❏ Doesn't apply

Comment:_____

The teacher makes clear what my child is expected to learn in this class.

❏ Usually     ❏ Sometimes     ❏ Rarely     ❏ Don't know     ❏ Doesn't apply

Comment:_____

The teacher contacts me promptly with concerns about my child's academic or behavioral performance.

❏ Usually     ❏ Sometimes     ❏ Rarely     ❏ Don't know     ❏ Doesn't apply

Comment:_____

As needed, the teacher and I develop a cooperative strategy to help my child.

❏ Usually     ❏ Sometimes     ❏ Rarely     ❏ Don't know     ❏ Doesn't apply

Comment:_____

My child's teacher assigns clear and meaningful homework.

❏ Usually     ❏ Sometimes     ❏ Rarely     ❏ Don't know     ❏ Doesn't apply

Comment:_____

The teacher shares my high expectations for my child's learning and behavior.

❏ Usually     ❏ Sometimes     ❏ Rarely     ❏ Don't know     ❏ Doesn't apply

Comment:_____

*Source:* Rochester Teachers Association.

on what we have solicited. Recall the use of the one-minute paper at Harvard, mentioned in Chapter Four. What some professors found most useful was preparing from these papers a summary of students' "big ideas" and questions and handing them out to all students at the next class. This technique suggests not only that teachers want to learn but also that student feedback is taken seriously.

By not seeking or by ignoring or distancing ourselves from feedback, we increase the likelihood of self-deception. And that self-deception is only abetted further by our routine isolation from other teachers, which breeds unease and defensive tribalism. We learn to resist formal review of our work as unneeded, a threat, or an intrusion. "No one could understand my kids, my classroom," we have all said at one time or another. "No testing or grading system could ever do justice to the achievements I've seen," I hear all the time in doing assessment reform work. These views, though understandable, begin to sound defensive and provincial when we become more dedicated to and sophisticated in our assessment work. All performance is measurable within tolerable margins of error. Interesting and helpful data always exist whereby we might better see our effect and how that effect matches our intent. As Mike Schmoker put it:

> Why do we avoid data? The reason is fear—of data's capacity to reveal strength and weakness, failure and success. Education seems to maintain a tacit bargain among constituents at every level not to gather or use information that will reveal where we need to do better, where we need to make changes. Data almost always point to action—they are the enemy of comfortable routines. By ignoring data, we promote inaction and inefficiency.[6]

In fact, an external validation of what we accomplish, grounded in data, is key to both credibility and improvement, as the story of Jaime Escalante of "Stand and Deliver" fame reminds us. Escalante's success, like that of all good coaches, was due to an external standard—the Advanced Placement test in calculus—having been targeted and conquered. Five years into Escalante's work, he and his colleagues at Garfield High School had more AP calculus test takers than all but three high schools in America, including all but one of the best nationally known independent schools. Once such targets are set and are aggressively addressed, surprising improvement becomes possible. Escalante's biographer, Jay Mathews, notes that

> It was not so much the test itself that made a difference. Standardized tests, even those as challenging and relevant as AP [c]alculus, have their flaws. What changed lives was the disciplined act of preparing for the test and the thrill of passing it. Students learned beyond any doubt that such obstacles, if taken seriously, could be overcome. Even students scoring 1s and 2s felt they had made progress.[7]

Perhaps more astonishing, less well known by readers, and more important for the argument than Escalante's own success is that once other teachers at Garfield High School become aware of what Escalante was doing, so many AP courses were developed that in the same year of the greatest calculus success, passing scores in history and other courses outnumbered the passing scores in mathematics! Seventy-four percent of the 329 Garfield student test takers passed their tests, including 200 non-calculus test takers.[8] External exams sometimes supply a needed standard, even if the test is constrained by the typical limits of national tests.

## Toward Results-Focused Job Descriptions

Let me put this even more provocatively: *Most educators still define their jobs in ways that keep them from understanding the effects of their teaching.* A *de facto* definition is ubiquitous in every workshop I teach: "Yes, but I *have* to cover the content. . . ." Indeed, the de facto job description of many teachers, as discussed throughout this book, is *coverage*—as if the *results* of teaching did not matter.

Contrast this view with what happens in any other job: "I have to follow this recipe"—even though many of the previous customers who ate it said the meal was distasteful? "I have to follow my medical school textbook"—even though the patient is not getting any better? For that matter, contrast it with coaching, something many of us do, whether on a field, in a debate room, or in a band room. Success on any test of performance, including standardized tests, is not primarily a function of what the teacher says and teaches but of what work is engineered for students and of the standards applied to that work. If feedback improves all performances, we need to ponder whether some formal feedback, against high standards, is in our and our students' interests.

Such thinking implies a host of ongoing questions: What are early performances revealing about how we might adjust things to meet final standards? How might we learn to adjust our teaching better, mindful of both performance results and client feedback en route? Recall the comment in Chapter Two by Marv Levy, the coach of the Buffalo Bills—and a former history teacher—that coaching is adjustment. That's how performance mastery is attained for teachers as well: our teaching, our syllabus, even our favored methods must be open to alteration when we respond to evident current need.

But this is not how teaching and schooling typically happen. "I have to march through the textbook"—in spite of results? In spite of the fact that the work builds sequentially, and that by simply marching on we have consigned many students to falling further and further behind? "I don't have time to write comments on papers"—in spite of the fact that the paper then has little educative value? (Imagine getting only generic feedback from a sports coach—two-word summaries of the mistakes made by most players. Who would ever improve?) When have we seen faculty redeploy people and alter program and methods to accomplish the goal *before it is too late,* that is, before end-of-year testing? Alas, the answer is almost never (in part, admittedly, because the results often are not credible or useful, but some sources of useful information nevertheless exist today and others can be created easily, for example, surveys).

The sad fact is that when our job description is coverage, our corresponding actions are *teach, test, and hope for the best.* Rely on habits. Do what we have always basically done and trust that it works out. If this is our real job description and these are our real actions, then it is fair to say, along with many of our harshest critics, that there is no accountability in education—not because we have no tests or policies or rules or people hassling us, but because we are not taking ongoing responsibility for adjusting our performance in a timely, effective fashion. We are simply satisfying our own private sense of how things are and ought to be going.

The key words here are *timely* and *performance.* To sense in November that half the class is in danger of failing Algebra I yet to make them persist with our style and methods is to value habits, teacher interests, and bureaucratic convenience over learning. To do major testing only once, at the end of the year, using simplistic exercises, and not using any ongoing challenges in which students have repeated chances to meet high exit-level standards, is to value teaching and routine over learning.

If teachers had job descriptions that valued fair and apt results we would see more faculty routinely pretesting students against exit standards, publishing samples of exemplary work for students to emulate over time, building in numerous opportunities and incentives to hand in quality work, and developing and using major assessments throughout the year rather than assessing only on the last day of the year, when the feedback is almost useless. And we would see major collective analysis and adjustment of routines, staffing, and methods when none of the preceding worked—in January, not in July.

An alarming corollary to the view that teaching is coverage is the claim that "we have to cover the material because we have to teach to the tests." As will be argued in Chapter Twelve, such a view rests on many misconceptions about testing. Where is the data to prove that we must teach poorly in order to increase test scores? (With valid correlations, which most decent state and commercial tests have, the opposite is true.) Where is the research to verify the idea that superficial teaching (which often accompanies coverage because of the amount of material to be dealt with) improves test score performance? How many teachers have done the necessary experiment to prove (or disprove) the idea that coverage actually maximizes performance? Teaching to the test is the rationalization of unexamined habits: most teachers have never done the key experiments necessary to answer the questions, How might I optimize student performance, given who the students are and what I teach? Which methods work best? When are my students most effective, most engaged, and so on?

Few of us have ever been accountable in this most basic sense. Despite all the hoopla about test scores and despite cases of heavy-handed administrators, as a group we educators rarely have to or choose to question our habits or styles, and schools rarely adjust their routines in light of any formal results. Performance appraisal systems—even "modern" portfolio systems—are often based on teacher actions rather than on performance results, their analysis, and consequent teacher adjustment. As it stands now, schools remain paradoxical: devoted to learning but impervious to feedback.

In light of the analysis presented throughout this book, it will be helpful to consider a simple rubric of indicators concerning learning systems and feedback. Following are the differences between what we can expect to see in our classrooms when we have effective feedback and what we see when we have ineffective feedback.

| *Effective Feedback System Indicators* | *Ineffective Feedback System Indicators* |
|---|---|
| Learner performance improves at all levels, especially novice. | Learner performance rarely improves much beyond what is typical. |
| Improved performance occurs more rapidly than expected. | Novices struggle to improve; they do not know "what you want." |
| Few quarrels occur about results; disputes are grounded in evidence. | Many quarrels occur about result credibility; anecdotes are more trusted than data. |
| Teachers and students both adjust performance in light of results, in a timely way. | Teachers make few changes of habit. |
| Norms and standards rise over time; what was considered extraordinary performance becomes more common. | Norms stay the same, standards rise, and the main result is that expectations are lowered. |

| Learners seek out feedback; they welcome and do not fear or resist it. | Learners fear, resist, do not seek, or ignore feedback. |
|---|---|

There are a few things we must do if we wish to improve the learning system of schools, hence its results significantly. (I do not pretend that these solutions by themselves will solve all problems, but they are a necessary part of solving the problems described in this book. Other proposals can be found in Chapter Thirteen.) We must focus more attention on the lowly job description, and we must build a performance appraisal system based on that description. The teaching job must be construed (as discussed in Chapter Two) in terms of performance improvement, or results—not in terms of what the curriculum plan and teachers intend to teach. The teacher's job, like that of the cook or the soccer coach, is not to "cover" or merely do what the curricular framework says, or what the teacher knows, habitually does, or only feels comfortable doing. The job is to cause specific results—in this case, increased understanding, competency, and intellectual maturity. Any accompanying teacher appraisal system must be grounded in a self-assessment and self-adjustment plan, derived from the core achievement targets, from the school mission, from the job description, and from the feedback solicited and provided by results broadly and credibly construed.

Similarly, we must write job descriptions for supervisors and building administrators that highlight ongoing data collection and troubleshooting, not mere program development. "How are we doing?" should be the mantra. Staff meetings should sound more like half-time locker-room discussions: open, shared, and ongoing inquiry into what works and does not work would be the norm in staff meetings once everyone agreed on these job obligations.

Assessment reform is obviously crucial here, just as it is in timely adjustment of real performance. When feedback from current tests is neither credible nor useful, there can be no adequate or useful feedback loop, hence no accountability. If there is only one-shot testing instead of longitudinal assessment against exit standards, there can be no useful feedback. If we persist in our testing methods and habits that typically produce data of little use or credibility to teachers, many teachers will continue to distance themselves from test scores, and later from all formal results, even those that are currently useful. And these colleagues of ours will feel justified in viewing their classrooms as unique—hence impervious to disinterested analysis and improvement. We must prove to them that this view is not justifiable, and not in anyone's best interests.

Habits run deep, the bad along with good. Building accountability out of once-a-year and end-of-year generic tests shows that policymakers do not understand accountability. If such state testing programs were apt and effective, they would yield significant gains in scores over time; they rarely do.[9] Nor do most of us educators understand—if we are to judge by actions—that tests should teach and that learning means trial and error. Otherwise more of us would choose to devote far more time to assessment and less to traditional teaching. More of us would labor over the design of performance tasks that elicit and evoke just the right information about student understanding. And more of us would take on "postgame" analysis to troubleshoot individual and group performance problems.

When we lament our lack of time to engage in this more intensive authentic assessment, we remain far from our goal of reform. This should tell us how deeply seated the coverage description of the teaching job really is. How can coverage be the best description of teaching when it leaves us little time for actions that are demonstrably central to effective learning?

What is so odd, of course, is that at some level every teacher who coaches anything knows this. But somehow the teacher in us does not grasp what we know as coaches. This has been true for me, too: I learned how to make continuous major adjustments on the athletic field and in music long before I even saw it as a problem in my classroom. And certainly it mattered that in athletics the "final" tests were known, many, ongoing, and repeated; there is a season of challenges to master and the questions to be answered and problems to be solved are never secret—the target is quite clear. As I have repeatedly pointed out and as we all in fact know from direct or indirect personal experience, athletes and musicians would be as unlikely to improve their performance as students if the only test were a secure one-shot proxy test of performance on the last day of the season.

We need to get at the blinders that prevent psychometricians and policymakers from seeing the ineffectiveness of conventional testing. It is not that its technical soundness is questionable but that it simply does not work as useful, rich, timely, and frequent feedback. It cannot ever provide true accountability, then, because the weeks-delayed scores, and arcanely derived and generically expressed results do not encourage or elicit our responsiveness and a feeling of responsibility.

Despite the views of some of my educator friends, assessment reform is not failing to take hold because of obstructionist psychometricians, impatient policymakers, or right-wing fanatics. Instead, as cartoonist Walt Kelly had Pogo say, "We has met the enemy, and it is us." Too many teachers and administrators have not examined their assessments and their results. And too many well-intentioned assessment reformers seem to think that this movement is about merely substituting one form of technique (performance testing) for another (multiple-choice testing) and thus do nothing about helping teachers acquire the leadership, understanding, resources, models, and inspiration to use assessments to improve learning. Worse, some reformers seem to think that data are what we need to get away from, that authenticity means we should downplay the actual results of performance so as to concentrate on scoring "process" and personal growth—as if performance were just good-faith effort. And far too many of us educators think that assessment reform means employing more nifty activities and projects that allow us to give students a few vague comments of supportive praise. The desire of many reform advocates to get rid of grades and scores altogether shows how poorly some educators understand the core function that assessment has in learning.

Surveying the state of education today, we have to conclude that we have the assessments we deserve.[10] Continued failure to truly reform assessment stems from failure to understand the purpose and value of assessment. If we knew, really knew and understood, that ongoing adjustment based on feedback is at the heart of all learning—for both student and teacher—then assessment would improve and we would find the time to do it well. Performance tests and portfolios will yield little of value until we understand that collecting more interesting student work by itself yields no further learning for anyone. Assessment will continue to be ineffectual and not justifiable until most of us recognize that our role as performance adjuster is as important as or more important than our role as teacher.

## Additional Tools

Beyond the need for explicit performance-based job descriptions to codify teachers' roles as performance assessors and adjusters, it must be ensured that each district has comprehensive policies about the design and use of good assessment and about the kinds of inquiries, discussions, and adjustments that are expected to facilitate timely and ongoing assessment and its results. Numerous documents on assessment standards are now available.[11]

One simple way to make teachers more responsive to assessment results—and more eager to reform assessment when current systems are lacking in credibility—is to take another page from the life of the coach and make student work more public. Games are highly public; academic performance is quite private. Most of us are unaware of the tests our colleagues design and of the patterns of results they get. Why is this so? Why do we allow student performance to be kept behind closed doors? Real accountability reform may be as simple as asking all teachers to publish their tests, assignments, and samples of student work with commentary; to formally self-assess its meaning; and to respond to parental, board member, and college professor comments. (The upcoming section on peer review suggests some practical ways to get productive, implementable commentary.)

With performance-based job descriptions, more credible forms of assessment, and policy statements with teeth in them, we can finally tackle teacher performance appraisal and make it work—in each school. Accountability in its practicable sense is only going to work at the site level. (Why do so many rabid advocates of local control in civic governance inconsistently call for lots of external state testing using simplistic generic instruments?) Furthermore, the issue is not firing or demoting people. Accountability involves making the teaching job one that obligates us to seek feedback and attend to it in order to succeed (especially when results are worse than we intended and expected), a job that makes it necessary and natural for us to seek feedback from students, next-level teachers, institutional clients, and parents. Such a feedback process naturally begins with the setting of standards: too few teachers and schools have measurable, worthy, and credible goals for student performance. The challenge is to make performance adjustment a more natural institutional and personal reaction than the current persistence in rationalized habits. Thus, as described at the beginning of this book, our challenge is also a moral one: as teachers we must learn to practice what we preach to students—self-assessment and self-adjustment against standards and criteria.

## Accountability in Assessment and Curriculum Design

What if a student came into your room and asked for a good grade merely for handing in a paper? What if student divers and gymnasts were able to judge and score their own performances in meets, and did so based on effort and intent? Unjustifiable ideas—yet this is just what happens in schools each year when faculty submit new curricular frameworks or design new assessments. Too many of our products as teachers are assessed, if at all, merely on whether we worked hard: Did we hand in a lengthy report, based on lots of discussion? Did we provide students with a test that we happen to like? We rarely demand that our products be formally self-assessed or peer reviewed against apt standards and criteria. But this is ironic at best, hypocritical at worst: we ask students to do this all the time. Once again, we need to practice better what we preach.

Effective schooling and reform involve our constant efforts to make our practice conform to stated ideals. Good intentions and lots of hard work are not enough: local design work requires rigorous self-assessment and continuous adjustment based on standards and apt criteria. Alas, one of the chief reasons that many mission statements, curriculum frameworks, and assessment systems produce a significant (and often apt) backlash is that such work is typically done without reference to specific standards for the resultant writing. We rarely assess and self-assess our faculty-generated documents against standards for such documents.

Think of a typical districtwide curriculum reform project. A group of twelve teachers and supervisors works part-time in meetings all school year. Their effort culminates in a report produced over a three-week period in the summer at district behest and with district financial support, resulting in a new local mathematics curriculum framework. They follow a time-tested process of scanning national reports, searching for consensus about themes and topics and logical progressions, and summarizing their findings and recommendations. But against what standards is their product (as opposed to their process) to be judged? The de facto answer is: against no broadly recognized standards at all, other than the implicit one that the writing be deemed complete by the authors.

By what standards and criteria should the curriculum be judged? At the very least if we think of this product as we do of any other public writing, we can say it should not be judged solely by the authors' standards or feelings, because the writing is meant to be of value to others. It is the same with assessments; almost every teacher operates by default under a view of test design and grading that, examined closely, boils down to "If I designed it and gave it, it must be valid and reliable." Yet we know from research and from our own observations that few teacher-designed tests and assessment procedures meet the most basic standards for technical credibility, intellectual defensibility, coherence with system goals, and fairness to students.

Standard-based reform forces us to have more demanding and appropriate criteria for judging our assessments and curricula: Does the work meet professional standards of curriculum design or measurement? If it is a joint product, does it meet the purposes laid out in a charge to the committee? (Alas, there typically is no charge that provides a useful purpose. It is just deemed time to do it in the cycle.) Most important, did the writers regularly self-assess and revise their work-in-progress against such criteria and standards? Did they regularly seek feedback from faculty affected en route? These are the same writing process questions we properly put to students.

Does our work cohere as described in Chapter Nine, and is it logically, not simply linearly or chronologically, thought through? Many of the districts involved in reform work around mission and outcome statements made the disastrous mistake of assuming that just because logic requires that we formulate global outcomes and then derive assessments and curricula from them, it follows that reform teams should treat such a logic as a sequential recipe for their work. Thus many groups blithely checked off outcome statements from their checklist of work without asking, In their present form are these statements useful? credible? clear in their implications for teaching and assessment?

Recall that design is always iterative, a process of constantly rethinking our work and clarifying our purposes based on feedback. Thus, in assessment design, as said throughout the book, teachers must think like assessors and ask, What evidence is needed? Is the proposed task likely to generate such evidence? and What must be done to improve the design in light of the gap? Thus we press ahead in our design work while every so often asking self-critical and refocusing questions that take us back to the standards. Have we predicted the inevitable misunderstandings of students? Will we able to validly discriminate the better from the worse answers?[12] And when we get down to designing scoring rubrics, have we avoided all the common errors discussed in Chapter Seven, such as turning a quality into a quantity, not transforming comparative or evaluative language into observable traits of performance, failing to maintain continuity in the distance between score points, coupling completely independent traits in the same descriptor, failing to distinguish criteria from indicators, and overemphasizing performance content and form and underemphasizing impact?

## Peer Review

As these questions suggest, one reason that we so need standards and peer review is that the designer of assessments always has a blind spot about something. I am sure that my task assesses for critical thinking; you ask a few simple questions of me to show that the task can be done by looking up all that is needed in the textbook. I am sure that the performance task assesses for knowledge of history; you show me that the scoring system pays little attention to the sophistication of the content used in the oral work and much attention to delivery and impact on audience.

At CLASS we have helped numerous faculties and groups of educators evaluate their final curricular and assessment designs over the past six years, not by teaching them mere procedures of design but by teaching them to peer review and self-adjust their curricular and assessment designs against educative and useful standards. This has led to better local designs, of course. It is also important that these educators have routinely commented on another profound result: the beginning of a truly professional relationship with colleagues. They have termed peer review one of the most satisfying (if initially scary) experiences in their careers. As a thirty-two-year veteran teacher put it, "This is the kind of conversation I entered the profession to have, yet never had. I'm rejuvenated. I'm optimistic."

What then is peer review, how is it best conducted, and against what standards should it be judged?[13] (Here, too, we need not only a process but standards.) The peer review process is designed first and foremost to help the designer improve the design. The peers serve as consultants to the designer, not as glib judges. The peer review process itself is evaluated against this basic criterion in support of that goal: the designer must feel that the design was understood and improved by the process, and the reviewers must feel that the process was insightful and team building. Using the following CLASS guidelines will help reviewers give specific, focused, and useful feedback and guidance to honor and improve the design as need be. The guidelines conclude with a set of peer review criteria.

Stage 1: Peer(s) review task without designer present (20 to 45 minutes).[14]

1. Designer states issues he/she wishes highlighted in the feedback session (Option: designer also self-assesses out loud), then leaves review group.
2. Reviewers read design material (tasks, rubrics, instructions, and so on).
3. Reviewers read and refer to assessment design criteria.
4. Reviewers consider strengths of design first, then weaknesses (in relation to the given design criteria, not reviewer tastes).
5. Each reviewer fills out the first sheet summarizing the design's strengths and weaknesses before discussion by whole review group.
6. Review group fills out a second sheet summarizing the group's key feedback and guidance, thus rehearsing the group oral report to follow. Reviewers rate the task against the task rubric, if appropriate.

Stage 2: Peers discuss review with designer(s) (25 to 45 minutes).

1. Establish roles (time-keeper/facilitator, and so on). The facilitator's key job is to ensure gently but firmly that the designer listens (instead of defends).
2. Designer clarifies any technical or logistical issues (without elaborating on context or justifying the intent, history, reasons for choices, and so on); the design must stand by itself as much as possible.
3. Reviewers give oral feedback and guidance, based on written outline from feedback and guidance sheets. They explain their analysis in light of the intent—the "targeted achievement" being assessed—and design criteria. Then they offer guidance: How might the design be improved, mindful of the designer's intent and the design criteria?

4. Discussion of feedback and guidance occurs with designer. Designer takes notes, asks clarifying questions of reviewers, and thinks out loud about possible implications, as appropriate.
5. A discussion by the peer review group and the task designer occurs concerning general design lessons and problems evoked, for later discussion with the faculty as a whole.

Criteria for peer review:

1. The core of the discussion involves considering the following: To what extent is the targeted achievement well assessed (versus a nice activity or project)? To what extent do the task and rubric meet the design criteria? What would make the assessment more valid, reliable, authentic, engaging, rigorous, fair, and feasible?
2. The reviewers should be friendly, honest consultants to the designer. The designer's intent should be treated as a given (unless the unit's goal and means are unclear, need to be clarified, or lack rigor).

*The aim is to improve the designer's idea, not substitute it with the reviewers' aesthetic judgments, intellectual priorities, or pet designs.*

3. The designer asks for focused feedback—that is, in relation to specific design criteria, goals, and/or problems.
4. The designer's job in the second session is primarily to listen, not explain, defend, or justify design decisions.
5. The reviewers' job in both sessions is first to give useful feedback (Did the effect match the intent?), and only then to give useful guidance (How might the gaps in intent versus effect be removed? How might the design be improved, given the intent?).

Key criterion for judging the success of the peer review:

*The designer feels that the design was understood by peers and improved by the critique and discussion.*

Note that this material distinguishes between feedback and guidance, a distinction stressed in Chapter Three. Feedback is information about how we did in light of what we attempted: intent versus effect, actual versus ideal performance. The best feedback is highly specific, descriptive of what we did and did not do in light of standards. What feedback most certainly is not is praise and blame or mere encouragement. As said before, try becoming better at any performance if all you hear is "Nice effort!" or "You can do better," or "We didn't like it." Whatever the role or value of praise and dislike, they are not the descriptive feedback needed in performance improvement. They can keep you motivated. They do not provide information to help you improve.

Feedback in teacher design work therefore involves commentary by reviewers in reference to criteria (or visible effects, as the design plays out with students): the reviewers describe where they saw the criteria being met and where they had concerns about criteria not being met (usually in relation to validity). No praise or blame here; nor are the reviewers' likes, tastes, and values relevant. What matters is judging the design against criteria related to sound assessment. Then the reviewers are free to offer concrete guidance—suggestions on how the design might be improved—assuming that the designer grasps and accepts the feedback.

Peer review is necessary to school reform but not sufficient. We need other feedback. Not just from teacher-designers or psychometricians, but also from students, parents, school boards, college admissions officers, and legislators. Now, what one group finds credible, another often does not. Such is the reality of schooling. There are different clients for information, and they have differing needs and interests in the data. A failure to meet such different needs is another reason that local assessment systems often end up inadequate and provincial, lacking sufficient outside reference. In addition, a failure to see that psychometric standards are often inappropriate for local assessment design has caused most local assessment systems to be inauthentic and ineffective as feedback because they improperly mimic large-scale audit testing methods.

In peer reviews, therefore, CLASS staff always ask designers to consider the different possible "customers" for the assessment information, to determine whether not just the task but also the reporting of results is apt and adequate. And we bug them to recall that the primary customer is always the student, because it is the performer who must learn from the task and the results.

## Embracing Accountability

Perhaps *embracing* is a bit strong, but those of us who now live in a much more public world of criticism know that if our work with people and our writing are really helping, then a great deal of the credit goes to the people who gave us feedback along the way, about what did and did not work. When we value accountability, we acknowledge that no one can be a good teacher unless he or she is a good assessor and a good self-adjuster—and we take the appropriate actions to make ourselves better and better teachers. As teachers worthy of the name, we do not allow assessment to be relegated to perfunctory and superficial testing that we do after teaching, or to be farmed out to external testers, making it less and less likely that either students or teachers will care about the results. We seek feedback from our clients and our peers, steadily improving our curricula and our assessments.

Do we fear true reform? Fear and doubt often mainly reflect unknowns: Where will the time come from? If I am an administrator, how will teachers react to such reform? If I am a teacher, who is going to be a resource for me? Do I have enough know-how about all the different task requirements? What can I do when those index cards come back each Friday describing all that did not work for my students? What if my peers don't like my curriculum design? There are two issues here. One is the initial tendency to think of the feedback we will get as personal, as something that will talk about our character. But like the feedback that educative assessment gives to students, the feedback accountability gives to us is directed at describing performance and product, not praising or blaming it. As the discussion of peer reviews illustrated, the questions are, Did it work or did it not? and in either case, How? The other issue is concern over learning something new and having to face the inadequacy of the old (and therefore, potentially, my own lack of imagination or wherewithal to change).

We can recognize such fears and doubts, and then we can overcome them. We have the information to understand what assessment and accountability should be and how to take the first steps. Specific resources are available to us (some of them supplied as templates and examples in this book). Let us begin a new era of professionalism by routinely and publicly modeling the very thing we demand of students—learning. Let it be central to our job description, and let us be accountable for our results in improving student performance.

# PART FOUR

# Changing the System

## CHAPTER 12

# Feasibility

## Real and Imagined

This chapter considers various issues of feasibility and strategy in assessment reform. For a variety of reasons, most educators new to the work described in this book believe the agenda to be impossible in their school, their classroom, their subject area. Although any reader who has come this far and still feels pessimistic is unlikely to be convinced in the final chapters, this chapter and the next close the book with numerous practical suggestions for how to make this work happen a step at a time—an incremental movement toward a distant-seeming standard—just as is preached about student performance.

While many reasons are often given for why the work called for in this book is not practicable, the most common complaints, as suggested in early chapters, involve the perceived lack of time. The next most frequent lament concerns the impediment of high-stakes standardized testing. The third most persistent objection concerns the problem of parents and school boards, and convincing them that educative assessment is not anti-accountability or harmful to little Joey's college chances. And finally, many educators sympathetic to the arguments in the book and willing to move forward nonetheless believe that the task is too daunting, especially when the district's or school's support, willpower, and talent are below par. This chapter responds to the arguments concerning these impediments and disincentives. The final chapter then offers a set of "next steps," courses of action for both individuals and entire faculties that can be undertaken to advance the agenda incrementally and successfully.

## Making Time _____

The use of judgment rather than machines in scoring, the use of collaborative designers and scorers, and the amount of time required for students to complete complex performance tasks all place great demands on teacher/assessor time. And insofar as the lives of teachers are very busy, it would seem that assessment reform simply demands too much of individuals and faculties.

The key to successful assessment reform, however, is not finding more time (to do the same things we now do) but to redeploy time, mindful of a new goal: working smarter, not harder, in the catch phrase of business and educational restructuring. Central to that rethinking and redeploying is coming to understand that noncontact time for teachers (that is, time when teachers are not obligated to students) is essential and must be planned for, yet it must be made feasible through incremental changes, first in schedules, then in contracts. In the short term, the trick is to make better use of available time.

Second, though teachers feel they have too little teaching time as it is, they need to see that student performance is not optimized by the habit of content coverage. More performance-focused work can ensure that content is well-learned, even if the assessment tasks take more time, as shown in earlier chapters. Just as it is worth our while in the end to tackle the steep learning curve of a new piece of powerful software, so too in assessment reform can we expect later gains in student performance and teacher productivity after the reform is finally up and running smoothly. We really do lose time to gain it.

But leave aside wholesale and uprooting redeployment of time. What always puzzles me about the constant naysaying over the issue of time is that almost all school faculties now have at least approximately thirty hours a year set aside for ongoing professional work. Staff in-service, faculty meetings, not to mention assemblies or special events that involve most children simultaneously can easily free up most people for a few hours per month. Just using half of those total hours toward better student assessment would make a profound difference. Reform begins, then, with a commitment to set aside available hours in, say, five four-hour blocks, spread out over the year, to enable performance tasks and rubrics to be well designed, and student work to be well scored by teacher teams. My colleagues and I have successfully worked with many entire faculties on such a schedule to produce an excellent shared library of tasks, rubrics, and anchor products.

Team, grade-level, and department meeting times are also available on a regular basis at present. These meeting times are ideal for peer review of draft tasks and rubrics and the scoring of student work. Again, all that is needed is some foresight and leadership at the site level to make an agenda for the year, mindful of some program-level, site-level, or district-level goals in assessment reform. Setting aside every other meeting for assessment-related business is typically enough to get such work off the ground. Simple beginnings include common grading of papers, the design of one or two common assessment tasks, or the development of a single rubric for a common achievement target (such as class participation, science lab work, essays, story writing, and so on).

But amidst these ideas, let us not reverse a key axiom and fail to practice what is preached in this book about work informed by purposes. If form follows function, then schedules suit purposes. For what, then, do we need the time? What kind of time is needed to do high-quality assessment, and what is implied for the schedule?

As these and many examples in the book suggest, assessment reform is fundamentally a team enterprise. We need design teams and scoring teams to make the work credible, useful, and feasible. That means ensuring a schedule conducive to regular (monthly, for starters) two-hour or half-day meetings devoted to collecting data about need, designing new forms of assessment, using them in classes, scoring student work, and analyzing results. Additional time is needed midyear to take stock of current student performance and to suggest midcourse corrections, and in the summer to revisit program goals.

A common error, however, is to give the team time only in the summer. Beware this mistake, which can reveal our misunderstanding of the iterative and feedback-based nature of learning. Because this is design work, we need to see our designs played out, with real kids, and to adjust our work, as has been said throughout this book. Designers badly need the feedback that comes from using the tasks; they need time to ponder the inevitable shortcomings of the paper blueprint; and they need a more timely loop than the one provided by trying the task out in November while having to wait until June to debug it.

In fact, the need to pilot tasks and rubrics a number of times, in quick cycles, is so vital for ensuring high-quality work that teams should work together to pilot the same task or rubric a few times, say, by having one teacher try out the first version, a second teacher try out the second version two weeks later in her class, and so on. In addition, teachers can use a subgroup of the entire class to try out the task, then try out the revised version on another subgroup a few days later, and so forth.

Beyond these commonsensical approaches to the use of currently available time, minor structural changes are possible that yield valuable time. For example, many staffs that the Center on Learning,

Assessment, and School Structure has worked with have simply built into the next year's calendar three half-days with early dismissal. Other faculties have used special all-school programs (such as the experiential education program Project Adventure or artists- and authors-in-residence) to free up all teaching staff for a morning. Still other faculties have copied the college schedule of having a "reading" period and an "exam" period during which teachers are freed from teaching to administer performance projects, oral exams, and so on. Whether or not you are free to do some of these things in your school, all of these changes involve a common tactic: challenging time-honored habits about the schedule and the use of personnel.

It is useful, I find, to pose these provocations as questions, such as, Where is it written that we must have

- Every day scheduled like every other day?
- Every week scheduled like every other week?
- Every month scheduled like every other month?
- Teacher schedules coincident with student schedules?
- Every class meeting every day (as opposed to a schedule in which each teacher or academic program gets one noncontact day per month, on a rotating basis, for assessment-related matters, with the schedule distributing students elsewhere for longer periods of time)?
- Grading and reporting periods for all students on the same schedule (as opposed to staggering the reporting periods over the course of a month by letters of the alphabet, thereby placing a far less demanding assessing and reporting burden on teachers)?
- Everyone tested on the same day (because many of the new tests will be known in advance or not need security)?
- The only assessor be the classroom teacher? (Why not use trained administrators, counseling staff, interns?)
- The only assessors be school staff? (Indeed, in South Brunswick's year-end sixth grade research and public presentation project, outside judges from the community and other school districts are trained for a morning to do the work; and in many science fairs, professional scientists are used as judges.)

As these questions suggest, so much of the debate over time is hampered by unexamined routines that need to be rethought, and by the view that schedule changes must be sweeping and nonpersonalizable. We need to have a more flexible schedule, especially because assessment is not a daily affair and not all subjects need the same assessment schedules. Thus we need not build a brand new daily schedule to accommodate all assessment-related purposes. It is possible to free blocks of time for assessment when we need them, as long as we are willing to endure the minor hassles of alerting students and parents well in advance to the need for special assessment periods or days. Though there are pedagogic plusses to block scheduling—positive factors that also relate to assessment, such as reduction in teacher-student load and more time for performance tasks—it simply is not necessary to get into the legitimate and sometimes contentious debate concerning its efficacy if we are willing to be more flexible in a traditional schedule one week or day per month.

But what if I am a reform party of one, where I have no power to effect such changes? A reasonable question, of course. While acknowledging that such conditions make many of the more systemic ideas discussed in this book difficult if not impossible to implement, individual teachers still have at their disposal professional development days; free periods; team, grade-level, and department meeting times; and the summer to work on their own designs. In addition, there are always a few sympathetic souls, even in the most hostile and barren of environments, who care enough about these matters to work together in an ad hoc research and development team. We find that even having as few as ten hours per year for a working team of three is enough to make significant strides and thus get folks over the fatalism that so pervades schools.

## Principles of Strategy

Regardless of one's power and influence or the culture of the district or school, there are three guiding principles that enable assessment reform to have the best chance of working: (1) get an early victory; (2) think big, act small; and (3) get it right before you go public. These three principles correspond to three helpful analogies: you need an early win in the primaries when running for president; engineers first build a few prototypes before moving into large-scale production; and software designers do "beta" testing with groups of users to debug software before it goes on the market.

"Get an early victory" means a few different things. First, it means *go where the real talent, interest, or obvious need is found.* As an individual, work on an area in which you have little to lose, a place in your syllabus where you are now unhappy with the results and the assessment. At the school level, do not arbitrarily imagine or mandate that all high school teachers or language arts teachers will produce a performance task by June if they are not the most likely producers of work that will inspire greater confidence in the reform effort. Do not bite off an extremely ambitious and controversial agenda (such as a graduation portfolio) as a first venture. Because there are many skeptics (even among the reformers!), it is vital to start with the design of something manageable in a short time (a task or a rubric). An early victory also means ensuring that there is oversight and feedback from nonparticipants who can serve as critical friends to the work. Not everyone is or needs to be a pioneer. But reformers often mistake sideline critics for enemies. On the contrary, many critics are anxious to see the reforms succeed, but in a quality way only. There is a fundamental difference between a skeptic and a cynic, in other words. Over the past decade I have seen many people on the sidelines join the effort in later years, once they were satisfied that the work was important and that the reformers had high standards. Reform groups must be on the lookout for critical friends and not shut them out. (Just as we need disinterested views of student work, we need them of our work.)

"Think big, act small" means that while the reform vision must be enticing, explicit, and sweeping in its eventual ramifications, the initial designs should be quite small, such as a task and rubric for a few courses or a program. Do not rethink your whole course, just one rubric or task. Do not rethink an entire program, just one final exam. Because the overall strategy is to build both competence and confidence, there must be both early victories and a sense that the vision is doable in increments. Too many assessment reform projects become both overwhelming and overwhelmed by issues of logistics and quality control.

That leads to the third principle, "Get it right before you go public." The software engineer knows that word-of-mouth from consumers about bugs in the software will kill the product, no matter what its virtues and value. It is vital for parent and school board credibility, therefore, that teachers and district officials not go public with tasks and rubrics until they have been tried out, reviewed, and refined. We at CLASS have seen many reform efforts derailed by poor quality products, in the misguided view that having lots of quantity of reform is the best way to get quality results. On the contrary, the credibility of the reform efforts is undermined by tasks and rubrics that make the mistakes described in earlier chapters. Whether it is skeptical parents or faculty on the sidelines watching the pioneers, it is vital to bring the fence-sitters on board, and the best way to do it is through a few polished assessments that strike disinterested observers, not the gung-ho designers, as worthy of emulation and large-scale efforts. The peer-review process, described earlier in Chapter Nine, and external reviews by credible outsiders are vital.

## Local Assessment and Standardized Tests_____

"All well and good in theory, but what about the standardized tests that we are held accountable to? We aren't able to have accountability tests play a less important role in our lives. We cannot anchor our work in authentic assessment when state and national tests call for simplistic out-of-context performance. So, given the need to cover all this stuff, we simply do not have the time or the mandate to do performance-based teaching and assessment." This second time-constraint argument is much different than the first. It is not based on an argument about the scarcity of time, really, but on the fear that in even the most hospitable of cultures, time "lost" to performance tasks and more in-depth teaching will cause a drop in test scores that emphasize out of context breadth of content knowledge and simple skills. Political realities would then demand that, even if time for adults were available for design and use, there is not enough time for students to get what they need. Assessment reform as called for in this book seems to run counter to the reality of the increased importance of standardized test scores.

Readers may be surprised to discover that I do not think this is a sound argument, despite my criticisms of American overreliance on standardized tests. In most (though not all) cases, I find these claims and fears to be based on a misunderstanding of testing and validity. The fallacy is suggested by the speaker's casting the matter as an apparent dilemma: teachers must either do what is desirable (authentic assessment) or teach to these simplistic tests. Because the latter tests are the public coin of the realm for accountability, we must do what is pragmatic. But this view is predicated on a misconception whereby causality and correlation in testing are confused. As plausible as the argument seems—and it is the most ubiquitous claim we at CLASS hear in all our work—it does not stand up to scrutiny, because the arguer implicitly assumes two things that are false: that effective performance-based teaching will not raise scores on simplistic tests, and that the best way to raise test scores is to cover content and test in the way the standardized tests test. Neither view is true.

Validity is always about inference. Given a result, what can we infer? Large-scale testers are always looking for the easiest ways to make great inferences, based on the most cost-effective, brief, and least-intrusive tests they can design—what I have been calling audit tests. Simplistic tests are thus meant to be quickly used indicators of more complex performance. If the rigor and complexity of local work increase, then test scores are designed to increase. An inauthentic test not only *can* give valid results, it *should* yield valid results—that is, correlations with performance ability—if the test is to be deemed valid. To put it bluntly (and to better show what is really being erroneously argued) teachers need not teach worse in order to make test scores better. We need to ensure that these facts are understood by educators, because the fears and mythology surrounding testing are some of the greatest obstacles to reform.

The misconception that we need to overcome, as mentioned throughout this book, is that the format of large-scale tests is important to mimic locally if we want to obtain higher scores. This is not so. This reverses the causality of causes and symptoms, indicators (be they test scores, economic indicators, or driver's license test results), and genuine achievement. In the same way that simple indicators like the driving and written test to get an automobile license do not and are not intended to represent all key driving performance challenges, so too are large-scale tests not designed to be authentic. They are designed to be valid and reliable only, that is, the results on such simplistic tests should adequately correlate with more direct performance.

The large-scale test maker, looking for a cost-effective way of assessing for the achievements we value, is using the same technique that political pollsters use, to invoke yet another analogy. These poll takers do not need to ask every conceivable question or watch how people act as citizens to predict what people think about candidates and what they will do in elections. Instead they get a small sample of political opinion with simple questions, and if their sampling techniques of population subgroups and simple questions are well chosen, they have then found a fast and relatively inexpensive way of assessing something validly that is in fact quite complicated. If the Gallup polls predict elections well, then they are valid, irrespective of how "inauthentic" a telephone interview is when compared with the act of voting.

Similarly, the large-scale test maker has available years of data from various kinds of student testing and, using this data, can correlate the results on a multiple-choice test of achievement (a small but highly targeted sample of a domain of accomplishments gathered by using simple questions) with more important results—assuming that the test maker has done the design and debugging work well and has correlated test results with more intellectually worthy results. No large-scale test maker believes that its test items are authentic, in other words. But taken together, those items can be proxies for significant predictive findings. Thus it does not follow that high test scores on simplistic and disparate tests require simplistic and scattershot teaching. Yet many teachers and administrators clearly talk and act as if this were true.

It makes sense, in fact, to ensure that large-scale testing is as efficient and unobtrusive as possible, hence built on indirect (inauthentic) items wherever possible. This auditing is important if we want to avoid spending all our days in school in testing or being tested.

Take the example of the National Assessment of Educational Progress (NAEP) writing assessment. NAEP test designers know how to use simplified large-scale testing to get results that are valid enough for reporting to Congress how students are doing as writers. The test uses fairly simple writing prompts devoid of a textual or experiential context, students have less than an hour to write, and they write in a single sitting (no feedback and revision). No one believes that this is how the best writing is actually produced. However, NAEP needs only to show that the level of writing a student produces under these less-than-ideal circumstances correlates positively with her or his level of writing under better conditions. These correlations are established through checking samples of NAEP results with data derived from either more in-depth assessments of writing or credible student grade point averages in school.

Yet as has been stressed throughout this book, we must as a society better recognize and act on the feedback that large-scale testing has an unanticipated but real effect of making many educators believe that the test requires a certain kind of (limiting) response. To teachers who are unaware of the fact that large-scale simplistic tests are valid only because they have been carefully designed to work as proxies for performance tests, for purposes that are basically non-educative in the sense discussed in this book, these tests send the unfortunate and unwitting message that this is an apt and accurate way to test locally. When teachers reverse the logic and assume that test scores are best optimized by teaching the way the test is formatted, they actually threaten performance results over the long haul. It is as if we stopped worrying about health and concentrated only on the items of the brief physical exam. When teachers teach to the test of simplistic items, they actually lower their standards and undercut test performance because the tester assumes that his or her indirect methods tap into a rigorous and demanding local program.

Leaving aside the rational fear that is bred in teachers by heavy-handed board members and test-score-fixated administrators, these misunderstandings are due in large part to educators' limited experience with formal assessment design, and reinforced by the historical lack of importance accorded to local assessment in this country. Given the prevailing view among policymakers that local assessment is much less trustworthy than large-scale, professionally designed "objective" tests, unfortunate consequences have been the failure to build local capacity in high-quality assessment and the needless dumbing down of local testing as it mimics those large-scale tests.

In addition to having such an influence over local testing practice, the prevailing mythology surrounding large-scale standardized tests also suggests to teachers that the smartest teaching strategy for ensuring good test results is to cover the content of the test in the kinds of random ways suggested by the seemingly arbitrary design of the test. But because these tests are deliberate samples, rigorous, coherent, and performance-focused teaching of the subject should always lead to good results on simplistic tests.

If it were true that the best way to raise scores on simple indirect tests was to teach to the test, then we should expect to see loads of multiple-choice tests in the best U.S. schools. But this is the opposite of what we see. As a consultant to some of the best private independent and public schools, I observe what I also know from my own teaching experience: that the most challenging, engaging, and authentic performance tasks are routinely found in our most demanding and successful classrooms and schools (as measured by standardized test results).

For example, it always struck me as a lovely irony that when Thomas Sobol was Commissioner of the New York Schools, he presided over one of the largest multiple-choice empires in the country, even though he had come from one of those excellent districts, Scarsdale, where he had been superintendent and teacher. Despite the paranoia all over the rest of New York State about state tests and Regents diplomas, a large majority of Scarsdale students neither take Regents exams nor receive Regents diplomas. Why? Because Scarsdale's local standards are higher, are linked to the admissions requirements of the most prestigious colleges, and involve more of the kinds of tests and standards that have been described in this book.

Educators have also feared that the national coin of the realm at the secondary level, College Board Scholastic Assessment Test (SAT) scores, will somehow be compromised if high schools begin to use more performance assessment. But this is an even more unfounded concern (in a rigorous program). The SAT not only tests the same skills that complex performance requires, it is also a general test of intellectual skill and, unlike the SAT II Achievement Tests, is deliberately not coupled to particular courses of study. Indeed, the current craziness over the SAT is sadly ironic because the test was initially developed in part to promote equity, to expand the pool of bright and able students lurking in the U.S. hinterlands who were likely to be eligible for Eastern colleges but who could not or would not go to each Eastern college for its admissions test. That is why it was originally called an "aptitude" not an "achievement" test: the purpose was and is to identify talent, irrespective of the particular content of the student's local academic experience.

A teach-to-simplistic-tests approach can only lower standards, fragment teaching, and discourage us from needed assessment reform. The best way to raise student test scores on all kinds of tests and assessments, ironically, is to offer a more rigorous, challenging, and engaging curriculum at the local level, anchored by worthy and valid performance assessment tasks. Yes, of course, give students practice in test taking. Of course there will be conventional quizzes and exams (now, however, properly in their place as subordinate to performance tasks at the heart of the content). But also understand that we have been unwittingly confusing face validity with correlational validity. If every local test were designed using the standards, criteria, logic, and processes described in these chapters, standardized test results would take care of themselves. They were designed to. That is how validity works. Yes, there is an unfortunate psychology and mythology surrounding these tests, and yes, some tests are flawed or inappropriately emphasize some easy-to-measure abilities at the expense of genuine intellectual performance and research (as in some advanced placement science exams). But far too much energy is spent in blaming external tests for impeding instructional innovation with reasons that are not supported by data or logic.

## Time and Testing

This lengthy aside was necessary to respond to the claim that teachers cannot afford the time needed to involve their students in more complex in-depth performance tasks. What the discussion should have made clearer is that the argument is based on a faulty premise: current standardized test scores tend to correlate with authentic performance results, and the choice is therefore not either/or.

A second faulty premise lurks behind teacher resistance to doing more performance assessment because of concern over time. That is the view alluded to earlier, that coverage of content tends to maximize test scores. In other words, the implicit claim made by many teachers who say they cannot risk jeopardizing test scores is that the greatest possible yield of aggregate student test scores is then supposed to come from a linear march through the syllabus and textbook. As has been argued in various ways and in various places throughout the book, this view is unproven at best or completely false at worst. The real enemy here is human psychology, summed up in the old saying noted previously, "If I taught it, they must have learned it." In short, coverage only *seems* to work because we fail to adequately distinguish, through credible assessment, between what we intended and what students actually took away as understanding and skill. We have a poor understanding of the yield of teaching. We have little data to support the claim that our current teaching methods optimize performance.

The argument on behalf of safe coverage would hold a lot more water if teachers had done the necessary experiments in their classes over the years to establish a particular strategy as optimal. But this rarely happens. Rather, teachers develop habits and approaches that are relatively untested, and as long as they seem to work adequately, they become tried and true methods. The comfortable is often confused with the effective. And as suggested in the chapter on accountability, a pervasive self-deception is possible in teaching whereby we easily confuse what we cover and understand with objective signs of student understanding. This egocentrism prevents significant reform more than any other phenomenon, because it seduces us into believing that our current efficient *teaching* methods are the most effective *learning* methods. And it is ironically only through more credible, disinterested feedback (from formal and informal assessment) that we will overcome such a prescientific view of our craft.

In this light, taking the additional time to do high-quality performance assessment has somewhat less risk than its opponents suggest. Because there is little evidence to support the view that the current yield of teaching is high—indeed, if "teach, test, and hope for the best" is an accurate view of things, the yield is far lower than it should and could be—and because many of the suggestions contained herein stand to make teaching and learning more coherent and rigorous, we should expect to see improved test scores if educators take the time to do these new assessments right. Indeed, as Fred Newmann and his colleagues have found, and as the results from the Third International Math and Science test suggest, this view is more plausible than the doubters' view.[1] Readers are invited to take careful, deliberate experimental steps to test the claim themselves. They are encouraged to experiment with a unit of study to see if overall student performance improves when the material is taught and assessed in a performance-based way (of course complemented by quizzes and prompts as appropriate), when standards are much higher than normal because secrecy is taken away, and when core content is needed to perform complex and demanding tasks.

The apparent impediment to reform in the minds of some critics that has not yet been addressed is that the great mass of teachers is neither adequately trained nor willing to do what it takes to make this agenda work. While current practice makes this view highly plausible, it too is based on a misconception. Nothing argued in this book is meant to suggest that assessment reform works out of the box. On the contrary, the goal in assessment reform is to establish a self-correcting system that is focused on the right set of principles and informed by more obligatory and routine feedback about our work.

This is, after all, what the book has stressed in terms of performance and its improvement. Students are not perfect or mature learners, and the proposed reforms do not assume so. Rather, they assume that students can be better motivated and become more competent if certain dysfunctional habits of testing and teaching are altered and if better feedback, guidance, and reiterative performance and understanding become more central to learning. So, too, with teachers and administrators. I do not assume that they are already highly knowledgeable about assessment or that they are highly motivated by mere moral suasion to do what is much harder than maintaining the status quo, even though it is better for kids. On the contrary, that is why making teacher assessment and student performance a more public act, with a clear set of design standards, peer review, and greater attention to job descriptions and performance appraisal systems, are so vital. We need to get the incentives right so that teachers will see that it is in their interest to experiment with better assessment and to learn from those experiments—as part of the job and as part of a state or district assessment system. That is why the portfolio system proposed for North Carolina (briefly described in Chapter Eight) requires teachers to score work in teams, to blend assessment methods, and to triangulate data from local, state, and national assessment. How else will we develop over time the expertise needed to make quality occur in its proper place, that is, locally, every day?

Common to all the proposed solutions in the book thus far, and to those sketched in the final chapter, is the view that change is incremental but not achieved step-by-step. In other words, reform is neither immediate nor formulaic. Rather reform depends on the generative tension created by a vision, the attempts to honor that vision, and feedback that reveals the gap between vision and reality and the need for adjustments. The vision—embodied in standards—is an essential spur to action and sustained effort. Feedback and adjustments are vital to achieving the goal. Incentives must exist in school structures, policies, and opportunities that influence people to do what is demonstrably harder than maintaining the status quo. None of these goals can be achieved by mere effort or will. Like any complex performance, we need to commit ourselves to a direction and then be willing to learn from our successes and mistakes.

Assessment reform therefore must be conducted according to the logic of performance, design, and teaching articulated throughout this book. We aim for a goal and reach it by trial and error. We succeed in reform as in any performance to the extent that we seek, find, and use feedback against a compelling vision. The standard may be far off, but it is not unrealistic or inappropriate. We will not manifest this or any other worthy vision tomorrow or next year. Even with the assessment illiteracy in our ranks, schools can develop educative assessment systems if they commit to working on the basis of standards, embodied in apt policies and more public and iterative design work. I do not dream of perfect schools, only of self-correcting ones—schools that are data-driven, not habit-driven.

In conclusion, schools are vital when they have integrity; that is, when they are true to their mission. Schools with integrity practice what they preach; policies make real what is valued; adults model the learning sought in students; teachers assess what they value and value what they assess. Attaining assessment integrity is certainly more difficult than testing what is easy to test, but consider its benefits to our goals, credibility, and self-respect. When people say that assessment reform is unrealistic, they misspeak ultimately. We might as well then say that it is unrealistic to expect moral conduct in individuals. When we commit ourselves to standards, we rightly reject a world judged merely against norms. In assessment reform, as in morality or education, writ large, then: The challenge is not to accept what is given but to strive for what might be. In the final chapter I propose some practical strategies for moving in the right direction and staying the course.

# CHAPTER 13

# Next Steps

This chapter concludes the book with a menu of strategies that individuals and faculties can use to leverage or advance assessment reform in light of the ideals and standards put forward in previous chapters. None of these approaches takes precedence over any other; there is no golden or straight road to reform. In fact, where possible it is best to employ these strategies in parallel, with each group reporting to one another and supervised by a steering committee composed of representatives from each reform strand. All the strategies assume that readers will take careful stock of their environment before selecting the most appropriate paths and timetables.

**Strategy 1. Turn tests into prompts and prompts into performance tasks.** This simple design strategy will make it more likely that you will see the strengths and limits of your current tests and the ease with which new forms of assessment suggest themselves.

**Keys to the strategy:**

> *Examining existing test questions carefully to see their limits in revealing the students' understanding.*

**Tactics:**

1. Take some multiple-choice questions and turn them into prompts by simply removing the four or five choices, requiring students to construct a written or oral response to the question.

2. Use a prompt that seems particularly well suited to a simulated challenge in a context—for example, a prompt concerning civil rights issues *(To Kill A Mockingbird, Letter From a Birmingham Jail)*—that can easily be turned into a mock trial.

3. Allow students to get exam credit for research or performance work that is brought to completion by exam day.

**Strategy 2. Begin to develop a few authentic assessment tasks, where there is most evidence or agreement of need.**   They should be seen as necessary—articulated with targeted achievements, yet missing from current testing—and credible to other faculty and school constituencies.

**Keys to the strategy:**

*Beginning where there is a strong sense of the inadequacy of current testing.*

*Developing credible tests that make accountability for more complex aims more possible, making it difficult to excuse poor performance by blaming the test.*

**Tactics:**

1. Examine current state and local tests to determine the targeted (and presumably valued) achievements that are falling through the cracks. Develop one or two tasks to determine how students fare on such performance-based assessments, and what the demands are on the designer(s).

2. Survey faculty and other constituencies to determine which state or commercial tests are seen as most and least credible. Determine how frequently and how well test data are now currently used to improve instruction in the building.

3. Develop some sampling strategies in which useful data about complex performance are obtained in a relatively cost- and labor-efficient way. For example, use the Seminar Rubrics from Chapter Seven (Figure 7.6) to assess three to four students per day on a rotating basis. Take brief notes during and after class, using previously prepared index cards for each student (putting a prepared printout of each student's name on a gummed label on each index card).

4. Develop an assessment policy statement for the school or district, to ensure that over time there will be an increase in the number of performance assessments.

**Strategy 3. Change typical (inauthentic) contextual constraints or limits on resources available during a test.**

**Tactics:**

1. Write the exam/final assessment before teaching a unit/course, then provide students with an overview of the final tasks/questions/portfolio guidelines from the first day of instruction.

2. Allow students to bring all notes to a test or exam.

3. Allow—encourage—students, as part of an assessment, to solicit and consider feedback from peers. Judge their work not merely on content and skill but on their ability to revise and produce quality work, based on self-assessment, peer critique, and self-adjustment.

4. Provide students with training in how to evaluate and score the work they must eventually produce. (Train them as if they were adult judges.)

**Strategy 4. Use exemplars and world-class benchmarks in evaluation to get beyond local norms or arbitrary expectations.**

**Key to the strategy:**

*Helping students (and colleagues) to understand the difference between standards and expectations.*

*Ensuring that everyone sees how local grades (hence transcripts) are not helpful or credible to outsiders because grades are not linked to clear, common standards. Getting them to see that imposed standardized tests are the inevitable result of school failure to set and uphold clear, shared standards.*

**Tactics:**

1. Collect and distribute copies of models—exemplary papers, products, performances—that would be used to better guide and standardize teacher grading. Use these models to anchor the scoring of work in the class or the building. Students should be given models and taught from them; parents should receive a booklet of models as well as guidance in helping students meet standards.

2. Ask the faculty in subject-area meetings to "holistically" grade the same piece of work on a 6-point scale, but using no agreed-upon scoring criteria and no anchors; then provide a set of papers, a 6-point scoring rubric with clear descriptors, and a set of anchor papers drawn from one of

your school's or district's best classes. Compare scores given in parts one and two to see how agreement on standards is possible.

3. Collect and distribute samples of work from your best (most desirable and admired) "institutional customers" to show faculties the expectations placed on your former students—that is, the work requirements and grading standards in force at the next level of schooling and/or employment.

4. Establish an exit-level assessment, anchored by the entry-level standards at the next level—the "institutional customer" (such as a writing task, with scoring rubric and anchor papers taken from a college course; a vocational course linked to entry-level job standards; and so on).

5. Establish a post-graduation committee to formally review performance of former students, to survey former students about preparation, and to report on testing, grading, and work-requirement standards of the better next-level programs in which your alumni are enrolled. (Alumni include your former elementary students in the middle school and high school.)

6. Develop an externally reviewed and equated assessment that is designed to provide credible accountability information to the public.

**Strategy 5. Don't reinvent the wheel.**    Borrow and modify what is already out there.

**Key to the strategy:**

*Keeping abreast of district, state, and national work in assessment reform, through Web sites (including the CLASS Web site at www. classnj.org), periodicals, and conferences.*

**Tactics:**

1. Many state tests now have some open-ended questions for which there are rubrics, many of them excellent. Use those rubrics (and anchors and prompts, where possible) in local work.

2. Get task ideas from performance-based organizations such as the Scout Merit badges, Odyssey of the Mind, and vocational programs.

**Strategy 6. Start with checklists before going to rubric design.**

**Key to the strategy:**

> *Understanding that rubrics begin with a list of criteria and indicators, and that students will profit from knowing those, at least.*

**Tactics:**

1. Develop a self-assessment checklist for students, in which the list involves key criteria, not merely a schedule or formal traits of the work. Sort the list into key criteria, with concrete indicators under each criterion.

**Strategy 7. Redefine *passing* to ensure that (at least some portion of) a grade is standard-based.** Devise credit standards so that quality performance is not an option. Establish a culture of quality in which every student is expected to produce quality work, in which major work products and performances are not done until they are done right, and in which practice, feedback, self-assessment, and revision are built into the design of the work requirements.

**Key to the strategy:**

> *Coming to see that if students are given clear standards and opportunities to meet them, the range of performance ability decreases and work quality increases.*
>
> *Getting faculty to see that many current testing, grading, and curriculum design practices unwittingly undercut the quest for quality.*

**Tactics:**

1. Ensure that any personal or school grading policy rewards quality over mere good-faith effort or begrudging compliance. This requires rewarding positive trends in performance rather than following the time-honored but dysfunctional habit of averaging all grades.

2. Examine such scoring systems as the music performance, athletic, and vocational scoring systems in which the degree of difficulty is separately scored from the quality of the performance. Determine how such systems might be incorporated into academic settings, such as through at least two separate rubrics for the assessing, grading, and reporting of work.

3. Conduct a small experiment whereby for a few assignments or tests the only grades are "to standard" or "incomplete."

4.  Conduct error analyses on a test and report findings to grade-level, team, or department members: What are the primary causes of student errors? How might these errors be better avoided in the first place? Try to get the group to formally set aside time each month for analysis of performance errors, their likely causes, and effective strategies for overcoming them.

**Strategy 8. Getting colleagues to "own" the problem of quality—** in terms of both *input* (the caliber of assessments and school performance indicators) and *output* (the quality expected of resultant student performance).

**Keys to the strategy:**

*Ensuring that all new initiatives are seen as solutions to problems raised by tangible and quantifiable problems—based on credible data about current performance, such as student papers.*

*Establishing dissonance through data to show discrepancies between current practices and intended achievement targets, between the faculty's beliefs and its practices.*

*Helping faculties to understand that local expectations for students are now uneven and divergent across teachers, courses, and tracks.*

**Tactics:**

1.  Have faculty or teams review existing policies for those not congruent with a mission focused on quality in student performance (such as those dealing with grading, promoting, scheduling, tracking, and so on).

    This can result in the development of an explicit building-level assessment policy to ensure that tests and grading are fair, appropriate, useful, reliable, credible, and consistent with stated achievement targets.

2.  School leaders should audit the quality of current tests— especially across tracks or levels: Do tests operationalize the current mission of the faculty?

    This can lead to annual reports to the faculty on the articulation of teacher tests with stated achievement targets and district goals, and in which the authenticity/engaging qualities of the tests is assessed.

    Solicit information from the students and parents about the quality of current testing, grading, and especially the quality of teacher feedback.

3. Distribute samples of the best, average, and worst student work from each grade or track. Ask faculty to grade the work, and discuss the quality and range of the work.

4. Distribute printouts of all grades given in the school or district. Balance this information against surveys to students, parents, and colleges about the quality of each school program. Ask faculty to assess results: Are the grades norm-referenced to the building (that is, A = what our best kids do) or truly standard-referenced?

5. Distribute any test score results that provide insight into an aptitude versus achievement comparison: Are we getting the most from our kids?

**Strategy 9. Go for scoring consistency:** ensure that as many teachers as possible "agree to agree" to use shared grading criteria and standards for assessing similar work.

**Key to the strategy:**

*Ensuring that faculties become aware of what students routinely experience, namely, that teachers often have differing expectations and standards and sometimes have too little objective basis or clear rationale for their grading practices.*

**Tactics:**

1. Agree that some major assignments will be collectively scored by faculty from across schools and grades, using the same scoring criteria and standards.

2. Establish one or two common performance and/or portfolio tasks to be required of all students as an exit-level requirement, scored collaboratively.

3. Report to the faculty on the consistency of teacher grading, having previously set up an experiment to compare grading.

4. Develop an assessment and grading policy statement that will provide students and parents with clear, common guidelines on how all tests should be designed to be valid, and how grades should be calculated to align with district objectives.

5. Establish some tests or evaluations in which student work is read blind by judges other than the classroom teacher.

6. Provide sanctioned opportunities for students to provide feedback about the fairness and appropriateness of teacher tests and grades. (Various college professors now make

this a test question for credit on the final exam!) Provide more informal opportunities for students to give you feedback, directly and indirectly, on what is and is not working.

7.  Leaders: establish grading reliability standards, that is, the "tolerance" margin of scoring differences between teachers that will be allowed on the same work.

**Strategy 10. Redefine individual course and overall school success to make it more honest and fair.**   Develop and employ more value-added assessments: In light of where students begin, how far have we taken them? How well have we optimized performance in light of the givens?

**Key to the strategy:**

*Making school reform work data-driven and credible.*

*Getting faculty to redefine their jobs as "achievers of results," given the students they have; ensuring that appropriate performance gains occur over time, in reference to exit-level standards.*

*Ensuring that faculty see that their job is to minimize the gap between their best and worst performers, whether in looking at individual students, classes, or subgroups of the whole student population.*

*Getting faculty to set yearly specific performance targets by repeatedly monitoring in terms of those targets through ongoing standard-referenced assessment.*

**Tactics:**

1.  Redesign the course grading or school report card to report current student performance against exit-level standards. Analyze the long-term and short-term trends, and how those trends compare against other cohorts.

2.  Develop longitudinal/developmental scoring criteria to evaluate student progress over time against fixed standards.

3.  More effectively distinguish between aptitude and achievement, growth and progress, in reporting the quality of student performance. (Get clearer on the value added by the school.)

4.  Establish team or department year-end and multiyear goals for monitoring, adjusting, and thus minimizing the gaps in student subgroup comparative performances.

5.  Use standardized tests to assess student progress over time (in a pretest/posttest way) instead of comparing aggregate performance of the current year's class to the previous year's.

6. Use high-quality high-standard national tests, on a sampling basis, to assess student performance against worthy targets (not just in advanced programs).

7. Develop indicators that compare the success of your schools against the success of similar schools (in terms of test scores, placement, and so on).

**Strategy 11. Know your institutional customers' expectations:** assess from the vantage point of the standards in force at the next level and at your most valued institutional customers. (Know with specificity the standards facing your former students.)

**Key to the strategy:**

> *Coming to see the actual requirements for success in valued programs and employment for your graduates (regardless of age).*

**Tactics:**

1. Collect samples of assessments and graded student work from the best programs and schools to which your graduates go.

2. Organize a field trip to the next level of schooling, local colleges, and employers to witness and discuss their operational standards, the tasks they face, the resources available, and so on. Don't just talk: get copies of assignments, assessments, and any rubrics and performance samples.

3. Develop a performance assessment in which students have their work assessed by faculty/staff/employers at the next level, grade, school, and so on.

4. Develop a committee composed in part of local people in the professions, trades, and universities to provide an external review of local standards and measures. Ask them to score important samples of student work occasionally, and compare their evaluation with teacher evaluation.

**Strategy 12. Make form follow function:** In incremental steps, begin to find the necessary resources to do assessment properly—by redeploying time and personnel.

**Key to the strategy:**

> *Moving incrementally, slowly but surely, toward a use of time and people that is optimal for assessment design, debugging, and scoring of work. This typically involves ensuring that there are at least five non-contact days spread through the year.*

*Challenging deep-seated assumptions about the use of time, especially the view that every day or week has to look like every other day or week.*

**Tactics:**

1.  Do a time-needs analysis by team, grade-level, or department. Survey colleagues on how many noncontact hours would minimally be needed for the design, debugging, use, and scoring of performance-based student assessments.

2.  Develop a plan to change the schedule over a three-year period in which two half-days of noncontact time are added each year.

3.  Since assessment occurs in cycles, develop a schedule that reflects the need for noncontact half days every six weeks or so.

4.  Challenge the assumption that courses need to meet every day. (Look at the collegiate model.)

5.  Challenge the assumption that only the classroom teacher, only teachers, and only school personnel should score student work. (Consider that in South Brunswick, New Jersey, they find more than one hundred educators and citizens from the surrounding communities to assist them in a major assessment of every sixth grade student's research and presentation ability, and that they get interrater reliability of better than .90.[1])

6.  Challenge the assumption that all students in a classroom, all courses, all departments, all grades, and so forth have to be tested simultaneously and have to have their reports sent home simultaneously. In the absence of secure multiple-choice tests, there is no need to do so. Indeed, time could be found to assess each child intensively if only a fourth of the class were assessed and reported on in a given month.

**Strategy 13. Establish a set of R & D task forces,** working in parallel on reform issues. Each task force reports to the others and to a steering committee (made up in part of representatives from each task force).

**Key to the strategy:**

*Avoiding typical committee gridlock and turf defense.*

*Ensuring that no committee can do its work without updates on work of other committees.*

*Requiring each committee to answer specific questions and address specific performance concerns or problem areas that lead to specific data collection, research, experimentation, and a final report with recommendations to the steering committee.*

*Setting firm due dates for final reports.*

**Tactics:**

1.  Focus the work of each group by using research-focus titles for groups such as a postgraduation committee, a prematriculation committee, a community standards committee, and so on.

2.  Insist that each committee use one or more of the tactics in the previous twelve strategies to ensure that their work is grounded in data. Each group should establish need and propose multiple solutions with respect to their topic.

3.  The result of each group's work should be the writing of an internal Request for Proposals that provides opportunities and incentives for any faculty members to propose solutions to the key problems identified by each task force and to pilot the proposed solutions. This ensures greater ownership of the analysis and proposals, and opens the door to greater creative entrepreneurship in the faculty.

**Strategy 14. Establish an explicit set of assessment principles and criteria.**   As an individual, give it to students on day one. As a system, develop quality control procedures to ensure that the policies are honored, whether considering the purchase, use, or local design of assessments.

**Key to the strategy:**

*Making it clear that assessment must be done according to appropriate criteria and rules for validity, reliability, fairness, rigor, and usefulness.*

*Establishing clear guidelines for making the difficult decisions involving the tension between necessary standards and discretionary practice.*

**Tactics:**

1.  Develop a districtwide and buildingwide committee system to formulate a policy statement on the purpose, nature, and exemplary use of assessment instruments and information.

2.  Ask faculty by department, team, or grade to study current practice in assessment (by survey, discussion, and so on)

and to make recommendations to one another about necessary uniformity.

3. Study policy statements from other districts and other countries, and ask faculty to react to them.

4. Study who is now versus who ought to be the primary customer for assessment data—if the aim of assessment is improved performance—and what the different (and conflicting) needs might be between primary and secondary customers.

**Strategy 15. Make self-assessment and self-adjustment more central to the job,** whether we consider the individual teacher or the faculty as a whole.

**Key to the strategy:**

*Making ongoing professional development the natural result of an exemplary assessment process (instead of isolated in-service work).*

*Getting faculty to provide students, parents, and community members with a published handbook of exemplary student work, with commentary.*

**Tactics:**

1. Develop a districtwide publication of exemplary and not-so-exemplary work, with commentary, as a way of communicating with clarity the standards and expectations of student performance.

2. Encourage faculty to volunteer for districtwide assessment scoring to ensure that more and more faculty share the same standards and criteria in grading similar work.

**Strategy 16. Provide opportunities, incentives, and requirements so that each teacher engages in more careful research into the effectiveness of their practice.**

**Tactics:**

1. What are the most and least revealing assessments you use? By what criteria are you judging the choices, that is, what do you consider to be revealing?

2. What are the most engaging assessments? What are the indicators?

3. What works? Model the soliciting and using of feedback. Get feedback from students on the effectiveness of your instruction, assessments, and feedback.

What was the most effective coaching, guidance, and feedback you gave students in the past year—in their view?

What did students think was the most/least challenging assessments you gave this year? What did they think were the most/least fair assessments?

What do they think are the most effective preparations/rehearsals and assessments?

# NOTES

PREFACE

1. See B. S. Bloom (ed.), *Taxonomy of Educational Objectives. Book 1: Cognitive Domain* (White Plains, N.Y.: Longman, 1954); and B. S. Bloom, G. F. Madaus, and J. T. Hastings, *Evaluation to Improve Learning* (New York: McGraw-Hill, 1981).
2. The theory is more fully elaborated in G. P. Wiggins and J. McTighe, *Understanding by Design* (Alexandria, Va.: Association for Supervision and Curriculum Development, forthcoming).

CHAPTER ONE

1. Ministere de Education, *Complementary Examination: English Language Arts 514–600* (Montreal: Gouvernement du Quebec, Ministere de Education, June 1995).
2. National Center on Education and the Economy and the University of Pittsburgh, *New Standards* (Pittsburgh: National Center on Education and the Economy and the University of Pittsburgh, 1997).
3. Department of Education and Science and the Welsh Office, United Kingdom, *National Curriculum: Task Group on Assessment and Testing—A Report* (London: Department of Education and Science, England and Wales, 1988); Department of Education and Science and the Welsh Office, United Kingdom, *English for Ages Five to Sixteen: Proposals of the Secretary of State for Education and Science* (London: Department of Education and Science and the Welsh Office, 1989).
4. P. Griffin, P. Smith, and L. Burrill, *The American Literacy Profiles: A Framework for Authentic Assessment* (Portsmouth, N.H.: Heineman, 1995); derived from *English Profiles Handbook* (formerly *Literacy Profiles Handbook*) (Melbourne, Victoria, Australia: Education Shop, 1991).
5. Report from the College Board.
6. As reported by G. F. Madaus and A. Tan, "The Growth of Assessment," in *Challenges and Achievements of American Education: The 1993 ASCD Yearbook* (Alexandria, Va.: Association for Supervision and Curriculum Development, 1993), p. 62.
7. As reported in *The New York Times*, Sunday, May 4, 1997, p. 19.
8. G. Wiggins, *Assessing Student Performance: Exploring the Purpose and Limits of Testing* (San Francisco: Jossey-Bass, 1993), chap. 3.

CHAPTER TWO

1. Earlier versions of these standards appear in Wiggins, *Assessing Student Performance*, pp. 228–230.
2. Bloom, *Taxonomy of Educational Objectives*, p. 125.
3. Bloom, Madaus, and Hastings, *Evaluation to Improve Learning*, p. 265.
4. Bloom, Madaus, and Hastings, *Evaluation to Improve Learning*, p. 268.
5. F. Newmann, W. Secada, and G. Wehlage, *A Guide to Authentic Instruction and Assessment: Vision, Standards and Scoring* (Madison: Wisconsin Center for Education Research, 1995).
6. Figure 2.2 is from North Carolina Education Standards and Accountability Commission, *Third Annual Report to the North Carolina State Board of Education, The North Carolina General Assembly and Governor James B. Hunt, Jr.* (Raleigh: North Carolina Education Standards and Accountability Commission, July 1996), p. 55.
7. Figure 2.3 is from North Carolina Education Standards and Accountability Commission, *Third Annual Report to the North Carolina State Board of Education, The North Carolina General Assembly*

*and Governor James B. Hunt, Jr.* (Raleigh: North Carolina Education Standards and Accountability Commission, July 1996), p. 56.

8. N. Frederiksen, "The Real Test Bias," *American Psychologist*, 1984, *39*(3), 193–202.

9. "A Question of Safety: A Special Report," *New York Times*, Sunday, November 13, 1994, Section 1, page 1.

10. H. Gardner, *Multiple Intelligences: The Theory in Practice* (New York: Basic Books, 1993); R. Sternberg, *The Triarchic Mind: A New Theory of Human Intelligence* (New York: Penguin Books, 1988).

11. Bloom, *Taxonomy of Educational Objectives*, pp. 120, 162.

12. Marv Levy, post-game radio interview, December 1992.

13. Newmann, Secada, and Wehlage, *A Guide to Authentic Instruction and Assessment*, p. 12.

14. Outward Bound is the international program in wilderness-based experiential learning, developed originally in Great Britain as survival training for sailors.

## CHAPTER THREE

1. W. James, *Talks to Teachers* (New York: Norton, [1899] 1958), p. 41.

2. "True or False: Testing by Computers Is Educational Progress," *The New York Times,* Sunday, June 15, 1997, Business Section, p. 10.

3. The reader is implored not to read this paragraph as advocating the withholding of praise or approval. Teaching, parenting, and relationships require praising. Here I am merely analyzing how feedback is *different* from any value judgment and more vital to performance improvement.

4. "Slocumb Off Closer Duty," *Boston Globe,* Thursday, June 5, 1997, p. C5. Alas, Mr. Slocumb could not apparently profit from the feedback and guidance. He was traded a few months later.

5. This example and others are further explained in Wiggins, *Assessing Student Performance,* chap. 5. Other sections of that chapter are also included in modified form in this discussion of feedback.

6. An earlier version of this list appears in Wiggins, *Assessing Student Performance,* pp. 194–195.

7. A version of this story appears in Wiggins, *Assessing Student Performance,* pp. 194–195.

8. This point is developed at length in Wiggins, *Assessing Student Performance,* pp. 184–190.

9. This story has an amusing postscript. Two years later Justin was with me while I was watching a video in which I tell the story and use his writing sample. "Who wrote *that?*" he asked. I laughed and said, "You did!" He shook his head and said, "Not a very good N. I can do better than that."

10. From Wiggins, *Assessing Student Performance,* p. 183. The word, of course, was *vague.*

11. V. Stallings and C. Tascione, "Student Self-Assessment and Self-Evaluation," *Mathematics Teacher,* 1996, *89*(7), 548–554.

12. Stallings and Tascione, "Student Self-Assessment and Self-Evaluation," p. 554.

13. Stallings and Tascione, "Student Self-Assessment and Self-Evaluation," pp. 553–554.

14. This is one of four different rubrics used for reading assessment in Monterey Elementary School, Colorado Springs, Colorado. Permission courtesy of Anne O'Rourke, Monterey Elementary School.

15. From *Measuring What Matters,* a videotape on assessment reform published by and available from the Center on Learning, Assessment, and School Structure.

16. Fairfax County Public Schools, *Assessing Primary Purposes: Language Arts Resource Guide* (Fairfax, Va.: Fairfax County Public Schools, 1995), pp. IV–64. Permission courtesy of the Fairfax County Public Schools.

17. From the video *Best of Standards, Not Standardization: Elementary* (Pennington, N.J.: Center on Learning, Assessment, and School Structure, 1996).

18. National Assessment of Educational Progress, "Narrative Scoring Guide," in *Exploring New Methods for Collecting Students' School-Based Writing: NAEP's 1990 Portfolio Study* (Washington, D.C.: National Assessment of Educational Progress, 1992), pp. 10–11.

19. For example, the work of New Standards—a private effort to develop exemplary assessments based on credible standards, developed over the past few years by the National Center on Education and the Economy and the University of Pittsburgh (in partnership with many states and districts)—is built on a mixture of standardized testing and classroom-based student portfolios (as discussed further in Chapter Eight).

20. R. Light, *Explorations with Students and Faculty About Teaching, Learning, and Student Life* (Vol. 1) (Cambridge, Mass.: Harvard University, 1990).

21. James, *Talks to Teachers*, p. 101.

22. Department of Education and Science, Assessment of Performance Unit, *Task Group on Assessment and Testing Report* (London: Her Majesty's Stationery Office, 1988), p. 78ff.

23. Department of Education and Science, Assessment of Performance Unit, *Task Group on Assessment and Testing Report* (London: Her Majesty's Stationery Office, 1988), science assessment, p. 81.

24. Department of Education and Science, Assessment of Performance Unit, *Task Group on Assessment and Testing Report,* science assessment, p. 119.

25. R. Camp, "Thinking Together About Portfolios," The Quarterly of the National Writing Project (Berkeley: University of California, 1989), pp. 8–14, 27; D. Wolf, "Portfolio Assessment: Sampling Student Work," *Educational Leadership,* 1989, 46(7), 35–39.

26. For further information on the Toronto Benchmarks see Toronto Board of Education, *Assessing, Evaluating, and Communicating with Parents* (Toronto: Toronto Board of Education, 1997).

27. The J. Peterman Company, *Owner's Manual No. 38a* (Fall 1995), p. 33. Catalogue. Permission courtesy of The J. Peterman Company.

28. The Carleton examples are also discussed in Wiggins, *Assessing Student Performance,* p. 168.

29. The South Brunswick examples are also discussed in Wiggins, *Assessing Student Performance,* p. 159.

30. Discussed in Wiggins, *Assessing Student Performance,* and in Chapter Six of this book.

31. On assessing for understanding, see also Wiggins and McTighe, *Understanding by Design.*

## CHAPTER FOUR

1. Bloom, *Taxonomy of Educational Objectives,* p. 120.

2. R. Gunstone and R. White, *Probing Understanding* (London: The Falmer Press, 1992), p. 45.

3. R. Nickerson, "Understanding Understanding." *American Journal of Education,* Feb. 1985, pp. 201–237.

4. T. Kuhn, *The Structure of Scientific Revolutions,* 2nd ed. (Chicago: University of Chicago Press, 1970), p. 172.

5. F. Sulloway, *Born to Rebel: Birth Order, Family Dynamics, and Creative Lives* (New York: Pantheon Books, 1996), p. 20. Howard Gardner notes that high school and college students persist in this misunderstanding in their study of evolutionary biology (see Gardner, *Multiple Intelligences,* p. 158).

6. Aristotle, *Metaphysics,* Book I, 981 a25–30, in J. Barnes (ed.), *The Complete Works of Aristotle: The Revised Oxford Translation* (Princeton: Princeton University Press/Bollingen Series, 1985).

7. D. Perkins, *Smart Schools: From Training Memories to Educating Minds* (New York: Free Press, 1992), p. 26ff.

8. H. Gardner, *The Unschooled Mind: How Children Think and How Schools Should Teach* (New York: Basic Books, 1981), p. 6.

9. National Assessment of Educational Progress, *The Mathematics Report Card: Are We Measuring Up? Trends and Achievement Based on the 1986 National Assessment* (Princeton, N.J.: Educational Testing Services, June 1988), pp. 31–32.

10. Reported in "Who Tops World Education Heap? International Math and Science Study Tests Forty-One Nations," *The Economist,* March 29, 1997. Reprinted in the *Trenton Times,* April 16, 1997, p. 14.

11. Reported in *The New York Times,* Sunday, May 4, 1997, p. 19.

12. Reported by A. Schoenfeld, "Problem Solving in Context(s)," in R. Charles and E. Silver (eds.), *The Teaching and Assessing of Mathematical Problem Solving* (Reston, Va.: National Council of Teachers of Mathematics/Erlbaum, 1988), p. 84.

13. A nice account of this phenomenon, using the example of heat, and of how to probe for student understanding and misunderstanding can be found in B. Watson and R. Konicek, "Teaching for Conceptual Change: Confronting Children's Experience," *Phi Delta Kappan,* 1990, 71(9), 680–685.

14. M. Schnep, *A Private Universe* (Santa Monica, Calif.: Pyramid Film and Video, 1989), videotape.

15. Gardner, *The Unschooled Mind,* p. 159ff.

16. Plato, *The Republic,* Book VII, in A. Bloom (trans.), *The Republic of Plato* (New York: Basic Books, 1968).

17. H. Gadamer, *Truth and Method* (New York: Crossroad, 1982), p. 185.

18. A test developed by D. Hestenes, M. Wells, and G. Swackhamer, "Force Concept Inventory," *Physics Teacher*, March 1992, pp. 141–158.

19. Gardner, *The Unschooled Mind*, p. 179.

20. Gardner, *The Unschooled Mind*, p. 181.

21. J. Dewey, *Experience and Education* (New York: Collier Books, 1938), pp. 82, 87.

22. Gardner, *The Unschooled Mind*, pp. 117, 145.

23. J. Piaget, *To Understand Is to Invent: The Future of Education* (New York: Viking Penguin, 1973).

24. P. Elbow, *Writing Without Teachers* (New York: Oxford University Press, 1973).

25. James, *Talks to Teachers*.

26. See, for example, J. Dewey, "Moral Principles in Education," in Boydston (ed.), *John Dewey—The Middle Works* (Vol. 4), pp. 289–290; J. Piaget, *The Moral Judgment of the Child* (New York: Free Press, [1932] 1965), p. 399ff.

27. J. Dewey, "How We Think," in Boydston (ed.), *John Dewey—The Middle Works* (Vol. 15), p. 290.

28. A more comprehensive account of the facets of understanding and their implications for teaching and assessment can be found in Wiggins and McTighe, *Understanding by Design*.

29. The College Board, *Advanced Placement U.S. History: Free Response Scoring Guide and Sample Student Answers* (New York: The College Board, 1991), pp. 25–26.

30. See more on essential questions in G. Wiggins, "Creating a Thought-Provoking Curriculum: Lessons from Whodunits and Others," *American Educator*, Winter 1987, pp. 10–17.

31. See Gunstone and White, *Probing Understanding*, chap. 2.

32. R. Light, *The Harvard Assessment Seminar: Explorations with Students and Faculty About Teaching, Learning, and Student Life* (First report) (Cambridge, Mass.: Harvard University, 1990), p. 36.

33. D. Perkins, *Smart Schools: Better Thinking and Learning for Every Child* (New York: Basic Books, 1993), p. 77ff.

34. Perkins, *Smart Schools*, p. 117ff.

35. See W. Perry, *Forms of Intellectual and Ethical Development in the College Years: A Scheme* (Austin, Tex.: Holt, Rinehart and Winston, 1970), for an elegant theory of the intellectual development levels that can be heard in college student responses to questions about their studies. This approach comes to a different kind of fruition in the work of such moral psychologists as Lawrence Kolnberg and Carol Gilligan.

36. As reported by Gardner in *The Unschooled Mind*, p. 247.

37. F. Bacon, *The New Organon* (New York: Bobbs-Merrill Publishers, [1620] 1960), Aphorisms 45–49, pp. 50–52.

## CHAPTER FIVE

1. This point is argued in greater detail in my previous book, *Assessing Student Performance*.

2. R. Marzano and J. Kendall, *A Comprehensive Guide to Designing Standards-Based Districts, Schools, and Classrooms* (Alexandria, Va.: ASCD, 1996). For a brief and helpful summary of Mastery Learning, Outcomes Based Education, and how both compare with standards-based learning, see Chapter Seven of this volume.

3. See the NYSSMA manual, *A Resource of Graded Solo and Ensemble Music*, 22nd ed. (New York: New York State School Music Association, 1988).

4. These points are further developed in Chapter Ten.

5. National Center on Education and the Economy and the University of Pittsburgh, *New Standards: High School English Language Arts Portfolio* and *New Standards: High School Mathematics Portfolio* (Washington, D.C.: New Standards, 1995).

6. A useful summary of international (as well as American) assessment practice can be found in Congressional Office of Technology Assessment, *Testing in American Schools: Asking the Right Questions* (Washington, D.C.: Congressional Office of Technology Assessment, 1992).

7. See Wiggins, *Assessing Student Performance*, and G. P. Wiggins, "Toward Better Report Cards," *Educational Leadership*, 1994, 50(2), 28–37.

8. H. Kirschenbaum, S. Simon, and R. Napier, *Wad-ja-get? The Grading Game in American Education* (New York: Hart Publishing, 1971).

9. Bloom, *Taxonomy of Educational Objectives*, p. 120.

10. Gardner, *Multiple Intelligences*, pp. 9, 117.
11. Discussed previously in Wiggins, *Assessing Student Performance*, chap. 5.
12. M. O'Neill, *The New York Times Magazine*, Sept. 1, 1996, p. 52.
13. J. Dewey, *How We Think: A Restatement of the Relation of Reflective Thinking to the Educative Process* (Lexington, Mass.: Heath, 1933), p. 74.
14. See Chapter Seven for further discussion of criteria, indicators, and good rubrics.
15. See Wiggins, *Assessing Student Performance*, chap. 6, for an extensive discussion of face validity and why this often-discredited notion needs to be seen for the moral and intellectual issue it is: students are entitled to tests that they can see as having value and resonance in relation to their prior work and future aspirations.

## CHAPTER SIX

1. *The Relevance of Education* (New York: Norton, 1973), p. 113.
2. *The Relevance of Education* (New York: Norton, 1973), pp. 111–112.

## CHAPTER SEVEN

1. This chapter is a greatly revised version of an article in dialogue form, "What Is a Rubric?" in R. Blum and J. Arter (eds.), *A Handbook for Student Performance Assessment in an Era of Restructuring* (Alexandria, Va.: Association for Supervision and Curriculum Development, 1996), pp. VI–5, 1–13.
2. This rubric uses a reading prompt and scoring rubric from the Colorado State University freshman placement exam. Permission courtesy of Heritage High School, Littleton, Colo.
3. California Assessment Program (CAP), "A Question of Thinking: A First Look at Students' Performance on Open-Ended Questions in Mathematics" (Sacramento: California State Department of Education, 1989), p. 53.
4. *English for Ages Five to Sixteen: Proposals of the Secretary of State for Education and Science* (London: Department of Education and Science and the Welsh Office, 1989). An updated version of these and other rubrics are available as *Consistency in Teacher Assessment: Exemplification of Standards—English, Key Stage 3, Levels 4 to 8, Reading and Writing* (London: School Qualifications and Curriculum Authority, 1995).
5. Reproduced courtesy of Sharon Baldwin, Cherry Creek Schools, Aurora, Colorado.
6. From American Council on the Teaching of Foreign Languages, *ACTFL Provisional Proficiency Guidelines* (Hastings-on-Hudson, N.Y.: American Council on the Teaching of Foreign Languages Materials Center, 1992). Used by permission of the ACTFL.
7. Alberta, Canada, provincial exam. This rubric concerns the quality of examples or cases used by the essay's author; other rubrics exist for quality of argument and historical accuracy.
8. National Assessment of Educational Progress, "Narrative Scoring Guide," in *Portfolio Assessment* (1992), p. 20.
9. "No set rules can be laid down in such matters. The way they are managed depends upon the intellectual tact and sensitiveness of the individual"—Dewey, *How We Think*.
10. Mechanisms for visually representing and reporting these distinctions can be found in Chapter Nine.

## CHAPTER EIGHT

1. See Koretz, Stecher, and Deibert, *The Reliability of Scores from the 1992 Vermont Portfolio Assessment Program* (Tech. Report 355), The National Center for Research on Evaluation, Standards and Student Testing (CRESST) at UCLA. A helpful brief summary of the problem and of portfolio assessment in general can be found in R. Marzano and J. Kendall, *A Comprehensive Guide to Designing Standards-Based Districts, Schools, and Classrooms*, chap. 5 (Alexandria, Va.: Association for Supervision and Curriculum Development, 1996).
2. The North Carolina Education Standards and Accountability Commission, *Third Annual Report to the North Carolina State Board of Education, The North Carolina General Assembly and Governor James B. Hunt, Jr.* (Raleigh: North Carolina Education Standards and Accountability Commission, July 1996).
3. Competency credits are (a) claimed by student's teacher or (b) assigned by portfolio reviewers.

## CHAPTER NINE

1. This chapter originally appeared in a different form as Wiggins, "Coherence and Assessment: Making Sure the Effect Matches the Intent," in *ASCD Yearbook 1995: Toward a Coherent Curriculum* (Alexandria, Va.: Association for Supervision and Curriculum Development, 1995), pp. 101–119.

2. J. Bruner, *Toward a Theory of Instruction* (Cambridge, Mass.: The Belknap Press of Harvard University Press, [1966] 1973), p. 65.

3. *Oxford English Dictionary,* 2nd ed. (New York: Oxford University Press, 1993).

4. J. Bruner, "Growth of Mind," *American Psychologist,* 1965, 20(17), 1007–1017. Quoted in J. Anglin, *Beyond the Information Given: Studies in the Psychology of Knowing* (New York: Routledge, 1973), p. 449.

5. See G. P. Wiggins, "Toward a Thought-Provoking Curriculum: Lessons from Whodunits and Others," *American Educator,* Winter 1987, pp. 10–17; and G. P. Wiggins, "The Futility of Teaching Everything of Importance," *Educational Leadership,* 1989, 47(3) for more on essential questions.

6. Many readers will no doubt recognize this as a restatement of the ideas of John Dewey and, later, Joseph Schwab. But the idea has a longer, complex history under the name of recapitulation theory, made popular by the theories of G. Stanley Hall at the turn of the twentieth century, derived from Haeckel's dictum in biology that "ontogeny recapitulates phylogeny." The sometimes insightful and sometimes foolish attempts to design curriculum in a way that recapitulates the intellectual progress of mankind goes back to Herbart, Pestalozzi, and Rousseau. Piaget and Bruner were also influenced by the work, and Dewey vacillated in his respect for the approach. See G. P. Wiggins, "Thoughtfulness as an Education Aim" (unpublished dissertation) (Cambridge, Mass.: Harvard Graduate School of Education, 1987) for a history of this approach to curriculum.

7. Adapted from *Chemistry: Study Design* and *Chemistry: Course Development Support Material* (Melbourne, Victoria, Australia: Victorian Curriculum and Assessment Board, 1990).

8. See, for example, J. Bruner.

9. L. Darling-Hammond et al., *Authentic Assessment in Practice: A Collection of Portfolios, Performance Tasks, Exhibitions, and Documentation* (New York: National Center on Restructuring Education, Schools, and Teaching, 1993), p. 217ff.

10. From Central Park East Secondary School portfolio guidelines.

11. R. Tyler, *Basic Principles of Curriculum and Instruction* (Chicago: University of Chicago Press, 1949), p. 44.

12. From definition of *coherence* in *Oxford English Dictionary.*

13. See Perkins, *Smart Schools* (1993) for further information.

14. J. Bruner, "Growth of Mind," *American Psychologist,* 1965, 20(17), 1007–1017. Quoted in J. Anglin, *Beyond the Information Given: Studies in the Psychology of Knowing* (New York: Routledge, 1973), p. 449.

15. P. Elbow, "Trying to Teach While Thinking About the End," *Embracing Contraries: Explorations in Teaching and Learning* (New York: Oxford University Press, 1986), p. 109. Written as part of a research project on competency-based higher education programs that was supported by the Fund for the Improvement of Postsecondary Education.

16. As described in F. Kliebard, *The Struggle for the American Curriculum, 1893–1958* (New York: Routledge, 1987), pp. 232–226.

17. See Kliebard, *The Struggle for the American Curriculum,* pp. 223–224. Kliebard wryly notes, however, that even here the idea of making curricula interest-centered had been corrupted somewhat from the more radical approach intended by "activity curriculum" proponents such as William Kilpatrick. To Kliebard it appears "open to question" whether the proposed sequence of topics "actually represented interests of children" or was a more benign but still arbitrary adult conception of how to order topics.

18. Using the now-discredited theory of recapitulation (ontogeny recapitulates phylogeny) as a basis for curriculum design was a fascinating attempt to make the entire K–12 experience more developmentally appropriate. Dewey was initially enamored of the view, although he never succumbed to the rigidity found in many of its proponents. See, for example, Dewey, "Interpretation of the Culture-Epoch Theory," in J. A. Boydston, (ed.), *The Early Works of John Dewey, 1882–1898* (Carbondale: Southern Illinois University Press, 1896), pp. 247–253. See also G. P. Wiggins,

"Thoughtfulness as an Education Aim" (unpublished dissertation) (Cambridge, Mass.: Harvard Graduate School of Education, 1987).

19. Dewey, *How We Think*, p. 127.
20. J. Dewey, *Democracy in Education* (Old Tappan, N.J.: 1916), p. 220.
21. Dewey, *How We Think*, pp. 86–87.
22. Textbook companies might legitimately complain that they provide reference materials in logical order. But this would be disingenuous because almost all publishers package textbooks as complete instructional programs, with exercises, test questions, and teacher's guides.
23. R. Descartes, "Rules for the Direction of the Mind," in J. Cottingham, R. Stoothoff, and D. Murdoch, trans., *The Philosophical Writings of Descartes* (Vol. 1) (Cambridge, England: Cambridge University Press, 1985), p. 19, Rule IV. It takes one to know one, by the way: Descartes was guilty of the same crime in his analytic geometry, as history shows and his own writings reveal.
24. G.W.F. Hegel, *Phenomenology of Spirit*, A. V. Miller, trans. (Oxford, England: Oxford University Press, [1807] 1977), pp. 25–26.
25. J. Piaget, "Comments on Mathematical Education," in H. Grubert and J. Voneche (eds.), *The Essential Piaget* (New York: Basic Books, 1971), p. 731.
26. J. Bruner, *The Process of Education* (Cambridge, Mass.: Harvard University Press, 1960), p. 33.
27. Bruner, *Toward a Theory of Instruction*, p. 60.
28. See J. S. Brown, A. Collins, and P. Duguid, "Situated Cognition and the Culture of Learning," *Educational Researcher*, 1989, *18*, 32–42; and Wiggins, *Assessing Student Performance*.
29. J. Bruner, "Growth of Mind," *American Psychologist*, 1965, *20*(17), 1007–1017. Quoted in J. Anglin, *Beyond the Information Given: Studies in the Psychology of Knowing* (New York: Routledge, 1973), p. 448.
30. This is not a minor point. The proof that there are different possible geometries that are as valid as Euclidean geometry depends on a clever repicturing of points, lines, and planes into segments of a circle—taking advantage of the lack of definition of the elements to show that other pictures are possible, that is, consistent with all other statements and propositions in the science. This is of course a highly sophisticated understanding of geometry. But it is an understanding we should not foreclose by downright misleading and dismissive textbook phrasings about undefined terms and postulates. No hint of interesting matters and history is put into most geometry textbooks. As the analysis in the previous chapters suggests, we should be more explicit and deliberate in trying to point toward higher levels of understanding, even as we work with novices.
31. Dewey, *Experience and Education*, p. 79.
32. Dewey, *Democracy in Education*, p. 184.
33. Newmann, Secada, and Wehlage, *A Guide to Authentic Instruction and Assessment*, pp. 28–29.
34. Newmann, Secada, and Wehlage, *A Guide to Authentic Instruction and Assessment*, pp. 31–35.
35. Information on a web-based prototype database of this kind is available from the author.

## CHAPTER TEN

1. See G. P. Wiggins, "Honesty and Fairness: Toward Better Grading and Reporting," in *ASCD Yearbook 1996: Communicating Student Learning* (Alexandria, Va.: Association for Supervision and Curriculum Development, 1995), pp. 141–177; and A. Goodnough, "New Report Cards Spell Out and Dress Up A's and F's," *The New York Times*, Jan. 12, 1997, p. 28 (Metro Section). The former is a yearbook devoted entirely to the subject; the latter is a lengthy article on report card reform in the greater New York tristate region. (This chapter is a revised version of my article from the yearbook.)
2. A. L. Lowell, "The Art of Examination," *Atlantic Monthly*, Jan. 1926, p. 61.
3. Bloom, Madaus, and Hastings, *Evaluation to Improve Learning* (New York: McGraw-Hill, 1981).
4. See J. S. Kendall and R. J. Marzano, *The Systematic Identification and Articulation of Content Standards and Benchmarks: Update* (Aurora, Colo.: Mid-Continent Regional Educational Laboratory, 1994) for an excellent cross-referenced compendium of all the national reports on standards and benchmarks. Note, however, that most of the reports focus on content standards, not performance standards.

5. National Council of Teachers of Mathematics, Commission on Standards for School Mathematics, *Curriculum and Evaluation Standards for School Mathematics* (Reston, Va.: National Council of Teachers of Mathematics, 1989).

6. National Council of Teachers of Mathematics, Commission on Standards for School Mathematics, *Curriculum and Evaluation Standards for School Mathematics;* and American Association for the Advancement of Science, *Benchmarks for Science Literacy* (New York: Oxford University Press, 1993).

7. From Wiggins, "Honesty and Fairness: Toward Better Grading and Reporting," pp. 150–151.

8. From private communications with numerous school heads and principals. The Educational Record Bureau (ERB) is in New York City.

9. Toronto Board of Education, *Assessing, Evaluating, and Communicating with Parents.*

10. From *The American Literacy Profiles: A Framework for Authentic Assessment* (Portsmouth, N.H.: Heinemann, 1995), pp. 108–117.

11. From *The American Literacy Profiles: A Framework for Authentic Assessment* (Portsmouth, N.H.: Heinemann, 1995), pp. 108–117.

12. Described in Wiggins, *Assessing Student Performance.*

13. Figure 10.6 is from School Curriculum and Assessment Authority, *Mathematics: Consistency in Teacher Assessment: Exemplification of Standards, Key Stage 3, Levels 4 to 8* (London: School Curriculum and Assessment Authority, 1995).

14. National Assessment of Educational Progress, *The Mathematics Report Card.*

15. National Assessment of Educational Progress, *The Mathematics Report Card.*

16. See G. P. Wiggins, "Rational Numbers: Scoring and Grading That Helps Rather Than Hurts Learning," *American Educator,* Winter 1988, pp. 20–48; G. P. Wiggins "Standards, Not Standardization: Evoking Quality Student Work," *Educational Leadership*, Feb. 1991, pp. 18–25; and G. P. Wiggins, *Assessing Student Performance,* chap. 4.

17. E. Thorndike, *Educational Psychology* (Vol. 1) (New York: Teachers College Press, 1913), pp. 288–289.

18. From the Cherry Creek Schools, in Wiggins, "Honesty and Fairness: Toward Better Grading and Reporting," pp. 157–158.

19. South Brunswick, New Jersey, Literacy Assessment Rubric, K–2 Reading/Writing Scale, Jan. 1991. Courtesy of South Brunswick Schools.

20. Term *word awareness writing activity* (WAWA) coined at the Cherry Creek Schools.

21. South Brunswick, New Jersey, Literacy Assessment Rubric, K–2 Reading/Writing Scale, Jan. 1991. Courtesy of South Brunswick Schools.

22. D. Meier, personal communication.

23. Rialto Unified School District.

24. Rialto Unified School District.

25. This public document can be obtained from any one of the over 400 private colleges using the common application form.

26. The *Exemplars* booklets in writing are available from the Center on Learning, Assessment, and School Structure (CLASS).

27. Making such a system user-friendly is now even more feasible through the World Wide Web. Parents could view data of varying levels of complexity just by clicking on the right buttons. The initial report might present only scores and grades with brief explanations of each. Clicking on each score or grade could take the parent to rubrics, sample work products, and anchors for the grading system as well as graphed data about historical performance in the class, grade, school, district, and state.

28. From *The American Literacy Profiles: A Framework for Authentic Assessment* (Portsmouth, N.H.: Heinemann, 1995), p. 145.

29. Figure 10.15 courtesy of the Center on Learning, Assessment, and School Structure.

## CHAPTER ELEVEN

1. This chapter originally appeared in a different form as two articles: in G. P. Wiggins, "Embracing Accountability," *New Schools, New Communities,* 1996, *12*(2), 4–10; and G. P. Wiggins, "Practicing What We Preach in Designing Authentic Assessment," *Educational Leadership,* 1996, *45*(4), 18–25.

2. J. Piaget, *The Moral Judgement of the Child* (Old Tappan, N.J.: Macmillian, 1965).
3. R. Osborne and P. Freyberg, *Learning in Science: The Implications of Children's Science* (Auckland, New Zealand: Heinemann, 1985), p. 153.
4. Osborne and Freyberg, *Learning in Science,* p. 151.
5. As reported in "Parents in New York District to Critique Teachers," *Education Week,* 1997, *28*(3), 3.
6. M. Schmoker, *Results: The Key to Continuous School Improvement* (Alexandria, Va.: Association for Supervision and Curriculum Development, 1996), p. 33.
7. J. Mathews, *Escalante: The Best Teacher in America* (New York: Henry Holt, 1988), p. 291.
8. Mathews, *Escalante,* pp. 300–302.
9. See *Testing in American Schools: Asking the Right Questions* (Washington, D.C.: Office of Technology Assessment, U.S. Congress, 1992), p. 61.
10. Argued previously in G. P. Wiggins, *Assessing Student Performance,* chap. 1.
11. See National Forum on Assessment, *Principles and Indicators for Student Assessment Systems* (Cambridge, Mass.: National Center for Fair and Open Testing [Fairtest], 1995); Kendall and Marzano, *The Systematic Identification and Articulation of Content Standards and Benchmarks;* and Wiggins, *Assessing Student Performance,* chap. 1.
12. A full development of a schema of understanding appears in Wiggins and McTighe, *Understanding by Design.*
13. Video and print material on the peer review process is available from CLASS.
14. Some may wonder about the utility or ethics of discussing the work without the designer present. We have found that this first stage is essential to give the peers freedom to express vague concerns and complete criticisms. When the designer is always present, we find that the session bogs down in the designer justifying and explaining all decisions. Given Stage 2 of the process, where the designer is present, and given the standard for judging whether the session was successful (that is, whether the designer feels that the session honored the design and helped to improve it), we find the two-part process more productive and ethical than people new to the process might imagine it to be.

## CHAPTER TWELVE

1. See Newmann, Secada, and Wehlage, *A Guide to Authentic Instruction and Assessment;* "Who Tops World Education Heap? International Math and Science Study Tests Forty-One Nations," *The Economist,* March 29, 1997.

## CHAPTER THIRTEEN

1. See R. Bridgeman, E. Chittenden, and F. Cline, *Characteristics of a Portfolio Scale for Rating Early Literacy* (Princeton, N.J.: Educational Testing Service, 1995).

# BIBLIOGRAPHY

Airasian, P. *Classroom Assessment*. (2nd ed.) New York: McGraw-Hill, 1994.

Alverno College Faculty. *Assessment at Alverno College*. (Rev. ed.) Milwaukee: Alverno College, 1985.

American Association for the Advancement of Science. *Benchmarks for Science Literacy*. New York: Oxford University Press, 1993.

American Council on the Teaching of Foreign Languages. *ACTFL Provisional Proficiency Guidelines*. Hastings-on-Hudson, N.Y.: American Council on the Teaching of Foreign Languages Materials Center, 1982.

American Psychological Association. *Standards for Educational and Psychological Testing*. Washington, D.C.: American Psychological Association, 1985.

Anderson, S. R. "Trouble with Testing." *The American School Board Journal*, June 1993, pp. 24–26.

Archbald, D., and Newmann, F. *Beyond Standardized Testing: Authentic Academic Achievement in the Secondary School*. Reston, Va.: NASSP Publications, 1988.

Astin, A. W. *Assessment for Excellence: The Philosophy and Practice of Assessment and Evaluation in Higher Education*. Old Tappan, N.J.: Macmillan, 1991.

Baker, E., and others. *Cognitively Sensitive Assessments of Student Writing in the Content Areas*. Los Angeles: National Center for Research on Evaluation, Standards and Student Testing, 1991.

Baker, E. L. "Questioning the Technical Quality of Performance Assessment." *The School Administrator*, Dec. 1993, pp. 12–16.

Baker, E. L., O'Neil, H. F. Jr., and Linn, R. L. "Policy and Validity Prospects for Performance-Based Assessment." *American Psychologist*, 1993, 48(12), 1210–1218.

Belanoff, P., and Elbow, P. "Using Portfolios to Increase Collaboration and Community in a Writing Program." *Writing Program Administration*, 1986, 9(1), 27–40.

Berk, R. A. (ed.). *Performance Assessment Methods and Applications*. Baltimore: Johns Hopkins University Press, 1986.

Berlak, H., and others. *Toward a New Science of Educational Testing and Assessment*. New York: State University of New York Press, 1992.

Bishop, J. "Why the Apathy in American High Schools? *Educational Researcher*, 18(1), 6–10.

Bloom, B. S. (ed.). *Taxonomy of Educational Objectives. Book 1: Cognitive Domain*. New York: Longman, 1954.

Bloom, B. S., Madaus, G. F., and Hastings, J. T. *Evaluation to Improve Learning*. New York: McGraw-Hill, 1981.

Bond, L., Friedman, L., and van der Ploeg, A. *Surveying the Landscape of State Educational Assessment Programs*. Washington, D.C.: Council for Educational Development and Research and the National Education Association, 1993.

Bracey, G. W. "Testing the Tests." *The School Administrator*, Dec. 1993, pp. 8–11.

Brandt, R. (ed.). *Performance Assessment: Readings from Educational Leadership*. Alexandria, Va.: Association for Supervision and Curriculum Development, 1992.

Burke, K. (ed.). *Authentic Assessment: A Collection.* Palatine, Ill.: IRI/Skylight, 1992.

California Assessment Program. "Guidelines for the Mathematics Portfolio: Phase II Pilot Working Paper." Sacramento: California Assessment Program Office, California State Department of Education, 1989.

California State Department of Education. *A Question of Thinking: A First Look at Students' Performance on Open-Ended Questions in Mathematics.* Sacramento: California State Department of Education, 1989.

California State Department of Education. *Writing Achievement of California Eighth Graders: Year Two.* Sacramento: California State Department of Education, 1989c.

Center on Learning, Assessment, and School Structure. *Standards, Not Standardization,* Vol. 3: *Rethinking Student Assessment.* Geneseo, N.Y.: Center on Learning, Assessment, and School Structure, 1993.

Center on Research in Evaluation, Standards, and Student Testing. *The CRESST Line,* Winter 1993.

Charles, R., and Silver, E. (eds.). *The Teaching and Assessing of Mathematical Problem Solving,* Vol. 3. Reston, Va: National Council of Teachers of Mathematics, 1988.

College Board. "Evaluating the AP Portfolio in Studio Art." In *Advanced Placement in Art.* Princeton, N.J.: Educational Testing Service/CEEB, 1986a.

College Board. "General Portfolio Guidelines." In *Advanced Placement in Art.* Princeton, N.J.: Educational Testing Service/CEEB, 1986b.

Collins, A., and Fredriksen, J. R. "A Systems Approach to Educational Testing." *Educational Researcher,* Dec. 1989, pp. 27–32.

Corbett, H. D., and Wilson, B. *Testing, Reform, and Rebellion.* Norwood, N.J.: Ablex, 1993.

Connecticut Department of Education. *Toward a New Generation of Student Outcome Measures: Connecticut's Common Core of Learning Assessment.* Hartford, Conn.: State Department of Education, Research and Evaluation Division, 1990.

Cronbach, L. J. *Essentials of Psychological Testing.* (5th ed.) New York: HarperCollins, 1989.

Department of Education, New Zealand. *Assessment for Better Learning: A Public Discussion Document.* Wellington, N.Z.: Department of Education, 1989.

Department of Education and Science and the Welsh Office (U.K.). *National Curriculum: Task Group on Assessment and Testing: A Report.* London: Department of Education and Science, England and Wales, 1988. [The brief *Digest for Schools* is also available.]

Department of Education and Science and the Welsh Office (U.K.). *English for Ages 5 to 16: Proposals of the Secretary of State for Education and Science.* London: Department of Education and Science and the Welsh Office, 1989.

Educational Testing Service. *The Redesign of Testing for the Twenty-First Century: Proceedings of the ETS 1985 Invitational Conference.* Princeton, N.J.: Educational Testing Service, 1986.

Educational Testing Service. *What We Can Learn from Performance Assessment for the Professions: Proceedings of the ETS 1992 Invitational Conference.* Princeton, N.J.: Educational Testing Service, 1993a.

Educational Testing Service. *Linking Assessment with Reform: Technologies That Support Conversations About Student Work.* Princeton, N.J.: Educational Testing Service, 1993b.

Elbow, P. *Writing with Power: Techniques for Mastering the Writing Process.* New York: Oxford University Press, 1981.

Elbow, P. *Embracing Contraries and Explorations in Learning and Teaching.* New York: Oxford University Press, 1986.

Ewell, P. "To Capture the Ineffable: New Forms of Assessment in Higher Education." In G. Gerald, *Review of Research in Education.* Washington, D.C.: American Educational Research Association, 1991.

Falk, B., and Darling-Hammond, L. *The Primary Language Record at P. S. 261: How Assessment Transforms Teaching and Learning.* New York: NCREST, Columbia University, 1993.

Feuer, M. J., Fulton, K., and Morrison, P. "Better Tests and Testing Practices: Options for Policy Makers." *Phi Delta Kappan,* 1993, 74(7), 532.

Finch, F. L. (ed.). *Educational Performance Assessment.* Boston: Houghton Mifflin, 1991.

Fitzpatrick, R., and Morrison, E. J. "Performance and Product Evaluation." In R. L. Thorndike, *Educational Measurement.* (2nd ed.) Old Tappan, N.J.: Macmillan, 1971. [Reprinted in Finch, F. L. (ed.), *Educational Performance Assessment.* Boston: Houghton Mifflin, 1991.]

Fox, R. F. "Do Our Assessments Pass the Test?" *The School Administrator,* Dec. 1993.

Frederiksen, N. "The Real Test Bias." *American Psychologist*, 1984, no. 3, 193–202.

Fredriksen, J. R., and Collins, A. "A Systems Approach to Educational Testing." *Educational Researcher*, Dec. 1989, pp. 27–32.

Gardner, H. "Assessment in Context: The Alternative to Standardized Testing." In B. Gifford (ed.), *Changing Assessments: Alternative Views of Aptitude, Achievement and Instruction*. Norwell, Mass.: Kluwer, 1989.

Gentile, C. *Exploring New Methods for Collecting Students' School-Based Writing*. Washington, D.C.: U.S. Department of Education, Apr. 1991.

Gilbert, T. F. *Human Competence*. New York: McGraw-Hill, 1978.

Glaser, R. "A Criterion-Referenced Test." In J. Popham (ed.), *Criterion-Referenced Measurement: An Introduction*. Englewood Cliffs, N.J.: Educational Technology Publications, 1971.

Grant, G. *On Competence: A Critical Analysis of Competence-Based Reforms in Higher Education*. San Francisco: Jossey-Bass, 1979.

Haney, W. "Making Testing More Educational." *Educational Leadership*, 1985, 43(2).

Haney, W., and Scott, L. "Talking with Children About Tests: An Exploratory Study of Test Item Ambiguity." In K. O. Freedle and R. P. Duran (eds.), *Cognitive and Linguistic Analyses of Test Performance*. Norwood, N.J.: Ablex, 1987.

Hanson, F. A. *Testing Testing: Social Consequences of the Examined Life*. Berkeley: University of California Press, 1993.

Hart, D. *Authentic Assessment: A Handbook for Educators*. Menlo Park, Calif.: Addison-Wesley, 1994.

Henning-Stout, M. *Responsive Assessment: A New Way to Think About Learning*. San Francisco: Jossey-Bass, 1994.

Herman, J., Aschbacher, P., and Winters, A. *A Practical Guide to Alternative Assessment*. Alexandria, Va.: Association for Supervision and Curriculum Development, 1992.

International Baccalaureate Examination Office. *Extended Essay Guidelines*. Wales, U.K.: International Baccalaureate Examination Office, 1991.

Kulm, G. *Mathematics Assessment: What Works in the Classroom*. San Francisco: Jossey-Bass, 1995.

Lesh, R., and Lamon, S. (eds.). *Assessment of Authentic Performance in School Mathematics*. Washington, D.C.: American Association for the Advancement of Science, 1992.

Linn, R., Baker, E., and Dunbar, S. "Complex, Performance-Based Assessment: Expectations and Validation Criteria." *Educational Researcher*, 1991, 20(8), 15–21.

London, R. *Non-Routine Problems: Doing Mathematics*. Providence, R.I.: Janson, 1989.

Lowell, A. L. "The Art of Examination." *Atlantic Monthly*, 1926, 137(1), 58–66.

Madaus, G., and others. *From Gatekeeper to Gateway: Transforming Testing in America*. Chestnut Hill, Mass.: National Commission on Testing and Public Policy, Boston College, 1990.

Macroff, G. "Assessing Alternative Assessment." *Phi Delta Kappan*, 1991, 73(4), 272–281.

Marzano, R., Pickering, D., and McTighe, J. *Assessing Student Outcomes: Performance Assessment Using the Dimensions of Learning Model*. Alexandria, Va.: Association for Supervision and Curriculum Development, 1993.

McClelland, D. "Testing for Competence Rather Than for 'Intelligence.'" *American Psychologist*, 1973, 28(1), 1–14.

McMillan, J. *Classroom Assessment: Principles and Practice for Effective Instruction*. Needham Heights, Mass.: Allyn and Bacon, 1997.

Mehrens, W. "Using Performance Assessment for Accountability Purposes." *Educational Measurement: Issues and Practices*, Spring 1992.

Messick, S. "Meaning and Values in Test Validation: The Science and Ethics of Assessment." *Educational Researcher*, 1989a, 18(2), 5.

Messick, S. "Validity." In American Council on Education, *Educational Measurement*. (3rd ed.) Old Tappan, N.J.: Macmillan, 1989b.

Mills, R. "Portfolios Capture Rich Array of Student Performance." *The School Administrator*, 1989, 11(46).

Ministry of Education, Victoria, Australia. *Literacy Profiles Handbook: Assessing and Reporting Literacy Development*. Melbourne, Victoria: Education Shop, 1990. [Distributed in the U.S. by TASA, Brewster, N.Y.]

Mitchell, R. *Testing for Learning*. New York: Free Press, 1992.

National Assessment of Educational Progress. *Learning by Doing: A Manual for Teaching and Assessing Higher-Order Thinking in Science and Mathematics.* Princeton, N.J.: Educational Testing Service, 1987.

National Education Commission on Time and Learning. *Prisoners of Time.* Washington, D.C.: Government Printing Office, 1994.

Newmann, F. Secada, W., and Wehlage, G. *A Guide to Authentic Instruction and Assessment: Vision, Standards and Scoring.* Madison: Wisconsin Center for Education Research.

Nickse, R., and others. *Competency-Based Education.* New York: Teachers College Press, 1981.

Office of Strategic Services Assessment Staff. *Assessment of Men: Selection of Personnel for the Office of Strategic Services.* Austin, Tex.: Holt, Rinehart and Winston, 1948.

Osterlind, S., and Mertz, W. "Building a Taxonomy for Constructed Response Test Items." *Educational Assessment,* 1994, 2(2).

Perrone, V. (ed.). *Expanding Student Assessment for Supervision and Curriculum Development.* Alexandria, Va.: Association for Supervision and Curriculum Development, 1991.

Resnick, D. P., and Resnick, L. B. "Standards, Curriculum and Performance: A Historical and Comparative Perspective." *Educational Researcher,* 1985, *14*(4), 5–21.

Resnick, L. B. *Education and Learning to Think.* Washington, D.C.: National Academy Press, 1987.

Resnick L. B., and Resnick, D. P. "Assessing the Thinking Curriculum: New Tools for Educational Reform. In B. Gifford (ed.), *Changing Assessments: Alternative Views of Aptitude, Achievement and Instruction.* Norwell, Mass.: Kluwer, 1991.

Rogers, G. *Validating College Outcomes with Institutionally Developed Instruments: Issues in Maximizing Contextual Validity.* Milwaukee, Wis.: Office of Research and Evaluation, Alverno College, 1988.

Rothman, R. *Measuring Up: Standards, Assessment, and School Reform.* San Francisco: Jossey-Bass, 1995.

Schmoker, M. *Results: The Key to Continuous Improvement.* Alexandria, Va.: Association for Supervision and Curriculum Development, 1996.

Schoenfeld, A. H. "Problem Solving in Context(s)." In R. Charles and E. Silver (eds.), *The Teaching and Assessing of Mathematical Problem Solving.* Reston, Va.: National Council of Teachers of Mathematics/Lawrence Earlbaum Associates, 1988.

Schwartz, J. L., and Viator, K. A. (eds.). *The Prices of Secrecy: The Social, Intellectual and Psychological Costs of Testing in America—A Report to the Ford Foundation.* Cambridge, Mass.: Educational Testing Center, Harvard Graduate School of Education, 1990.

Shanker, A. "A Good Job for Good Grades." *The New York Times,* Mar. 5, 1989.

Shavelson, R., Carey, N., and Webb, N. "Indicators of Science Achievement: Options for a Powerful Policy." *Phi Delta Kappan,* 1990, 71(9), pp. ??.

Shepard, L. "Why We Need Better Assessments." *Educational Leadership,* 1989, *46*(7), 4–9.

Sizer, T. R. *Horace's Compromise: The Dilemma of the American High School.* Boston: Houghton Mifflin, 1991a.

Sizer, T. R. *Horace's School: Redesigning the American High School.* Boston: Houghton Mifflin, 1991b.

Speech Communication Association. *Speaking and Listening Competencies for High School Graduates.* Annandale, Va.: Speech Communication Association of America, 1994.

Stiggins, R. "Assessment Literacy." *Phi Delta Kappan,* 1991, *72*(1), 534–539.

Stiggins, R. *Student-Centered Classroom Assessment.* New York: Merrill, 1994.

Terenzini, P. "The Case for Unobtrusive Measures." In Educational Testing Service, *Assessing the Outcomes of Higher Education: Proceedings of the 1986 ETS Invitational Conference.* Princeton, N.J.: Educational Testing Service, 1987.

Tierney, R., Carter, M., and Desai, L. *Portfolio Assessment in the Reading-Writing Classroom.* Norwood, Mass.: Christopher-Gordon, 1991.

U.S. Congress, Office of Technology Assessment. *Testing in American Schools: Asking the Right Questions.* OTA SET-519. Washington, D.C.: Government Printing Office, 1992.

U.S. Department of Labor. *What Work Requires of Schools: A Secretary's Commission on Achieving Necessary Skills Report for America 2000.* Washington, D.C.: Government Printing Office, 1991.

University of California. "Assessment Alternatives in Mathematics: From EQUALS and the California Mathematics Council, Lawrence Hall of Science." Berkeley, Calif.: University of California, 1989.

Wiggins, G. "Rational Numbers: Scoring and Grading That Helps Rather Than Hurts Learning." *American Educator,* 1988, *12*(4), 20–48.

Wiggins, G. "A True Test: Toward More Authentic and Equitable Assessment." *Phi Delta Kappan*, 1989a, *70*(9), 703–713.

Wiggins, G. "Teaching to the (Authentic) Test." *Educational Leadership*, 1989b, *46*(7), 41–47.

Wiggins, G. "Standards, Not Standardization: Evoking Quality Student Work." *Educational Leadership*, 1991, *48*(5), 18–25.

Wiggins, G. "Creating Tests Worth Taking." *Educational Leadership*, 1992, *49*(8), 26–33.

Wiggins, G. *Assessing Student Performance: Exploring the Purpose and Limits of Testing.* San Francisco: Jossey-Bass, 1993.

Wittrock, M. C., and Baker, E. L. *Testing and Cognition.* Upper Saddle River, N.J.: Prentice Hall, 1991.

Wolf, D. "Opening Up Assessment." *Educational Leadership*, 1987/1988, no. 4.

Wolf, D. "Portfolio Assessment: Sampling Student Work." *Educational Leadership*, 1989, *46*(7), 35–39.

Wolf, D., Bixby, J., Glen, J. III, Gardner, H. "To Use Their Minds Well: Investigating New Forms of Student Assessment." In G. Grant (ed.), *Review of Research in Education.* Washington, D.C.: American Educational Research Association, 1991.

Zacharias, J. R. "The People Should Get What They Need: An Optimistic View of What Tests Can Be." *The National Elementary Principle*, 1979, *58*, 41–45.